Indexing from A to Z

Hans H. Wellisch

Indexing from *A* to *Z*

Second edition, revised and enlarged

H. W. Wilson
New York, Dublin   *1995*

Printed in the United States of America

Library of Congress Cataloging-in-Publication Data

Wellisch, Hans H., 1920–
    Indexing from A to Z / Hans H. Wellisch. — 2nd ed., rev. and enl.
      p. cm.
    Includes bibliographical references (p.   ) and index.
    ISBN 0-8242-0882-X
    1. Indexing. I. Title.
  Z695.9.W45 1995
  025.3—dc20   95-46720
                                              CIP

*The labour and patience, the judgement
and penetration which are required to make
a good index, is only known to those who
have gone through this most painful, but
least praised part of a publication.*

WILLIAM OLDYS (1696–1761)

*It is easy enough to make an index, as it is
to make a broom of odds and ends, as
rough as oat straw; but to make an index
tied up tight, and that will sweep well into
corners, isn't so easy.*

JOHN RUSKIN (1819–1900)

*When I tell people that I am working on an
index to a book, they tend to hang their
heads in sorrow. I tell them that compiling
an index for a book is a lot more fun than
writing a book could ever be, a relaxing
jaunt from A to Z compared with a jerky
stop-start trek without maps.*

CRAIG BROWN, COLUMNIST,
in *Times Saturday Review*,
21 July 1990

CONTENTS

PREFACE TO THE SECOND EDITION

This revised and enlarged edition is the result of several factors. First and foremost, it was necessary to accommodate the many and often substantial changes that have taken place in rules and standards pertaining to indexes and indexing since the publication of the first edition in 1991. Specifically, the publication of the American National Standard NISO Z39.4, the International Standard ISO 999 (in the elaboration of both I was involved as a member of the relevant committees), and the 14th edition of the *Chicago manual of style* resulted in many rule changes. Second, reviewers and users made valuable suggestions for adding or expanding sections. Third, changes in terminology and other developments resulted in relocations or deletions.

New sections deal with AUTOMATIC INDEXING, THE CONTINUUM OF VERBAL TEXTS, DEPTH OF INDEXING, INDEXING LANGUAGES, LEGAL TEXTS, MEDICAL TEXTS, and TECHNICAL MANUALS AND REPORTS. Substantially expanded sections are COSTING, DISPLAY OF SUBHEADINGS, EDITING, EXHAUSTIVITY, PREPOSITIONS, and PROFESSIONAL INDEXING. Two sections have been renamed: ALPHANUMERIC ARRANGEMENT (formerly Filing) and LEAD TERMS (formerly part of Keywords). Many minor changes have been made in most sections to clarify meaning or to correct mistakes.

A new CLASSIFIED LIST OF SECTIONS provides a systematic approach to related sections that are inevitably separated by the alphabetical arrangement of the book; I am indebted to Trudi Bellardo (1993) and her students for this valuable suggestion. A larger number of examples and references to the recent professional literature as well as to older but still relevant sources, also requested by many users and particularly by students, has been provided.

On one relatively minor issue, the treatment of "and" in sub-headings, I changed my mind in favor of retaining the word at the beginning (but only if that cannot be avoided by suitable rephrasing of the subheading) in order to avoid mental inversion of a subheading.

In the discussion of principles and practices of indexing, care has been taken to consider the indexing of texts not only in book form but also those in other formats wherever applicable, ranging from periodicals through nonbook media, databases, and hypertext (a medium that will undoubtedly be of increasing interest to indexers in years to come).

Computers are now used by virtually all professional indexers as well as by most amateurs, but discussions of indexing by means of cards have been retained for the benefit of those who may still wish to use the time-honored method; after all, only a few pages have been devoted to the humble tools that predominated the techniques of indexing for several hundred years.

Finally, I hope that the index will this time be reasonably free from the misprints, mistakes, and omissions that marred the previous one (though reviewers mercifully did not remark on these blemishes).

I am again indebted to friends and colleagues who gave freely of their time to provide valuable advice and constructive criticism, and especially to those who reviewed entire sections. My thanks go to Trudi Bellardo, Linda K. Fetters, Trisha L. Feuerstein, Rachel In, William G. Jenson, Frances L. Lennie, Jessica L. Milstead, Brian L. Porto, Lillian R. Rodberg, Dorothy Thomas, John Vickers, Bella H. Weinberg, and Ceci Wittmann. None of them is to blame for omissions, errors, and outrageous opinions, for which the usual suspect is to be apprehended.

Last but not least, I am grateful to Bruce R. Carrick, my editor, and to Laurie Brown, my copy editor, as well as to other members of the staff at the H. W. Wilson Company, who spared neither time nor effort and expenses to convert a rather messy manuscript into a pleasingly produced and typographically well-designed book.

H. H. W.

LIST OF TABLES

LIST OF FIGURES

DEFINITIONS

Terms that have their own definitions in this list are *italicized*. Definitions marked by an asterisk (*) conform to those in the *Proposed American National Standard: guidelines for indexes and related information retrieval devices* (NISO Z39.4–199X); those marked by a dagger (†) are from the International Standard *Guidelines for the content, organization and presentation of indexes* (ISO 999); and those marked by a paragraph sign (§) are from the International Standard ISO 5127, Parts 1, 2, & 3a, *Documentation and information—vocabulary* (International Organization for Standardization 1981, 1983*a, b*). Some definitions are slightly abridged or modified, though without affecting their meaning.

alphanumeric arrangement. The arrangement of *headings* in a sequence in which words, written in Roman letters, are displayed in alphabetical order, and numbers, expressed by Arabic numerals, are displayed in arithmetical order.

*concept. A unit of thought, formed by mentally combining some or all of the characteristics of a concrete or abstract, real or imaginary object. Concepts exist as abstract entities, independent of *terms*.

†cross-reference. A direction from one *main heading* or *subheading* to another.

*document. A medium on or in which a message is recorded.
NOTE: The term applies not only to written or printed media, but also to all nonprint media such as microforms, pictures, audio and video recordings, films, machine-readable records, multi-media and natural or humanly made objects intended to convey *information*.

*entry. A record in an *index*, consisting of a *heading* (if necessary, defined by a *qualifier*) and followed by a *locator*.

*entry array. A sequence of *entries* sharing the same *heading*.
NOTE: Each *locator*, in combination with the heading, represents a single entry.

*feature. An aspect of a *document* other than a *concept* or *topic*.
NOTE: Features include such aspects as authorship, style, language, format, publication date, etc.

*heading. One or more *terms* representing a *topic* or *feature* of a *document* in an *index*.

indented style. The display of a *multilevel heading* in which each *subheading* and *sub-subheading* begins on a new line, progressively shifted to the right under a *main heading*. Also known as entry-a-line, line-by-line, or set-out style.

§index. An *alphanumerically* or otherwise systematically ordered arrangement of *entries*, different from the order of the *text* of the indexed *document*, and designed to enable its users to locate *information* in the document.

§indexing. An operation intended to represent the results of the analysis of a *document* by means of a controlled or natural *indexing language*.

*indexing language. Any vocabulary used for *indexing* and the rules of syntax for its application.

§information. A message used to represent a *concept* within a communication process in order to increase knowledge of a recipient.

locator. An indication, following a *heading* or *subheading*, of the part of a single *document* (page, column, paragraph, section, chapter, plate, frame, or serial number) to which that heading or subheading refers. Also, a complete bibliographic citation or serial number of a document in a collection to which a heading or subheading refers.

*main heading. The first *heading* in a *multilevel heading*.

*multilevel heading. A *main heading* that is modified by one or more *subheadings* which in turn may be modified by one or more *sub-subheadings* at successive levels of subordination.

*qualifier. A word or phrase added to a *term* in order to distinguish among homographs or to clarify the meaning of a term.
NOTE: A qualifier forms part of a term.

run-in style. The display of a *multilevel heading* in which *subheadings* are arranged in a single indented paragraph under a *main heading*. Also known as run-on or paragraph style.

NOTE: In this style, sub-subheadings cannot be displayed except by use of special punctuation or in a hybrid style, mixing indented subheadings and run-in sub-subheadings.

*sub-subheading. A modifying *heading* subordinated to a *subheading* in a *multilevel heading*.

*subheading. A modifying *heading* subordinated to a *main heading* in a *multilevel heading*.

subject. *See* topic.

†term. A word, phrase or symbol used to denote a *concept*.

*text. Any organized and meaningful pattern of symbols as manifested in a *document*.

NOTE: A text may be verbal (a representation of speech), visual (a picture), aural (a sound recording), or a mixture of these (as in a film, video recording, or multi-media presentation).

topic. A *concept*, theme, or idea treated explicitly or implicitly in a *document*.

NOTE: Although the term *subject* is better known and more often used than *topic*, and is virtually synonymous with it, its meaning in traditional library practice is much broader than that of *topic* as used in this book. For example, "United States—History—1861–1865—Civil War—Fiction—Bibliographies" is considered as a single "subject" in library catalogs, but it is a conglomeration of five (or perhaps six) topics in indexing.

ABBREVIATIONS FOR STANDARDS AND RULES

When a topic is covered by standards or rules prescribed by major national and international authorities, the relevant numbered sections of such documents may be referred to in the text, and they are listed at the end of a section on that topic. In these annotations, the publication date is omitted. Full bibliographic data for all standards and rules will be found in the Bibliography.

The following abbreviations are used for standards issued by national and international standardizing organizations, as well as for cataloging and alphanumeric arrangement rules which are frequently cited. These abbreviations are also used in bibliographic references in the text.

AACR2   *Anglo-American cataloguing rules.* 2nd ed., rev. (American Library Association, Canadian Library Association, Library Association [London] 1988)

ALA   *ALA filing rules.* (American Library Association 1980)

BS   British Standard (British Standards Institution)

ISO   International Standard (International Organization for Standardization)

LC   *Library of Congress filing rules.* (Rather & Biebel 1980)

NISO   American National Standard (National Information Standards Organization)

The national and international standards on indexes and indexing which are frequently cited throughout the book are abbreviated as follows.

BS 3700 British standard recommendations for preparing in-dexes to books, periodicals and other documents. (British Standards Institution 1988)

ISO 999 Information and documentation—Guidelines for the content, organization and presentation of indexes. (International Organization for Standardization 199X)*

NISO Z39.4 Indexes and related information retrieval devices. (National Information Standards Organization 199X) NOTE: This standard is at the time of writing still in draft form. For this reason, no section numbers for specific rules have been given in the text. The latest draft is available in printed or electronic form from NISO. After publication of the standard, readers may wish to add the relevant section numbers to the "NISO Z39.4" line that appears at the end of many chapters.

---

*The standard was approved in 1994, but had not been published when this book went to press. The cited section numbers are those of the last draft.

CLASSIFIED LIST OF SECTIONS

The alphabetical order of sections in this book disperses related topics throughout the text. Some readers of the first edition, particularly students, suggested to list the sections also in classified order, so as to bring together related sections. The following list of ten main topics is an attempt to fulfill this request. However, the sections under each main topic are still listed alphabetically, because it would be nearly impossible to arrange them according to some further classification. Main topics that are also sections are marked with an asterisk.

Texts   Bibliographies at ends of books. Bibliographies in book form. Biographies. The continuum of verbal texts. Cookbooks. Fiction. Legal texts. Letters and diaries. Loose-leaf publications. Medical texts. Newspapers. Nonprint materials. Periodicals. Poetry. Technical manuals and reports.

Indexable matter*   Appendixes. Chapter headings. Footnotes. Illustrations. Maps. Symbols. Tables. Titles.

Types of indexes   Automatic indexes. Bad indexes. The continuum of verbal texts. Cumulative indexes. Multiple indexes. Narrative indexes. String indexes.

The indexing process*   Depth of indexing. Editing. Exhaustivity. Specificity.

Indexing techniques*   Abbreviations. Bad breaks. Cross-references. Display of subheadings. Double entries. Errors. Introductory notes. Length of an index. Locators. Revision of indexes. Standards.

Terminology   Adjectives. Adverbs. And. Compound headings. Homographs. Index: the word. Indexing languages: natural

INTRODUCTION TO THE FIRST EDITION

Indexing does not come naturally, like breathing. It is rather more like playing the fiddle: some learn to do it reasonably well, a few will become virtuosi, but most people will never know how to do it at all. This simple truth seems to be lost on publishers and editors, who almost always assume that someone who can write a book will also be able to index it. But this assumption, enshrined in most authors' contracts, is tantamount to the belief that an author can also design and cut the type from which the book will be printed, as the British literary critic and writer Bernard Levin (1989) has remarked.

This book is aimed at a broad range of audiences, from people with no or little experience in indexing to professional indexers. Among the former is the author of a book who must or wants to compile an index to it but has never done it before. To be sure, virtually every author will at one time or another have used indexes and will therefore be somewhat familiar with their format and style. Nevertheless, not all indexes are good examples, nor will the index to a reference book be a good model for one to a historical work, for example. Index-making is not as simple as picking out names and words from a text and putting them in alphabetical order—two tasks that can be performed by a computer (sometimes with disastrous results).

An author who must index his or her book while still weary from the arduous task of writing it does not want to read a whole book on how to do it. A few hints on how to start and how to tackle specific problems as they arise may be all that an author may wish to get. For that reason, this book is arranged by topics: it is not intended to be read from cover to cover, but rather to be browsed as the need arises. The novice indexer may wish to start with THE

INDEXING PROCESS and INDEXING TECHNIQUES, and may perhaps take a look at PERSONAL NAMES or PLACE NAMES, and then set out to compile the index entries. While engaged in this task, it may become necessary to look up CROSS-REFERENCES and LOCATORS, and perhaps also COMPOUND HEADINGS or SPECIFICITY. When all entries are ready, it may be useful to have a look at ALPHANUMERIC ARRANGEMENT and DISPLAY OF SUBHEADINGS, two details that should preferably not be left to the tender mercies of a general-purpose word-processing program without first making the modifications necessary for the special requirements of indexing, and to pay close attention to EDITING, which no computer can do as yet.

Another group of people who may need advice on both basic and specialized aspects of indexing are those who want to compile indexes as a hobby—to provide access, for instance, to their collection of video tapes and compact discs, to a stamp collection, to a sound archive of bird calls, the family photo album, or graphic materials from etchings to comic books. People in this group may wish to combine information on various technical aspects of indexing with advice offered under NONPRINT MATERIALS.

Students in library and information science courses may find the book useful as a source of practical information on the technical aspects of indexing, complementing the largely theoretical and sometimes pretty abstruse lectures that often constitute their sole acquaintance with the topic. The examples showing the application of arrangement rules, the treatment of difficult or complex personal, corporate, and place names, the proper structure of cross-references, and solutions for various other technical problems—all provided in easily accessible form—will supplement the various standards, codes, and rule books which are often difficult to understand for the beginner and are not always easily available to students.

People who want to do indexing as a part-time activity, but do not quite know how and where to begin, are another audience. During my term as president of the American Society of Indexers, at least once a week the mail brought letters from recently retired persons (often librarians) or from housewives with a college education and two kids but no outside job, asking how to get started in indexing. Frequently, these people wanted to perform a service to their community, such as compiling an index to the newsletter of their congregation, the local paper, the archives of a genealogical society, and the like. Many inquirers also indicated that they hoped to earn a little extra money by doing part-time indexing. Although some of the proposed projects were much too ambitious to be undertaken by beginners or even a single person, many of them could indeed be tackled by an intelligent person with a flair for the task, if properly guided by explanations of the problems that might arise in the indexing of PERIODICALS and NEWSPAPERS and made aware of the available solutions without their having to reinvent the wheel. To be sure, neither this nor any other book alone can be a substitute for formal training in indexing or for the school of hard knocks provided by practical experience, but I hope to have covered enough ground to help the indexer who is an amateur (in the original and best sense of the word) to avoid some of the worst pitfalls. Readers in this category as well as in the next one may also benefit from the business-oriented sections on CONTRACTS, COSTING, and COPYRIGHT.

The professional indexer, finally, will not need much if any advice on basic issues but may wish to dip here and there into the book when encountering a particular technical problem whose treatment may be subject to divergent opinions as to how it is best handled or which may call for innovative and unusual methods.

Whether they are novices, professionals, or anything in between, I hope that my readers will enjoy the occasional digressions on historical and linguistic matters. Though these may not necessarily make them better indexers, I believe that it is good to know how and where things originated, and to understand how languages of written communication can be translated into the languages of indexing.

My recommendations regarding what to do and what not to do are in most cases the same as those of the relevant national and international standards, which are the fruit of many years of experience and labor by indexers and other workers in the field of information. These standards are authoritative not only because they are sponsored and backed by national and international organizations, but also because they are subject to mandatory review and revision every five years or so; they are, therefore, not just sanctioned by hallowed tradition, but are also reasonably sure to be in tune with current technical as well as social conditions and developments.

Unfortunately, the provisions of standards are too little known, both among indexers and among publishers and editors, and their recommendations may even be rejected in the realms of printing and publishing, which are among the most conservative enterprises in modern society. This may be only natural in an occupation and trade that can look back proudly on an unbroken tradition of more than half a millennium and among whose earliest products are books of enduring beauty and materials unmatched by any printed today, even with sophisticated electronic devices and huge machines that dwarf Gutenberg's humble and primitive hand press. Yet, despite the extensive use of computers for the physical production of books, periodicals, and other printed materials, some typographical traditions and rules of arrangement which affect indexes in particular continue to be used and enforced even though they are no longer useful (if ever they were) or have lost their justification. Letter-by-letter filing, for example, which is particularly unsuitable for indexes, is such a relic from earlier times; some presses and publishers are reluctant to abandon it, although the most prestigious and widely used encyclopedias are now arranged word-by-word, the method always used in library catalogs and therefore best known to the general public, as well as recommended by all current standards.

I have therefore attempted to make indexers as well as editors and publishers more aware of standards by citing relevant sections whenever they pertain to a particular topic, while dissuading them from following outmoded and counterproductive rules.

In addition to the practices and procedures dealt with by standards, I relied on the experience and insights of many of my predecessors, inasmuch as these are still useful and valid. I find myself in the same situation as Samuel Miller, a New Jersey clergyman, who stated in his book *A brief retrospect of the eighteenth century*, published in 1803:

> Though the greater part of this work consists of compilation, yet the writer claims to be something more than a mere compiler. He has offered, where he thought proper, opinions, reflections, and reasonings of his own (1803: 2, ix).

Whenever I recommend a practice or procedure, I try to justify it by stating my reasons, rather than relying merely on tradition or custom. Time and again in my research into the origins of various rules and practices widely accepted as gospel in the library field and in the more specialized one of indexing, I find that they were the ideas of (mostly anonymous) persons who imposed them following their own predilections or idiosyncrasies but seldom if ever based them on facts, observation, collection of data and their interpretation, or on research into causes and effects. (Nevertheless, the same persons usually claimed to work in a field they loved to call library *science*.)

My foremost criterion for judging a rule or procedure regarding its usefulness and viability is to ask the basic question "Is this rule necessary?", following in the footsteps of Seymour Lubetzky, whose valiant attempt in the 1950s to clean out the Augean stables of library cataloging rules has always been an inspiration to me. (Sad to say, his endeavor to simplify and streamline those rules was buried under an avalanche of even more rules, resulting in the present second edition of the *Anglo-American cataloguing rules* (1988)—but this, as Kipling used to say, is another story, and one with which indexers need not be overly much concerned.)

Having found a rule to be truly necessary, my next question is, "Does it work?" That is, will it help users to find what they are looking for in the best possible way—quickly, effectively, and without any prior knowledge of arcane rules? If a rule or a procedure is or contains an exception, I am particularly suspicious. Is this exception necessary? What happens if it is not made? Will it then be easier or more difficult for users to find desired information? If the exception is made "because we have always done it this way", this makes it a candidate for a good, long look at its usefulness and, if found wanting, for throwing it on the scrap heap.

If there are several different practices or possibilities to achieve a certain aim or effect, I have tried to analyze the reasons for and against their use in different circumstances as objectively as possible, and again without regard to prevailing customs or purportedly ancient traditions. I may not have succeeded in this endeavor in all such cases, but at least I have tried to look at controversial issues from different angles so as to justify my views and recommendations on the basis of their usefulness and not on that of my personal predilections.

The topic of the physical equipment necessary for indexing used to be treated by textbooks and manuals written in the B.C. (Before

Computers) era in a few short paragraphs, unless an author wanted to trot out some eccentric hobby-horses, such as thumb-indexed ledgers, ingeniously ruled foolscap sheets, perforated and gummed labels, metal frames for movable cardboard strips, and similar contraptions which might now be preserved in a museum of indexing if there were such an institution. Since this book is being published in the last decade of a century that has seen mankind's greatest technological achievements since the invention of the wheel, it is not easy to strike a reasonable balance between the traditional tools of the trade which at this time are still being used, and computers which will no doubt be dominant if not mandatory and ubiquitous as indexing tools by the end of the century or earlier. Since there are still indexers who either do not want to use a computer or do not need one for the very limited indexing they are doing as a hobby rather than as a business, I decided to deal briefly with cards and typewriters (but not with handwritten slips or batches of cards submitted as index manuscripts, which were still seriously considered only a little more than a decade ago).

Regarding computer-assisted indexing, I have tried to deal with its various aspects in general terms rather than in detail, being well aware of the fact that the extremely rapid developments in hardware and software would make any specific treatment obsolete even before this book reaches its first readers. On various technical aspects I sought the advice of friends and colleagues who were very generous (though not always unanimous) in bringing me up to date on the present state of the art, but any mistakes or questionable details should not be blamed on my advisors but on my limited understanding of these issues.

I must ask my readers to bear with some redundancy in the treatment of certain issues, which is virtually unavoidable in a book organized alphabetically by topics. Cross-references—printed in small capitals to avoid the repeated use of *see* and *see also* as much as possible—have been liberally employed so as not to overload any section with details treated elsewhere at greater length. This is particularly the case in the section on ALPHANUMERIC ARRANGEMENT, which would otherwise have swelled to a size out of proportion relative to other sections.

The index, compiled by myself—thus, not taking my own medicine —almost certainly suffers from the fault of overindexing. This was done on purpose, in order to illustrate as many indexing problems as possible. Nevertheless, users may occasionally look for some issue or detail but will not find it in the index. For such omissions, as well as for other mistakes, the blame rests with me rather than with any of the friends and colleagues to whom I owe thanks for their advice.

Acknowledgments

I am indebted for advice and constructive critique to Dr. Bella H. Weinberg, who suggested the title of the book, Dr. Karl F. Heumann, and Ms. Mary F. Tomaselli, all of whom read the entire manuscript, saving me from making many mistakes of omission and commission. I am also grateful to Mr. Bruce R. Carrick, my editor, who improved my style in many instances, pointed out errors and ambiguities, and saw the book through all stages of production. Other friends and colleagues who gave freely of their time and shared their experiences with me are K. G. B. Bakewell, Hazel K. Bell, Linda Fetters, Lotte Goldman, John Gordon, Sally S. Grande, Susan Klement, Jane and Hugh Maddocks, Max McMaster, Bill Pitt, Dr. Richard Randall, Frank Shulman, Kenneth Kazuo Tanaka, Dorothy Thomas, and Bill Wilson.

I also wish to thank the Society of Indexers for permission to reprint, with minor editorial revisions, my article "Index: the word, its history and meanings", as well as excerpts from the feature "Indexes past", which appeared in *The Indexer*.

The quotations from Stephen Leacock's *My remarkable uncle* are reprinted by permission of The Bodley Head, London; Dodd Mead & Co., New York; and McClelland & Stewart, Toronto.

My wife Shulamith helped, as usual, to check and recheck the index, but was much more importantly involved in the progress of the work through her loving care during my several periods of severe health problems. At times these threatened to inhibit or to slow down the writing of the book, which was begun as a pleasant way to spend my time in retirement but became a challenge to overcome what seemed to be almost insurmountable obstacles.

H. H. W.

ABBREVIATIONS

An abbreviation is a shortened or contracted form of a word or a phrase, used to represent the whole. Abbreviations appear in three different forms, namely, as *truncations, initialisms,* and *acronyms.*

Typical *truncations* are "Bull." for Bulletin, "Proc." for Proceedings, "Tr." or "Trans." for Transactions, "Govt." for Government, "Dept." for Department, and so on. They are always to be treated exactly as written and not "as if" spelled out in full.

An *initialism* is a set of initials representing parts of a name, with each letter pronounced separately (mostly because of a lack of vowels which could make the initialism pronounceable). Typical initialisms are BBC for British Broadcasting Corporation, DDT for dichlorodiphenyltrichloroethane, and NFL for National Football League. Sometimes, nicknames may develop from otherwise unpronounceable initialisms: FNMA (Federal National Mortgage Association) is fondly known in financial circles as "Fanny Mae".

An *acronym* is a name formed from the initial letters or groups of letters or words in a name or phrase. It is intended to be pronounceable and may, in the course of time, become a word or proper name in its own right, e.g., *radar* (originally an acronym for *r*adio *d*etecting *a*nd *r*anging) or *Unesco,* which underwent a metamorphosis from U.N.E.S.C.O. to UNESCO to Unesco, standing for *U*nited *N*ations *E*ducational, *S*cientific and *C*ultural *O*rganization; in this case, the organization itself decided to change its acronym to a proper name.

All abbreviations pose three problems in indexing: (a) when should they be used as main headings (and sometimes as subheadings)?, (b) how should they be punctuated?, and (c) where and how should they be alphabetized? The answer to (a) depends on several factors. Using an abbreviated form of a name or phrase will save space, particularly if the heading is followed by more than a few locators as well as by subheadings. For the latter, initialisms or acronyms are often preferable because of their brevity. In the following example, the spelled-out subheadings require turnover lines and the entry takes up seven lines, whereas the abbreviated subheadings result in an entry of only four lines and no turnover lines, which is easier to read.

Abbreviations as subheadings	*Subheadings spelled out*
indexing standards	indexing standards
ANSI 13, 56	American National
BSI 15, 27, 56	Standards Institute 13, 56
ISO 16	British Standards
	Institution 15, 27, 56
	International Organization
	for Standardization 16

Initialisms or acronyms may, however, be used in this manner only if they are expected to be well known to the users of the index, and a cross-reference from the full form of the name of an organization, project, material, etc. must be made in the index even if the full form is not given in the text. For initialisms or acronyms which are not widely known, or which may have been specifically invented by an author, it is preferable to index the full form, followed by the abbreviation in parentheses. A cross-reference from the abbreviation to the full form must be made if the full form is followed by many locators or by one or more subheadings. If the full form has only a few locators, say, no more than three, it is better to make DOUBLE ENTRIES, which may save two or even three lines, especially if the full form of an organization's name, for example, is rather long; it will also save the user's time, because no secondary lookup of a *see* reference will be necessary:

United Nations Relief and Rehabilitation
  Administration (UNRRA) 112, 120
        .
        .
        .

UNRRA 112, 120
  not
UNRRA *see* United Nations Relief and Rehabilitation
  Administration

Problem (b), PUNCTUATION, depends on the usage of the text. Most initialisms and all acronyms are now written without periods, but if periods are used in the text (as in the U.N.E.S.C.O. example above), they should also be written in the index. If usage varies and both punctuated and unpunctuated forms are found in the text, e.g., in a periodical, the most prevalent or the latest form (Unesco in the example) should be used, with cross-references to other forms if necessary.

The answer to problem (c), alphabetizing of initialisms and acronyms, has been the subject of heated debates. The relevant rules have changed more than once during the past few decades, to the utter confusion of indexers and index users alike. Fortunately, the solution has now become very simple and straightforward: all arrangement rules and indexing standards published since 1980 by national and international organizations and national libraries in the English-speaking world prescribe that the initialisms and acronyms be alphabetized exactly as written, and that any punctuation be disregarded; that is, they file as simple words. The only exceptions to this are initialisms or acronyms written as strings of letters separated by spaces, e.g., A B C, which makes each *letter* a "word"; such a heading may, however, only be used as a cross-reference, never as a main heading, as shown in the example below. These rules invalidate all older and often very complex and inconsistent rules regarding the alphabetizing of initialisms and acronyms, such as to group them before any other word or name beginning with the same letter, or to arrange them "as if spelled out".

Admittedly, the impetus for the formulation of the new and simple rules came from attempts to make alphabetization of index entries of all kinds amenable to automation, thereby eliminating the tedious and highly error-prone task of shuffling and reshuffling cards or slips, and reducing human intervention in alphabetizing to an absolute minimum. But it was also realized that the old rule "arrange abbreviations as if spelled out", though sounding quite simple, was in fact shot through with inconsistencies, contradictions, and problems of a linguistic nature. Thus, while *Mr.* is indeed uniformly spelled and pronounced (aloud or silently) as "Mister", such is not the case for a wife as *Mrs.*, never pronounced or arranged as "Mistress". (One of the many exceptions in the old ALA rules [ALA 1968] was an instruction to arrange *Mrs.* "as written", that is, exactly what the present rules say.) Going from Mr. and Mrs. to their liberated daughter *Ms.*, one wonders what the old-timers would have done with it had it already been invented in their time.

And what about *Dr.*, which may be spelled as Doctor, Docteur, Doktor, Dottore, etc. (e.g., in the many translations of *Dr. Zhivago*)? *St.* may be spelled out variously as Saint, Sainte, Sankt, Santa, Santo, etc. even in a strictly English index if names of places or churches in different countries are involved. To make matters a little bit more complicated, certain abbreviations widely used in scholarly writings date back to a time when every educated person knew Latin, but they are now "pronounced" (again, aloud or silently) in their English *translation:* e.g. [*exempli gratia*] is read as "for example", not "ee jee"; i.e. [*id est*] is read as "that is"; and there are a number of other such Latin abbreviations read not as written but as translated. Although they may not often be index entries, they might have to be indexed in an English grammar or style manual. In this instance, the old rule "arrange as if spelled out" breaks down altogether.

Even the *Chicago manual of style* (1993, 17.92, 17.107) has at long last come around to prefer alphabetization of abbreviations as written, though it still permits to arrange the abbreviation "St." occurring in personal and place names as if spelled out.

The following example shows the arrangement of abbreviations and acronyms according to the post-1980 rules, all of which prescribe or prefer word-by-word arrangement:

A B C *see* A.B.C.	No and yes
Aarhus	*No, Fernando*
Abacus	*Number 10, Downing Street*
A.B.C.	Number line
Abdera	R. Accademia
Cmdr. Smith	filarmonica
CO_2 lasers	RCA-Victor
Commander Brown	Regia Galleria di Firenze
Doctor Who	Sailors
Doktor, William	Saint, P. K.
Doktor Faustus	Sainte-Beuve, Charles Augustin
Dr. Jekyll and Mr. Hyde	San Francisco
M. Flip ignorait sa mort	Sankhya
Marine Maritime	*Short Title*
Academy (M.M.A.)	*Catalogue (STC)*
M'Bow, A. P.	SS. Pietro e Paolo
Mister Abbott	SS (Schutzstaffel)

Mistress Anne
Mlle. Henriette
M.M.A. *see* Marine
  Maritime Academy
Mme. Pompadour
Modern Poetry
  Association (M.P.A.)
Mons veneris
Monsieur Verdoux
M.P.A. *see* Modern
  Poetry Association
Mr. Adams
Mrs. Miniver
Ms.
M'sieu Gustave
No. 10, Downing Street

St. Louis
St. Moritz
*STC see Short Title
  Catalogue*
Ste. Geneviève Co.
Stearin
x rays
Xmas
Yemen
Y.M.C.A.
Yuan
YWCA
Zambia
z.B.
Zn
zoos

ALA: 3
BL: 2.4
BS 1749: 5.3
BS 3700: 5.2.1.3; 6.2.1.5; 7.1.4.3
Chicago manual of style: 14.1–57; 17.90
ISO 999: 7.3.6
LC: 10
NISO Z39.4:

ADJECTIVES

V irtually all textbooks and standards agree that an adjective *standing alone* should not be used as a main heading.

	Not this	*But this*
	optical	optical illusions 74
	illusions 74	optical rotation 36
	rotation 36	

Adjectival nouns, however, may be used as headings:

> food
>   additives 15
>   colors 23
>   preservatives 47

This entry could also (and with one line less) be displayed as

> food additives 15
> food colors 23
> food preservatives 47

but the indented subheadings in the first example are more easily scanned than the three headings in the second one, because the eye must "jump", as it were, across the first word to find the distinguishing part of the heading. This applies to printed pages as well as (or perhaps even more) to screen displays.

On the question of whether or not to invert headings consisting of an adjective and a noun, *see* COMPOUND HEADINGS.

ADVERBS

Adverbs should not be used as headings, except in those rare instances when they happen to be the first word of a set phrase used as a term, e.g., "Very high frequency band". Adverbs may, of course, also form the initial word in entries of title indexes, in first-line indexes of POETRY, and in indexes to linguistic texts in which adverbs are treated as topics.

ALPHANUMERIC ARRANGEMENT

No other issue in librarianship and indexing has evoked more heated debates, has been bedevilled by more arcane and silly rules, has been the target of more well-deserved satire* and ridicule, or has frustrated users more than the arrangement of headings in catalogs and indexes. Before 1980, filing rules were not based on the sequence of letters in the Roman alphabet alone but contained dozens of complex and sometimes contradictory rules intended to file certain words or groups of words and letters by their *meaning* rather than by their graphic representation and to arrange abbreviations and numbers as they were *pronounced*, not as they were written. All of this needed not only special rules but also dozens of exceptions which human filers were expected to remember unfailingly, though most of these unfortunate clerks neither did their job correctly nor understood what they were doing and why. The rules were, however, not designed in order to fool the "enemy"—the users of alphabetic files—but out of an earnest and sincere desire to make entries in catalogs and indexes easier to find. Alas, though, they had the opposite effect. The plethora of special rules and exceptions resulted in such confusion that even trained librarians and indexers were often unable to make sense of an alphabetical arrangement, while the general public was baffled and exasperated, because more often than not people could not find what they were looking for, especially in card catalogs in which only one entry at a time could be seen.

When it became obvious that the tedious task of alphabetizing could be performed by computers which were admirably suited for repetitive operations following strict and logical rules, it turned out that the arcane exceptions and special provisions of the arrangement rules, stipulating, for example, that certain words should be arranged "as if" transposed to a different place in a heading or even "as if" they did not exist at all, could not be translated into programs that computers could execute.

Rules and Standards

Partly because of the need for computer-compatible arrangement and partly because of the even more urgent need for simplification of the rules, by 1980 all national arrangement rules and standards

*One of the funniest is Herbert H. Hoffman's "How the indefatigable H*Y*M*A*N K*A*P*L*A*N got filed by the foiling rules" (1976).

in the English-speaking world had been thoroughly revised and streamlined. For example, the *ALA rules for filing catalog cards* of 1968 contained 37 main rules, having from three to a dozen or more subrules and filling 260 pages; they were stripped down in the *ALA filing rules* of 1980, a slim 50-page pamphlet, to only 10 main rules and a few subrules, only seven or eight of which are sufficient for most alphabetizing purposes.

All alphanumeric arrangement rules and standards issued after 1980, namely, *ALA filing rules* (ALA), *BLAISE filing rules* (BL), BS 1749:1985 *Alphabetical arrangement . . .* , the *Library of Congress filing rules* (LC), and both the international standard ISO 999 and the American standard NISO Z39.4 on indexing (which contain rules for alphabetical arrangement) consider only the graphic representation of symbols, numbers, and words, but not their meaning or pronunciation. A new NISO standard, *Alphabetical arrangement of letters, and the sorting order of numerals and other symbols*, which is currently being developed, will be based on the same principles.

In alphabetical files kept in the form of cards (which are now rapidly disappearing from the scene) the old rules are often still being followed because of the impossibility of rearranging tens of thousands or millions of cards according to the current rules. But that is fortunately not the case for indexes to books which ought to be arranged by the current rules. Regarding indexes to PERIODI-CALS, these too need not be arranged by the old rules for the sake of continuity, but can be arranged by the current rules, beginning with a new volume.

Since 1980, when the current alphanumerical arrangement rules were published, they have proven their effectiveness. Indexers should firmly insist on the exclusive application of these rules, not only because they enable a computer to relieve an indexer from the tedious and error-prone task of alphanumerical arrangement but also, and most importantly, to make it possible for users of an index to find what they are looking for quickly and easily.

At this point, the reader may well ask: why bother about arrangement rules, old or new? Are not word processors equipped with sorting programs which will automatically put all headings in their correct alphabetic place? The answer to this is, unfortunately, no.

Commonly used all-purpose software, sorting headings by ASCII*
codes, will not produce alphabetic sequences suitable for indexing
and may actually wreak havoc with index entries.

This may happen because a term enclosed in quotation marks (either single or double) will precede all numerically or alphabetically
sorted terms; hyphens and commas will sort after spaces; and all
terms beginning with a capital letter will be arranged before those
beginning with lowercase letters. The result would be the following
sequence of headings:

> "hyperion" (Keats)
> *1066 and all that*
> Alabama
> Mainland
> Zoological Society
> alabaster
> mainland
> mean time
> mean, arithmetic
> sick leave
> sick-berth
> zoology

Only sorting software specially designed for indexing will produce
properly arranged entries, and, even then, human intervention may
sometimes be necessary to "nudge" headings into their correct alphanumeric position by formatting them in a special way, e.g.,
names of chemical compounds (discussed below).

Terminology

Filing, the most general, and formerly the most widely understood,
term still graces the titles of several current standards and codes of
practice for alphanumeric arrangement. Unfortunately, it has become ambiguous, because the term "file" is being used in the context of data processing in an entirely different sense; it is therefore
no longer suitable and has been largely replaced by *alphanumeric*

*For an explanation of ASCII see p. 460.

arrangement. The term *alphabetization,* frequently employed in this book, is not comprehensive enough, because it applies solely to the arrangement of a sequence of letters forming words, phrases, and abbreviations. *Sorting,* the term used when the arrangement is performed by a computer, pertains not only to the arrangement of symbols, numerals, and letters but in certain systems it distinguishes also between their shape and size (upper- and lowercase); this feature is not only irrelevant for the purpose of arranging index headings but is actually counterproductive if rigorously applied, as shown in the example above.

Symbols

All current arrangement rules stipulate that symbols other than letters and numerals (except for a few punctuation marks in some rules) have no ordering value and should be disregarded in alphanumeric arrangement (ALA, 1.2; BL, 1.1.1; BS 1749, 4.1; BS 3700, 6.2.1.3(c); LC, 1.3, 18). Headings beginning with a symbol are therefore currently arranged by the first letter or word following the symbol, and a symbol occurring anywhere after the first word of a heading is disregarded. However, this rule, while simplifying computerized sorting, makes such headings in effect unfindable, as shown in Figure 11, p. 462, and is, therefore, entirely unsuitable for the arrangement of index headings.

Instead, any symbol in a heading otherwise written with letters or numerals or both should be explicated by its name in brackets, e.g. the title *100% American* should be alphabetized as *100 [percent] American.* This is also the reasoning behind the optional exception made by the arrangement rules cited above, namely for the AMPERSAND which may be explicated and arranged as the word "and" or its equivalent in other languages (see Table 1, p. 23).

The forthcoming NISO standards on indexing and on alphabetical arrangement will prescribe that all symbols (including PUNCTUATION marks) are to be considered the *equivalent* of a space for arrangement purposes, and not to be treated as if they did not exist.

Various methods for the arrangement of symbols when these have to be shown in an index (e.g., the various icons used on monitors to generate pictures, which must be indexed in a software manual) are discussed under SYMBOLS.

Numerals and Numbers

All numbers are arranged after spaces or their equivalents (dashes, hyphens, and diagonal slashes) and before any heading beginning with a letter (ALA, 1; BL, 1.2.3.1; BS 1749, 4.1; 4.2; BS 3700, 6.2.1.2(c); ISO 999, 8.3; LC 1.2; NISO Z39.4). Roman numbers are written in the customary manner by means of capital letters but are arranged with other numbers according to their numerical value (ALA, 8.5; BL, 1.2.3.5; BS 3700, 6.2.1.2(c), 6.2.1.4; LC, 16.2; ISO 999, 8.3; NISO Z39.4). However, this cannot be achieved automatically and needs human intervention, namely the flagging of Roman numerals as such; once strings of capital letters have been identified as not being "words" but Roman numerals, computers can sort them arithmetically, provided that an algorithm for that purpose is part of the sorting program.

Example:

0 (zero)	*Le XXme siècle*
2-phase flow	*The XXnd Olympic Games*
3-D scale drawing	*25 short stories*
3.1416 and all that	*Nineteen Eighty-Four*
3M Company	*Three men in a boat*
17 days to better living	XX *see* powdered sugar
Der 18. Oktober	zero-sum games

Punctuation used to aid in the readability of a number is ignored, e.g., 1,765,348 is filed as 1765348. Slashes, fraction lines, hyphens, and colons in numerical expressions (any of which may appear as first elements of titles, but also in other contexts) are treated as spaces, e.g.,

Heading	*Arranged as*
1:00 a.m.	1 00 a m
1–14–90	1 14 90
½	1 2
⅓	1 3

(ALA, 8.6; BL, 1.2.3.1; BS 1749, 4.2.2; LC, 16.1, 16.4).

Subscript and superscript numerals are treated as if they were printed on the line but preceded by a space; they are then treated as any other numeral, that is, before any following letter; e.g.,

Heading	Arranged as
10^6	10 6
C_3H_8	C 3H 8
$CaCO_3$	CaCO 3
cadmium	cadmium
CO	CO
Coast Guard C^4I system	Coast Guard C4I system
CS_2	CS 2

(ALA, 8.6; BL, 1.2.3.4; BS 1749, 4.3; LC, 16.6). *See also* NUMERALS.

Modified Letters

Any letters modified by DIACRITICS (marks written above, below, through, or inside a letter in order to distinguish it from the basic letter, and using it to represent a different sound) are alphabetized as if they were basic unmodified letters, that is, à, á, â, ä, ā, ă, å, ą are all arranged as a simple a, ç as c, ñ as n, ø as o, and so on (ALA, 1.1; BL, 1.2.4.1; BS 1749, 4.1; BS 3700, 6.2.1.3(d); LC, 1.1.1). Diacritics must, however, be printed, and may not be omitted, as is so often the case because printers seem to think that these outlandish squiggles are unnecessary and can be dispensed with.

Single-Word Headings

The alphabetization of headings consisting of single words would not seem to need a rule other than the most basic one, namely, that such a heading be arranged according to the sequence of its constituent letters. But what is a "single word"? Normally, it is a string of letters, preceded and followed by a space, representing a vocabulary item of a language. But the matter is not always as clear-cut as that. Thus, both "ground" and "water" are single words; "groundwater" is technically also a single word, but the alternative spellings "ground water" and "ground-water" are not. Both are compound headings, since there is a space in the first one, and a hyphen is the equivalent of a space in alphabetization (*see also* HYPHENATION). Abbreviations, initialisms, and acronyms such as Proc., BBC, or NATO may or may not qualify as single words, depending on the way they are printed (with or without periods or spaces between letters). For more details *see* ABBREVIATIONS.

Compound Headings

Headings consisting of two or more words are COMPOUND HEAD-INGS, which are alphabetized by the letters of the first word; if two or more headings share the same first word, the next word is alphabetized, and so on, until each heading occupies its unique place in an alphabetical sequence. The best-known example is the arrangement of names in a phone book, where persons having the same surname are distinguished by forenames, and if they share the same forename, then other distinguishing elements come into play, such as address or occupation. The apparent simplicity of this system has often led people to ask why index entries cannot similarly be alphabetized in a way that is simple and easily understood. The answer to that is that the vast majority of index entries are indeed alphabetized in the same or in a similar manner, but that some types of entries have to be treated differently, such as hyphenated headings and abbreviations (discussed above) as well as some others. In addition, there exist two different systems of alphabetization, a fact that is not very widely known among people other than librarians and indexers (and even they are not always sure which is which and why), because children are never taught that such is the case when they are first initiated into the mysteries of the alphabet and its ordering function.

Word-by-Word and Letter-by-Letter Alphabetization

Index entries were not always alphabetized by considering every letter in a word from beginning to end, as people are wont to do today. Most early indexes were arranged only by the first letter of the first word, the rest being left in no particular order at all. Gradually, alphabetization advanced to an arrangement by the first syllable, that is, the first two or three letters, the rest of an entry still being left unordered. Only very few indexes compiled in the 16th and early 17th centuries had fully alphabetized entries, but by the 18th century full alphabetization became the rule, so that every heading was arranged by all letters in its LEAD TERM and mostly also by the following words if the first ones were common to two or more headings. Once this principle had become a common practice, two systems of alphabetizing also evolved and have been a contentious issue ever since. Their merits and demerits have been hotly debated, generating more heat than light, and they have been either recommended or rejected for certain types of indexes.

In the word-by-word system, each compound heading is first alphabetized by the letters of its lead term; if two headings share the same lead term, the next word is alphabetized, and so on. If any two lead terms share the same letter sequence, but one is longer by one or more letters, the shorter one precedes the longer one, e.g., DOT files after DO and before DOTS. The system is also popularly known as "nothing before something" because a space ("nothing") always precedes a letter or word ("something") in alphabetization.

The other system known as letter-by-letter, treats a compound heading as a single "word", disregarding any spaces or punctuation marks; its popular name is, therefore, "all-through".

At first sight, there may not seem to be much if any difference between the two systems because both are, of course, based on the principle that a word is alphabetized by the sequence of its letters, and it is actually futile to argue that one is better than the other as an ordering device. Both achieve their intended purpose, namely, to arrange headings in a predictable pattern that assures a unique place for every heading, no matter how long or complex an index may be.

Neither system is more "natural", as has sometimes been claimed, because the order of the alphabet itself is artificial and arbitrary; it is based on a decision probably made by the ancient Phoenicians who left us no clue for the grounds on which they decided that the letter *alef* should be the first, followed by *beth*, and so on.

The important difference between the two systems is that word-by-word alphabetization keeps headings beginning with the same name or word together, while letter-by-letter alphabetization tends to disperse them, depending on the first letter following the end of the initial word. Since this would, however, wreak havoc with the alphabetization of homographic surnames (which must normally be kept together in a single sequence, differentiated only by their forenames), letter-by-letter alphabetization needs a special rule regarding commas in order to avoid a faulty arrangement such as

Brown, Charles
Browne, John
Browner, Anne
Browne, Thomas
Brown, George
Browning, Jane
Brown, Johnson, Miller & Co.

The rule given in the *Chicago manual of style* (1993, 17.97) states that

alphabetization continues across spaces between words and stop at the first comma preceding a modifying element or an inversion. . . . Parentheses enclosing definitions, alternatives, explanations or cross-references also interrupt letter-by-letter alphabetization. But . . . alphabetization continues across hyphens, slashes, apostrophes, and . . . serial commas.

People other than professional editors or proofreaders will probably not know that such distinctions between punctuation marks are made in alphabetization, nor that there are two classes of commas, a subject not taught in English grammar lessons, neither in grade school nor at college level.

The aim of keeping names and headings with the same spelling together in an unbroken alphabetical sequence is automatically achieved by the word-by-word system, in which no special rules for punctuation are needed, since, for example, the shorter name Brown will always precede the longer names Browne, Browner, Browning, etc., regardless of which forenames follow them:

Brown, Charles
Brown, George
Brown, Johnson, Miller & Co.

Browne, John
Browne, Thomas
Browner, Anne
Browning, Jane

In both systems, alphabetization is carried only to the end of a heading; *see* and *see also* cross-references following immediately after a heading are never alphabetized with it.

The different arrangement of headings resulting from the choice of one system or the other matters little if any in a brief index. In long indexes, however, particularly in those containing personal names with prefixes and in indexes to scientific and technical publications, it may make a tremendous difference, as can be seen in the following examples.

Word-by-word	*Letter-by-letter*
gas	gas
gas burners	gas burners
gas engines	gas engines
gas heating	gas heating
gas pipes	gaskets
gas supply	gasoline
gas turbines	Gaspé peninsula
gas welding	gas pipes
gaskets	gas supply
gasoline	gastrectomy
Gaspé peninsula	gastric juice
gastrectomy	gastritis
gastric juice	gas turbines
gastritis	gas welding
gasworks	gasworks
La Fayette, Gilbert	Laas, Ernst
La Fontaine, Jean de	Labé, Louise
La Tour, Maurice	Lafayette, Charles
Laas, Ernst	La Fayette, Gilbert
Labé, Louise	Lafont, Pierre
Lafayette, Charles	La Fontaine, Jean de
Lafont, Pierre	Lafontaine, Louis
Lafontaine, Louis	Latouche, Joseph
Latouche, Joseph	La Tour, Maurice

The word-by-word system has always been used in library catalogs, whereas the letter-by-letter system is invariably employed in the arrangement of dictionaries. In the past, letter-by-letter was also used in many encyclopedias, but since 1980 virtually all major general encyclopedias, foremost among them the *Encyclopaedia Britannica*, followed the example of the *Encyclopedia Americana* and the *Academic American encyclopedia* and switched to the word-by-word system for the arrangement of entries both in the text and in the indexes. The claim that one system is preferable for a certain discipline or field is belied by the diametrically opposed statements made by practitioners or authorities in those fields. Thus, the letter-by-letter system is said to be "used almost without exception" by American lawyers (Thomas 1983, p. 168), while "in general, the word-by-word system is preferred" according to a British legal expert (Hewitt 1969, p. 165). The style manual of the Council of Biology Editors shows an example of both methods in its section on indexes and states that "Alphabetizing terms letter by letter is generally preferred" (*Scientific style and format* 1994, p. 702), but without providing evidence for that statement or discussing the advantages and disadvantages of the two methods. On the other hand, the *Encyclopedia of science and technology* (1992) arranges both its entries and its index word-by-word.

The best evidence for the superiority of the word-by-word system for title and subject indexes is found in the introduction to the index volume of the 15-volume *Encyclopaedia of world art* (1959, v. 15, p. li):

> Alphabetization of the index . . . is in dictionary style, letter by letter. . . . There is one important exception. Titles of works of art are alphabetized word by word. . . . In a strict letter-by-letter arrangement a title that begins *"Christ healing"* would be followed by approximately three hundred lines of entries and subentries for "Christianity" before the next title, which begins with the words *"Christ in."* *"Man and"* would be separated from *"Man of "* by nearly four hundred lines, including all material on "mannerism." . . . [T]he advantage of finding all titles beginning with *"Christ"* in one sequence is more important than the inconsistency [of] this arrangement.

Had the indexer employed the word-by-word method throughout this index, she would have avoided many other inconsistencies

inevitably caused by the letter-by-letter system, which is now rapidly losing ground. Even the arch-conservative *Chicago manual of
style* (1993, 17.98), which prefers the letter-by-letter system, grants
that the press is "willing to accept indexes compiled on the word-
by-word principle". The letter-by-letter system is still used in most
gazetteers on the grounds that it keeps place names such as New
Haven and Newhaven together; but this is a specious argument,
since these are indeed different places, one in Connecticut, others in
England and in Scotland. It is difficult to understand what is gained
by listing them close together. If deemed to be necessary, a
cross-reference "New Haven *see also* Newhaven" can always be
made, and the same device can be used for names such as La
Fayette/Lafayette.

All current alphabetization rules (ALA, BL, and LC) are predicated on the word-by-word system, and the national and international standards (BS 1749, BS 3700, ISO 999, and NISO Z39.4) recommend it strongly. The forthcoming NISO alphabetization
standard will also follow the same principle.

A survey of 255 frequent index users (librarians and college professors) found that 90% of the librarians and 68% of the professors
preferred word-by-word alphabetization (Diodato 1994). Un-
daunted by this clear preference of users, most American publishers
still ignore the recommendations of the current alphabetization
rules and standards (Mulvany 1994, pp. 59–62), mainly because the
letter-by-letter system is favored by the *Chicago manual of style*. British publishers, however, prefer mostly the word-by-word system
(Simpkins 1990).

The choice of one or the other alphabetization system will thus
most often depend on the house style of a publisher and the preference of an editor; only seldom will an indexer be allowed to make a
decision on this matter.

Whichever system is chosen, it must be applied rigorously and
consistently. One of the worst mistakes in indexing is the mixing of
the two systems, which may leave even an experienced user with
knowledge of both systems baffled and exasperated because entries
cannot be found in their expected places.

Since it is not always obvious by which system an index has been
alphabetized, the INTRODUCTORY NOTE should make it clear which

system has been used. In this book, all examples and the index are alphabetized according to the word-by-word system.

Names

In relatively short indexes, and when only a small number of names is involved, proper names may be intermingled with other headings; but if two or more name headings begin with the same word, each homograph must be printed separately. Under no circumstances should long dashes be printed for the repeated keyword, as in the following horrible example:

London, Arthur
———— bridge is falling down
————, Jack
———— Transport Co.
————, Zelda

In long indexes containing many homographs (identical forenames, surnames, corporate names, place names, and topical headings) it may become necessary to arrange them in two or more separate consecutive alphabets (as is the custom in large library catalogs). The rules for such classified arrangements are discussed in more detail under HOMOGRAPHS.

Complex personal names—those that are hyphenated, begin with prefixes, articles, or prepositions in different languages, or are of non-Western origin—pose many difficulties regarding their proper entry word, which are discussed under PERSONAL NAMES. But once the form of a name and its proper first element have been established according to the relevant rules, it is generally not difficult to alphabetize them the same way as any other compound heading. *See also* CORPORATE NAMES and PLACE NAMES.

Prepositions and Conjunctions in Subheadings

Subheadings beginning with the function words *and, as, at, for, in, on, under,* and other prepositions or conjunctions should as far as possible be avoided because the function words are in most cases superfluous and self-evident, as discussed under PREPOSITIONS. If, however, a preposition is needed for the sake of clarity, it should be alphabetized the same as any other word in a compound heading. The advice given in older textbooks and in the *Chicago manual of style* (1993, 17.104), namely that prepositions and conjunctions in subheadings should be disregarded and the subheadings arranged by the word following the function word, is no longer supported by the current arrangement rules and standards, none of which recommends that anything be disregarded in alphabetizing.

Disregarded Elements of Headings in Biology and Chemistry

Names of chemical compounds often have prefixes or infixes such as numerals, italicized letters, capital letters standing for elements, small capitals, Greek letters, or verbal prefixes such as *meta-, ortho-, para-*, and others, all of which should be disregarded in alphabetization unless they are the only differentiating elements in otherwise identical names of chemical compounds (*Scientific style and format* 1994, p. 702), as shown in the following example:

acetyl benzoyl peroxide
acetylcarb
N-acylneuraminic acid
O-acylneuraminic acid
butanol
1-butanol
1-butanol, 1 cyclohexyl-
1 butanol, 2 cyclohexyl-
2-butanol
tert-butanolysis
16,17-butanomorphinan
3-ethyl-4-picoline
4-ethyl-α-picoline
ribonucleic acids
*m*RNA
*t*RNA
ortho-xylene
para-xymene
zeolites

Disregarding prefixes of names and other words in alphabetization is a practice strictly limited to the disciplines of biology and chemistry, and may not be extended to headings in any other discipline or field.

Nonalphabetical Order of Headings

Although indexes are normally arranged in alphabetical order, there are instances in which other arrangements are needed or are more suitable. Even in alphabetic indexes, separate sequences have to be established for NUMERALS and SYMBOLS, and subheadings may have to be arranged in CHRONOLOGICAL ORDER, CLASSIFIED ORDER, evolutionary order, or canonical order, all of which are discussed and exemplified under the relevant sections and under NONALPHABETICAL ORDER.

Non-Roman Letters and Headings

In the disciplines of astronomy, biology, chemistry, and physics, as well as in various other fields of study, Greek letters are often used as prefixes or infixes of scientific names; in mathematics, Hebrew letters may also be used. Depending on the traditions of these disciplines and fields, Greek letters may either be ignored (as in biology and chemistry, discussed above), Romanized (e.g., in astronomy), or arranged in a separate index, as discussed in detail under GREEK SCRIPT.

Entries in other non-Roman scripts may either be rendered in ROMANIZATION or arranged in separate indexes for each script, e.g., in texts dealing with the Bible and the Apocrypha there may be a need for a regular Roman index, followed by a Hebrew and Greek index for citations from Scripture. Under no circumstances should entries in different scripts be mixed in the same sequence, the non-Roman ones being arranged as if they had been Romanized. An example of this confusing practice is the *British union catalogue of periodicals* (1955–1958) and the *ABHB: the annual bibliography of the history of the printed book and libraries* (1973–   ) which should not be emulated in this respect.

BS 1749
BS 3700: 6.2
ISO 999: 8
NISO Z39.4:

AMPERSAND

The symbol & or *et* is a contraction of the letters *e* and *t* (*et,* Latin for "and"), one of many such devices invented by medieval scribes in order to speed up writing and to save precious space on parchment or vellum, their costly writing materials. The ampersand is the only one of these contractions that has survived until our days, though it is now used only in the names of commercial firms or, very rarely, in fancy titles of books or poems. Sometimes it is used in index subheadings for the same reason the scribes invented it: to save space on a line. Its peculiar name, ampersand, once written "ampussy", is also a (badly mangled) contraction of "and per se and", that is, "[the symbol] & by itself [stands for] and". It is the nearest the Western world has come to the Chinese writing system: the character & is written the same way wherever the Roman alphabet is used, and its meaning as a connective is uniformly recognized, but its pronunciation varies with the language—and that is just one half of the problem which the little squiggle poses in indexing. The other half is: since it is neither one of the 26 letters of the English alphabet nor a numeral, where and how should it be arranged in an alphanumeric sequence?

Before 1980, all rules prescribed that & should be arranged "as if spelled out". This rule sounded simple and had the advantage of uniformity. Actually, it was far from simple, because it meant that both the indexer and the user had to know the spelling of "and" in those languages in which the ampersand is being used (*see* Table 1, p. 23). It may even become impossible to determine the pronunciation of an ampersand unless extraneous information on the language of the heading is provided; for example, in a title index there may be two identical entries *Arte & cultura,* one of which is Italian (& to be arranged as "e"), the other Spanish (& to be arranged as "y"), as shown in the example on p. 24.

Since 1980, alphanumeric arrangement rules have been designed so as to make the ampersand amenable to automatic sorting, but unfortunately these rules are not uniform. Three widely used arrangement rules, namely BS 1749, BL, and LC, assign the lowest arrangement value among alphanumeric characters to the ampersand, that is, the symbol & follows a space and precedes numerals or letters.

When automatic sorting is performed by using ASCII codes, the ampersand has value 038, which puts it after space (032) and before some other symbols and the numeral Ø (048), thus achieving essentially the same effect as the three arrangement rules just mentioned.

The odd man out is ALA, which treats the ampersand as any other symbol by "ignoring" it, that is, as if it did not exist at all (*not* as a space). The resulting arrangement of names or titles is probably more difficult to understand for most people, and is therefore not recommended for indexes.

All rules permit as an alternative the arrangement of an ampersand as if it were spelled out (at least for cross-references, if needed). If only English names or titles are indexed, this can still be done automatically by appropriate software, but if foreign languages are also involved, it is less time-consuming and error-prone to manually post-edit an automatically sorted sequence of entries containing ampersands. Table 1 will be helpful in applying the option to arrange an ampersand as spelled out for languages other than English.

Table 1. The Word "And" in Some Foreign Languages

Language	& spelled as	Language	& spelled as
Afrikaans	en	Icelandic	og
Catalan	i	Italian	e
Croatian	i	Latvian	un
Czech	a	Norwegian	og
Danish	og	Polish	i
Dutch / Flemish	en	Portuguese	e
Estonian	ja	Romanian	şi
Finnish	ja	Slovak	a
French	et	Spanish	y
German	und	Swedish	och
Hungarian	es	Welsh	a, ac

Note: languages written in non-Roman scripts do not use the ampersand.

The following examples show a sequence of entries, some of which contain an ampersand. In the left column, the & is arranged following a space and preceding a numeral or letter; in the right column, the & is arranged as spelled out in the respective language (explicated only for non-English languages).

Automated sorting of &	*Arrangement of & as if spelled out*	
& so to bed	*007 James Bond*	
007 James Bond	A 22	
A. & A. Enterprises, Inc.	A 22 & 23	
A. & H. Rodriguez	A. & A. Enterprises, Inc.	
A. & P. Schultze, GmbH	A B C see A.B.C.	
A. & R. Leblanc frères	A. & R. Leblanc frères	[et]
A 22	A. & P. Schultze, GmbH	[und]
A 22 & 23	A. & H. Rodriguez	[y]
A B C see A.B.C.	AAB (Army Air Base)	
AAB (Army Air Base)	Abbott & Co.	
Abbot & Co.	A.B.C.	
A.B.C.	*& so to bed*	
Art & commonsense	*Art & commonsense*	
Art &c	*Art &c*	[etcetera]
Arte & cultura [Italian]	*Arte & cultura*	[e]
Arte & cultura [Spanish]	*Arte e historia*	
Arte e historia	*Arte & cultura*	[y]

ALA: 1.2; 1.3
BL: 1.2.2
BS 1749: 4.1
LC: 18.1
NISO Z39.4:

AND

The second most frequent word in English nonfiction prose is also quite often found in main headings and even more in subheadings, probably because it seems to be such a brief and convenient way to express a link between two concepts or names treated together in the text. The little word is, however, often of little help for the index user, and it should be avoided as far as possible.

Of course, no one would argue against "and" when it joins two parts of a name heading, such as "Black and Decker" (most often in the form of an AMPERSAND), or in set phrases such as "black-and-white films" or "savings and loan associations". In title and first-line indexes, "and" must be part of a heading even if it is the first word: *And* is the entire title of two poems listed in the *Columbia-Granger's index to poetry* (1990) and the same work contains several columns of first lines beginning with "and"; *And so to bed* (Havlice 1987) is the title of a bibliography of diaries.

But when should "and" not be used?

1. In phrases linking entities and activities (or agents) by joining two words derived from the same root, such as "Banks and banking". This heading may be justified when the text deals with the two concepts in one and the same context and on the same pages; otherwise, two separate headings should be made, even though they may come close together in the alphabetical sequence. If necessary, *see also* CROSS-REFERENCES may be added, e.g.,

bank holidays 77
banking 20, 35, 47 *see also* banks
banknotes 122
bankruptcy 208, 337
banks 24, 37, 45
   accounts 73
   failures 38
   insurance 49, 53
   security 133

2. In phrases linking a term and its antonym, e.g., "reward and punishment", "sobriety and drunkenness", or linking two terms for concepts that are thought to be closely related, as in the following examples (all culled from the *New York Times* index):

behavior and training
books and literature
decisions and verdicts

> laboratories and scientific equipment
> sales and contracts

Most of these express relationships that obtain only in certain circumstances but not generally: users looking for behavior may not be interested in training and vice versa; not all books deal with literature, nor is all literature published in books; decision making is not necessarily tied to the deliberations of a jury; scientific equipment is not used in laboratories only; not all contracts are related to sales, and so on. But the establishment of arbitrary or spurious relationships in "and"ed index headings is not the worst part of it; much more serious is the fact that the second term in "and"ed phrases is effectively hidden and made inaccessible for an index user who may remember that a book or article dealt with punishment, drunkenness, training, or contracts but who does not know that these terms can only be found by hitting upon quite different terms to which they have been linked by "and". Even if a *text* may frequently link together two antonymous or related concepts, the *index* must list each of them separately or at least provide cross-references, the more so since the two parts of a linked phrase will not come close together in an alphabetical sequence, as is the case in instance 1 above.

3. In hackneyed phrases (often taken from outmoded subject heading lists) implying some unspecified relationship between two broad concepts, such as "Church and State" or "Religion and science", and for the same reasons as in instance 2.

4. In subheadings beginning with "and", indicating a modification of or relation with the concept expressed by the main heading:

> obesity
>   and diet
>   and heredity
>
> Churchill, Winston S.
>   and gold standard
>   and Palestine

In instances 3 and 4 the word "and" does not tell the user what kind of relationship obtains, only that two concepts are somehow treated together in the text, and that is often not enough, nor does it save the user's time. In the "Church and State" example, the text may say "When Church and State were legally separated . . .", but the index heading does not make that clear, whereas

Church	*and*	State
separation from State		separation from Church

result in unambiguous entries.

In the "obesity" example, does the text deal with diet as its cause or with a slimming diet? Did Churchill institute a policy on Palestine or did he just give his opinion on the country? Did he abolish or return to the gold standard? The relationships should be made explicit by suitable paraphrases of the text, even though this may result in subheadings that are slightly longer than the "and"ed ones, e.g.,

obesity	*or*	obesity
dietary factors		diets
hereditary		as a cause
slimming diets		for weight loss
		hereditary

with corresponding entries

diets	heredity
obesity caused by	diabetes
slimming	obesity
vegetarian	syphilis

For the "Churchill" entry, the following subheadings may be suitable:

Churchill, Winston S.
  Palestine policies criticized
  gold standard reinstated

Thus, "and" should preferably not be used as the first or last word of a subheading, because that renders it almost meaningless. Users will be better served by subheadings that explicate and specify their relationship to the main heading by suitable wording. This will also enable users to scan subheadings more rapidly, because their essential initial terms will appear in the proper alphabetical sequence, and not tucked away behind a tedious sequence of "and"s.

A special case of phrases in which "and" connecting two terms should be retained is their use in LEGAL TEXTS, discussed on p. 265.

ANONYMOUS PERSONS

Depending on the libel laws of a country, it is sometimes not possible for the author of a biography or a political work to mention persons still living or only recently deceased whose doings may have been sinister and well-documented but who had never been convicted in open court, or whose sexual habits were uncommon, or who had any other personal traits the revelation of which may be grounds for a libel suit by the person himself or his or her heirs. Likewise, in a book reporting the history of a major crime a state witness who has been given a "new identity" in exchange for his or her testimony cannot be mentioned by name, whether former or present. Persons serving in a country's security service must also often remain anonymous.

Nevertheless, such anonymous persons, whose real names may be indicated in the text only by a long dash or three asterisks or some such typographical device, must be indexed, as they are often frequently mentioned throughout a book. One way of doing this is to list all such references under the main heading "Anonymous persons" and to provide subheadings based on the context which describes the persons (often in an only thinly veiled manner). The following example is adapted from an actual index published in 1987 which was, however, so badly alphabetized that it must itself remain anonymous:

    anonymous persons
      bisexual Lord 121
      Conservative MP 118, 133, 212
      Conservative Secretary of State 213
      former MI6 operative 151–3

friend of Lord Astor 161
Hungarian woman 191
lesbians 149, 217
member of the Royal Family 211
minister who offered to resign 4, 209
model 54
solicitor 209

Some of the subheadings in the example could also be used as main headings with the subheading "anonymous", e.g.,

lesbians 159, 210, 305
    anonymous 149, 217

but this may become somewhat cumbersome and tedious if the text deals with many persons who cannot be named because the author is afraid of libel suits.

APOSTROPHES

Any word or name written with an apostrophe is filed only by its letter sequence, disregarding the little (but not unimportant!) symbol. All arrangement rules and style manuals agree on this, but the British arrangement standard and rules provide an exception for M' in Scottish and Irish names (for which *see* MAC). In the following example all apostrophes are disregarded.

Cox, A.
Cox, F.
Coxe, B.
Cox's apples
Coxsackie virus
Jacaranda
J'accuse
Jackobowski, M.
Jack-o'-lantern

MacKenzie, S.
Mayer, Barbara
M.B.A.
M'Bow, Amadou
McAllister, David
McKenzie, Arthur
Meyer, Fritz
M'Kenzie, William
M'Puono, A.
oboes
O'Boyle, Patrick
Ocala
O'Connor, Tom

ALA: 6
BL: 1.1.1; 2.3
BS 1749: 4.1
BS 3700: 6.2.i.3(a)
LC: 15; 20

APPENDIXES

Should they be indexed? Most writers on indexing seem to think that they can safely be omitted from an index, together with other parts of a book, such as the table of contents, a dedication, a fore- word, a brief introduction, or a glossary. But Knight strongly recom- mends indexing appendixes as well as any other textual matter that may be of potential interest to a reader (1979, p. 52).

Here, as so often in similar cases, no hard and fast rule can be laid down, and the indexer must make a judicious decision. A book on the political history of Egypt and Israel during the 1970s contains the entire text of the Camp David agreement as an appendix on 23 pages of fine print. The pages, by the way, are unnumbered, so it would be difficult to refer anything indexed to a place where the user would be able to find it quickly. But this is really not necessary, because the conditions of the historic agreement are discussed in the book in much detail. Anyone interested in the exact wording of the peace treaty can find its place in the book through the table of contents, and specific issues in the treaty are indicated by its section headings and subheadings.

On the other hand, in a book on the libraries of U.S. presidents, there is an appendix of TABLES showing data not summarized elsewhere in the text, such as holdings of each library, their physical size, etc. In this case, the topic of each table needs to be indexed under "Holdings", "Areas", and so on, both as main headings and as subheadings under "Presidential libraries".

AUTHOR-PUBLISHER-INDEXER RELATIONSHIPS

The relationships among these three persons can be displayed schematically as an inverted triangle, subtly implying that the indexer at the bottom is at the mercy of the two people on top:

AUTHOR   PUBLISHER

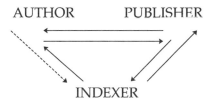

INDEXER

As in many *ménages à trois* in real life as well as in fiction, they are subject to frequent ups and downs, achievements and frustrations, or love and hate.

Books constitute the majority of works for which indexes are individually commissioned. The following discussion focuses therefore on authors as individual writers of books; on publishers and their editors who are in the business of transforming an author's manuscript into a book; and on indexers hired by either author or publisher to compile an index. However, the terms "author" and "publisher" pertain in this context also to the creation and production of other works. Many texts, such as TECHNICAL MANUALS AND REPORTS are "authored" by teams of scientists or engineers, and the "publisher" may be a government agency, a manufacturer, a hospital, an insurance firm, or a bank. The role of author and publisher may also often be combined by means of desktop publishing, especially for smaller or ephemeral publications or for those that must be frequently revised and updated, such as software manuals. In these cases, it is more appropriate to substitute the term "client" for those of author and publisher, although the relationships and their problems remain essentially the same as those which obtain among traditional authors, publishers, and indexers of books.

It all starts with an author who has produced a work that needs an index. If the author has been lucky enough to find a publisher who will take the risk of publishing, the latter will often encourage the author to index the work him- or herself, assuming that "the author, having written the work, is also the best-prepared person to index it properly". Such a phrase or words to the same effect actually appear in authors' guides put out by some major publishers. In an ideal world populated by ideal authors (and, not to forget, ideal publishers) this would be true, and no indexers, ideal or otherwise, would be needed. Yet, in the real world, this assumption flies in the face of most publishers' (and indexers') actual experience with author-produced indexes and is akin to Samuel Johnson's dictum on second marriages being "the triumph of hope over experience". Unfortunately, authors are often not only admonished but actually forced by the terms of their contracts either to index their work themselves or to find an indexer and to pay the costs of indexing out of their own pockets, whereupon many an author starts compiling an index that turns out to be woefully inadequate or that has to be abandoned after some feeble and often misguided attempts. The reasons for such failures are easy to understand. The author may be exhausted from the arduous work of writing and finishing the book (often against a tight deadline) as well as proofreading it, and has neither the inclination nor the experience to undertake the time-consuming and tedious task of indexing. Authors are also in most cases too close to their own work and may fail to index important facts, events, relationships, or even names, assuming either that "everybody knows that" or "nobody will ever look for this". In a comparative study of the SPECIFICITY of index terms assigned to medical articles by their authors and by professional indexers it was found that the indexers' terms, taken from a thesaurus, were more specific than those provided by authors (Rasheed 1989). Conversely, authors may sometimes index every last trivial bit of information, often without giving the context, or they may indulge in listing nouns and adjectives in page order as interminable subheadings, not to mention the equally bad enumeration of dozens if not hundreds of undifferentiated page numbers after the name of their hero or main topic and some of the other mistakes listed under BAD INDEXES. In brief, writing a book and indexing it are two quite different skills, and rare is the person who has mastered both.

Experienced authors will, therefore, disregard some publishers' suggestion that they compile their own indexes. Rather, they ought to heed the advice of Bernard Levin, a British essayist, literary critic, and champion of good indexes, who considers the notion of authors indexing their own books to be a

> Delusion indeed; indexing is a highly skilled science, and it would be as foolish for a writer unversed in its mysteries to compile his own Index as it would be for him to attempt, without the requisite knowledge, to cut the type from which his book is to be printed (Levin 1989).

Authors, unless proficient in indexing, should either let their editor find a competent indexer or may themselves commission an index from a freelancer or other suitable person. Sometimes, the person chosen for the task is the author's wife, daughter, cousin, or uncle; there is, of course, nothing inherently bad about a family relationship between author and indexer, and such collaboration can be very useful, provided that the family member really knows how to index. This is, however, seldom the case, as witness many a relative-produced index of deplorable quality. (Indexes compiled by members of the author's immediate or extended family are easily spotted because the author's acknowledgment or dedication makes this fact publicly known.)

An author's relationship with his or her indexer may range from very little or none whatsoever (and that is why the downward

arrow in the triangle is shown as a broken line) to highly cooperative and helpful. Unfortunately, authors may also be meddlesome if
not outright destructive; for example, some authors will highlight
or underscore dozens of words on each page (and even color-code
them), demanding that the indexer include every last one of these
words in the index, or else! (Gibson 1989). There are also authors
who seem not to care whether and how their books are indexed,
which is remarkable, seeing that the cost of indexing is normally
borne by them. Others will readily reply to an indexer's occasional
queries and may even be grateful if inconsistencies (e.g., in the
spelling of names or the dating of events) are pointed out to them.
Yet other authors may not only want to read the index manuscript
(which is their legitimate right) but may also insist on making
changes which contravene good indexing practice, thus sometimes
ruining an experienced indexer's work. Such conflicts can occasionally be resolved more or less amicably by the publisher's editor, but
no protracted discussions can take place, and the indexer may often
draw the shortest straw in such a situation, because the editor
wants the index—the last part of the book to be printed—to go into
production without any further delay.

Enter thus the editor, who is the actual person representing the
publisher's interests and the one with whom the indexer has to
deal. A few large publishing houses have special index editors, but
most publishers leave decisions regarding indexes to the manuscript or production editor who deals with a work from the submission of a manuscript to the final product, the printed book. Thus,
the editor must decide whether or not the work needs an index. For
reference works, technical and scientific books, and legal treatises,
an index is virtually a necessity. But for books in the social sciences
and humanities, and for those aimed at the public at large, an editor
may consider an index as an unnecessary frill that only adds to the
production costs of a book. If a book can be expected to sell well
whether or not it has an index, it may be published without one,
however badly its subject matter (and its readers) may need one.
On the other hand, many publishers seem to have come to the
conclusion that an index is an asset for almost any nonfiction work,
and that it is a marketable commodity: publishers' promotional
material for a book now often stresses the fact that an index has
been provided.

Having decided in favor of an index, the editor must find a suitable indexer. Three factors matter most in the choice of an indexer: skill and experience in the indexing of a particular type of work (e.g., monograph, textbook, reference work, instruction manual); familiarity with the discipline or field covered by the work; and immediate availability so that the index can be compiled right away and finished in time to meet the printer's schedule and deadline.

The indexer chosen will often be a freelancer who has previously worked for the editor. It happens, however, not infrequently that the indexer first approached by the editor cannot accept the job because of previous commitments. Since time is of the essence, the editor may then have to fall back either on another (but perhaps less experienced) indexer who happens to be available or on someone on a roster of people who have offered their services as indexers to the publisher. This may provide an opportunity for novice indexers to prove their mettle, and many successful business relationships between indexers and editors have been established this way.

When an able and willing indexer has been found, the editor will provide him or her with either galleys or page proofs, and with technical details such as the approximate number of pages allotted, the number of columns per page, and the width of an index line. If the index manuscript is to be submitted in machine-readable form on a disk, the indexer must ask the editor for the disk and file format and any specifications which the typesetters may use in order to convert the indexer's disk into a printed index without any reprocessing. Some publishers provide instructions for the submission of index manuscripts on disk, but these are seldom complete and must often be adapted to the special requirements of a particular index. If the publisher requires the indexer to insert machine codes which will be used directly by the typesetters' formatting program, this should result in a higher remuneration, because the indexer will then actually do much of the highly-paid work of the typesetters and may even be held responsible for coding mistakes that result in faulty index entries.

Many publishers have their own house style, a set of rules intended to ensure consistency in the indexes compiled for their books. The house style determines, among other things, details such as the system of ALPHANUMERIC ARRANGEMENT, PUNCTUA-

TION, CAPITALIZATION, alphabetical or CHRONOLOGICAL ORDER of entries, and DISPLAY OF SUBHEADINGS, etc. The editor will generally ask that the indexer follow these provisions, but to many an indexer's regret and despair, the house rules are often antiquated or cumbersome and will mar an index rather than enhance its appearance and usefulness. If the editor insists strictly on such house rules, the indexer is often in no position to object, though it may sometimes be possible to persuade the editor that current codes and standards are different from the publisher's long-standing practice and that following the newer practices will make the index a better retrieval tool. Here, as in all other negotiations between indexer and publisher, diplomatic tact and gentle persuasion, as well as reliance on examples of other indexes, may sway even rather stern editors.

Experienced indexers have found it useful to submit their own list of index specifications, covering the most common technical details that may have to be clarified and explicitly stated before an indexing job is undertaken. Most editors will indeed welcome such a list, because it may include details not previously considered by them, and will in any case prevent misunderstandings and potentially costly corrections and changes after the index has been delivered. Figure 1, pp. 38–39, shows a specimen of such a list.

Some publishers prefer to have an index proofread by their own proofreaders and fail or even refuse to send copies of the page proofs to the indexer, relying on the *Chicago manual of style* (1993, 17.64) which tells the indexer that "It is likely that you will not have a chance to proofread the index yourself, as that is frequently done in the publishing office to save time . . . for the same reason you may not see the final, copyedited form of your index. . . ." But it is the indexer who should do the PROOFREADING, because more than just checking for typos and correct SPELLING is involved, such as BAD BREAKS that must be resolved without impairing the structure of the subheadings involved, the proper setting of (CONTINUED) LINES, and other details specific to the printing of indexes. Many editors are, however, pretty flexible in this respect and will agree to have the proofreading done by the indexer rather than by their in-house proofreaders, especially since the indexer's hourly fee may be lower than the wages of professional proofreaders.

One thing to which publishers ought to agree easily, though surprisingly few of them do, is recognition of an indexer's work by displaying his or her name on the first page of the index. This does not cost anything other than setting one line of print, but it is of great value for every indexer who can claim to produce an index of high quality. At the least, the indexer ought to be named in the acknowledgments or in a listing of editorial staff, though this is only a poor substitute for the naming of the indexer as author of the index.

Whatever the form in which the index manuscript is going to be delivered, the editor will generally ask the indexer to submit an estimate of the remuneration, based on the technical details and specifications, and a time limit will be set for the submission of the index. Once these conditions have been agreed upon, the editor may ask the indexer to sign a CONTRACT, or will sometimes just confirm in a letter that the indexer agreed to index a work for a certain fee and to deliver the index manuscript by a certain date. Although such a letter is the legal equivalent of a formal contract (in case a dispute should arise), it is much preferable to rely on a document that clearly stipulates all conditions, obligations, and duties on the part of the publisher and the indexer. A freelancer should insist politely but firmly either on the relevant provisions of the *Recommended indexing agreement* (1990) published by the American Society of Indexers or a contract closely resembling it. In general, an indexer should not undertake a job on the strength of a phone call or a friendly handshake alone, without any written stipulation of the technical conditions of the work and without any safeguards for the indexer's professional, financial, and legal interests.

Contract negotiations are less often about payments than about time limits, which may vary from (horrors!) a couple of days or even less to an average of from two to four weeks to an open-ended assignment for large reference works and cumulative indexes. Most disagreements between indexer and publisher arise on this matter of deadlines, and it is often not easy to arrive at a mutually agreeable compromise. Though it is true that tight production schedules often leave the editor no choice but to set a short deadline for the completion of an index, delays caused by printers or by other factors should not become a pretext for giving the indexer less time than originally planned to make up for lost time.

If some of the foregoing sounds as if indexers' relations with authors, publishers, and editors were nothing but a constant

Index Specifications

Preliminaries

Title _____
Contact _____   Phone # _____
Publisher _____   Author _____
Subject _____   Type _____

Type: business ☐   text ☐   el-hi ☐
scholarly ☐   trade ☐   college ☐
technical ☐   other ☐

Arrival date _____

Return date _____   Page proofs: none ☐   yes ___ no ___ expected # ___
other ☐   sending sample index: yes ___ no ___

Style of Index   house ☐   Chicago ☐

Kind of Index   subject ☐   name ☐
single ☐   multiple ☐

Format   indented ___   run-in ___

headings   caps   1 ☐   lc ☐
subheadings   levels: 1   2   no limit ☐
order: alpha   pg   chrono. continuum

Alphabetization   letter ☐   word ☐   words ☐   numbers ☐
numbers ☐   words ☐

special conventions   names ☐   Chicago ☐   house ☐   other ___
St. / Saint ☐   Mc / Mac ☐

Cross-References

See   from subentry: yes ___ no ___   follow: Chicago   house   other

See also   from subentry: yes ___ no ___   follow: Chicago   house   other
after main ___   last subhead ___
paren ___

General
Under
special conventions

yes — no —
yes — no —
roman if italics follow: yes no
acronym posting @ spellout @ acronym
names common to proper proper to common

Indexable Matter
footnotes/endnotes ___ Locator format
charts/tables ___ Locator format
illus/maps ___ Locator format

Page Range Format
full — elided — follow: Chicago house other

Length
limit: yes no **Line count**
Characters per line

Delivery Format
ms.
disk (IBM)
typed, double-spaced ___ camera-ready ___
3 1/2 □ 5 1/4 □ low □ high □
text file format: IBM Mac □

ASCII □ Cindex □ Microsoft RTF □ PageMaker □ □
Macrex □ WordPerfect □ Ventura
Paradox □ WordStar □
XyWrite □
other ___

typesetting codes
maximum size of file ___ sending code list: yes no
Chicago □ ANSI/NISO □ simple □ house □ other

modem
phone # ___ Procomm ___ protocol ___
MNP5 □ other

© 1992 Elsie Lynn
J.E. Lynn Associates
P.O. Box 4471
Somerville, MA 02144

Figure 1. *Index specifications.* © J. E. Lynn Associates, P.O. Box 4471, Somerville, MA 02144. Reproduced by permission.

struggle, it should in fairness be said that publishers also have their well-founded complaints about authors as well as indexers. Authors, quite apart from all other quarrels they may have with publishers, may cause them delays by starting to compile their own indexes only to abandon them because of lack of time and experience, whereupon the publisher must find an indexer at the very last moment to complete the index or even to start one from scratch if the author's index turns out to be unusable. Publishers' complaints about indexers concern over-indexing, which may require more pages than originally allotted to an index (but what constitutes over-indexing is, of course, a matter that is debatable). Sometimes an indexer may not keep an agreed-upon deadline, causing the publisher to miss the pre-arranged time slot at the printers, resulting in delays in the publication of the book and additional costs. Contrary to what indexers sometimes think, remuneration is not a major source of disputes. Most reputable publishers are quite willing to pay fair and reasonable fees for a good index compiled to their specifications and delivered on time. In fact, publishers complain sometimes about the difficulty of finding really competent and reliable indexers and claim that they are willing to pay such people handsomely if only they can get and retain them. On the other hand, publishers have publicly complained about the lack of standardized methods of payment and established scales of fees for indexing. Here the SOCIETIES OF INDEXERS still have a lot of work to do in order both to safeguard the interests of their members and to provide publishers (especially smaller ones) with equitable and reasonably flexible methods and scales of remuneration set by a professional body.

Authors, publishers, editors, and indexers seem to know surprisingly little of each other's occupation, although all of them are so closely involved in the creation and production of books and other documents. *What publishers do* (Graham 1992) and *Editors on editing* (1993) describe and explain the role these people play in the long and complex process of book production, and some of the problems that indexers may encounter in their relations with them are discussed in the chapter "The author and the index" of *Indexing books* (Mulvany 1994b).

Though all parties in the triangular indexing relationships seem forever to remonstrate with each other, in the end they will all agree with what an anonymous Latin versifier put in a distich and an equally anonymous translator rendered in an English heroic couplet:*

Absente auxilio perquirimus undique frustra
Sed nobis ingens indicis auxilium est.

(Without a key we search and search in vain
But a good index is a monstrous gain.)

BS 3700: 4.5; 7.1.1
ISO 999: 6.4
NISO Z39.4:

AUTOMATIC INDEXING

Almost from the time when computers became available as general-purpose machines, attempts were made to harness them to the task of indexing, based only on the words of a text, and with no or only little human involvement. The earliest practical application was the KWIC index, invented in 1958 by Hans Peter Luhn at IBM, which used KEYWORDS in the titles of documents and stop lists of "unimportant" words. From these crude beginnings, automatic indexing (AI) has been developed into more sophisticated retrieval tools, intended to supplant the admittedly fallible, error-prone, and costly human indexing operation.

*G. Norman Knight, the founder of the Society of Indexers, asked in a letter to the *Times Literary Supplement* of 6 January 1978 whether anybody could shed light on the authorship of the distich and its translation, because he wanted to use them in his book *Indexing, the art of* (Knight 1979). Apparently, his quest for the elusive poet went unanswered, because the verses grace the title page of the book without any attribution.

The Nature of Automatic Indexing

In order to understand the nature of automatic indexing it is necessary to abolish a tempting but false analogy all too often encountered in most popular articles, but unfortunately found even in
serious writings on the topic. The false analogy is between a car
transmission and indexing. Cars have either manual or automatic
transmissions; both are mechanical devices that perform the *same*
operation, namely, reducing the speed of the motor to that needed
to move the car at desired speeds. "Manual" indexing (the unfortunate misnomer for the work of a human mind) is, however, *not*
performing the same operations as "automatic" indexing, but entirely different ones (and the role of hands is actually the same in
both—pounding a keyboard—though in AI it is the user who has
to do the hard work).

Indexing, as performed by a human being, is a mental process of
intellectual analysis, based on understanding the meaning of a text,
with the aim of rearranging its conceptual structure in an easily
searchable format, resulting in the construction of a parallel but
differently organized text. All AI methods, on the other hand, are
essentially *search strategies*, primarily designed with the aim of finding words used by searchers in their queries and matching them
with the same words occurring in natural-language texts. Such
finding and matching methods can, of course, also be used to "index", as it were, natural-language texts in a rough-and-ready approximation of human indexing, but it must be realized that (a)
what is offered by bibliographic database systems as AI is virtually
always an array of various search strategies, and that (b) the matching of words (or parts of words) and phrases will not always find
words or phrases with the meaning intended by the searcher and
may therefore fail to retrieve relevant documents. It is thus not
entirely unreasonable that AI has been said to be an oxymoron
(Mulvany 1994*b*, p. 245).

Be that as it may, it is unfortunate that the term "automatic indexing", originally coined for the algorithmic assignment of index
terms to natural-language texts, was retained when the same methods were later used for the automatic *retrieval* of documents. Consequently, most users of retrieval systems are now convinced that
applying various search strategies for the retrieval of relevant documents in answer to their queries is somehow automatically "index-

ing" these documents. But although neither printed nor other eye-legible indexes are produced, the term AI is now so firmly entrenched for what is actually automatic retrieval that it would be futile trying to change the terminology.

It is self-evident that the full natural-language texts to be searched by AI methods must be accessible and stored in machine-readable form. This, in effect, limits the type of texts on which AI is being performed to articles, reports, and other relatively short documents; most books are currently not available on public-access databases, primarily because of copyright restrictions, but current AI methods are in any case not capable of producing acceptable back-of-the-book indexes comparable to humanly compiled ones.

Both human and automatic indexing have the same goal: making documents retrievable for those who need or want them. AI puts the burden of retrieval on the enduser who must necessarily find the words actually used in a text or be otherwise out of luck. None of the currently employed AI methods offer the searcher synonyms for the terms used in a text, nor can they display relationships among concepts dispersed in a text, or concepts that are only implicit in a text, that is, those that can only be inferred from the context. In order to compensate to some extent for these deficiencies of AI, some retrieval systems provide endusers with access to an online thesaurus as a source for synonyms and conceptually related terms. Thesauri are, however, not part of any AI method as such, but are components of a retrieval system. Moreover, thesauri, which are exhibiting a network of related topical terms, do not exhaust all or even most of the terms that may be crucial to successful retrieval. They are also highly sophisticated tools, primarily aimed at professional indexers, not endusers who, even if they bother to look up thesaurus terms (which happens only seldom) rarely know how to use these tools to best advantage. Needless to say, no thesaurus can provide access to concepts that are only implicit in a text.

Human indexing, on the other hand, provides not only the terms for concepts that are mentioned in a document but also their synonyms, and their relationships to other concepts in a systematic and largely predictable structure. It does that by means of multilevel headings, by cross-references, and other devices that are part and parcel of the index structure, and do not have to be consulted separately by the enduser.

Automatic Indexing Methods

All AI methods, even the most sophisticated ones, are predicated on the occurrence of *words* in texts. At this point, it is necessary to clarify what constitutes a "word" for the purposes of AI. In principle, it is any written unit of text, separated from other units by spaces or by punctuation. There are, however, several exceptions to this rule, mainly concerning PUNCTUATION marks such as hyphens, periods, commas, and parentheses which, depending on the AI method and the sorting algorithm of the computer used, may either form part of a word or are disregarded.

Keyword searching. This is the oldest AI method, originally used, as mentioned above, for the retrieval of document titles only. It was simplistically thought that the titles of articles and reports would express their topics—an assumption that may not have been justified even for the reports written by IBM engineers in the late 1950s, and one that obviously does not hold for most documents, no matter in which discipline.

All keyword indexing methods rely also on stop lists of words that are considered to be unimportant or unnecessary for particular retrieval purposes, such as function words (articles, pronouns, prepositions, conjunctions, and adverbs), which occur very frequently in texts and which, taken only by themselves, are meaningless or almost so. Some stop lists may contain hundreds of words, including nouns and adjectives, if these are considered to be trivial in a particular context. It seems, however, that the larger the database, the smaller a stop list should be, containing no more than 8–10 words at most. Moreover, excluding, for example, the English article *a* may prevent the retrieval of a document on "vitamin A".

Adjacency and proximity commands permit users to specify that two terms must either be close to each other in order to be retrieved, or that they should occur within a certain distance (number of words) from each other. This method is, strictly speaking, not part of AI as such, but is rather a feature of certain retrieval systems, but it supports and sometimes enhances searching of texts by AI methods.

Stemming. A refinement of the raw keyword searching method is the use of algorithms which allow a searcher to specify only the roots of words that may have various prefixes or suffixes, e.g.,

```
        co-operat-ion
        co-operat-ive
           operat-ing
           operat-ion
           operat-ive
           operat-or
     post-operat-ive
      pre-operat-ive
```

Although users like this search method and employ it frequently, it is not always cost-effective, and does not necessarily improve search results.

Truncation is closely related to stemming. It allows a user to perform word-fragment searching, lopping off either beginning syllables (left truncation), e.g., all words ending in "cycline" (to find documents on antibiotics having that ending), or eliminating endings (right truncation), e.g., all words beginning with "evapor", which will find evaporable, evaporated, evaporating, evaporation, and evaporator(s). There is also infix truncation, e.g., "di—amine", which can be used to find related but unspecified chemical compounds in the middle.

Boolean logic (named after its inventor, the 19th-century British mathematician George Boole) enables a user to formulate a search for correlations of several terms in three different ways, as shown in Fig. 2. Because of the unconventional use of the words AND and OR, and the various combinations in which these operators may be used to satisfy a complex search formulation, e.g.,

((A AND B) OR C) NOT D

many endusers do not apply Boolean logic correctly.* The method is best left to trained intermediaries who know how to translate a user's search request into the appropriate Boolean search statement.

Term weighting is one of the more sophisticated AI methods, developed since the early 1960s, in order to overcome the crudity of keyword searching. Various statistical and probabilistic methods are employed to rank terms according to their frequency in a do-

---

*The U.S. National Library of Medicine found that in 245,521 searches in its GRATEFUL MED retrieval system 27% of the searches retrieved no citations at all; 57% of these failures were caused by wrongly ANDing terms (A and B and C and D . . .) which inevitably ended in zero retrieval (Kingsland et al. 1993, p. 179).

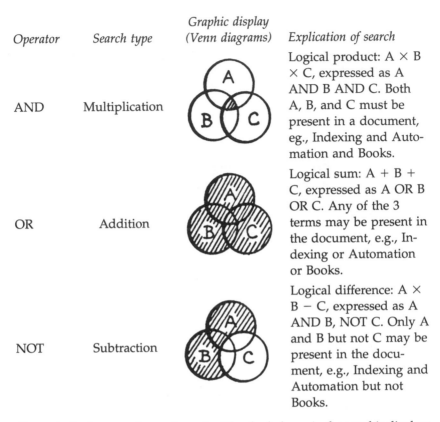

Operator	Search type	Graphic display (Venn diagrams)	Explication of search
AND	Multiplication		Logical product: A × B × C, expressed as A AND B AND C. Both A, B, and C must be present in a document, eg., Indexing and Automation and Books.
OR	Addition		Logical sum: A + B + C, expressed as A OR B OR C. Any of the 3 terms may be present in the document, e.g., Indexing or Automation or Books.
NOT	Subtraction		Logical difference: A × B − C, expressed as A AND B, NOT C. Only A and B but not C may be present in the document, e.g., Indexing and Automation but not Books.

Figure 2. *Boolean operators and searches.* The shaded area in the graphic displays indicates a document that answers the respective search statement.

cument collection, so as to find those documents that are most relevant to a query. These methods have mostly been applied to relatively small collections of documents but fail to produce significantly better results than the simpler methods when employed in large databases that contain records of millions of documents.

Linguistic methods, such as phrase matching, syntactic parsing of text segments, and even some semantic analysis with the aid of dictionaries and thesauri have also been tried experimentally, but their practical value is doubtful. In one such laboratory project, aimed at the automatic recognition of adjectival noun phrases in the subject area of computers, the system was unable to recognize that in the phrase "hierarchical computer architecture" it is the architecture that is hierarchical, not the computer (Vickery & Vickery 1992); one might add that it would also have been unable to distinguish between the metaphorical use of the word "architecture" in the phrase and the literal use of the same word, which may very well occur in a text on the use of computers in architecture.

Although linguistic methods of AI may ultimately have some potential for at least partial success in specialized fields that enjoy a relatively stable and uniformly employed terminology, they are currently not used in any commercial or large-scale retrieval system.

A combination of several AI methods is generally thought to be the most cost-effective way of searching large document collections, but so far nobody has come up with a recipe for the optimal mix of the ingredients.

A more detailed survey of the state of the art of AI methods, their advantages and disadvantages, has been provided by Harman (1994).

Evaluation of Automatic Indexing

Despite the efforts of hundreds of researchers during several decades, resulting in an enormous mass of articles, reports, and books, nothing much has changed *in principle:* automatic indexes are still based on the occurrence of terms in verbal texts and on their manipulation in various ways. However, they cannot fulfill some of the functions that are regarded as essential for an effective index. Specifically, they cannot indicate ideas, concepts, and features that are not expressly stated in a text but are only implied, and they cannot distinguish between major and minor topics, except by statistical methods based on word counts which is a rather crude and often unreliable way of ascertaining the importance or otherwise of a topic in a given context (Weinberg 1981).

Automatic indexing is based primarily on two rather simplistic assumptions, namely: (a) that words and terms in natural language texts always have precise and unique meanings in a given context, and (b) that human languages can be reduced to a set of logical propositions and transformations. However, the matter is not so simple and straightforward:

Natural language is a neural mechanism, apparently the result of genetic and social evolution. While it is sometimes regular, logical and precise, it is as often irregular, non-logical, and imprecise, and oftener still a mix of the two. It blends intellect with instinct, logic with inspiration, and the standard with the varied. Logic is closely associated with language and . . . is an essential tool, but one cannot deduce from this usefulness that it is the sole or even primary means by which language can be understood (*The Oxford companion to the English language* 1992, p. 626).

Thus, the methods employed to achieve automatic indexing do not take into account the infinite variety, complexity, and even sheer intractability of human language which relies on much more than the mere concatenation of words in order to convey concepts in the mind of an originator and to make them meaningful to a recipient.

Admittedly, the crudeness of early keyword searching has been mitigated by the improvements beyond mere stop lists, discussed above. Depending on their skill (or lack of it) in manipulating various search strategies, users may or may not hit upon the words and phrases that correspond to those in the documents stored in a database, and consequently to citations of those documents that may be relevant to their requests. But the most frequent and most intractable obstacle to effective searching of a database indexed by automatic methods is the great variety of possible search terms in virtually every field of inquiry, even in the supposedly "hard" sciences and in technology (Gomez et al. 1990).

In an extensive investigation of the way people name things, it was found that two persons agreed on the same term for an object less than 20% of the time, and that an average of 15 terms was needed to achieve an average of 80% agreement. The researchers found that *"there is no one good access term for most objects. The idea of* an 'obvious,' 'self-evident,' or 'natural' term is a myth! . . . *there can exist no rules, guidelines or procedures for choosing a good name, in the sense of 'accessible to the unfamiliar user.'"* (Furnas et al. 1987, p. 967 [emphases in the original]).

The corollary of this finding is the following: because AI methods *as such* can only find those terms that are actually used in documents but not any of their potential synonyms or paraphrases, only that fraction of all stored documents can be found in which the terms chosen in a user's search formulation do indeed occur. (Some retrieval systems provide searchers with synonyms or nearly equivalent terms which have been added as a result of previous searches; however, such augmentation is a system component, not something that can be achieved by any AI method itself. Most endusers do not know how to use such searching aids effectively, nor do they care.) Consequently, a large number of searches in an automatically indexed database will be of the "quick and dirty" type, missing all relevant documents whose terms happen to be different from those employed by an enduser.

At first sight, this conclusion seems to fly in the face of the well-publicized success of databases for LEGAL TEXTS (JURIS, LEXIS, WESTLAW, and others) which do rely on keyword searching, stemming, truncation, and proximity commands, dispensing entirely with human indexing. But although legal terminology is indeed fairly stable, and must be as unambiguous as possible, this is not true for terms describing the facts and circumstances of individual cases which are as much subject to change and ambiguity as any other terms in general, specialized, scientific, technical, or scholarly texts. This problem and other serious failures of unindexed legal databases, relying only on the retrieval of words and phrases, have been exposed by Dabney (1986a, b). It has also been shown that lawyers familiar with a specific case who searched a legal database for documents pertaining to that case thought that they had retrieved at least 75–80% of relevant references, while their actual recall rate ranged only from 12 to 20% (Blair & Maron 1985; Blair 1986; 1990, pp. 87–112).

Machine-Aided Indexing (MAI)

Major databases covering entire disciplines, such as BIOSIS, Chemical Abstracts Service, and MEDLINE, or those covering specialized but extensive fields such as American Petroleum Institute, NASA, and several others do not employ any of the fully automatic systems for the indexing of their millions of stored references. Rather, they rely on highly trained teams of human indexers whose work is supported by machine-*aided* indexing systems. These systems minimize the time needed by indexers to execute repetitive tasks and to look up terms in thesauri. Some MAIs index taxonomic terms, names of chemical compounds, organs of the human body, place names, and other objects or facts that have standardized names or numbers held in authority files. Other MAIs seek to enhance indexing consistency by scanning natural language texts with the aid of advanced linguistic AI methods and then suggesting suitable index terms to the human indexers who must still apply their understanding, knowledge of the topic, and skills to the final indexing of texts (Hodge 1992, 1993; Humphrey 1994; Silvester et al. 1994). But even these advanced systems have limitations and are sometimes not cost-effective. The U.S. National Agricultural Library found that an MAI system took more time to scan the text of documents and to choose index terms for them from a thesaurus than human indexers given the same task. Moreover, the machine-assigned terms had to be post-edited by indexers who thought that the system was confusing rather than assisting them (Edwards 1993).

The Future of Automatic Indexing

The limits of automatic indexing based on mechanical, logical, and statistical methods, and the insurmountable obstacles to completely automatic content analysis, interpretation, and understanding of natural language texts were reluctantly recognized even by Gerald Salton, one of the foremost researchers on information science in general and on statistical and probabilistic AI methods in particular:

> The free manipulation of unrestricted natural language data is not a likely prospect for the foreseeable future. In particular, no agreement exists about the best way of formalizing document content, about the world knowledge (above and beyond the specialized knowledge in a given subject area) that may be needed to understand texts and interpret natural language statements, and about reasoning strategies, inferences, and deductions that may be needed in order actually to respond to user inquiries (Salton & McGill 1983, p. 420).

Nothing has happened since this was written that would render Salton's conclusion invalid. Quite to the contrary: exactly ten years

later, a study of artificial intelligence methods for automatic indexing ruefully stated in its conclusion that

> The major limitations of . . . these systems is that they are restricted
> to indexing material from a very narrow domain. A fully automatic
> indexing system that operates without human intervention and in-
> dexes general text has not yet been developed, mainly owing to the
> large size of the knowledge base required, and the difficulty in repre-
> senting commonsense knowledge (Schuegraf & Van Bommel 1993).

The conclusion of an investigation into the use of automatic indexing methods by major American and European databases was
that, despite many research efforts, "fully automatic indexing will
not be practical for large databases in the foreseeable future" (Milstead 1992b, p. 428). This seems to indicate that even the most
advanced methods are now probably approaching the limits of
what can be achieved for the AI of articles in large bibliographic
databases. Regarding the automatic compilation of indexes to textbooks, monographs, treatises, and other lengthy and complex texts,
no AI method that has been tried during the past four decades has
been able to produce indexes that are even remotely comparable to
those compiled by competent human indexers. Attempts at AI of
TECHNICAL MANUALS AND REPORTS, e.g., for computer manuals,
resulted almost invariably in woefully inadequate and even ludicrous conglomerations of terms which are no more than caricatures
of real indexes, and whose only function is to frustrate hapless
users (Mulvany 1994a).

There is an interesting parallel here with automatic translation,
which was thought to be a cinch in the 1960s: just build a bilingual
dictionary into a computer, feed a Russian document in one end,
and an English translation will come out the other. Today it is well
known that fully automatic translation of just any text is not feasible, unless the text has been simplified in advance by using a restricted vocabulary and syntax, or unless post-editing is performed
by a human editor; literary texts (essays, novels, poetry) defy any
attempt at automatic translation.

Since indexing is essentially also a translation process—
transforming the text of a document into a condensed and differently structured parallel text—it is not surprising that AI has developed along similar lines. It works for certain types of documents,
provided that the search results need not be exhaustive, and that a

low degree of both recall (the proportion of relevant documents retrieved) and precision (the proportion of retrieved documents that are relevant) is acceptable to endusers. The majority of endusers do indeed accept these conditions and they are generally satisfied with a few more or less relevant documents in response to a query (Wilson 1977, pp. 94–99; White 1992, p. 275–276). This general acceptance by users as well as the economic incentive for retrieval systems management to use the cheapest and quickest retrieval methods will ensure that every year hundreds of thousands of articles, reports, and ephemeral publications will be indexed automatically to serve users who need rapid access to information that is mostly focussed on narrow topics and which has a half-life of less than a year or so.

Documents considered by users and database producers alike to be of vital interest, that is, those dealing with topics in biology, medicine, chemistry, and some other fields, are for the time being still indexed by human indexers, aided by automatic support services. This symbiotic system results in higher indexing quality and better retrieval results which seem to justify the effort and expense of human indexers and it may well last for quite some time, provided that the necessary financial support will be available. Lastly, book-length documents which are essentially sifting, filtering, and condensing the large mass of articles and reports in databases that have been indexed either automatically or by computer-assisted methods, and which present it in a more manageable and longer-lasting format of higher quality, need thorough and exhaustive analysis of their topics and cannot be indexed at an acceptable level of quality by currently available automatic indexing methods.

The basic reason for the ineluctible limits of both automatic translation and indexing is that mechanical or electronic devices can extract words from a text, they can manipulate them one way or another—but they cannot understand them. Like Hamlet, they read only "words, words, words". The human faculty of understanding, the grasping of meaning and context, is a process that depends on "knowledge of the world", a vast microcosm of experiences, memories, relations, and intuitions—on the "image" in Kenneth Boulding's sense.* We still know next to nothing about how the creative mind works, nor do we know much about how understanding

*The image (Boulding 1956).

occurs. But we do know that these processes cannot be reduced to mere algorithms, as has been demonstrated by the great mathematician and physicist Roger Penrose in his books *The emperor's new mind* (1989) and *Shadows of the mind* (1994). The workings of the human mind when indexing texts can neither be successfully performed nor even approximated by machines, despite ludicrous claims to the contrary by enthusiasts of artificial intelligence methods who often falsely equate this term with just about any AI method, as has been pointed out by Lancaster (1991, p. 245) and Fugmann (1992).

The matter has been aptly summarized by Bella H. Weinberg, one of the editors of a collection of papers on online searching (*Gateway software* 1988, p. 112):

> The reader may secretly delight in the ambiguities of natural language that defy automatic resolution and in the difficulty of programming common sense and real-world knowledge into computers which guarantees the employability of human search intermediaries in the foreseeable future.

"Indexers" may legitimately be substituted for "search intermediaries", because the role played by the latter in online searching, working face-to-face with inquirers, is essentially similar to that of an indexer, with the important difference that an indexer must work for a largely unknown audience.

Human indexers, despite all their shortcomings, are thus in no danger of being eliminated by computers (Milstead 1992a), no matter how many dire predictions to that effect may from time to time appear in the popular and sometimes even in the professional literature. After all, books, articles, and other documents are created by human minds, and they are addressed to and intended to be understood by other human minds. Is it not fitting that the keys to finding information in documents should also be forged by human minds?

BAD BREAKS

When a main heading is on the last line of a left-hand column but its subheadings start at the head of a right-hand column (assuming a two-column layout of the index), you have, in typographers' jargon, a "bad break". If such a break occurs between the bottom of a right-hand (odd-numbered) page and the top of a left-hand (even-numbered) page, it is an even "badder" break. Trouble is, these ugly beasts can be discovered only when the index is in page form, by which time it is sometimes too late to do anything about them. Moreover, moving the "orphan" heading to the top of the right-hand column involves not only some adjustment of the left-hand column, but will also occasionally lead to *new* bad breaks at the foot of the right-hand column or on some of the following index pages where formerly there were none! This will happen according to a law which is a corollary to the well-known one formulated by the legendary Murphy, to wit: any correction of a bad break will result in other bad breaks down the line.

If a bad break can be corrected without any further trouble, the left-hand column, now short one line, can be brought up to its specified length by several methods. One is the insertion of an extra blank line, preferably at a break between two letters of the alphabet, where in any case one blank line is customarily inserted. Another method is the insertion of more space ("leading") between a few lines which, if properly done, will be hardly noticeable but will also achieve the desired effect. Lastly, a one-line heading or subheading, perhaps discarded in editing to save space, can be "resurrected" and inserted into the line that has become available. This can, of course, be done only if all entries, including those not used, are saved until the page proof stage. This is what any prudent indexer will do anyway, just in case the index manuscript has been eaten by the publisher's or printer's dog or has been swallowed by a computer virus.

Chicago manual of style: 17.139

BAD INDEXES: A BAKER'S DOZEN OF COMMON MISTAKES

The quality of indexes, like that of any other product, varies widely from excellent and exhaustive to run-of-the-mill and mediocre, and down to outright bad, which does a disservice to both authors and users of a text. The standing feature "Indexes reviewed" in *The Indexer* inevitably lists many more indexes that were judged by reviewers to be mediocre, deficient, or bad than those that were deemed to be good to outstanding.

The reasons for the existence of so many bad indexes have been analyzed by Bakewell (1979) and are discussed under STANDARDS as well as throughout this book whenever outmoded or unhelpful practices are being dealt with. Among the worst indexes (some of which hardly deserve that name) are those produced by simple word-processing programs without any human intervention whatsoever, short perhaps of a stop list for certain "unimportant" words. But human indexers also commit sins of omission and commission when compiling indexes, even when using computers and special indexing software. The following is a baker's dozen of the most common mistakes. While a few of them, notably numbers 1, 11, and 12, can be avoided by using a computer, only an indexer's accuracy and skill can prevent other mistakes.

1. Bad alphabetization of entries: mixing word-by-word and letter-by-letter arrangement.
2. Wrong locators.
3. Long strings of undifferentiated locators.
4. Relevant proper names not indexed.
5. Misspelled names.
6. No or too few topical entries.
7. Bad synonym control: the same topic indexed under different terms.
8. Page-order arrangement of topical subheadings in run-in style, when the topics are not chronologically related to each other.
9. *See* cross-references instead of double entries when only one or a few locators are involved.
10. No entries for illustrations, maps, tables, glossaries, or appendixes.
11. Circular cross-references: Persia *see* Iran; Iran *see* Persia.
12. Blind cross-references: from an unused term to a non-existing heading.

13. No introductory note explaining any special features other than the simplest alphabetical arrangement.

BIBLIOGRAPHIES AT ENDS OF BOOKS OR CHAPTERS

The authors (or titles) of works listed in end-of-the-book or end-of-chapter bibliographies are seldom indexed, though there is no good reason not to do so, and there is at least one good reason *for* the indexing of items in bibliographies. In most instances, an author or a title (for multi-author works) referred to or cited is mentioned at least once in the text of a book, albeit sometimes only in the form of a brief reference to a full citation in the chapter or end-of-the-book bibliography, e.g. (Smith 1976) or Smith[5] (referring to endnote 5). In the index, Smith will, therefore, have one or more locators for the textual references; listing also the page number for the full citation will add only one more locator to the entry. A good reason for doing this is the convenience for the reader who knows the name of an author and wants to find or to verify only the bibliographic data of a work, not necessarily the place in the text where that work is cited. The locator for an end-of-the-book bibliography will always come last in an index entry, no matter how often the author is mentioned or cited in the text, so users interested only in bibliographic data can turn straight to that page and find immediately what they are looking for—which is what a good index is supposed to do. For end-of-chapter bibliographies this will obviously not work the same way, but it will nevertheless be useful to have the LOCATORS for full bibliographic data included among those for textual references. Alternatively, the bibliographic locators can be singled out by printing them in italics (if that device is not used for other purposes, such as indicating illustrations) or by adding the letter *b* (for bibliography); such identifying devices must, of course, be explained in an INTRODUCTORY NOTE to the index.

"Hidden" bibliographies in the form of widely dispersed references to sources of FOOTNOTES are seldom if ever indexed, and more's the pity because users often remember having seen such references but are unable to find them easily.

BIBLIOGRAPHIES IN BOOK FORM

Author bibliographies, listing all or most of an author's works, are often published without any supporting indexes, which is a great disservice to users. At the very least, a title index is needed, especially if one or more of the listed works have been published in several editions or if an author's works have been translated, adapted, or have been the subject of commentaries and other derivative writings about them. In bibliographies of older works, particularly those published before 1800, it is often necessary to index the names of printers or booksellers, and there may also be a need for an index of persons and places dealt with in an author's work as well as for the names of those to whom a book was dedicated, as was the custom from the 16th to the 18th century.

In subject bibliographies, an index (or more likely MULTIPLE INDEXES) are virtually indispensable, unless the subject is very narrow and the number of entries is not very large, say, less than a hundred or so. Some subject bibliographies are arranged by first author's name, and that may seem to make an author index superfluous; but, since nowadays most articles, reports, and even many nonfiction books are the fruit of collaboration of several authors, it is advisable to compile an index of coauthors. Classified subject bibliographies need both an author index and a detailed subject index which brings together aspects and relationships that are separated by the classified arrangement, where each item is generally listed only once under its principal subject, though it may also treat several other subjects or aspects and relationships. Since users of a classified bibliography seldom study the structure of its classification (which is not always self-explanatory, and may often be obvious only to the compiler of the work), it is important to include in the index also the main headings under which items are classified.

In large bibliographies, author and subject indexes should preferably be separate, since the author index alone may run to several hundreds of names whose alphabetization may be difficult, especially if the bibliography is international in scope and problems of ROMANIZATION of names originally written in non-Roman scripts compound the difficulties. In fields which employ taxonomies, e.g., botany, zoology, pharmacology, and others, a separate index of taxonomic terms may also be needed.

Items in bibliographies are in most instances consecutively numbered, and the index entries must refer to those numbers as LOCATORS. Page or column numbers would be almost useless, because a dozen or more items may appear on each page. If items are not numbered, there is no choice but to use page numbers as locators; the approximate place of an item on a page can then be indicated by dividing a page into two parts (or four quarters if there are two columns per page) and labeling them by letters, as is sometimes done in encyclopedic works, e.g.,

a
b

a	c
b	d

resulting in entries such as

    abstracts
        author-supplied 38a, 47c, 163b
        automatic translation 50c, 54a, 63d
        editing 82c, 93a

Many issues here are also valid for serial bibliographic databases (printed or online). The indexing of these is almost always performed by a team of in-house indexers who have an extensive professional background in the field covered by a database. The employment of outside indexers is generally limited to language specialists who scan and index journals, patents, and reports in lesser-known languages. Since indexing is performed by a number of people and on a continuous basis, a thesaurus (or other controlled vocabulary) as well as a clear set of indexing rules and policies are indispensable in order to ensure a maximum of uniformity and consistency of indexing.

The organizational and management aspects of indexing for bibliographic databases are outside the scope of this book.

BIOGRAPHIES

Paradoxically, the indexing of biographies has as much in common with that of FICTION (which, regrettably, is very seldom indexed) as it does with the indexing of reference works—two types of writings that are otherwise poles apart. Biographies resemble fiction (especially the genre once known as *Bildungsroman*) in that they are written in narrative prose centered on one person's experiences, works, and achievements, as well as on family, friends, and acquaintances. The readers of a biography, having followed the person's life from birth to death or at least through a significant period, may in fact not need an index overly much because, after having finished the book, they now know what happened to its protagonist and will not refer to it any more. But those who have not read the biography, yet are seeking information on a person and on certain events in his or her life, expect to find it by means of a detailed index—and this is exactly how a reference work and its index are used. Thus, the number of people who have read all six volumes of Dumas Malone's *Jefferson and his time* (1948–1981) is probably smaller than that of people who turn to the indexes of that work in order to find a particular detail in Jefferson's long life.

In many respects, the indexing of biographies is different from that of other nonfiction works. Facts, data, and events often cannot be indexed by the precise terms in which they are dealt with in the text but have instead to be paraphrased or summarized under headings that do not appear in the text as such, e.g., "character", "health" (which may be an umbrella term for all manner of diseases and afflictions briefly mentioned here and there, any of which would not merit a separate index entry), or "marriage" if there are only occasional references to the biographee's wife or husband.

PERSONAL NAMES may pose difficult and time-consuming problems: forenames are sometimes not provided in the text, and if a person has not been so famous as to merit an entry in a biographical dictionary the author may have to be asked to supply the missing details. Family relationships must be clearly indicated as QUALIFIERS when several people bearing the same surname appear in a biography, e.g., Johnson, Michael (father of Samuel). Women may marry, be divorced (sometimes several times), remarry (also several times), and end up in a convent, thus going through a number of name changes, all of which have to be linked by cross-references to one and the same person; the same goes for pseudonyms, of which some writers have several.

Subheadings under the names of persons for any topics concerning them are generally arranged in CHRONOLOGICAL ORDER, but the name of the main protagonist will be mentioned on almost every page, and must therefore be dealt with in a different way. The name of the biographee ought not to be followed by long strings of undifferentiated locators (as shown in Figure 8, p. 280) nor by an unbroken sequence of dozens or even hundreds of subheadings in page order. There are two schools of thought on how to handle this problem.

Some indexers prefer a GROUPED ORDER of subheadings under appropriate general headings such as "childhood", "education", "travel", "military career", "political career", and the like. Others recommend restricting subheadings for the central character as much as possible and displaying references to the biographee under the subheadings for other persons with whom he or she may have had relations or subheadings for events experienced, works written, stages in a career, and so on. A drawback to the latter approach may be that all persons mentioned in a biography will then have more or less elaborate and extensive index entries while the biographee will have only a few under his or her name, which would be incongruous.

The problems and pitfalls of which an indexer of a biography must be aware have been discussed by Bell (1989, 1990). A revised version of these two articles is Bell (1992b).

CAPITALIZATION

The questions of what and when to capitalize are amply (though not quite uniformly) covered by style manuals and cataloging codes, e.g., *Anglo-American cataloguing rules* (1988, Appendix A), the U.S. Government Printing Office *Style manual* (1984, ch. 4), and the *Chicago manual of style* (1993, 7.24, 17.15–16). The indexer may turn to any of these if the text of the document itself is not clear or is inconsistent on this issue. Generally, an author's way of capitalization should be followed also in the index of the work. If a CHAPTER HEADING is used as a main index heading, only the first word may be capitalized. The same rule applies to certain LATIN TERMS, especially Latin titles of books.

A problem not yet considered by any of the reference sources cited above is the capitalization of commercial names and trademarks for computer hardware and software and for databases. These are variously written fully capitalized or as if they were proper names: even in the same text one can sometimes find DIALOG and Dialog, BIOSIS and Biosis, SCI-MATE and Sci-Mate. To make matters worse, there are also odd combinations of upper- and lower-case letters, such as dBASE, MeSH, and PSYCHinfo (also appearing as Psychinfo). If only a single text is to be indexed, the spelling preferred by the author should be followed, provided that it is consistent. But in the index to a periodical or a conference proceedings where different authors may spell the same name in two or more forms, the indexer must decide on a single style. It seems that full capitalization has now become the preferred form for the names of hardware and software, as well as for databases. This, in turn, leads to a problem of layout, TYPOGRAPHY, and legibility: index columns with many fully capitalized entries liberally sprinkled among lower-cased ones look rather untidy and are less easily scanned. This effect can be lessened somewhat by the use of small capitals.

Opinions are divided on the question of whether or not main headings should be capitalized. In the past, most guides and textbooks recommended capitalization of the first word of main head ings but not subheadings (unless these happen to begin with a name or word that must be capitalized), e.g.,

Immigration
Indians
  agriculture
  Delaware
  Eliot's Bible for
  fighting methods
Indigo

However, a good case has been made for printing main headings in lowercase, because in a combined name and subject index it is easier to pick out the capitalized names among the lowercased subject entries (Holmstrom in *Training in indexing*, 1969, p. 121). Index headings in many scientific and technical books have for a long time been lowercased, and since the 1980s this practice seems to have been adopted more frequently also for indexes to other types of books. The decision on capitalization of index headings will often depend on a publisher's house style.

The question of the arrangement of capital letters has been uniformly resolved by all arrangement rules: capital and lowercase letters have equal arrangement value. Consequently, names written with capital letters inside a lowercase sequence are arranged as if written in all lowercase after the first capital letter, e.g., MacKey files the same as Mackey. Only the given name determines the order; if also the given name is the same (as may happen in very large name indexes), dates or other QUALIFIERS (e.g., occupation) may have to be used to determine alphabetizing position (but *not* capitalization), e.g.,

Leclerc, Jean
LeClerc, Pierre
Macauley, George
MacBride, Sean
Macdonnell, Mary
MacDonnell, Susan
Mack, Robert
MacKay, Charles (poet)
Mackay, Charles (senator)

Computers and word processors normally sort by ASCII code, that is, all capital letters are arranged before any lowercase letters. Obviously, this would result in separate sequences for names and topical headings if the latter are lowercased, and it would also sort all capitalized subheadings before all other subheadings. For this reason, only software that assigns the same sorting value to capitals and lowercase letters should be used for the alphabetization of indexes.

ALA: 1
BL: 1.2.4
BS 1749: 4.1
Chicago manual of style: 7.24; 17.15–16
ISO 999: 7.2.2.3
LC: 1
NISO Z39.4:

CHAPTER HEADINGS

What an author decides to tell you up front, as it were, on the topics that will be dealt with in a chapter should, at first sight, make useful material for an index entry. This is indeed often, but by no means always, true, and the indexer must decide the matter on a case-by-case basis. Even in the same book, some chapter headings may be suitable as index headings while others are not. A case in point may be Winston Churchill's *History of the English-speaking peoples* in the one-volume abridgment by Henry S. Commager (1983). The topic "The Norman invasion" is treated in one chapter and is therefore suitable as an index entry (minus the article). Yet, other chapter headings in the same book, such as "The lost island" or "The round world" are obviously not useful as index headings.

Rejecting some chapter headings as unsuitable is, however, a far cry from not including any of them in an index as a matter of principle. The introductory note to the index of a recent book (on librarianship, at that!) states that "those topics which are identified by specific headings in the table of contents are not included here". No conceivable purpose is served by such an arbitrary limitation, and users searching the index may be baffled by the absence of just those headings that would have led them to the principal topics of the book.

A chapter heading for a fairly long chapter, when used as a main heading, should be followed by inclusive LOCATORS for the entire chapter as well as by locators for the principal topic of that chapter occurring in other chapters. It must often be supplemented by subheadings indicating more specific issues dealt with in the chapter. Thus, in a book on the mind, "Consciousness" is the heading for a long chapter (pp. 69–149), but the topic is also dealt with in other chapters:

> consciousness 23, 47, 69–149, 213, 318
>   awareness 72–78
>   location 73, 110
>   nature of 76, 187, 318–22

The reader looking up the heading "consciousness" is immediately made aware of the fact that the most comprehensive treatment of the topic is indicated by the inclusive pages 69–149. This effect can be further enhanced by printing those locators in boldface:

> consciousness 23, 47, **69–149**, 213, 318

Chapter headings are often constructed on the pattern "X and Y" (e.g., "Reform and free trade" in Churchill's book mentioned above). This is quite appropriate for a chapter in which the various relationships between X and Y are explained, and the reader will become aware of them when proceeding through that chapter. But such a heading should not be taken unchanged into the index, because there the word "and" between seemingly unrelated concepts does not convey any information on the nature of the relationship considered by the author (*see also* AND).

Closely related to chapter headings are section and paragraph headings which are often found in TECHNICAL MANUALS AND REPORTS. Because of the instructional nature of these texts, the headings are often formulated in terms of an action, e.g., "How to clean the air filter", "How to remove the air filter", and so on. Such headings should never be used unchanged in an index, because people are normally not in the habit of looking up index entries

beginning with "how". The proper way of dealing with such headings is their conversion to a noun or noun phrase and a modifying
subheading, e.g.,

    air filters
        cleaning
        removal

and corresponding DOUBLE ENTRIES

        cleaning   removal
            air filters   air filters
            windshields   oil filters

An extended discussion of this otherwise neglected issue is by
M. D. Anderson (1969, reprinted in *Indexers on indexing* 1978,
pp. 67–69), who cites several good examples.

CHRONOLOGICAL ORDER

While virtually all main headings in an index (except those beginning with a numeral) are arranged in alphabetical order, this is not
necessarily always true for subheadings. In historical and biographical works, chronological arrangement of subheadings is often more
useful than alphabetical order. The subheadings are then almost
always displayed in run-in style (because there is generally a large
number of them) and their locators are given in the sequence of
page numbers. Care must be taken, however, to list all locators for a
particular event or topic together with the first one so as not to
disperse references to the same event or topic throughout a large
(and superfluous) number of subheadings, each of which has only
one locator. (This should be almost self-evident, but it is amazing
how many indexes to historical works are faulty in this respect.)
The following (abridged) example from a biography of Charles
Dickens (CD) is a good example:

Dickens, Elizabeth (CD's mother)
CD's birth, 1–2; CD's relation with, 3, 6–8, 13, 72, 78–79, 281–282, 440; appearance, 7–8; courtship and marriage, 10; teaches CD, 27, 29; opens school, 65; . . . decline 873–874; Helen D. takes care of, 881; death, 935, 937; portrayed as Mrs. Lirriper, 936

Chronological arrangement of subheadings can be particularly useful in a biographical account that does *not* relate the events in the life of a person in the order in which they happened. In the following fictitious entry, the subheadings for Flavia have been arranged by successive stages in the life of the Queen, although they have been treated differently in the text, e.g., her engagement is dealt with early in the narrative on page 30, while her childhood is discussed much later, on pages 56–58, and her death is mentioned earlier than her family life as well as at the end:

Flavia, Queen of Ruritania: birth 10; childhood 56–58; betrothed to Henry of Slobovia 30; marriage with King Charles 207; daughters born 225; separated from husband 223; widowed 275; death and burial 86, 280

Despite the apparent ease with which chronologically arranged subheadings can be made in historical works and biographies, they must be handled judiciously. If necessary, they must be broken up into manageable "chunks", either by starting new paragraphs at appropriate points or by GROUPED ORDER under collective headings, e.g., "Early years", "Education", "In London", "On the Grand Tour", etc. If chronologically arranged subheadings become more numerous than about a dozen or so in every "chunk", then they are difficult and tedious to scan; an unbroken listing of many dozens or even hundreds of subheadings becomes totally useless. A frightful example can be found in Winston S. Churchill's monumental *The second world war*, vol. 4; *The hinge of fate* (1950): the entry for the author himself runs to six closely printed columns with more than 300 subheadings in run-on style from page 5 to page 830! If users want to know, say, what Churchill said about the bombing of Germany, they must wade through about $4\frac{1}{2}$ columns of fine print until hitting the relevant locator, pp. 678–680—which, of course, nobody in his right mind will be prepared to do because of the enormous waste of time involved. As early as 1942, Stephen Leacock, a Canadian humorist, poked fun at chronological arrangement of subheadings in biographies:

> The name of the person under treatment naturally runs through almost every page, and the conscientious index-maker tries to keep pace with him. This means that many events of his life got shifted out of their natural order. Here is the general effect:
>
> *John Smith:* born, p. 1; born again, p. 1; father born, p. 2; grandfather born, p. 3; mother born, p. 4; mother's family leave Ireland, p. 5; still leaving it, p. 6; school, p. 7; more school, p. 8; dies of pneumonia and enters Harvard, p. 9; eldest son born, p. 10; marries, p. 11; back at school, p. 12; dead, p. 13; takes his degree, p. 14 . . . (Leacock 1942, p. 213)

A special case of chronological arrangement is *evolutionary order,* which may be useful in indexes to works on geology, mineralogy, paleontology, and related subjects, e.g.,

Fossil insects
  Permian 127
  Triassic 138
  Cretaceous 141, 145
  Tertiary 148

The subheadings are here displayed in line-by-line style because this is the predominant one in indexes of scientific or technical texts and also because the number of subheadings is relatively small, but run-in style is also possible.

A third type, *chronologico-numerical arrangement,* is often employed for the subarrangement of numbered sequential events or documents, e.g.,

World Zionist Congresses: First (Basle, 1897) 87–91; Second (Basle, 1898) 103–5; Fourth (London, 1900) 156; Sixth (Basle, 1903) 198–203

Philatelic Society 14, 19–24, 48
  First annual report 19
  Second annual report 26
  Fifth annual report 52, 55

But, since this deviation from alphabetical order may be confusing, it is preferable to use ordinal numbers, even if the actual titles have spelled-out numbers. This has the additional advantage of shortening the subheadings.

It cannot be stressed too strongly that chronologically arranged subheadings in run-in style, whether following the page order of the book or rearranged by date, are suitable only for historical or biographical texts but not for any other treatment of topics where neither chronological nor evolutionary sequences or aspects are involved. Alas, frightful examples of pseudo-chronological arrangement of subheadings in page order are all too often found. The following example is from *The modern researcher* by Jacques Barzun and Henry F. Graff (revised edition, 1970):

> Sentences: faulty, 34–36; topic, 273; euphony in, 279–80; overabstraction in, 279–80; rhythm in, 294, 299–300, 308–9, 312, 313; characteristics of, 295 ff; relation of, to words, 296–7; undefinable, 296–8; must move, 297; contents vs. meaning, 298; first rule governing, 298–9; emphatic places in, 299–300; tone of, 299–300; periodic, 300; rules of thumb for, 300, 306–8; [etc., etc. for another dozen subheadings, ending with] final revision of, 361

Quite apart from the ludicrous style of the subheadings and their occasional irrelevancy and some other mistakes, this jumble of unrelated or redundant subheadings, dutifully set out in page order of the text, offers almost no help for the reader who wants to find what the authors have to say on a specific topic, such as "periodic sentences". That reader must wade through thirteen entirely unrelated subheadings before hitting, more or less accidentally, "periodic", and it is of little or no concern to him or her that "tone" or "rules of thumb" are discussed in the same section of the book.

It is ironic, to say the least, that the authors of this book admonish their reader to "make your index such as to prevent the reader's saying that he could not find again a choice passage he came across in its lively pages. . . . [An index] will provide a clue to every single item of interest . . . By the care of its preparation, the index shows the author's pride in his work and his regard for other researchers. Both it and they deserve better than to be slighted at his hands" (pp. 378–379). Golden words of wisdom indeed (though marred by being addressed to male author-indexers exclusively) but not heeded by the book's indexer.

Although arrangement of subheadings in page order was criticized, and alphabetical arrangement recommended instead as early as 1902 (Cragg 1902), it seems that pseudo-chronological order of subheadings gained the upper hand and became the accepted form of display until the 1950s: several textbooks and guides on indexing, among them the often-cited works by Spiker (1953) and Wheeler (1957), exhibit examples of model indexes in which almost all subheadings are arranged in page order, whether or not topics are treated historically. Spiker does not even consider alphabetical arrangement of subheadings, even though her only detailed example deals with a scientific subject, namely poisonous spiders. Perhaps some of this predilection, if not preoccupation, with chronological order may have been sheer laziness on the part of indexers who did not bother to alphabetize the slips or cards on which they had noted modifications or subsidiary aspects as they went through a text.

It seems, however, that pseudo-chronological arrangement of subheadings is now on the wane: Collison (1962) barely mentions it, Carey (1963) gives only a facetious example of it, and neither his successor Anderson (1971) nor Cutler (1970) mentions it as a possibility; Collison (1972) again deals with it very briefly, and only in a really chronological context; Hunnisett (1972), though concerned exclusively with the indexing of historical records, does not deal at all with subheadings in chronological or pseudo-chronological order, nor do the textbooks by Borko and Bernier (1978), Cleveland and Cleveland (1990), and Lancaster (1991), while Mulvany (1994b, pp. 124–125) strongly warns against it, except for historical or biographical texts. Regrettably, a few publishers (among them Stanford University Press) still insist on having subheadings arranged chronologically, irrespective of the topic. There is, however, some hope that pseudo-chronological arrangement of subheadings in page order will disappear altogether towards the end of the century, not least because of the use of computers, which have changed the alphabetization of subheadings in run-in style from a tedious chore into a task that can be achieved, almost literally, at the touch of a button.

BS 3700: 6.3
Chicago manual of style: 17.54, 17.105
ISO 999: 8.6
NISO Z39.4:

CLASSIFIED ORDER

Classification is in many respects fundamental to indexing as well
as to any other information retrieval technique, but it ought not to
be employed in the arrangement of topical index headings. The
main reason for this is that, however "logical" or "natural" a classified arrangement in hierarchical form may seem to be to the classi-
fier, it may not be so to other people who are not privy to the
principles of division and subdivision employed by the maker of
the classification. Moreover, even in disciplines such as botany or
zoology, where laymen tend to assume that hierarchical genus-
species classifications, such as Vertebrates—mammals—felines—
cats—Siamese cats, are natural and stable, this is by no means
always the case: taxonomies are frequently changed when it comes
to fine subdivisions or when new species are discovered, and the
experts cannot agree on their proper and exact classification.

Under no circumstances should an alphabetical arrangement of
headings be interspersed with a classified array of subheadings, as
in the following example of an index to a book dealing with all
types of road vehicles:

    motor vehicles
      freight vehicles
        tankers
        trucks
        vans
      passenger vehicles
        buses
        limousines
        sedans

> sports cars
> taxi cabs
> special purpose vehicles
>   ambulances
>   fire engines
>   hearses

There are two serious objections to such a classified display of index headings. The first has already been mentioned: the user does not know the criteria by which the indexer-classifier has chosen to divide a generic concept into species or subgroups. In our example, though the subdividing of Motor vehicles into Freight vehicles, Passenger vehicles, and Special purpose vehicles may make sense, it is neither "natural" nor "logical", and it is in any case not clear what the criterion of subdivision is. Perhaps that first subgrouping was made arbitrarily, while the sub-subgroups are clearly arranged in alphabetical order, presumably because no other "logical" principle of further subdivision could be found. If so, how is the user to know where, for example, Taxi cabs are indexed unless the whole classified display is scanned almost from top to bottom?

Second, it would be inconsistent with the basic principles of classification (and technically difficult) to index *associatively related* (i.e. nonhierarchical) aspects of any subheading; if attempted, this disrupts the hierarchical genus-species sequence and may result in sub-sub-subheadings, thus effectively hiding indexable and sought concepts and relationships from the user. Assuming that the book on road vehicles also deals with details such as hazardous cargoes carried by tankers or special valves for the loading of fluid materials, this would need, in the above example, the sub-sub-subheadings

> motor vehicles
>   freight vehicles
>   tankers
>   hazardous cargoes
>   valves for fluid loading

Clearly, neither hazardous cargoes nor valves are subspecies of tankers, so they don't belong in the hierarchical display; moreover, they are now third-level subheadings, tucked away where a user will not necessarily expect them to be indexed.

The proper way to index the concepts in the road vehicle book is to list each and every one of the subheadings in the classified example shown above as a separate heading in its alphabetical place and to provide subheadings for related concepts as needed, e.g.,

> tankers
>   hazardous cargoes
>   valves for fluid loading

which now becomes legitimate, because direct access to the main heading is provided and no classified hierarchy needs to be searched; separate entries for Hazardous cargoes and Valves (or Loading valves) may also have to be made if warranted by the extensiveness of the treatment in the text or by the special needs of the prospective users of the book.

The case against classified arrangement of topical index headings has been made most eloquently by J. E. Holmstrom (*Training in indexing* 1969, p. 119):

> If what ought to be a straight alphabetical sequence of terms denoting different things is interrupted by pockets of attempted systematic classification of the things themselves—"concealed classifications" as they have aptly been called—the only effect is to bewilder the user of the index by leaving him in doubt as to where he ought to look for what he wants.

The only defensible application of classified headings is in indexes of biographies or historical works containing extensive biographical accounts, as discussed under GROUPED ORDER.

COMPOUND HEADINGS

A compound heading, defined in the most general way, is one composed of more than one element, e.g.,

40-hour week
Brown, John
Gascoyne-Cecil, Robert Arthur James, 5th Marquis of Salisbury
North Pole
optical illusions
water pipes

In linguistic terminology, a compound heading is a *noun phrase*, that is, a phrase consisting of a noun that is modified by another word, generally an adjective, adverb, pronoun or other noun, or several of these. The noun part of a compound heading that is modified is known as the *genus term* or *focus*; it identifies the broad class of things or events to which the term as a whole refers. The modifying part is the *species term* or *difference*; it identifies a characteristic which narrows the meaning of the focus and thus specifies a subclass of it.

Compound headings may take one of two forms:

1. *Adjectival phrases,* in which one or more adjectives or adjectival nouns modify a noun or gerund, e.g.,

electrical engineering
gross domestic product
life support systems
personnel management
steel pipes

2. *Prepositional phrases,* in which a preposition and its object (a noun or a noun phrase) is modified by another noun, e.g.,

Bible in English literature
burden of proof
hospitals for disabled children
strength of materials

Inversion

The very fact that a compound heading has two or more parts inevitably raises the question whether or not to invert such headings in an index, so as to bring the second part to the fore. General agreement exists only on one type of compound heading regarding its inversion in indexes: personal names in the familiar form of given name(s)-surname are normally indexed in inverted form, as in the Brown, John example above, but—as the Gascoyne-Cecil example shows—things can get complicated even for Western names, not all of which follow the same pattern, not to mention African and Asian names (*see* PERSONAL NAMES and PLACE NAMES).

Yet regarding compound headings for topics, and whether they should be listed in direct or inverted form, there is probably no other issue that has led to more heated debates and headaches for indexers and index users alike, and there will probably never be full agreement, because the treatment of topical compound headings will depend on the nature of the text and its intended audience. It is safe to assume that few people would argue in favor of inversion for "40-hour week" or "North Pole". But is "optical illusions" better or worse than "illusions, optical" as an index heading? And are people interested in pipes better served by headings such as:

pipes, concrete	pipes, sewer
pipes, copper	pipes, steel
pipes, gas	pipes, water
pipes, plastic	pipes, wooden

than by the direct headings "concrete pipes", etc.?

The answers to these questions can now be given with more confidence than was the case a few decades ago, but they demand more mental effort on the part of the indexer than the snap decisions often made in the past regarding direct versus inverted form of compound headings. Until the late 1970s, most textbooks and indexing guides gave vague and highly subjective advice on the matter of compound headings (and some of them still do). Indexers were advised to put the "more important" or "logical" part of the heading first and to invert the rest of it. It was not realized that importance, like beauty, is in the eye of the beholder and that there is nothing inherently "logical" about the preference of users in looking for one component rather than another of a compound heading. Thus it came to pass that *Library of Congress subject headings* (LCSH), the most prestigious and virtually unrivalled subject heading list used by American libraries, contained until 1988 the headings "Jewish libraries" and "Libraries, Catholic" as valid ones, with "Libraries, Jewish" and "Catholic libraries" as invalid forms given only as cross-references.* There were hundreds of similar incongruous pairs of valid headings in LCSH which simply shows that the subject catalogers who designed these headings a long time ago had diametrically opposed views of what was "more logical".

Research into the structure and use of printed indexes (Keen 1977, 1978; Austin 1984) has convincingly shown that inverted headings cannot be constructed according to objective criteria, nor are they particularly helpful for index users. Consequently, *inverted headings should be avoided altogether in indexing,* and this is exactly what current indexing standards recommend. Quite simply, English-speaking people in search of information think and speak in phrases that put modifying adjectives before and not after nouns; they ask or search for "optical illusions", not for "illusions, optical". The inverted form, if used in an index, forces them to transform it mentally into its natural form ("illusions, optical"—ah, that really means "optical illusions").

Moreover, adjectives and adjectival nouns modifying a noun in a compound heading may multiply:

> water pipes
> polyvinyl water pipes
> extruded polyvinyl water pipes

which, when inverted, may lead to headings beloved by quartermaster general clerks but utterly unintelligible to other mortals:

> pipes, water, polyvinyl, extruded, small bore

(Note that "small bore" is left uninverted because it is somehow intuitively felt to be some kind of "unit" that should not be split up.†)

---

*"Jewish libraries" appeared first in the 5th edition of 1948, while "Libraries, Catholic" made its appearance only in the 6th edition of 1957; the latter heading was finally cancelled and converted to "Catholic libraries" in 1989.

†The reasons for this phenomenon are complex and have long been the subject of linguistic research. A popular (and amusing) discussion of adjectival order is in Crystal 1971, pp. 128–141.

Furthermore, since the main headings of indexes are arranged in alphabetical (or alphanumerical) order, any arrangement such as the one in the "pipes" example above is a misguided attempt to introduce a (concealed) classification into the alphabetical sequence. (In the example, there are actually two classifications, mixed up by alphabetical order: one is by material, the other by fluid conveyed.) Although classified displays of related concepts are eminently useful for an overview of the structure of a discipline or field, their proper place is in classification schemes or in the classified part of a thesaurus (where the classification forms the basis of its structure), but these must be kept strictly apart from alphabetical arrangements of terms. *See also* CLASSIFIED ORDER.

An amalgamation of the two systems, known as an alphabetico-classified index, was a form sometimes used around the turn of the century, but it has been long since discarded as unhelpful and confusing.

Still, it is an indisputable fact that users of an index may wish to find a concept expressed by that part of a compound heading which is not the first one in its direct form, such as the noun in an adjective-noun phrase. When and how is this to be done? The following discussion, which will try to answer these questions, may at first seem to be difficult for those who have not previously been exposed to this kind of analysis, but the effort involved will be worthwhile, as it will result in better indexing and higher satisfaction on the part of index users.

Adjectival Phrase Headings

As already stressed, compound headings in the form of adjectival phrases should always be listed first of all in their natural language order. There are three types of adjectival phrase headings for which this is the only form necessary.

1. Compound headings containing proper names, e.g.,

Alzheimer's disease
Freudian slips
Salvation Army

2. Compound headings in which the adjectival phrase has be-

come so familiar in common use or in the specialized vocabulary of a field that it can be considered as a term for a single concept, e.g.,

data processing
deoxyribonucleic acid
gross domestic product
very high frequency waves

3. Compound headings in which the difference of the adjectival phrase has lost its original meaning, e.g.,

cabinet making
first aid
trade winds

Double Entries and Cross-References

The decision on a DOUBLE ENTRY or CROSS-REFERENCE for a compound heading in order to bring its focus to the fore will depend on the nature of the text and on the intended audience, but it is better to err on the side of making a double entry or a cross-reference than to omit one that users will desperately look for. Several methods can be used to formulate double entries for compound headings of the adjectival phrase type.

1. Determine whether the relationship between the difference and the focus is one of the following four types:

to be (genus-species or predicative)
to have (whole-part or possessive)
to do (active/passive)
to occur at/in (locative)

The compound headings "small airplanes", "jet airplanes", "cargo airplanes", and "Japanese airplanes" illustrate the four types which look deceptively similar in structure but are actually quite different regarding the kind of relationship between the adjective and the noun. Small airplanes *are* small ("to be"); jet airplanes *have* jet engines (the term "engines" being implied in "jet"); cargo airplanes *carry* cargo ("to do"); and Japanese airplanes are *in* or come *from* Japan. Any compound headings of these four types do not normally need cross-references from their inverted forms. A single *see* reference from the focus as a generic term to the more specific compound heading(s) is all that is needed, e.g.,

   airplanes *see* cargo airplanes, Japanese
     airplanes, jet airplanes, small airplanes

If the concept represented by the focus is also treated separately in the text, the cross-reference must be *see also:*

   airplanes 56, 73, 128
      see also cargo airplanes, Japanese
        airplanes, jet airplanes, small airplanes

However, no double entry featuring the focus as a main heading and the differences as subheadings should be made. Therefore,

   airplanes
     cargo
     Japanese
     jet
     small

would be wrong, and should not be confused with subheadings that indicate concepts that are *associated* with the main heading in a relationship other than the four listed above. Thus,

   airplanes
     history 36
     maintenance 128, 156, 211
     recreational use 78, 89

is correct. Note that the last subheading is itself a compound one of the "to be" type that does not need any further cross-references from the noun "use". The *see also* references in the example above may be combined with subheadings for associative concepts:

   airplanes 56, 73, 128
      see also cargo airplanes, Japanese airplanes, jet airplanes,
        small airplanes
     history 36
     maintenance 128, 156, 211
     recreational use 78, 89

2. Make a *see* reference from the inverted form of a compound heading to its direct form. This seemingly rather obvious and simple method is, however, not always the best or most appropriate one, nor is it even always needed, as shown in the examples of method (1). An inverted heading followed by a *see* reference should be employed only if the main heading in direct form is followed either by a large number of locators or by at least one subheading. But if the direct form has only one or two locators it is uneconomical in terms of space, and cumbersome for the user, to make a *see* reference. Assuming that "optical illusions" is treated only on page 74 and is illustrated on page 75, the entry

illusions, optical 74, 75

takes up only one line and provides the user immediately with the sought information, whereas the entry

illusions, optical *see* optical
    illusions

occupies two lines and forces the user to turn to a different part of the index, perhaps several pages away, in order to find the two locators. *See also* CROSS-REFERENCES.

3. A third method of making a double entry for the noun in an adjective-noun phrase is to drop the adjective altogether and to add instead a QUALIFIER, which may also serve to distinguish between possible HOMOGRAPHS, e.g.,

Instead of	*Noun + qualifier*
auditory illusions 237	illusions (audiology) 237
optical illusions 74, 75	illusions (optics) 74, 75

4. Index only the focus without the modifying difference. This is a rather poor solution, because it is not specific enough; it may have to be used in a pinch (e.g., if space for the index is severely limited), but only when the compound heading has only one or two locators, so that the user will find the modification in the text. Thus,

illusions 74, 75

leads to those pages where the user will see that the text deals with *optical* illusions, accompanied by an illustration of the phenomenon.

This also presupposes that the text contains no discussion of other types of illusions, such as auditory or hallucinatory ones.

It could be argued that method (3) also involves inversion and that typographical layout (line-by-line subheadings, indentions) and different punctuation are just substitutes for the simple comma, but this is not so. An inverted heading of the noun-comma-adjective type is always the product of a subjective decision as to what is "more important" or "logical" for a potential user—and users may or may not agree with that decision and may or may not be helped by it. The use of double entries in any of the forms shown above, based on the application of objective criteria governing genus-species, whole-part, active/passive, or locative relationships distinguished from associative ones, will result in internally consistent and linguistically correct displays of compound headings and their parts which are helpful for the index user.

Prepositional Phrase Headings

Compound headings in the form of prepositional PHRASES are frequently found in traditional subject heading lists of the *Library of Congress subject headings* type. They have therefore also found their way into subject indexes, but they should only seldom if ever be used as main headings. The only exceptions are prepositional phrases which have become common terms for a single concept, either in everyday usage or in the specialized vocabulary of a field. "Cream of tartar" and "milk of magnesia" are not dairy products, but the name of a chemical (potassium bitartrate) used in baking powder and in the galvanizing industry and the trade name of a laxative, respectively. "Birds of prey" and "Medal for Merit" are other examples of prepositional phrases which may be used as main headings and do not need any double entries or cross-references. "Strength of materials", if used in a scientific or technical text, would not need a cross-reference from the inverted form because it signifies a single concept often used in the titles of treatises and textbooks, and neither would "burden of proof" in a legal text.

Prepositional phrases often appear in texts as CHAPTER HEADINGS, but they should not be transferred to the index unchanged. Rather, the best way to deal with them is to split them up (or to "factor" them) into their components and to use these as main headings, modified by subheadings which may take the form of preposition + object (or vice versa, as the context demands). Thus, the phrase

hospitals for disabled children

should be factored into its three components, as follows, particularly if there are also other aspects of hospitals and of disabled children in the text:

hospitals 26, 58, 103
   for chronically ill 217, 238–241
   for disabled children 257–261
   management 75–81

disabled children 37, 48
   hospitals 257–261
   prosthetic devices 157, 178
   training 148–155

Access to the third topic, "children", may be provided either by a cross-reference

children *see also* disabled children

or, if several types of medically treated children are mentioned, and the heading "disabled children" has also several subheadings (as above), by an entry

children
   autistic 305
   disabled *see* disabled children
   retarded 298, 301

The structure and scope of a text as well as its intended audience will determine which type of factoring is the most suitable one. If the topic "hospitals for disabled children" appears in a text only once (say, in a travelogue in which the author briefly mentions having seen such an institution) a prepositional phrase may be used, especially when space for the index is limited and the entry itself is of marginal value, but factoring would still be the preferable approach because it would provide equal access to all components of the phrase.

Inverted phrases, such as

children, hospitals for disabled *see* disabled children, hospitals for

should not be used at all because they suffer from the same limitations as those discussed above under inverted adjectival phrases,
and may easily succumb to the "quartermaster general syndrome"
mentioned earlier, e.g.,

children, disabled, hospitals for

which, though still intelligible, is clumsy and forces the user to do
some mental gymnastics.

PREPOSITIONS at the beginning or end of the subheadings for
factored phrases should as far as possible be avoided, unless they
are necessary in order to prevent ambiguity, e.g.,

education
    for teachers
    teachers of

BS 3700: 5.2.2.3
ISO 999: 7.2.2.1; 7.2.2.4
NISO Z39.4:

(CONTINUED) LINES

Any index in which entries are printed in two or three columns per
page will almost inevitably have some breaks between the last main
heading with one or more subheadings on the bottom of a right-
hand (odd-numbered) page and the rest of the subheadings on top
of the first column on the following left-hand (even-numbered)
page. In this case it is absolutely necessary to repeat the main heading as the first line on the left-hand page, followed by the word
continued (often abbreviated to *cont.*) in parentheses, e.g.,

[*on bottom of right-hand page*]	[*on top of left-hand page*]
tuberculosis 126, 131	tuberculosis (*cont.*)
bones 449	joints 450
checkups for 533	prevention 428
contraction 426	symptoms 427
hospitalization 338	treatment 429

If this is not done, the user must turn back to the previous page in order to find the main heading and all subheadings before the one on top of the left-hand page. If the subheading "joints" (in the example above) starts the page, users may even be misled to think that they have opened the index somewhere at the letter *J* while actually being somewhere near the end of *T*; although the mistake is soon discovered, it is annoying.

In scientific, technical, and legal works, in which subheadings have sub-subheadings and even sub-sub-subheadings, all of these must be carried over to the next page followed by (*cont.*):

fire prevention codes (*cont.*)
   combustibles (*cont.*)
      open fires 172
      paints 76
      petroleum 47

This is the practice recommended by the relevant standards and style manuals. Some standards, e.g., BS 3700, make the use of (*continued*) optional for breaks between columns on the same page and for breaks between the last column on a left-hand page and the first one on the facing right-hand page, but most well-designed indexes use (*continued*) lines for these breaks as well, especially if there are more than two columns per page.

Before 1970 or thereabouts, all this was almost self-evident, and good printers would insert (*continued*) lines where necessary, even without special instructions on the part of the indexer. Unfortunately, computerized typesetting and the increasing use of desktop publishing often result in incongruous breaks between index columns. It is therefore necessary to give explicit instructions regarding column and page breaks and the use of (*continued*) lines when submitting the index manuscript; this is especially important if the index is in machine-readable form, because column and page breaks cannot be foreseen by the indexer, and the (*continued*) lines must be inserted separately at the typesetting stage. It is also useful to remind the typesetters that at least one subheading must remain with the last main heading at the end of a page or column before a break is being made, because otherwise the result would be a BAD BREAK. For instructions to typesetters, *see* EDITING.

The word *continued* or *cont.* is always set in lower-case italics and is either enclosed in parentheses or preceded by an em-dash:

tuberculosis (*cont.*)   *or*   tuberculosis—*continued*
joints 450   joints 450

BS 3700: 7.2.6.3
Chicago manual of style: 17.139
ISO 999: 9.4.1.5
NISO Z39.4:

THE CONTINUUM OF VERBAL TEXTS

The basic principles of indexing—the analysis of a text, the identification and naming of relevant concepts, the indication of their relationships, and the systematic arrangement of the resulting index entries—apply equally to books and periodicals. However, books and periodicals are not just two different physical embodiments of text, appearing either as bound volumes or as individual issues of periodicals (which are in principle also intended to be bound into volumes, though this is not always being done). Rather, books and periodicals are the endpoints of a continuum of verbal texts whose several different forms of presentation are blending into each other as far as their indexing is concerned. Each of these forms poses different challenges to the indexer, and makes it necessary to employ different indexing techniques.

Books

On one end of the continuum stand books. A book has been defined as a "Document having more than 48 pages and forming a bibliographic unit" (ISO 1983b). This rather narrow definition, designed primarily for book publishing statistics, must for the purposes of indexing be expanded to encompass not only a set number of printed sheets under one cover and bound volumes but also pamphlets, TECHNICAL MANUALS AND REPORTS, instruction booklets, and other minor publications, regardless of their physical extent, being published only once in the same form, and conveying an amount of information that makes it necessary or desirable to provide them with an index.

Books written by a single author or a small team. The majority of commercially published books falls into this category. Generally, they present the indexer with a more or less well-defined central topic at a certain level of specialization (popular, for the educated layperson, or for specialists). The topic of a book is in most cases expressed by a fairly uniform terminology chosen by the author or by a small team of coauthors, say no more than two or three, who are presumably agreed on a consistent terminology throughout the book. By "uniform terminology" is meant that the author is not only more or less consistent in using the same terms for the same topic, but that she or he also employs consistent SPELLING, HYPHENATION, ABBREVIATIONS, and other writing conventions that may be subject to variant usage. Although an author's terminology may be deemed to be difficult, esoteric, weird, or offensive, between the covers of one book it will probably be consistent. Using an author's terminology does not, however, relieve the indexer from seeking to provide synonyms for topical terms where those exist, and to provide the necessary CROSS-REFERENCES. Synonyms for the indexing of texts aimed at the general public can be found in *Roget's thesaurus* or similar reference works, while specialized texts may make it necessary to consult an indexing thesaurus covering the topic.

Books written by multiple authors. Conference proceedings, anthologies, and other collective works are the most common representatives of this type of publication which has traditionally been issued in book form. Similar to books written by one author, collective works deal mostly with a specific topic, often one that is highly focused or very narrowly circumscribed, and is aimed at specialists in a particular field. Yet, even though presented in the form of a bound book, this type of text exhibits, as far as its indexing is concerned, one of the salient characteristics of periodicals, namely a nonuniform terminology.

The various and often quite numerous authors of conference papers often do not agree on calling a spade a spade, but may variously describe it as a gardening tool, a digging device, or a soil aeration implement, not to mention the terms bêche or Spaten, if the conference had international participants and the editor allowed authors to submit their papers in their own vernaculars. The lavish use of synonymous terms is common in the humanities, particularly in philosophy, history, and literary criticism; it is notorious in the social sciences where the followers of one guru and his or her followers may not understand the mentor of a rival school, though both purportedly are using the English language; and it affects also science and technology, especially in biology, chemistry, and medicine, where names of plants and animals, compounds, drugs, and diseases may have dozens of synonymous forms. The indexer may thus be confronted with a variety of terms for the same topic, only one of which must be chosen as the principal or preferred one, all others being relegated to cross-references.

Added to these problems are vagaries of spelling (not only American vs. British, but occasionally also Canadian and other variants), hyphenation (which affects alphabetical arrangement), and abbreviations or acronyms which are often used indiscriminately without explication in full, the author blandly assuming that "everybody in our field knows what QPSX means". An experienced editor would eliminate such hurdles to effective indexing and easy retrieval, but most conference proceedings are either not edited at all, the papers just being printed in the order of their presentation, often reproduced from (sometimes nearly illegible) camera-ready copy, or the editor is a scientist, engineer, or scholar who organized the event but lacks any experience in editing and does not have sufficient time to devote to the task. It then falls to the indexer to straighten out the mess, which may entail extensive and time-consuming research in reference works or inquiries with the authors in addition to the normal indexing tasks that must be performed against a deadline set by the publisher.

Encyclopedias. A subspecies of books written by multiple authors, encyclopedias are still most often published in book form, though they are increasingly also accessible on CD-ROM, through an electronic database or in video format. As far as their indexing is concerned, the text of an encyclopedia has much in common with that of books by single authors, but also with that of periodicals. This may sound paradoxical, seeing that an encyclopedia is written by a large number of contributors, but each article is written by only one author (or at most two) whose terminology is uniform within that article and does not depend much if any on that of other contributors. The terminology of an encyclopedia index will therefore as far as possible follow that of its individual articles. A measure of consistency may be imposed by a specially designed thesaurus, prepared in advance for an encyclopedia. Its editor will then admonish contributors to stick to prescribed and preferred terms, so that the use of exotic synonyms and idiosyncratic terminology is kept to a minimum.

Common characteristics of book indexes. In almost all books, the index is an integral part of the physical volume, generally placed in the back (hence the popular term "back-of-the-book index", though some indexes may appear in the front matter or, as in commercial catalogs, in the middle and before or after each section). It is thus immediately available to users of a printed book. Such is, however, not the case for microfilmed books in which the index appears at the end of a reel or on the last frames of a microfiche, thus making it tedious and cumbersome to use (one of the reasons why scholars hate microforms). Similarly, the index of a book on CD-ROM is not as easily scanned and referred back to a page as is the case in a printed book.

Book indexes are normally compiled by a single person, most often a freelancer who specializes in the topic dealt with by an author or in a collective work; some publishers employ their own in-house indexers for books intended for the general public, but hire freelancers for specialized books. The sometimes enormous bulk of an encyclopedia or other major reference work makes it almost always necessary to employ a team of indexers who often work with the support of various automated aids and use methods that allow the compilation of the index while the text volumes are being edited and printed, so that the index can be published simultaneously with or shortly after the printing of the last text volume, often as a separate volume.

Periodicals

At the other end of the continuum of verbal texts are articles and other contributions in newspapers, journals, magazines, newsletters, bulletins, and other serials. A serial is defined as a "publication in print or in nonprint form, issued in successive parts, usually having numerical or chronological designations, and intended to be continued indefinitely, whatever the periodicity" (ISO 1983b). This definition covers also publications such as yearbooks, almanacs, annual reports, and the proceedings of regularly held meetings and conferences, but these, as discussed above, are for the most part published in the form of books by multiple authors.

Only a relatively small part of the world's enormously large output of PERIODICALS is provided with indexes. Even many professional journals have indexes only for the names of authors or titles which are easy to produce automatically from machine-readable input without almost any human effort, but do not offer indexes to the topics of articles. Those periodicals that do have such indexes, publish them in several different forms.

Bibliographic volume indexes. The index to one bibliographic volume of a periodical generally comprises one calendar year, but may cover a different twelve-month period, half a year or a number of years, depending on the date of the first issue of a volume or the period assigned to one volume. It is either compiled for each successive issue and the entries are cumulated after the last issue has been indexed, or the index is compiled only after the volume is complete. In the first case, the index will be almost ready when the last issue is being printed and can be included at the end of that issue with only little time lost (though the indexer will have to work very quickly at the cumulation). If the issues are bound to form a physical volume, the index is then similar to a back-of-the-book index and serves the users of the periodical in the most convenient way and with as small a time lag as possible (though that time lag will still be more than a year for articles in the first issue of a volume and at least a month for those in the last issue). If the index is compiled only after the completion of the bibliographic volume, the time needed to do that may make it necessary to publish the index either in one of the issues of the next volume (which makes it impossible to bind it with the previous volume, unless the pages are detachable) or as a separate booklet, sometimes featuring a title page and a table of contents, intended to be separated into these parts and bound with the issues of the volume. In either case, such indexes may appear weeks or even months after the last issue of the indexed volume, thereby increasing the time lag between the appearance of an article and its indexing to such an extent that it may become an exercise in futility for those scientific and technical fields in which developments occur rapidly.

In the past, some periodicals published CUMULATIVE INDEXES, but the availability of indexes in the form of electronic databases and the resulting capability of performing retrospective searches, limited only by the extent of a database backwards in time, have made massive printed index cumulations virtually obsolete, especially in science and technology. However, cumulated indexes from the period before the advent of electronic databases still fulfill an important task, and cumulations of only several months are still being produced for topical newsletters and other small periodicals.

Index production. The compilation of a one-volume index to a periodical is in most cases a task for a single indexer, either a freelancer or a person in the service of the publisher. Even the compilation of a fairly large cumulative index may be performed successfully by a single indexer if time is not of the essence. But if the amount of material and the time span covered are large, the project may have to be done by a team of indexers, convened specially for that task, and special techniques may have to be devised for such a project (Bliss 1990).

The Present State of Indexes to Verbal Texts

Verbal texts of a length that cannot easily be remembered have always been in need of devices that make it possible to find and retrieve names, facts, and passages from the texts. The techniques of doing this may have originated with the ancient Egyptians who seem to have used red ink to indicate titles, sections, and subsections in medical texts (Kilgour 1993), while their contemporaries in Mesopotamia incised brief cuneiform indications of the contents of clay tablets on the containers of such tablets. From these early indexes developed the finding tools for written texts that have been with us since the Middle Ages in more or less unchanged form.

The advent of nonprint media and electronic display of texts, as well as the growing variety of forms of printed texts are now changing the shape and character of indexes. The indexing of books written by single authors or by a small team is becoming increasingly different from that of collective works, which in turn exhibit more and more the features of periodicals. The indexing of hypertext (briefly discussed under NONPRINT MATERIALS), will probably add yet other features to the character and the compilation techniques of indexes.

Table 2 displays some of the features of verbal texts and their indexes. The further down on the list of texts, the more they exhibit nonuniform terminology; they may be indexed not by a single indexer but by a team; they may be published separately from the text; and they may be available in both printed and electronic form, or in the latter form only. Only one thing remains unchanged: as long as human beings will produce verbal texts, indexes to them will be needed.

CONTRACTS

No indexing job should ever be accepted by a freelance indexer without a written contract or with one that does not clearly spell out the mutual duties and obligations, especially regarding conditions of payment. It is amazing how often this essential principle is neglected by otherwise quite experienced indexers—be it because the author is a good friend who asked to have his or her work indexed and so the indexer feels embarrassed to ask for the conditions in writing, or because the publishing house is a well-known and reputable firm which may be relied upon to fulfill its obligations and to honor its word. But friendships may founder on the rocks of

Table 2. The Continuum of Verbal Texts and Features of Their Indexes

Form of text	Terminology		Index production		Form of index		Publication	
	Uniform	Non-uniform	By a single indexer	By a team	Published with text	Separate from text	Printed	Electronic
Books								
By single author	X		X		X		X	
By multiple authors		X	X		X		X	
Periodicals								
One bibliographic volume		X	X		X	X	X	
Cumulated volumes		X		X		X	X	X
Current issues		X		X		X	X	X

Reprinted by permission from Hans H. Wellisch, "Book and periodical indexing", *Journal of the American society for information science* 45 (1994), p. 626. Copyright John Wiley & Sons, Inc.

unfulfilled expectations, and payments may be delayed or never made; as to publishers, long delays of payments are not unknown even among highly regarded firms, and cancellation of a publication in midstream while part of the index has already been compiled or a publisher's sudden bankruptcy is unfortunately neither a rare nor an unusual occurrence.

While a carefully drawn-up contract is no absolute defense against such calamities, its existence makes it much easier to prevail, if necessary in court, against an author or publisher who does not fulfill his or her part of the bargain struck when the index was commissioned. A contract will of course also force the indexer to live up to its provisions, compiling the index according to specifications and delivering it on time.

An indexer who is being commissioned by a publisher will often be asked to sign a standard contract whose "boilerplate" provisions are intended to be suitable for most indexing jobs, while at the same time safeguarding the publisher's interests; those provisions do not necessarily take into consideration the interests of the indexer and the specific concerns relating to a particular indexing job. Every indexing contract should therefore be carefully scrutinized and, if necessary, amended or complemented by inserting provisions that will protect the indexer's concerns and interests. The *Recommended indexing agreement* (1990) published by the American Society of Indexers is an excellent model for such provisions, and it should also be used when drawing up an indexing contract directly with an author.

Certain items and conditions must always be clearly stipulated in every indexing contract, while others are optional and will depend on the nature of the indexing job.

The essential items are:

1. The name and address of the author or editor of the work.
2. The title of the work.
3. The actual or estimated extent of the work.
4. The time schedule or date of delivery of the index manuscript.
5. The type of fee and the method of payment. For most back-of-the-book indexes, it is customary to stipulate payment within 30 days of delivery of the index manuscript. For large jobs, such as CUMULATIVE INDEXES to a multivolume work or sev-

eral years of a periodical, a schedule of regular payments should be agreed upon.

6. The display of the indexer's name on the first page of the index. Although this is still far from being customary, it ought to be made mandatory, especially since it does not cost any money. A note of thanks among the author's acknowledgments, welcome though it may be, is no substitute for the prominent display of an indexer's name.

Optional items may include the following:

1. The form of the index manuscript: typewritten, word-processed, or on disk. If disks are to be formatted for electronic typesetting and / or transmitted electronically to the publisher, separate payment for this service and the cost of transmission should be agreed upon.
2. Supply of the text on galleys, to enable the indexer to become acquainted with it before indexing from page proofs is undertaken.
3. Specification of typographical details for the index: number of columns, type size, width of lines, and number of lines per page.
4. Notification about substantial changes in the index proposed by the author or editor before such changes are set in type.
5. PROOFREADING of index galleys and page proofs by the indexer, not the publisher's own proofreaders.
6. Assignment of COPYRIGHT in the index.
7. A complimentary copy of the published work.

Some of these provisions, especially the last three, may meet with stiff resistance on the part of publishers as being unheard-of and contrary to long-established practice. But the times they are a-changing, and such demands are certainly not unreasonable, particularly since proofreading by the indexer is intended to enhance the quality of an index at the expense of the indexer, who must devote much time and effort to the task. Every indexer will have to decide in the light of circumstances whether to insist on some optional condition at the risk of losing the job or to give in and do the job on the publisher's terms. Here, as elsewhere in life, tact, diplomacy, and gentle persuasion will sometimes yield results in the face of initially abrupt refusal. *See also* AUTHOR-PUBLISHER-INDEXER RELATIONSHIPS.

COOKBOOKS

Cookbooks are one of the most ancient types of nonfiction books: four of them and their authors are specifically mentioned by the Greek chronicler Athenaios as having been cataloged in the Alexandrian library in the 3rd century B.C.; we also know that they were all on cakes, then as now a favorite of cookbook writers.

The oldest cookbook that has come down to us is the work of an otherwise unknown author by the name of Apicius who probably lived in the 2nd or 3rd century A.D. The book was very popular in Antiquity as well as in the Middle Ages and is preserved in several manuscripts dating from the 9th to the 15th century.* Though these did not contain any indexes, the second printed edition, published in Basel in 1541, proudly announced on the title page *"cum indice copiosissimo"* (with a most plentiful index) which occupied some 14 pages. Later editions also had indexes, ranging from a dozen to 70 pages. Thus both the compilation and the indexing of cookbooks can look back on a long history.

The indexing of cookbooks has until recently not been treated in the professional literature, except for one brief article (Grant 1990), perhaps because it was thought to be quite simple and straightforward or because cookbooks are not held in particularly high esteem in the literary world. Yet cookbook indexes are probably searched more often and by more people than many others, and their compilers must be aware that prospective users will be novices as well as experienced cooks, housewives as well as professional chefs. This means that recipes must be made accessible by almost every

---

*The work has been translated into English (Apicius 1936).

conceivable clue, which translates into a fairly large number of headings for each recipe; but space for the index is more often than not severely limited. A cookbook indexer is, therefore, frequently caught between a rock and a hard place: the editor may have allotted 1,000 index lines to a book containing more than 300 recipes, which means about three headings for each of them—scarcely enough to index the name of a dish, its type of food, and one major ingredient. Most recipes need more than that, and it is left to the indexer's ingenuity and skill to make this possible (for methods of squeezing more entries into a given space, *see* LENGTH OF AN INDEX).

The indexing of cookbooks must be performed at a high level of EXHAUSTIVITY and SPECIFICITY, because people will look under all possible (and some impossible) entry words in order to find a recipe or picture of a dish they may have seen a long time ago but remember only vaguely.

For example, "Aunt Nellie's shrimp aspic mold with apple-potato-walnut salad" may need entries under apples, aspic, potatoes, shrimp, and walnuts, and perhaps also under seafood and molds, but Aunt Nellie may safely be omitted, since nobody but the author will know who she is or was.

Recipes should generally be indexed by the following features:

1. Type of food, e.g., appetizers, soup, fish (unless the entire book is on a single type of food or dish).

2. Name. Generally, the heading under which a recipe appears in the book, but excluding nondistinctive initial terms such as "old-fashioned", "homestyle", or "quick" (the latter is a particularly ambiguous and often misleading term: whether a dish can be prepared quickly depends on the cook's skill and on someone's idea of a short period of time). Initial adjectives indicating the method of cooking, such as baked, broiled, grilled, or steamed, should likewise not be the first words of a heading; rather, they should be used as subheadings under the main heading for a foodstuff, e.g.,

fish
  baked
  broiled
  deep-fried
  poached

Names of persons, such as "Aunt Nellie" in the example above, should be omitted unless such a name has become an integral part of the name by which a dish is known, e.g., beef à la Stroganoff or Sacher torte.

3. Ingredients. Of course, not everything that is listed under a recipe needs to be indexed, but ingredients that are specific or unusual need index entries. For example, "Mocha surprise", a chocolate cake, must be indexed under chocolate, which is the main ingredient and the one that will probably be best remembered by most people who have read the recipe or seen its picture but may not recall "mocha". Unfortunately, there are as yet no THESAURI for the thousands of ingredients and foodstuffs used in contemporary cooking, so it is up to the indexer (who should also be an expert cook) to think of synonyms for the terms used by cookbook authors. Common ingredients like salt or flour will obviously not need index entries referring to specific recipes, but when the advantages of coarse salt rather than refined table salt are discussed in a cookbook on bread, salt will need its own index entry and so will the various types of flour used in baking bread.

4. Region or place. If the book mentions that a dish is typical for a certain region or originated in a particular country, province, or city, the name of the region or place should be indexed. This is particularly important for regional cookbooks, which are mostly arranged by type of food, not by place; for example, in a book on American Southern cooking, New Orleans should be indexed for those recipes said to come from or be typical of that city's cuisine.

5. Illustrations. Most cookbooks have ILLUSTRATIONS, often in color, and people may remember them better than the recipe or the name of a dish. It is, therefore, important to index pictures of dishes or methods of preparation, but, unfortunately, indexers are seldom provided with them together with the page proofs, because illustrations are separately printed (often by a different printer or in another country) and are not yet ready when the index is being compiled. The editor may not even know at that stage where exactly the color plates will be inserted and bound into the book or may not realize that this information is necessary for the index. A cookbook indexer must therefore always ask about illustrations and insist on their delivery, at least in the form of a sketch or some other preliminary form, e.g., as black-and-white photos of final color plates. Illustra-

tions should have clearly marked LOCATORS; boldface numerals are much better than the usual italic numerals often used for the same purpose because they stress the importance of pictures. The index to that staple of millions of American households, *The joy of cooking* (Rombauer & Becker 1975), uses this feature; that index is commendably thorough and clear, justly honored by a prize, and thus a good model for cookbook indexers.

Upon completion of an index to a cookbook, the indexer may have experienced not only the joy of indexing but also the sense of having made an important contribution to the joy of cooking.

COPYRIGHT

Can indexers claim copyright in the indexes they compile for other people's work? The answer is: maybe, depending on where you happen to live, but don't count on it.

Copyright laws in their modern form were first enacted in England in 1710 (the "Statute of Queen Anne"). They protect the rights of authors to their written, musical, or artistic works against unauthorized copying, translation, or adaptation. It is important to realize that this protection pertains only and exclusively to the *form* of a work, and not to the ideas or information expressed or contained in it. Thus, the protection covers not *what* has been said but *how* it has been said. The types of works protected by copyright, inasmuch as indexes can be compiled for them, are: literary works; musical works, including any accompanying words; dramatic works; pictorial and graphic works; motion pictures and other audiovisual works; and sound recordings.

The current laws in the major English-speaking countries are: the U.K. Copyright, Designs, and Patents Act of 1988, which went into effect in 1989; the United States General Revision of the Copyright Law of 1976 (Public Law 94–553), a complete revision of Title 17 of the U.S. Code, effective since 1978 and slightly revised in 1988; and the Canadian Copyright Act (Statutes of Canada C-15), also enacted in 1988. Adherence of these countries to the Berne Convention of 1887 and the Universal Copyright Convention of 1952 assures copyright protection in more than 90 countries.

The U.K. Copyright Act allows for the possibility of the copyright in an index to be owned by the indexer provided he or she is not an employee of the publisher but works as a freelancer. However, the Act makes this provision only implicitly, and so, in order to be on the safe side, the indexer should obtain from whoever commissions an index—the author or the publisher—an explicit, written waiver of any rights in the index. The Act, for the first time, also grants to authors two basic "moral rights" required by the latest revision of the Berne Convention, namely, the *right of paternity* (in the Act called "the right to be identified as an author") and the *right of integrity* (in the Act "the right to object to derogatory treatment of a work"). Both rights have important implications for indexers. The paternity right (which must be claimed explicitly) means that the author of a copyrighted work has the right to be so identified whenever the work is published commercially. While it is unlikely that the author of a book will be denied the privilege of having his or her name prominently displayed on the title page, the names of indexers are generally not given such treatment, despite the fact that this would not cost the publisher anything; but now an indexer, having obtained a copyright in his or her index, may demand that his or her name be printed on the first page of the index, not as a mere courtesy, but as a right. The integrity right is even more important, because "derogatory treatment" means any addition to, deletion from, alteration, or adaptation (other than an authorized translation) of a work. Thus, any changes made by an editor in a copyrighted index without the knowledge or consent of the indexer amount to a distortion or mutilation of the work or are otherwise prejudicial to the honor and reputation of the indexer, constituting an infringement of the integrity right. A guide to the U.K. Copyright Act has been provided by Wall (1993).

The U.S. Copyright Law, quite different from the British one, specifically states that indexes are "supplementary works". If an index is "made for hire", (that is, commissioned by the author or publisher), no separate copyright can be claimed; in principle, the law grants the copyright in an index to the copyright owner of the indexed work. To understand why this is so, one must first consider some of the definitions in ¶ 101 of the Law:

> A "compilation" is a work formed by the collection and assembling of preexisting materials or of data that are selected, coordinated, or arranged in such a way that the resulting work as a whole constitutes an original work of authorship. A "derivative work" is a work based upon one or more preexisting works. . . . A work consisting of editorial revisions, annotations, elaborations, or other modifications which, as a whole, represent an original work of authorship, is a "derivative work".

In the definition of a "work made for hire", indexes are specifically mentioned:

> A "work made for hire" is (1) a work prepared by an employee within the scope of his or her employment; or (2) a work specially ordered or commissioned for use as a . . . supplementary work . . . *if the parties expressly agree in a written instrument signed by them that the work shall be considered a work made for hire.* . . . A "supplementary work" is a work prepared for publication as a secondary adjunct to a work by another author . . . such as . . . *indexes* . . . . [Emphasis in this and the following quotations added.]

These definitions make it absolutely clear that (1) an index compiled by an employee of a publisher is not separately copyrightable; and (2) an indexer commissioned by an author (or publisher) to compile an index cannot claim a copyright in that index; the copyright in such a "supplementary work" belongs to the author of the indexed work. A commentary on the 1976 Copyright Law concludes that "Authors presumptively own all rights in works made for hire, absent an express written agreement signed by them stating otherwise" (Angel & Tannenbaum 1977, p. 59). This means that an indexer who wishes to obtain the copyright in an index that he or she compiled must include an explicit statement in the CON-TRACT stipulating that the author or publisher waives copyright in the index. It may be relatively easy to persuade an author who was neither willing nor able to compile an index to his or her work to waive the copyright in an index compiled by another person, but it may be much more difficult to get a publisher to relinquish a part of the copyright.

Once this has been successfully achieved, an index can then presumably be considered a "compilation" or "derivative work", whose author (that is, the indexer) can claim copyright in it according to ¶ 103(b) and ¶ 106(2). ¶103(b) states that

> The copyright in a *compilation* or *derivative work* extends only to the material contributed by the *author* of such a work, as distinguished from the preexisting material employed in the work. . . . *The copyright in such work is independent* of . . . any copyright protection in the preexisting material.

¶ 106(2) gives the author "exclusive rights to do and authorize . . . to prepare derivative works based upon the copyrighted work . . . ."

It would seem that the definitions of ¶ 101 and the provisions of ¶¶ 103 and 106 mean that (a) only the holder of the copyright in a work, i.e., the author or the publisher can commission or authorize an index; and that (b) such an index is then to be considered either a "compilation" or a "derivative work", the author of which (that is, the indexer) may claim copyright in it provided that, as discussed above, the author expressly waives his or her copyright in the index.

A United States Supreme Court decision handed down in June 1989 may have important implications for freelance indexers. The case, *Community for Creative Nonviolence vs. Reid*, no. 88–293, concerned the copyright of an artist in a sculpture that had been commissioned by an association. The association claimed that, since the sculpture was a "work made for hire", they could do with it whatever they liked, including destroying it. But the Court held that, although the artist had been commissioned to create a sculpture, he was not engaged in an employer-employee relationship; he worked in a skilled occupation, had supplied his own tools, and worked in his own studio in Baltimore while the association was in Washington, thus making daily supervision of his work impossible; he was retained for less than two months, during which time the association could not engage him in other projects; the association paid him a specific sum upon completion of the job, but paid no Social Security taxes or unemployment insurance for him and provided no employee benefits. All of this made the sculptor an independent contractor, not an employee, and he could therefore retain the copyright in his creation.

It stands to reason that these criteria would apply equally to freelance indexers commissioned to compile an index, but it must be borne in mind that no case concerning copyright in indexes has ever been brought to or adjudicated anywhere in a court of law and that therefore all opinions on whether or not indexes are copyrightable when compiled by freelance indexers are just that—conjectures without the force of court opinions.

Most indexers may not be too much concerned about the copyright to their indexes because virtually all indexes are commissioned by an author or publisher for a specific edition of a work only (since another edition would need a different index); the indexer receives a fee upon completion, and that is normally the end of the process. The chances that the index may be translated, adapted, or set to music seem somewhat remote, so why bother about copyright? The issue is, however, far from being a trivial one. It may happen, for instance, that the index to a hardcover edition of a work is being reprinted in a paperback edition by a different publisher (and often in a different country); the original publisher may have assigned or sold the copyright in the work to the paperback publisher, but does that also include the right to print the index? Unless the indexer claimed copyright to the index, the publishing company may indeed do with it whatever it likes, and the indexer's fee for the hardcover index will not compensate him or her for the use made of the index in the potentially much larger (and more lucrative) paperback edition. Not only may the indexer be deprived of any additional remuneration, but the paperback index may have been abbreviated, compressed or otherwise altered, thus impairing its quality and damaging the indexer's reputation. An actual case of such a blatant infringement of an indexer's "moral right" occurred when Peter Ackroyd's biography *Dickens* was reissued as a paperback (Bell, 1992a).

Since the copyright in an index is still a somewhat murky and as yet undecided issue, an indexer who expects that further use may be made of an index by a publisher may wish to include a clause in the original contract stipulating some adequate and equitable remuneration for such future use, rather than rely on the protection (or otherwise!) of existing copyright laws. Whether a publisher will agree to such a clause is, of course, another story.

If copyright has been successfully claimed in an index, the by-line, e.g., "Compiled by Jane Roe", which is now an indexer's "moral right", must also be preceded or followed by the copyright symbol © or the word "Copyright", because the Universal Copyright Convention stipulates the display of that symbol in order to protect the rights of an author in all signatory countries to the same extent as is the case in the author's homeland. However, the Berne Convention (joined by the United States only in 1988, effective 1989) does not require any symbol or word in order to establish an author's copyright, which is acquired automatically "as soon as he lifts the pen from paper", as one commentator put it.

CORPORATE NAMES

These names are actually not "corporate"; they are the ones borne by "corporate bodies", a concept invented by lawyers and adopted by librarians for "an organization or group of persons that is identified by a particular name and that acts, or may act, as an entity. Typical examples of corporate bodies are associations, institutions, business firms, nonprofit enterprises, governments, government agencies, religious bodies, local churches, and conferences" (AACR2, Appendix D). The treatment of corporate names in indexes varies in many respects from that of PERSONAL NAMES, mainly because a corporate body is quite different from a real warm body and enjoys some advantages denied to the latter: corporate bodies may legally use several different names (sometimes in more than one language); they may change their name suddenly and as often as they please; they may marry other corporate bodies and take or change their names; they may split into a number of different corporate bodies, each of which may or may not retain all or some of the parent body's name; they may spawn branches, departments, divisions, offices, and other children; and they may die, yet do not always go to corporate heaven but may be resurrected after some time with the same or a different name, to live happily ever after.

Order of Entry

The most conspicuous difference between the indexing of personal and corporate names is that the latter are always entered in the order of all words, that is, *without any inversion.* This practice pertains also to names of commercial firms, institutions, or foundations, even when the first part is a forename or initials standing for a forename, e.g.,

> D. G. Jackson Advertising Services
> John Hanson Savings & Loan Bank

Inverted forms of a corporate name are used only for cross-references if these are deemed to be necessary because the first word of a name may not always be the one that users would look up or remember. Thus, for the examples just given, cross-references or double entries like these would be made:

> Jackson (D. G.) Advertising Services
> Hanson (John) Savings & Loan Bank

The enclosure of the inverted name or initials in parentheses and the absence of any commas is now standard practice (AACR2, 26.3A3).

INITIAL ARTICLES in corporate names are not transposed but they are disregarded in alphabetization, e.g.,

> The Library Association [alphabetized at L]
> La Rose Limousine Service [alphabetized at R]

Form of Name

In back-of-the-book indexes the form of a corporate name chosen by the author will in most instances be the one given as a main heading, and cross-references from other forms may not always be needed, except when ABBREVIATIONS are used as main headings, for which cross-references *must* be made. In indexes to periodicals in which different authors may refer to the same corporate body by various forms of name, and even more in indexes of trade directories and similar compilations consisting only or predominantly of corporate names, cross-references from all possible access points for a name (including inverted forms) must be made. Cross-references in inverted form for the distinctive part of a corporate name should also be made when the first word of the name is a very general and commonly used one. Names beginning with Academy, Association, Council, Foundation, Institute, Institution, and Society (to list only a few of the most common ones) and their counterparts in other languages (Institut, Société, Gesellschaft, etc.) are easily confused by users searching for a corporate name. Is it the Institute or the Institution of Mechanical Engineers? Is it the Association of American Publishers or the American Publishers' Association? It is therefore important and sometimes indispensable to provide cross-references such as:

> American Publishers, Association of
>   *see* Association of American Publishers

and perhaps also

> Publishers, Association of American
>   *see* Association of American Publishers

Cross-references for corporate names may also have to take other forms. Commercial enterprises (especially shops and restaurants) often choose fancy forms of names to attract the attention of customers, such as

> AAA Cleaning Service
> Bar-B-Q Chef

which may need cross-references from

> Triple-A Cleaning Service
> Barbecue Chef

Both a corporate body itself and the general public may use a corporate name in an abridged form because the full official name is long and cumbersome and will therefore appear only on highly formal documents or seals, but not in everyday use. Thus, the full name of the Hudson's Bay Company as chartered in 1670 is Governor and Company of Adventurers Trading into Hudson's Bay, but probably no one will look for the venerable company under "Governor", and even a cross-reference may be superfluous here. Another example are the Franciscans, whose original Latin name is Ordo fratrum minorum but who are also sometimes referred to in English as the Order of St. Francis or the Minorites, from all of which cross-references may have to be made.

Several Names

A vexatious problem is posed by corporate bodies that have and use more than one official name. These are generally international bodies, such as the United Nations and its many agencies (with five official names), the European Economic Community (with more than a dozen names for each of its member countries), or international professional organizations, such as the International Federation of Library Associations and Institutions (which has also French, German, and Russian names, but only one acronym—IFLA).

Yet another instance of multiple corporate names may be that of bodies in bi- or multilingual countries, such as Belgium, Canada, or Switzerland. In all cases where a corporate body may be referred to by different names, the form and language chosen by the author of a book will govern the form of a main heading, but in indexes to periodicals, especially international ones which accept articles in more than one language, one form (mostly the English or the most prevalent one) must be chosen and cross-references be made, e.g.,

Communauté économique européenne, *see* European Economic
    Community
Bibliothèque nationale de Suisse, *see* Schweizerische
    Landesbibliothek

Changes of names occur frequently, especially in commercial corporate bodies. Normally, the latest name will be used, but even in the same text the corporate body may be dealt with under both the current and previous names. In such cases, all names need main headings with *see also* cross-references to previous or later names. Cross-references may be expanded to explain their purpose, e.g.,

> Agricultural College of Pennsylvania 56–58
> > *See also its later names* Pennsylvania
> > State College; Pennsylvania State
> > University
>
> Pennsylvania State College 77, 83
> > *See also its previous name* Agricultural
> > College of Pennsylvania
> > *See also its later name* Pennsylvania
> > State University
>
> Pennsylvania State University 113–118, 257
> > *See also its previous names* Agricultural
> > College of Pennsylvania; Pennsylvania
> > State College

Governmental Agencies

The often long, intricate, and frequently changing names of governmental agencies are among the most difficult ones to index. In principle, all government departments, divisions, offices, sections, etc. should be listed first under the name of the jurisdiction (country, state, province, city, etc.), e.g.,

> United States. Department of Transportation
> Maryland. Department of Transportation
> Baltimore. Department of Transportation

This example shows why it is necessary to give the name of the jurisdiction first. The name of the country is, however, often omitted if the text deals with only one country, since there will then be no risk of confusion.

The form of headings for governmental bodies, especially their subordinate bodies, which may constitute long and complex hierarchies (the delight of bureaucrats who invent them and the despair of ordinary citizens, including indexers, who have to deal with them), are covered in great detail in AACR2, 24.17–26; although these rules pertain primarily to library catalogs, they may also be applied in indexing. A relatively simple example of a hierarchy of subordinate units is

> Baltimore. Department of Transportation.
> Interstate Division. Design Section

where the entire chain must be given because each of its links has a nondistinctive name that may also belong to quite different units elsewhere.

Romanization

Last but not least, there is the problem of ROMANIZATION. Corporate bodies in countries that do not use the Roman alphabet, e.g., those in the former U.S.S.R., East Asia, and the Middle East, are rendered in English texts in Romanized form, unless a corporate body uses its own English (or other European language) form of name in its publications intended for use outside its own country.

In most instances, the Romanized form of a corporate name used by the author of a book will also be the one to be used in the index, although the existence of standardized or authoritative Romanization systems for many non-Roman scripts is not always known to authors, who may blandly use their own schemes or may mix different Romanization systems. In periodical indexes, however, a single Romanization system must be used, preferably one that is widely known and accepted as a standard, primarily those used by the British Library or the Library of Congress. Their catalogs, now accessible both in print and online, may often serve as authoritative sources for foreign corporate names, especially those of governmental bodies.

It is, however, often not enough to list the name of, say, a Japanese or Soviet institution in Romanized form only, since most users will not know Japanese or Russian and so be quite ignorant of the meaning of the institution's name, especially if it also appears in the form of an acronym (of which the Russians are very fond). An English translation of the name or an explication of its acronym, if not already given in the text itself, should be added to the Romanized form and also added as a double entry:

International Society for Educational Information (Kokusai Kyōiku
    Jōhō Senta) 48
Kokusai Kyōiku Jōhō Senta (International Society for Educational
    Information) 48

All-Union Institute of Scientific and Technical Information (VINITI)
    33, 51
VINITI (All-Union Institute of Scientific and Technical Information)
    33, 51
Vsesoyuznyi Institut Nauchnoi i Tekhnicheskoi Informatsii
    (VINITI) (All-Union Institute of Scientific and Technical
    Information) 33, 51

Here, as in other instances where the heading is fairly long but may have only one or a few locators, it is more economical of space and less cumbersome for the user to make double or multiple entries rather than *see* references.

AACR2: Chapter 24
BS 3700: 5.3.2
ISO 999: 7.3.2
NISO Z39.4:

COSTING

Once upon a time, in the era known as B.C. (Before Computers), indexers did not worry much about costing. Most of them thought that they only had to charge for time spent on indexing, because their expenses for equipment were fairly low (except for major projects lasting many months or even years, which also consumed lots of cards, typewriter ribbons, paper, etc.). Shoeboxes cost nothing and lasted a long time, and cards were relatively cheap and could be used at least twice (some indexers even claimed that they could reuse cards up to four times!). And since indexing was (and still is) a cottage industry, often performed on the kitchen table in one's own home, indexers tended not to take into consideration things like rent, utilities and property taxes, insurance, and other "incidentals", like supplies, which in reality affected their costs.

All this changed when personal computers began to be used for indexing in the early 1970s. Now virtually all professional indexers and most parttime freelancers use computers and specially designed indexing software for their work. Consequently, not only the time spent on indexing but also the cost of equipment, its repair and amortization, the cost of materials and other incidental costs must be recovered by the fee charged for an indexing job.

Time Spent on Indexing

In the early days of computer-assisted indexing the professional literature was full of statements claiming that the use of a computer saved 50% or more of the time needed to compile an index on cards. This was comparable to the signs often seen at shopping mall outlets for cheap jewelry "50% off!" which don't tell you off *what*. If only the mechanical stages of indexing are considered (writing entries on cards, filing and refiling them), the saving of time may indeed be as high as 50% compared with the same operations performed on a computer. But this is not the whole story. Even though indexing on cards is now almost extinct, it is still instructive to analyze the time spent on *every* stage of the indexing operation when performed with cards and to compare it with computer-assisted indexing.

A fairly average indexing job would be one for a popular historical work, 390 pages long, with an 8-page index containing about 800 headings. The operations to be performed when using cards or a computer, respectively, as well as data pertaining to the time needed and savings in time achieved by using a computer are shown in Table 3. The time spent on each operation is based on the number of hours for such a job as reported by experienced indexers. Beginners would probably need more time, especially if they have not had previous experience with computers, programming, and

Table 3. Comparison of Indexing Times Using Cards versus a Computer

	Cards		Computer		
Operation	Hours	Percent of total time	Hours	Percent of total time	Percent of time saved
(a) Quick first reading of text	4	9	4	14	0
(b) Reading and marking passages	9	21	9	31	0
(c) Writing or key-boarding headings	7	16	5	17	29
(d) Alphabetizing	4	9	0.5	2	88
(e) Editing	5	12	5	17	0
(f) Typing manuscript/ printing computerscript	8	19	0.5	2	93
(g) Final checking	2	5	1	3	50
(h) Proofreading printed index	4	9	4	14	0
Total	43	100%	29	100%	33%

the use of specialized indexing software, whose manuals (often comprising several hundred pages) must be carefully studied. It is unlikely that anyone would spend considerably less time on this job if it is properly done, that is to say, not just indexing personal and place names but also events, as well as political, social, cultural, and economic issues discussed in the text.

Regarding each operation:

(a) A first rapid reading or at least scanning of the text is needed to get a general idea of the work, its structure, level of exposition, and occurrence of names, events, and ideas;

(b) and (c), the marking of terms and phrases on the pages and the writing or keyboarding of headings, can often be combined by experienced indexers. If cards are used to write the headings, considerably more time is needed than for keyboarding because of the constant filing and refiling of the cards. The addition of subheadings to main headings on cards will also take more time than the same operation performed automatically by indexing software, which thus achieves a considerable saving of time.

(d) Alphabetizing cards involves some preliminary editing, as redundant headings are eliminated, subheadings consolidated, etc., while the cards are being arranged. Saving of time when a computer is used amounts theoretically to 100% because the software sorts all headings automatically as they are keyboarded; but, since the program has to be set up for the requirements of each specific job (the alphabetization system to be used, characters to be ignored in sorting, the display style of subheadings, etc.), and there will also be inevitable and time-consuming snags, mishaps and even—heaven forbid—crashes or other calamities, a minimum of half an hour has been allowed for automatic alphabetization. In addition, the quick preliminary editing possible on cards is not always feasible to the same extent on a computer (depending on the sophistication of the software), so the actual saving of time for the arrangement operation—shown as 88%—may be less.

(e) This includes only the editing of main headings, subheadings, and cross-references and the elimination or consolidation of redundant headings, not the entire sequence of steps described under EDITING.

(f) The time of 8 hours for typing 800 lines is not excessive, considering that locators must be carefully typed and checked and that indentions for subheadings and turnover lines slow down typing somewhat. Depending on their proficiency as typists, some indexers may need even more time to produce a clean typescript. Thus, the saving of time when using computers, again allowing half an hour for incidental chores, amounts to 93% in the example.

(g) Final checking has also been allotted relatively little time, especially if the manuscript has been typed from cards, which will inevitably cause typos that must be detected and corrected. If the word-processing software includes (as it should) automatic spelling correction, the resulting saving of time has already been taken into consideration at (f), but even a computerscript will have to be checked for possible mistakes.

(h) Proofreading will obviously take the same time, no matter how the index has been compiled.

The example shows that the time saved by using a computer as compared to cards amounts to 14 hours, or 33%. This translates into $3\frac{1}{2}$ hours spent on each final printed index page for computer-assisted indexing versus almost $5\frac{1}{2}$ hours for each page produced on cards. The saving of time by a computer is achieved by four operations, namely, the keyboarding of headings (29%), the arrangement of headings (88%), the printing of the computerscript (93%), and the final checking (50%). The *percentage* of time spent on input operations (a) to (d) is 55% for cards versus 64% for computer, and for editing operations (e) to (h) it is 45% versus 36%, respectively; this means that computer-assisted indexing allows the indexer to spend relatively more time on the intellectual tasks of analyzing a text, while less time needs to be spent on editing and final checking.

The example in Table 3 is a fairly common one concerning the hours spent on the various operations. It so happens that one of the professional indexers who provided data on their work kept a detailed log of time spent on 10 back-of-the-book indexing jobs done during 1988. The books were all on highly specialized scientific and technical matters, intended for an audience of engineers. They ranged in size from 135 to 2,272 pages; excluding that very big one, the average length of the other nine books was 400 pages. The big book needed a total of 328 hours, the nine others an average of 64 hours; the shortest book of only 135 pages needed 29 hours. The average of 64 hours for 400 pages is more than double the amount of time for the popular historical work of comparable length in the example if using a computer, but scientific and technical books contain many more terms and need more subheadings; moreover, the number of pages alone does not allow a meaningful comparison, because scientific and technical texts are generally printed on larger pages, in smaller type, and with less leading (space between lines) than popular works, so that the number of words in the former may be almost double that of the latter on the same number of pages. Thus, while the amount of time spent on the indexing of the nine actual books is not directly comparable to the example in Table 3, the *percentages* correspond fairly well. (The indexer's breakdown of operations shown below is different from that used in Table 3, so that the categories used there and the times spent on them have been given in parentheses.)

Reading text and marking headings	40%	(a + b = 45%)
Keyboarding headings	23%	(c = 17%)
Editing and miscellaneous	37%	(e + g + h = 34%)
Total	100%	

Time saved on the various stages of indexing is, however, not the primary advantage of computer-assisted indexing. Rather, features that are not directly measurable in terms of hours but result nevertheless in faster and better production, such as automatic setting of indentions and listing of locators in ascending order, control of double entries, eliminating of alphabetization errors, and the possibilities of transmitting an index in machine-readable form and electronically to publishers and other clients have made the computer rather than the card tray the indexer's tool of the trade. That tool must now be considered in costing.

Depreciation and Incidental Costs

A reasonable depreciation period for hardware and software (exclusive of upgrading) is four years, i.e., for every $1,000 of initial costs of equipment the annual cost charged against income must be at least $250. To this must be added incidental costs, such as supplies (disks, paper, ink cartridges, etc.), repairs of defective chips, boards, hard disks, lasers, etc., and upgrading of hardware, software, and ancillary equipment. The annual cost of incidental expenses should be computed at no less than 10% of the total cost of hardware and software, and may amount to much more if extensive repairs must be made. The effects of tax provisions regarding depreciation must also be taken into consideration, for which the services of a tax accountant may be needed.

What Is an Adequate Fee?

From time to time, the SOCIETIES OF INDEXERS conduct surveys among their members to find out about current indexing methods and fees. Invariably, these surveys reveal that many indexers, even those with several years' experience, accept woefully inadequate fees which may make authors and publishers happy but are harmful for all indexers because they put those who charge reasonable fees at a disadvantage. Indexers who charge low fees do so not because of cut-throat competition but either because they are novices eager to get their first indexing jobs and to gain experience even though actually losing money—paying in fact an apprenticeship

fee—or because they are ignorant of the various methods of remuneration and the real costs of doing the job. This is particularly true
of those who take on occasional part-time indexing jobs just to
make a little extra money in their spare time, without bothering too
much about things like overhead and a reasonable return on their
investment in electronic equipment.

Experienced professional indexers in the United States could expect to earn hourly fees of $30–35 in 1995. Indexing jobs of unusual
complexity, and those demanding highly specialized knowledge on
the part of the indexer, or rush jobs would add 10–20% to these
amounts. The following computations are based on an hourly fee of
$30, on the assumption that, even at a relatively slow but inescap-
able rise of inflation, before the end of this millennium that amount
will probably be not a high but only an average remuneration.

Does a full-time freelance indexer really earn as much as $60,000
or more per year, assuming a work year of 50 weeks @ 40 hours =
2,000 hours per year? The answer, unfortunately, is: no, a hard-
working freelancer with a steady flow of work, and assisted by a
trusty and not too failure-prone computer and software, will generally make no more than *half* of that money. How come?

Assuming that the freelancer is working at home, the following
factors will constitute costs that have to be deducted from the gross
earnings. All figures are based on data provided by several experienced freelance indexers who keep accurate records.

Non-working time. First of all, there are not 2,000 working hours in
a year (even with two weeks' vacation already taken into consideration) but somewhat less than that. Deduct:

Holidays	10 days per year
Sick days	10 " " "
Other	5 " " "
Total	25 days per year

This is the equivalent of five work weeks per year, so that the actual
number of effective work weeks per year is 45 or 1,800 hours, thus
10% less than the maximum number of normal work hours. The
indexer could, of course, decide to forgo holidays and vacations,
but sooner or later (and depending on the indexer's age and health)

this may add to the number of sick days, so that in the end nothing is being gained. If the indexer decides to work overtime, for example, in order to finish a rush job, this may not always result in a higher hourly fee.

Overhead. The following costs, which will vary with an indexer's age, health, location, work habits, and tax bracket, must be taken into consideration:

Retirement fund contributions
Social Security payments as a self-employed person
Personal insurance (medical, dental, life, disability)
Rent and home insurance, pro-rated for the space used (but
    disregarding possible tax deductions for partial use of a home
    as office, because regulations vary from year to year and in
    different countries)

Amortization of electronic equipment and
    supplies
Utilities (electricity, gas, water)
Telephone   } All pro-rated for
Office supplies (stationery, business cards)   indexing only
Postage
Travel

These costs will normally amount to about 20–25% of gross annual earnings. The gross hourly fee will thus be reduced by the costs of non-working time + overhead = 30–35%, or an average of one third, leaving only two thirds in net earnings. But this is still not the end of deductions from the gross.

Non-billable time. Inevitably, there will be some activities resulting from indexing as a business which cannot be billed directly to the customer, yet will take up a considerable part of a freelance indexer's time. Some of these are:

Business meetings with the customer
Correspondence
Record-keeping
Professional activities (attending meetings, upgrading one's
    computer skills, promotion, etc.)

These and other necessary but time-consuming tasks may take up to one quarter of business time (not counting walking the dog, changing baby's diapers, preparing lunch and dinner, all of which have to be done during "business" hours and will thus add to the length of the actual working day).

The bottom line. Thus, only ¾ of ⅔ = ½ or 50% of gross income will remain as net earnings. Now the theoretical annual earnings of $60,000 look considerably less glamorous, because they may actually amount to no more than $30,000 or less—and that's before taxes! If an indexer is living—as some indeed do—somewhere in rural New Hampshire, in a fishing village on the coast of Scotland, or among the wheat fields of Saskatchewan, such an annual income may be adequate, though not overly comfortable; but, evidently, it would not be possible to make ends meet in New York, London, or Montreal.

It will now readily be seen why an hourly fee of, say, $20 must be considered too low for professional high-quality indexing. Let us, therefore, state the following rule of thumb, which is readily adaptable to whatever hourly wages are specified as the legal minimum, and which is independent of location, taxation, and legislation, yet will avoid aggravation, frustration, and starvation:

An hourly indexing fee should always be at least five times the wage one can earn by flipping hamburgers at a fast-food emporium, and it should be no less than six to eight times that amount for indexing which demands high or unusual skills and an intimate knowledge of a field or discipline (even though this may be an ideal level of remuneration which can only seldom be achieved).

Methods of Remuneration

Various ways have been tried by indexers in order to arrive at a method of remuneration that is both equitable and acceptable to authors and publishers who commission an index. Although the methods may at first sight look somewhat different, all can ultimately be reduced to a single common denominator: time spent on the indexing job. The five most commonly used methods are the following:

1. A fixed fee, agreed upon in advance between author or publisher and the indexer. This method can be used only if the indexer has been given enough time to study the text and to assess its

difficulty, the probable number of entries per page, the time needed for research on names and other data that may have to be verified, and time for unforeseen problems. Unless an indexer is very experienced in the type of text to be indexed, this method is risky because the lump-sum payment, when ultimately converted to an hourly fee, may turn out to be far too low. This method is not recommended for novices, although some publishers may insist on it, claiming that they do not know the indexer as yet, much less the quality of his or her work, and therefore do not want to take a risk. The lump-sum offered may then be ridiculously low. *Caveat index.**

2. Payment by the number of text pages. This method, which is the one preferred by many publishers, is only a variant of method (1), and may also turn out to be to the disadvantage of a less-experienced indexer. It is easy to underestimate the number of entries per page that will have to be made because the number of subheadings under each main heading is often difficult if not impossible to assess in advance. Authors who do not wish to compile their own indexes sometimes propose this method because it seems to them the most natural one, and one that is easy to verify. But unless the index is to be a very simple one, consisting mainly or even exclusively of names of persons and places (no topics and few if any cross-references), this method, too, may entrap the indexer in an arrangement that results in less than the legal hourly minimum wage.

3. Payment per 1,000 locators, where "13–16" counts as 4 locators. This method seems to have the advantages of being a fair reflection of the amount of work involved and easy to verify, but it is actually quite cumbersome because the counting of the locators is a tedious and time-consuming chore which must also be charged for if the indexer is not to lose on the deal. Since the final number of locators will not be known until the index is finished, it is necessary to keep an accurate time log so that the number of hours spent per 1,000 locators can be translated into an adequate hourly fee.

4. Payment by the number of index lines or number of columns. Since the number of lines in a full column will practically be the

*In classical Latin, *index* meant a person who reveals or points out. The other meanings of the word were later derived from that principal one, as discussed in INDEX: THE WORD, ITS HISTORY AND MEANINGS.

same throughout an index except for the first and last page, it is easier and quicker to count columns rather than lines, and it is certainly much quicker than counting locators; otherwise, this method is only a variation of (3), although the fee per column may be negotiated in advance and not after the completion of the index, as in method (3). In order to make an estimate of the size of an index and to calculate an adequate fee, the indexer needs to know in advance the size of a page, the size of type in which the index will be set, and the number of columns per page (*see* Table 5, p. 271). This method is the one preferred by many indexers for the following reasons: it is flexible in terms of an indexer's time (a slow indexer, especially a novice, will have to settle for earning less per hour than an experienced and fast-working one); if the depth of indexing has to be changed during compilation (that is, the text turns out to need either a more detailed or less extensive index than initially assumed), the fee per column need not be re-negotiated; and the total remuneration is easily verifiable by the publisher. When negotiating a fee per column in advance, the indexer should retain the right to charge more if it should become necessary to change the type size (say, from 8 pt. to 7 pt.) in order not to exceed the available number of pages.

5. Payment by the number of hours spent on the index. This method, finally, is the one to which all others can be reduced, because all of them boil down to a fee per hour of actual work. An accurate time log of hours spent is as indispensable for this method as it is for method (3).

An indexer choosing to work for a fee negotiated in advance, as in methods (1) through (4), must of course also keep track of time spent, if only to see whether the job at hand has been adequately paid for or perhaps to charge more for the next job. Needless to say, method (5) is the only reasonable one for lengthy and time-consuming jobs, such as an index to an encyclopedia or other reference works, a cumulative index to a periodical or multivolume work, or a major biographical or historical work.

The only difficulty with method (5) is to get an author or publisher to agree to it if the indexer and the quality of his or her work is not already well known to them. Well-established publishers have, of course, experience with indexes and indexers and will generally agree to an hourly fee charged by an indexer only after completion of the index, based on the type of text, its difficulty, the experience and speed of the indexer, and the format of the index manuscript (e.g., typed sheets, camera-ready copy, or diskette coded for typesetting). Less experienced publishers may fear that they will be overcharged or that they will have no control over an indexer's working methods, and individual authors (who may have to pay the indexer out of their own pockets) may also be reluctant to rely on an hourly fee charged by someone they do not know. As in all negotiations on matters of money, some friendly persuasion on the part of the indexer coupled with tact and flexibility will be necessary to come to a satisfactory agreement based on mutual trust.

Quoting a Fee

Whichever method of payment is preferred by the indexer or pre-scribed by the publisher (except for methods 1 and 2), the indexer should submit a cost estimate of the fee for the job before starting to work on it. Experienced indexers may occasionally be able to make a reasonable estimate based on previous jobs of approximately comparable type, size, and difficulty. But in most cases it will be better to index a representative chapter or section of no less than about 20 pages, and to record the time it will take to scan the text, mark indexable items, and keyboard or type the entries. Adding at least 30% to the raw indexing time should normally cover the addi-tional time that will have to be spent on cross-referencing, editing, printing, proofreading, and mailing the index or transmitting it by modem. If extensive generic markup of the computerscript beyond that which can be executed automatically by indexing software is required, an additional percentage of time would have to be added. The same goes for complex and difficult texts, or for those contain-ing an unusually high number of names. The resulting amount must then be computed for the actual length of the book in order to arrive at a reasonably accurate estimate of the total fee.

The advantages of this method are: a) the estimate can be submit-ted to the client within a few hours or at most a day after the receipt of the page proofs; b) if the estimate is accepted, one chapter of the book has already been indexed—a saving of the indexer's time.

The disadvantage of the method is that in case the estimate is rejected, the indexer will have spent a few hours' time without remuneration.

The author or publisher, as is customary in most commercial transactions, may either accept the estimate, may try to haggle over it, or reject it as too high. In the latter instance, under no circumstances should an indexing job be undertaken for an amount that is way below the current average hourly fee. However hungry the indexer may be, accepting a low fee just to get the job is a disservice to fellow indexers and the profession at large.

Once the fee for a job has been agreed upon, it is of the utmost importance to specify both the method and the amount, as well as the conditions of payment in a written CONTRACT. An indexer who relies on an oral agreement for payment of fees—even one made between old friends—is courting financial disaster.

Renegotiation of a Fee

Despite careful computation of a fee for a particular indexing job, an indexer may occasionally find that the task turned out to be much more time-consuming than originally estimated, so that consequently the fee quoted would result in a loss. This may happen not only to novices but even to experienced indexers. In such a case, it is by no means necessary to absorb the loss, and to write it off as a "learning experience". In most instances, if done early enough and on the basis of hard facts (e.g., the number of index terms per page) as well as with the necessary tact, it may be possible to renegotiate the contract. This may result in a fee that will at least cover the time spent on the compilation of the index and the out-of-pocket expenses for its production, though perhaps not in a profit.

Nonpayment of Fees

Even when a contract has been signed between the indexer and the publisher (or author), things may go wrong. If the agreed-upon fee for the index has not been paid 30 days after the date of the bill, a polite but firm phone call or letter to the person responsible will

often yield results. If this does not work, a stern letter from the
indexer's attorney (which normally is not too expensive) may help.
Next, the threat of legal action may be effective, although that step
must then be followed up by an actual law suit if it is not to be
perceived as a hollow threat. This poses a dilemma: while nonpayment of an earned fee should not go unpunished, in many if not
most cases the amount in question will be too small to warrant the
expense of a law suit.

Nevertheless, an indexer who has not been paid does have certain legal rights, not all of which are widely known. First, simple
nonpayment of a contractually agreed-upon fee for an index delivered according to specifications gives the indexer the right to sue
for the amount owed. That much is obvious, but other actionable
issues may also be involved. If the indexer claimed COPYRIGHT in
the index, the publisher may additionally be sued for copyright
infringement (for which the damages awarded may be higher than
the fee alone). If the index was compiled according to specifications
but the publisher either rejected it or failed to publish it, an action
for damages may be brought. In both cases, the publisher may be
forced, in addition, to either publish the index or return it to the
indexer so that no unauthorized use can be made of it. All these
legal actions require, of course, the services of an attorney which, as
noted above, may not be economically worthwhile or feasible.

A less expensive way to enforce payment of a fee (if no questions
of rejection or nonpublishing are involved) is to hire a collection
agency which may get results where the indexer's pleas alone may
be disregarded. Although these agencies may charge a third or
more of the amount collected, positive results may still be worthwhile for the indexer, both in terms of money recovered and in
order to get even with the recalcitrant publisher.

Finally, a claim can be filed in small claims court, where no
attorney is needed and only a nominal filing fee has to be paid by
the indexer who must, however, be prepared to buttress the claim
by providing all relevant documentation and, if necessary, expert
witnesses. A judgment in favor of the indexer must then be followed up by the separate step of collection which may or may not
yield results, but in case the publisher goes bankrupt, the small
claims judgment may be the indexer's only recourse for the recov-
ery of at least some part of the fee owed.

These are not pretty matters to consider, but since occasionally they do happen, an indexer should know what course of action to take when relations with those who commissioned an index turn sour.

CROSS-REFERENCES

Cross-references are so well known and so ubiquitous in reference works and indexes that most people, including indexers, think they need little if any explanation or discussion. Yet there are several aspects of cross-references that are often poorly understood or badly mishandled by indexers. Despite their obvious usefulness in certain situations, cross-references should be used sparingly, and only if they will actually save the user's time and result in better information more quickly found. Before sprinkling them liberally throughout an index, the indexer should always ask whether it would not be better (and briefer!) to refer directly to the text, that is, to a particular name, synonym, or related topic and their locators rather than forcing the user to turn index pages back and forth.

All cross-references have one purpose in common: they lead a user from a heading that is either not used, incomplete, or different in form or content to another heading under which relevant information (including locators) will be found. They fall into two separate categories: *see* references, which are prescriptive and require the user to look in another place; and *see also* references, which are suggestive, that is, the user may or may not wish to follow up on them.

"See" References

See references are used for the following purposes:
1. Synonym control:

aspirin *see* acetylsalicylic acid

(or vice versa, depending on the intended audience of the text). This presupposes that all text occurrences of the drug under whatever name (there are more than a dozen, including $C_9H_8O_4$, its chemical formula) have indeed been brought together by the indexer under "acetylsalicylic acid".

2. Antonym control:

softness *see* hardness

Although in everyday usage "soft" is the antonym of "hard", in science and technology there is only a hardness scale for testing materials, the lower end of which measures what the layman (and toilet paper commercials) call "softness".

3. Personal names with variant spellings, forms, fullness, or other differences from the form chosen as a main heading:

Smyth, John *see* Smith, John
Hohenheim, Theophrastus Bombastus von *see* Paracelsus
Vinci, Leonardo da *see* Leonardo da Vinci
Arundel, earl of *see* Fitz Alan, Richard
Roncalli, Angelo Giuseppe *see* John XXIII, Pope

4. Pseudonym control:

Arouet, François Marie *see* Voltaire
Clemens, Samuel Langhorne *see* Twain, Mark
Publius (pseud.) *see* Hamilton, Alexander; Jay, John; Madison, James

5. Provision of different access points for corporate names:

IBM *see* International Business Machines Corporation
Mechanical Engineers, Institution of *see* Institution of Mechanical Engineers
Commonwealth of Massachusetts *see* Massachusetts

6. From generic to specific terms:

dams *see* concrete dams; earth dams; masonry dams

This may be done only if "dams" in general are not indexed at all. In most instances, a book on dams will have some text passages dealing with these structures in general before treating different types of construction; in this case, a *see also* reference may be more appropriate:

> dams 17, 20–25
>   *see also* concrete dams; earth dams; masonry dams

This presupposes that concrete, earth, and masonry dams are not indexed as subheadings under "dams" but appear as main headings with their own subheadings, e.g.,

> concrete dams
>   construction
>   cooling
>   drainage
>   intake structures

(The fact that "concrete dams" has its own subheadings makes it desirable to index it as a main heading rather than having sub-subheadings under "dams".)

As briefly mentioned above, and stressed throughout this book wherever *see* references are discussed and exemplified, they should be used only if (a) the heading to which they refer has more than three locators; or (b) the heading to which they refer has subheadings. Otherwise, a double entry for a synonym, a variant form of a name, or topic with only two or three locators (often only one) or a main heading with only one subheading will not only save space (which is almost always at a premium in an index) but will also save the time of the user for whom, in Carey's oft-cited phrase, "it is always irksome to be made to take two bites at a cherry" (1963, p. 11). Regrettably, even in otherwise well-designed indexes this simple rule is often disregarded: thus, in the index to a book published by the National Geographic Society one can find:

> Zaire: fishing industry 174, 175; history 164, 166, 179; independence
>   164; President *see* Mobutu, Sese Seko; schools 169, 170, 171

Turning back, one finds "Mobutu, Sese Seko 164, *164*" (the italicized locator indicates that his picture appears on the same page). Indexing in the third line of the example "President Mobutu 164, *164*" or even only "President 164, *164*" would not only have saved one line but, more importantly, the user would have been saved a tedious second look-up.

Obsolete forms. The form *see under* instead of *see* should not be used at all, although it has been recommended by Knight (1979, p. 111) among others; like several other rules and guidelines in his book, this one has not stood the test of time. The idea was that *see under* should be used to direct the user to a subheading rather than the main heading to which, however, the cross-reference necessarily had to be made, for how else could users have found the subheading to which they were referred? *See under* is therefore practically identical with *see,* which has the advantage of being shorter. Few if any users will notice the fine distinction between *see* and *see under* as applied according to Knight, because the majority of index users are not indexers and many know barely what a *see* reference is or how to use it. A better way of directing users to a particular subheading is the use of a *see* or *see also* reference (as the case may be) to the main heading, followed by the relevant subheading, e.g.,

air pressure *see* tires: air pressure

The colon sign between the main heading and its subheading may indicate that this is not just an inverted heading (the use of which is now deprecated by current indexing standards).

Another form, now fortunately only seldom seen because it is so antiquated, is the abbreviation *q.v.* (Latin *quod vide,* "which see"). This form, too, should not be used in modern indexes. If at all needed, a special cross-reference should be given in English and without any abbreviation, so as to be immediately intelligible, even though it will then take up more space. The following example is from a genealogical index:

Smith, Adam, husband of Mary (*see below*) 27
   Charlotte 58
   David 13
   George 67
   Henry 56
   Mary, wife of Adam (*see above*) 29, 31

Typography. The word *see* is normally set in lowercase italics, so as to make it stand out between the first and the second part of the cross-reference. But in indexes in which headings referred to and from are both italicized (e.g., in botanical, zoological, medical, or linguistic works), the word "see" is set in lowercase roman, e.g.,

hebephrenia see *dementia praecox*

Contrary to earlier usage, all indexing standards recommend that no PUNCTUATION whatsoever should precede the word *see* which follows naturally and without a break after the heading from which it refers to another one. However, the *Chicago manual of style* (1993, 17.15) prescribes that *see* when following a main heading should be capitalized and preceded by a period, but when following a sub-heading should be lowercased and be enclosed in parentheses. It is doubtful that this fine distinction is noticed by users or that it is any more useful to them than a simple space before the word. Research into the use of cross-references revealed the somewhat unexpected fact that readers do not seem to have great trouble finding them, but are more often than not puzzled by their purpose and meaning (Liddy & Jorgensen 1993).

"See Also" References

See also references are made from a heading with its own locators (and subheadings) to another heading with locators (and subheadings) in order to show the user that more and different information may be found under the heading referred to.

For a long time, it was not realized by the compilers of traditional subject heading lists that *see also* references are of two different kinds, but thanks to research on the structure of THESAURI this is now generally recognized. The two kinds are:

1. *General-to-specific cross-references.* These are used to link a class to its members or a genus to its species. The latter are best known in the form they take to indicate relationships that exist in biological taxonomies which are strictly hierarchical. Such a *see also* reference may be made in general form:

mammals 81, 85, 105
    see also names of individual
        mammals

This may be done when the text refers to mammals in general but deals also with a large number of different mammals, each of which has a separate index entry. In this case it is normally not necessary to make a reciprocal *see also* reference to "mammals" from every mammal between aardvarks (beloved by crossword puzzle fans) and zebras, because users may be expected to know that these animals are mammals, and the latter are only dealt with briefly in the text.

A more specific *see also* reference of this type would be:

horses 204–215
    see also racing horses; riding
        horses; work horses

In this case, reciprocal *see also* references should be made from "racing horses" etc. to "horses" because some important information on horses in general may be given there which is not repeated under racing, riding, and work horses:

racing horses 235, 238–241
    see also horses
riding horses 189–192
    see also horses
work horses 120, 125
    see also horses

2. *Associative cross-references.* These refer from one topic to another that is often thought of in *association* with the first one but belongs to a different class or category. Such *see also* references should almost always be made reciprocally because if, while thinking of A one may also think of B, it follows that while thinking of B one may also think of A. The following are the most frequently encountered types of associative relationships which may need *see also* references:

a. whole-part relationships:

automobiles *see also* engines; transmissions
New York City *see also* Bronx; Brooklyn; Manhattan
Protestants *see also* Baptists; Methodists
zoology *see also* anatomy; physiology

b. fields of study and phenomena studied:

astronomy *see also* galaxies; planets
botany *see also* flowers; shrubs; trees

c. activities and their agents or instruments:

surgery *see also* anti-coagulants; heart-lung machines

d. activities and things acted upon:

dentistry *see also* gums; teeth

e. activities and their products:

carpentry *see also* chests; tables

f. occupations or professions and people working in them:

librarianship *see also* catalogers; indexers

g. The same concept, separated in an index by headings beginning with a noun and a synonymous adjective:

female . . . *see also* women
agricultural . . . *see also* farming

It could be argued that in some instances a reciprocal *see also* reference would be superfluous, e.g., in the examples listed at (c). Would

anti-coagulants *see also* surgery

be necessary? Perhaps not. Still, subheadings under "surgery" may
turn out to be useful, leading a user to topics not previously thought

of. However, most *see also* references do need reciprocals and these can be generated automatically by an appropriate computer program which will ensure that no needed reciprocal reference is missed. The relatively few unnecessary reciprocal references that may be generated automatically will not hurt (except taking up a line of space) while the lack of a needed *see also* reference may be a serious flaw.

A third kind of *see also* references, quite unrelated to the former two, is

3. *Cross-references between synonymous names:* Synonymous names of persons or places are normally linked by a *see* reference, as shown in the examples above. But sometimes a *see also* reference may have to be made to and from the synonymous names if the person or the place are dealt with separately in a text because of intrinsic differences. For example, in a biography of King Karl XIV Johan of Sweden and Norway who was born a French citizen by the name of Jean Baptiste Bernadotte, it may be necessary to make cross-references from the royal name to the civilian one and vice versa, because he had a brilliant career as revolutionary general, French ambassador to Vienna, Napoleon's minister of war, and Marshal of France before being elected Swedish crown prince:

> Karl XIV Johan, King of Sweden and Norway *see also* Bernadotte, Jean Baptiste Jules
> Bernadotte, Jean Baptiste Jules *see also* Karl XIV Johan, King of Sweden and Norway

Similarly, in an historical account of Russia from earliest times to the present it may be necessary to make the cross-references

> Russia (Republic) *see also* Russia (Empire); Soviet Union
> Russian S.S.S.R. *see also* Russia (Empire); Russia (Republic)
> Soviet Union *see also* Commonwealth of Independent States; Russia (Empire)

If this looks complicated, don't blame the indexer but the unpredictable course of history. It is the indexer's duty to guide the reader through the maze of relationships that may exist in a complex text.

Typography. See also references are set in lowercase italics, and they are *not* separated from the heading or its locators by any

PUNCTUATION, but the *Chicago manual of style* (1993, 17.16) stipulates the same punctuation as for *see* references discussed above, p. 126. Whichever style is chosen (and that may depend on a publisher's house style), *see also* references can be displayed in two different styles:

1. indented 2 ems under the main heading (whether or not it has locators) and before any subheadings:

> maintenance 8–10
>> *see also* boats, cars, garden tools
>> importance 16
>> intervals 25
>> safety precautions 36–38

The 2-em indentation of *see also* distinguishes it from the subheadings which are indented only 1 em (*see also* DISPLAY OF SUBHEADINGS).

2. at the end of a main heading with few (two to three) locators, and followed by subheadings, if any:

> bears 17, 21 *see also* grizzly bears
>> hibernation 25
>> hunting 34

Whichever style is chosen, the *see also* reference should be put *before* any subheadings, not after the last subheading. Opinions on this issue have been divided among indexers, some arguing that *see also* references at the end of all subheadings are more logical, telling the user, as it were, "now that you have seen all subheadings, there are still other places in which to look". But if there are large numbers of subheadings (and sub-subheadings) perhaps spilling over onto another page, the user may miss the *see also* reference tucked away at the very end of the entry. If the same reference is presented up front it cannot be easily missed, and the subheadings following it will still be noticed.

Mistakes

Common mistakes in the application of cross-references are:

1. Making *see also* references between synonyms (except in the special case of synonymous names of persons or places discussed above):

aspirin *see also* acetylsalicylic acid

Here, the indexer failed to collocate all text references to the drug and their locators under only one of the names, as discussed above under *see* references.

2. Listing the same locators for the heading *from* which the cross-reference is made, and for the heading *to* which it refers:

lathes 27, 29 *see also* turning
turning 27, 29 *see also* lathes

This can easily happen when both "lathes" and "turning" are first mentioned on the same pages and two separate entries with a *see also* reference are prepared because the indexer anticipates that both the tool and the operation will be dealt with separately on further pages; but no more is said about them, and in the final editing of the index the *see also* references should have been eliminated, leaving only two different main headings.

3. Finally, there are (or rather, there ought not to be) "blind" cross-references which lead the baffled user to a heading that does not exist:

dromedaries *see* camels

but when one turns to "camels", "there is no there there" as Gertrude Stein said. Even worse are "circular" cross-references, leading the hapless user from one heading to another and back again in a ring-around-the-rosy:

Iran *see* Persia
Persia *see* Iran
endless loop, *see* loop, endless
loop, endless, *see* endless loop

or even

maintenance *see* care
care *see* protection
protection *see* maintenance

Such atrocities, caused by sloppy EDITING, are unfortunately not figments of the imagination: the second cross-reference above appeared in the index of a software manual.* Such mishaps will almost never occur in indexes compiled with the aid of dedicated indexing programs, because these provide automatic cross-reference validation. The Canadian satirist Stephen Leacock wrote a hilarious piece on this phenomenon, "The perfect index: there is no index, and why—":

> What is the real title or name of a thing or person that has three or four? Must you put everything three or four times over in the Index, under three or four names? No, just once, so it is commonly understood; and then for the other joint names we put what is called a cross-reference, meaning, see this, or see that. It sounds good in theory, but in practice it leads to such results as *Talleyrand, see Perigord* . . . and when you hunt this up, you find—*Perigord, Bishop of, see Talleyrand*. The same effect can be done flat out, with just two words, as *Lincoln, see Abraham* . . . *Abraham, see Lincoln*. But even that is not so bad because at least it's a closed circle. It comes to a full stop. But compare the effect, familiar to all research students, when the circle is not closed. Thus instead of just seeing Lincoln, the unclosed circle runs like this, each item being hunted up alphabetically, one after the other—*Abraham, see Lincoln* . . . *Lincoln, see Civil War* . . . *Civil War, see United States* . . . *United States, see America* . . . *America, see American History* . . . *American History, see also Christopher Columbus, New England, Pocahontas, George Washington* . . . the thing will finally come to rest somehow or other with the dial pointing at: See *Abraham Lincoln* (Leacock 1942, p. 212).

Tracing of Cross-References

The mistakes listed above can easily be avoided by *tracings* (also known as "inverted cross-references"). These are intended only for the use of the indexer, and should never show up in an index. For example, for the cross-reference

dromedaries *see* camels

a tracing

camels, dromedaries *see*

*The advanced programmer's guide to dBase II and III+.

is made; likewise, for the cross-reference

   lathes *see also* turning

the tracing would be

   turning, lathes *see also*

When editing the index, each *see* or *see also* cross-reference is looked up in the tracings file under the heading referred to, so as to make sure that the heading exists. Tracings are also invaluable when headings are being changed while the index is being compiled, e.g., from a subheading to a main heading or vice versa, or from a scientific term to a popular one. The tracings will immediately show which cross-references have to be changed or eliminated, as the case may be.

All tracings should be stored in a separate computer file, unless the indexing software already provides this feature. In a card file, cards of a different color should be used for tracings.

Statistics of Cross-References

In a sample of 300 books, chosen randomly from many branches of knowledge, Diodato (1991) found that 46% of all cross-references were used for synonym control, 19% were links from general to specific terms or vice versa, 15% served to indicate related activities, their agents, products, or things acted upon, 7% were used to show whole-part relationships, 3% linked disciplines or studies with objects studied or applications, 2% were regrettably "blind" or otherwise unintelligible references and 8% were cross-references not fitting any of the categories of the study.

The total of 2,247 cross-references was divided into 1,169 *see* and 1,032 *see also* references, while 46 references were of a different kind, e.g., *cf*, *see below*, and *see under*, etc. The overall ratio of roughly 1.2 to 1 between *see* and *see also* references was, however, not typical for 218 indexes in which both types of cross-references appeared; in these indexes, the overall ratio was 3.8 to 1, and in 74 of the 218 indexes using both forms, *see* references were used at least twice as often as *see also* references.

BS 3700: 5.1.5; 5.5
ISO 999: 4(i); 7.5; 8.7
NISO Z39.4:

CUMULATIVE INDEXES

The indexes to each year or volume of a periodical are sometimes combined or form the basis for cumulative indexes, covering five, ten, and even a hundred years or more.* The indexes to large works, published in several individually indexed volumes, are sometimes also cumulated into a single comprehensive index. Both types of cumulative indexes are generally published as separate volumes, are expensive to produce, and have only a limited market, mainly libraries and research institutes. They are therefore compiled only for PERIODICALS or books of lasting value.

The compilation of a cumulative index is not a task to be undertaken by a novice in indexing, and it cannot be done by a simple mechanical amalgamation of existing entries in the underlying partial indexes. Although some periodicals, especially those carrying only abstracts, generate annual indexes from the machine-readable entries in their monthly indexes by simple computerized cumulation without any editing, the resulting product is often difficult if not impossible to use because frequently many dozens or even more than a hundred locators may accumulate under a single heading (the computer will not by itself generate subheadings to modify a main heading and its mind-numbing multitude of locators).

On the other hand, it is today virtually inconceivable to produce a cumulative index without the aid of a computer, simply because of the very large number of entries for a run of 5, 10, or 20 years of a monthly journal. Assuming that each issue has 50 to 70 pages of text, a 5-year index would have to cover from 3,000 to 4,200 pages, a 10-year index from 6,000 to 8,400 pages, and a 20-year index from about 12,000 to 16,800 pages. If, on the average, there are three to

---

*The weekly journal *The Engineer* published a cumulative index spanning a period of 104 years, from 1856 to 1960.

four indexable items per page, the number of headings and locators becomes staggering (although, in the past, such indexes have been compiled using only vast quantities of cards over a period of several years). There will, of course, always be a sizable number of entries in the annual or partial indexes which can be transferred unchanged to the cumulative index, particularly proper names, but even regarding those, some changes may have to be made, as discussed later on. If a cumulative index is to be kept within reasonable limits of economic feasibility and yet be of practical value, intellectual decisions regarding most entries will have to be made before they can be input to a computer, especially regarding terminology.

Terminology

In the course of several years, and certainly during a decade or more, terminology changes in virtually every sphere of human activity, and a multi-year cumulative index must therefore contain both the terms currently used by readers of the periodical and cross-references from those terms that have become obsolete. For example, in a medical journal the term "consumption" may have been used in the early part of the century, while the disease is now referred to as "pulmonary tuberculosis"; similarly, a geographical journal will have used the terms "Northern Rhodesia" and "Southern Rhodesia" for what is now "Zambia" and "Zimbabwe". Double entries should preferably not be made in a cumulative index because the risk of dispersing information under different main headings and subheadings is much greater than in an index to a single work.

Changing terminology is less of a problem in a work by one author, published in several volumes, each of which has its own index, because one person will probably be more consistent in his or her choice of words. Still, since a multivolume work is written over a long period, some changes in terminology concerning the same topic will be inevitable and must be dealt with in a cumulative index by cross-references to the terms most prevalent in the entire work. Multivolume works written by several authors are in principle no different from long runs of periodicals as far as varying and changing terminology is concerned.

A related issue that must sometimes be resolved is the variant SPELLING of words composed of two or more elements, such as "ground water", which may also have been written "ground-water" or "groundwater" (depending on a journal's editors and their preferences at different times). There may also be variant forms of specialized terms, such as "hyperlipidemia" vs. "hyper-lipemia", both of which refer to the same medical condition. Most often, such a problem can be solved with the help of a special dictionary or encyclopedia, but sometimes such reference works contradict each other or allow the use of both terms, in which case the indexer must make a decision on a preferred term.

Depth of Indexing

The EXHAUSTIVITY and SPECIFICITY of a cumulative index covering a period of several years will almost always have to be at a higher level than for an index to the same material covering only one year or a single volume. Even so, the cumulation of entries from many years may result in a large number of locators for a single heading; in this case, modifying subheadings must be added to keep the number of locators for each heading at a manageable level.

Typography

Cumulative indexes covering a number of years or even decades are always quite voluminous, and publishers therefore often print them in very small type and in three or even four columns per page. But, in the interest of legibility, the type size used should not be less than 6 pt. and there should not be more than three columns at most, because the shorter the width of a column the more headings will have turnover lines, thus defeating the aim of squeezing more headings onto each page, as shown in Figure 15, p. 493. A detailed description of the problems involved in editing and producing a large cumulative index has been provided by Bliss (1990).

BS 3700: 5.5.3
ISO 999: 7.5.3
NISO Z39.4:

DEPTH OF INDEXING

The quality of an index can be evaluated by its depth of indexing which is the product of its EXHAUSTIVITY and SPECIFICITY. The two are twin sisters, though not identical twins. They were born in the mid-1960s in Cranfield, England, to a clever don who sired them while busy on a research project aimed at finding out which factors enhanced or diminished the quality of indexes and their capacity to retrieve information from documents.

Depth of indexing is defined in the International Standard ISO 5127/3a-1981 as "The degree to which a topic is represented in detail in an index" (International Organization for Standardization 1981) and in NISO Z39.4 as "The result of the combined effects of exhaustivity and specificity in an index". It is thus not, as stated in some textbooks, merely the equivalent of exhaustivity (the number of terms representing a document in an index). It is a function of both the indexer's assessment of the amount of detail needed and the degree of specificity of the INDEXING LANGUAGE employed to index a document.

To measure the depth of indexing it is not enough just to count the number of terms assigned to a document, which is rather easy to do. It is also necessary to establish the specificity of the index terms, and that is a qualitative judgment which is somewhat more difficult to make. Only the interplay of exhaustivity and specificity, together with suitable CROSS-REFERENCES, result in a certain degree of depth. A small number of terms which are fairly general, with only a few or even no cross-references, will result in an index of rather shallow depth, but it will be quick and easy to do, will take up little space, and will be inexpensive. An example would be the card catalog of a small library in which the topics of a book or other items may be indexed by only two or three subject headings at most, with only a few cross-references from unused synonyms to the subject headings. A large number of terms, each of which is also highly specific, together with ample cross-references, will result in a large depth of indexing, taking more time and care to compile, occupying more space, and being more expensive. An example would be the detailed index to a treatise or textbook, containing specific main headings, modified by subheadings and perhaps sub-subheadings, with ample *see* references from unused to preferred terms and *see also* references from and to related topics, resulting in a 10% ratio of index pages to text pages, and sometimes even more; some TECHNICAL MANUALS AND REPORTS or reference works may have an index to text page ratio of 20–25%.

Examples of both high and low exhaustivity and specificity will be found in the relevant sections, beginning on p. 175 and 439 respectively.

NISO Z39.4:

DIACRITICS

Diacritical marks, or *diacritics* (a word derived from a Greek verb meaning "to distinguish"), are the little dots, dashes, strokes, tails, squiggles, and wiggles appearing above, below, through, or inside letters of the Roman alphabet in order to distinguish them from the plain basic letters because they are to be pronounced differently or stressed in a certain way. Diacritics are used in the writing systems of every language using the Roman script, except in the original Latin and in English. Since they do not normally occur in written English (other than in some proper names, such as Brontë, or in loanwords like *blasé* or *tête-à-tête*), they are often considered outland-ish frills and are simply omitted if printers' typesetting equipment does not have the necessary type. The assumption, particularly in the United States, seems to be: if English can do without these strange little marks, why cannot all foreign languages do likewise? Does it make any difference? The answer is: Yes, very much so.

Far from being unnecessary frills, diacritics are of vital impor-tance in the writing systems of all modern languages written in Roman script in order to indicate stress, pronunciation, or the mean-ing of words. For example, the French letter sequence *c o t e* has different meanings depending on the diacritics: *cote* (no diacritics) means a quota or share; *côte* means a rib or coast; *côté* means a side;

and *coté* means marked, classed. Why the English writing system is the only one not making use of any diacritics has never been satisfactorily explained, but it is certainly not because diacritics would not serve useful purposes, especially by indicating different stress patterns for homographs, e.g., *récord* (as a noun) vs. *recórd* (as a verb).* English dictionaries do, of course, use diacritics extensively to indicate stress and pronunciation, but that is a highly sophisticated and specialized application of a writing system that exists outside of formal English orthography.

As far as indexing is concerned, diacritics will most likely be encountered in names of persons or places. First of all, diacritics must be written and are not simply to be omitted. This means that in typewritten index copy some diacritics may have to be inserted by hand, although daisy-wheels for electronic typewriters or printers are available that carry at least the most common diacritics used in French, German, Italian, and Spanish (though not those used in Slavic languages). Word-processing software is usually able to handle commonly occurring diacritics, and specially designed software is available for virtually all modern languages, including those written in non-Roman scripts. Most diacritics can also be generated by using the generic codes prescribed in the American National Standard *Electronic manuscripts: preparation and markup* (NISO Z39.59), but if more than a few names or phrases are involved, this becomes a tedious and time-consuming chore.

Getting diacritics printed may often turn out to be a losing battle if, as already mentioned, the printer does not have the necessary types and therefore substitutes basic letters for the modified ones, the result being, for example:

Angstrom, Jonas Anders *instead of the correct form* Ångström

(the name of a famous Swedish physicist, in whose honor the unit of measurement for wavelengths Å is named).

---

*Actually, there is at least one known use of a diacritic in English. Until the 1930s, a dieresis was sometimes used to indicate separate pronunciation of two adjacent vowels in words like *coöperate* (to avoid the pronunciation of the first two syllables as in cooper), but this typographical practice has now largely been abandoned.

Alphabetizing names in which modified letters occur has fortunately never been a problem. Both previous and current filing codes always prescribed that all diacritics should be disregarded in alphabetizing (but not omitted in print!) and only the basic letter be taken into account. Thus,

à, á, â, ä, ā, ă, å, ą are all alphabetized as a, ç as c, ł as l, ñ as n, ø as o, and so on.

One of the most common diacritics is the *dieresis* (two dots on top of a vowel), also known by its German name *umlaut.* In German (and *only* in this language) ä, ö, ü may be written as ae, oe, ue; these digraphs must, of course, be employed if the bearer of a name, e.g., the very common one Müller, prefers it spelled Mueller. Since these two spellings may be quite widely separated from each other in an alphabetical sequence, it may be necessary to make cross-references from one form to the other; this can be done either in a general way, referring from and to the surname only (particularly if there are many bearers of that name in both forms) or specifically to a surname-forename if the same name (but not the same person) appears in different spellings, e.g.,

Mudd, John
Mueller, Fritz *see also* Müller, Fritz
Muffley, Beth

.

.

.

Mulkey, Berta
Müller, Fritz *see also* Mueller, Fritz
Muller, George
Müller, Robert
Mulrooney, Sean

The substitution of ae, oe, and ue for ä, ö, and ü is, however, *not* permitted in other languages which use diereses on vowels to indicate a certain pronunciation, namely Dutch, Estonian, Finnish, Hungarian, Norwegian, Spanish, Swedish, Turkish, and Welsh.

Occasionally, authors who are only vaguely familiar with the orthography of languages that use umlauts (particularly German) will write umlauts where none are needed or put them on the wrong vowels when citing names or titles. Such mistakes should not be repeated in an index, but the correct SPELLING should be substituted if it can be ascertained from reference works or from other reliable sources.

ALA: 1.1
BL: 1.2.4.1
BS 1749: 4.1
LC: 1.1.1
NISO Z39.4:
NISO Z39.59

DISPLAY OF SUBHEADINGS

Multilevel headings are those that consist of a main heading and one or more subheadings which may in turn be further subdivided by sub-subheadings. All subheadings, as their name implies, must be visually subordinated to the main headings they modify. This is achieved by means of indentions, that is, by printing subheadings somewhat to the right of the flush left margin at which the main headings are printed. The purpose of indentions is to guide the user's eye in scanning a number of subheadings.

Printers measure the depth of indentions in *ems,* that is, the width of the letter *m* in the type style and size used. In typewritten manuscripts it is best to use two spaces to indicate an indention of 1 em, since the width of only one space may easily be overlooked by a typesetter. If it is important to draw attention to a specific depth of indention, it may be marked on the manuscript in drawing squares, each of which indicates an em:

Bacon, Roger ("Doctor mira-
□□□□bilis") 77
□contribution to

□□philosophy 753
□□□Aristotelianism 71
    empiricism 619
□□science 32
    technology 480
□□□explosives 276
    telescope 751
□views on alchemy 78

In a computerscript the width of indentions is set by the relevant software code which must be inserted as appropriate by the indexer.

Indented Style

In this style all subheadings are normally indented 1 em, sub-subheadings 2 ems, sub-sub-subheadings 3 ems, and so on; any turnover lines are indented 1 em more than the deepest indention used in an entry. Thus, if an entry consists of a heading and sub-headings only (indented 1 em), any turnover lines are indented 2 ems; if an entry has sub-sub-headings (indented 3 ems) any turn-over lines are indented 4 ems, as shown in the second line of the example above. Care must be taken not to make deeply indented index lines too short because this will inevitably lead to many turn-over lines which are difficult to scan and add to the length of an entry. For this reason, some publishers prefer that the indention of a subheading be only 1 en wide (that is, half an em) with multiples of an en at each subsequent level of subheading or turnover line.

If a main heading is not followed by locators or cross-references, the first subheading should not appear on the same line, even if there is enough space for it; all subheadings, including the first one, should always be indented under the main heading, because other-wise the entry may become ambiguous, e.g.,

        not this   *but this*

    Pakistan, education 103   Pakistan
        finances 124   education 103
                                    finances 124

In the faulty example, are the finances those of education or of Pakistan in general? In the correct example, the indention of both subheadings show at a glance that both modify the main heading.

The indented style of subheading display is predominantly used for scientific, technical, biomedical, and legal texts in which not only subheadings but also sub-subheadings and so on, down to a fourth or even fifth level, are not uncommon; it is also employed in the indexes to reference works. Users of these types of works are primarily interested in facts and data, the terms of which or their synonyms are mostly well known to them, so that scanning a column of indented subheadings (and sometimes further indented sub-subheadings) will provide the easiest and quickest access to a desired index heading. The main drawback of the indented style is the fact that it takes up much more space than the run-in style, to which an index originally designed in indented style may have to be converted if space is at a premium. This will almost always entail a sacrifice of clarity and legibility, particularly regarding sub-subentries which are difficult or even impossible to accommodate in the run-in style.

The simple typographical rule governing indented display, namely, to set subheadings indented 1 em under the main heading, sub-subheadings indented 2 em, and so on, is unfortunately not always followed. All manner of embellishments, flourishes, and variations on the theme have been invented by printers and book designers in order to enhance, as it were, the appearance of indexes, but virtually all of them have had the opposite effect: they generate visual clutter, waste space, and do not aid the user, who is best served by a straightforward and uniform layout of index entries. One of the "improvements" often found in older indexes but still occasionally used, particularly in indexes to legal works, is the insertion of dashes, graphically indicating each successive indention, e.g.,

stereotype 201–205
—casting box 202–204, 263
—flexible mold 203–205
——and rotary presses 204, 263
—plates
——curved 204, 205

——duplication of 294, 355
———for platen jobber 265
——edition 313
—specialists in 205

This style is now considered obsolete and should be avoided.

Another obsolete style is one in which the subheadings are set flush with the end of the first word of the main heading. This wastes precious space, may cause unnecessary turnover lines, and gives the index entries an untidy look, as shown in the following example (Ridehalgh 1985, p. 171):

Legibility in lettering, 104
Lettering, 38, 55, 59, 102
            contrast, 98
            hand-drawn, 100, 160, 164
            in design, 4, 59, 67, 73, 84, 92, 100
            on roughs, 59
            position of, 46, 59, 106
Letterpress posters, 92, 102, 128, 162, 165
            printing, 165
Life studies, 66, 77
Light and colour, 70, 182–183
        artificial, 185–186
        day, 100, 185
Lighting of posters, 100, 131
            studio, 150
Limitations, design, 60
            personal, 63
            technical, 63, 132, 193
Line and mass in design, 64, 83, 91, 126
        blocks, 162

Similar to the previous "improvement", but of quite recent vintage, is a style in which only a single indention is used for everything, including turnover lines, the first word of which may then be thought to be misfiled as a new subheading. The example below is an excerpt from an index to a desktop publishing product where the word-processing software evidently provided only a single indention for all subheadings or turnover lines:

Twain, Mark
   on accuracy 1
   on direct experience vs. book-
   learning 63
   on grammar 74
   on revising and cutting out the
   superfluous 118
   on simplicity 127

All of the indention styles shown in the three examples above should be avoided.

Run-In Style

In the run-in style, the subheadings form a paragraph that is indented 1 em under the main heading; if the main heading is not followed by locators or cross-references it does not need any PUNCTUATION. The subheadings are separated from each other by semicolons, but the last one remains without any punctuation after the last locator, e.g.,

Campbell-Bannerman, Sir Henry
   character of 322; Prime Minister 427;
   supports disarmament 323, 324, 326–327;
   Balfour and 432; on House of Lords 441;
   resigns and dies 442

If, in order to save space, the main heading is followed immediately by the first subheading on the same line, a colon must separate the main heading from the subheading; the example above would then appear as follows:

Campbell-Bannerman, Sir Henry: character
   of 322; Prime Minister 427; supports
   disarmament 323, 324, 326–327; Balfour
   and 432; on House of Lords 441; resigns
   and dies 442

Comparing the two examples, it is evident that no space has been saved, since the indented paragraph of subheadings still takes up four lines under the main heading. A saving of perhaps one line may be achieved in short paragraphs of no more than two to three lines, but at the expense of making the main heading less easily discernible. The style shown in the first example is therefore preferable to that in the second one.

The run-in style is often used to save space when many main headings are followed by large numbers of subheadings, because it is, of course, much more compact than the indented style. It is the style preferred for indexes to works in the humanities and the social sciences, where a CHRONOLOGICAL ORDER of subheadings may be more useful than an alphabetical one. It is also better suited for NARRATIVE INDEXES of biographies and historical texts, because the consecutive and uninterrupted sequence of subheadings seems to fit the narrative style better than an indented display, which has been said to result in a "staccato" effect (Bell 1989, p. 170).

Its main disadvantage, as mentioned above, is the difficulty of accommodating sub-subheadings so that they will not be confounded with subheadings. Special punctuation, such as parentheses enclosing sub-subheadings or a colon between the last locator of a subheading and its sub-subheading is awkward and will easily be overlooked by busy users, who are not likely to pay attention to typographical niceties such as the difference between a semicolon and a colon when looking for a name or a fact in an index. The only practical solution to this problem is a hybrid style of display.

Hybrid Style: Indented and Run-In

In this style, each subheading begins on a new line, indented 1 em, the sub-subheadings following it in run-in style and indented 1 em under each subheading. This display saves a good deal of space compared with indented display, as shown in the example below, but it may be less easily scanned.

The displays on the next page have been chosen to exemplify the hybrid style, but they are actually not representative of good indexing practice. It would be better to use "education" only as a heading for general discussions of that topic, with *see also* references to "colleges", "elementary schools", etc., which should appear as main headings followed by their subheadings.

Indented display	*Hybrid display*
education	education
colleges	colleges: enroll-
enrollment 95, 97	ment 95, 97; faculty
faculty 83–88	83–88; students 91–93
students 91–93	elementary schools: curricu-
elementary schools	lum 41; pupils 38, 40;
curriculum 41	teachers 35, 37
pupils 38, 40	high schools: curricu-
teachers 35, 37	lum 53; faculty 61–62
high schools	universities: facul-
curriculum 53	ty 156, 158; financing
faculty 61–62	148; private 203; state
universities	205; students 160, 163–165
faculty 156, 158	
financing 148	
private 203	
state 205	
students 160, 163–165	

A survey of 255 index users (librarians and college professors) found that 93% of the librarians and 95% of the professors preferred the indented display of subheadings (Diodato 1994). Indexers should therefore seek to persuade their editors (particularly those of reference works and textbooks) to accept indexes in the indented format even though they need more space.

Length of Multilevel Headings

The design of subheadings which modify a main heading is one of the two principal factors that determine the utility and user-friendliness of an index. (The other one is the formulation and terminology of the subheadings.) The best-formulated subheading may remain unread and therefore unused if it appears too far away from its main heading, especially if that heading is on the recto of one page and some or most of its subheadings appear on the verso of that page or on the next page, or if it becomes visible only on the fourth or fifth screen of an electronic display.

It is, however, virtually impossible to stipulate a magic number of subheadings in a multilevel heading without taking into consideration the form of display, the physical format, and the use of an index. What may look somewhat long but still manageable on the page of a hardbound book, say two dozen subheadings, preceded and followed by other headings on the same page, may be too crowded for the same text in a smaller paperback edition, and will be far too much for one screen.

Users of multilevel headings should in principle be able to scan them easily from beginning to end, because in most instances a user does not know which subheadings have been listed or which terms have been used as LEAD TERMS. Only by scanning the entire hierarchy of a multilevel heading can a user be sure that no possible modification or relationship has been overlooked. Relatively short multilevel headings, say those having no more than six subheadings, are easily scanned. The number of subheadings in a multilevel heading that is acceptable and comfortable to users will vary with their visual acuity and their training in scanning an index, but it will also depend on the nature of the text. For example, indexes to LEGAL TEXTS, particularly those to statutes and regulations, often contain headings that are subdivided down to four, five, and more levels, so that a sub-sub-sub-subheading may appear several columns, pages, or screens away from the governing main heading. This does not seem to bother lawyers who are the principal users of such indexes, whereas indexes to textbooks and most reference works generally make do with a maximum of three levels, i.e., down to sub-subheadings.

Ideally, the number of subheadings under a main heading should be no larger than the amount that can be accommodated on a single index page, although there will, of course, always be instances in which a larger number of subheadings cannot be avoided. (Nothing can be done about entries that are split between two pages or screens because of the unpredictable sequence of lines that will fit into one column, but it is self-evident that the smaller the number of subheadings, the less the risk of a split.)

A rule of thumb may be to assign no more than half the amount of total lines in a column to the subheadings of a main heading. This will ensure that, depending on the number of turnover lines among the subheadings, about a third to a quarter of the available lines in a column will be left for single main headings or those with only a few subheadings. The limitation to no more than half a column of subheadings under any main heading may in many cases also prevent the splitting of a multilevel heading between two pages.

Achieving such a limited display of subheadings will often challenge an indexer's ingenuity. When faced with too large a number of subheadings, an attempt may be made to divide them into two or three groups by suitable modification of the main heading, e.g., when the main heading "bridges" has more than three dozen subheadings, it may be possible to devise modified main headings such as "bridge construction", "bridge design", and "bridge maintenance", each with only a smaller number of subheadings.

An excessive number of subheadings is sometimes the result of clumsy overindexing. An index should not repeat every last detail of a topic, nor should it belabor the obvious. Subheadings that just repeat the locators of a main heading are only cluttering up an index and lengthen it unnecessarily without providing essential information, as in the following ridiculous example, taken from an encyclopedia of library history:

```
Laos, 331
   history, 331
   libraries, 331
      academic, 331
      national, 331
      public, 331
   outlook, 331
```

The sub- and sub-subheadings simply repeat the text of the article in a kind of telegraphic keyword style, but do not provide any information that a user may not reasonably expect to find in an article actually occupying no more than half a page!

Sub-Subheadings

Some multilevel headings for topics dealt with extensively and from many different points of view may become unduly long, particularly when subheadings are further modified by subsubheadings. Clearly, an occasional sub-subheading is sometimes the best and most economical way of indicating further modification of a subheading, but if too many sub-subheadings tend to clutter up a multilevel heading, it may be better to eliminate them. This can be done by converting modified subheadings to main headings (to which only cross-references are made under the original main heading), thereby changing the former sub-subheadings to subheadings. This may sound complicated, but is actually quite simple, as shown in Figure 3, first schematically and then by an actual example.

The drawbacks of this method are (a) that a user, instead of finding all modifications of a main heading in one place, is forced to look up second-level modifications in another place which may be annoying and is in any case more time-consuming, thus less user-friendly; and (b) that the index will be somewhat longer. An indexer must therefore weigh carefully which method is the more convenient and economical one from the point of view of the user—a matter that will again largely depend on the nature of the text and on the habits of users. As mentioned above, lawyers find nothing wrong with multiple levels of subheadings, probably because time is of the essence for them more than it is for most other index users.

The issue of sub-subheadings may become moot in case an editor stipulates that modification of main headings may not be made beyond the level of subheadings. An indexer faced with such a restriction may wish to use the method displayed below in order to avoid any sub-subheadings.

		Broken up into	
Entry 1	*Entry 2*	*and*	*Entry 3*
main heading A	main heading A		main heading X
subheading B	subheading B		subheading D
subheading C	subheading C *see*		subheading E
sub-subheading D	main heading X		
sub-subheading E	subheading F		
subheading F			
subheadings 57, 107	subheadings 57, 107		display of sub-
ambiguous 311	ambiguous 311		headings
display 20, 72	display *see* display		line-by-line 98
line-by-line 98	of subheadings		run-on 100
run-on 100	editing 109		
editing 109			

Figure 3. *Conversion of sub-subheadings to subheadings.*

Subheadings in Electronically Displayed Indexes

The dichotomy between indented and run-in format virtually does not exist in indexes displayed on a screen (with the exception of those used by indexers in their own work). The vertical size of a screen, generally limited to 24 lines or less, imposes a severe limitation on the number of subheadings that are simultaneously visible. The user may therefore be uncertain whether or not all subheadings have been shown. If the last visible subheading on the first screen starts with the letter R, is this really the end? Clicking on the next screen will, of course, provide the answer, but then the main heading will have disappeared since it was shown only on the first screen. Consequently, the number of subheadings is (or ought to be) much more limited in electronic indexes than in printed ones, perhaps to no more than 15–20 lines, if splitting of multilevel headings is to be avoided or minimized. Obviously, this will not always be feasible.

BS 3700: 5.2.3.2; 7.1.3.4; 7.2.6.2; 7.2.7
Chicago manual of style: 17.4; 17.51–56
ISO 999: 9.1.2.3; 9.1.2.4; 9.5
NISO Z39.4:

DOUBLE ENTRIES

Whenever a name appears in different forms or a compound heading must be referred to by its component words, there is a choice between a double (or multiple) entry and a *see* reference. A double entry should be made when (a) a heading has only a few locators (no more than three); (b) a heading has no or only one subheading; and (c) when the double entry would take up no more space than a *see* reference. Double entries save the time of the user but editors sometimes disallow them because they may increase the length of an index. However, a double entry may actually save space, as the following example shows.

Double entries	*See reference*
Bath, 1st Marquis of 177, 230	Bath, 1st Marquis of *see*
Weymouth, 3rd Viscount 177, 230	Weymouth, 3rd Viscount
	Weymouth, 3rd Viscount 177, 230

The *see* reference forces the reader to use a double look-up (in this case almost at the opposite end of the index), while the double entry is not only saving the reader's time but also one index line.

Double entries are therefore "neither a problem nor an evil" (Cutler 1970, p. 22); it has also been found that in the indexes of science and technology books multiple entries are much more often used than *see* cross-references and that such double entries were more likely to be made by professional indexers than by authors who indexed their own books (Bishop et al. 1991; Liddy et al. 1991). A survey among librarians and college professors found that the former preferred *see* references, while the latter preferred double entries; the rate of preference was 58% in both groups (Diodato 1994*b*). An examination of 1,100 *see* cross-references in 202 books found that 22% of these references should have been converted to double entries according to the criteria mentioned above (Diodato 1994*a*).

Double or multiple entries are particularly useful in the following cases.

1. *Compound headings* in the form: Main heading followed by a single subheading:

lungs 58–60	cancer 85, 89, 93
cancer 87	lungs 87

2. *Double-barrelled names:*

Trevor-Roper, Hugh 36, 43	Roper, Hugh Trevor- 36, 43

3. *Titles of nobility vs. family name:*

Pitt, William 26	Chatham, Earl of (William Pitt) 26
Chesterfield, Earl of (Philip Dormer Stanhope) 48	Stanhope, Philip Dormer, Earl of Chesterfield 48

4. *Changes in place names:*

Beijing 51–63   Peking 51–63

5. *Legal cases,* especially when listed in "Tables of cases", where the first name is always that of the plaintiff, and the second is the name of the defendant; the inverted double entry must, by convention, preserve that relationship:

Able vs. Willing 51   Willing; Able vs. 51

For this particular type of double entry special indexing software is available that will automatically convert one form to the other.

6. *Acronyms and their explication,* when the heading is followed by no more than one or at most two subheadings, so that the user need not look up a cross-reference from the acronym to the full form or vice versa:

ASI (American Society of Indexers)   American Society of Indexers (ASI)
    annual meetings 26   annual meetings 26
    publications 31   publications 31

The additional two lines (or sometimes only one if a heading plus cross-reference would need a turnover line) may not unduly lengthen an index, but if there are more than two subheadings, a cross-reference from the acronym to the full form will indeed save space (though not the time of the user).

7. *Topic vs. place.* It is sometimes difficult to decide on the relative importance of a topic and a place when formulating an index entry. In the past, double entry was recommended in almost every case, but current indexing practice favors entry primarily under topic and only secondarily under place, if at all. A broad ranking of topical categories as they are more or less significantly affected by place has been established by Coates (1960); it has stood the tests of time and practical application remarkably well, especially in periodical indexes. The ranking is as follows:

1. Geography and biological phenomena
2. History and social phenomena
3. Language and literature

4. Fine arts
5. Philosophy and religion
6. Technology
7. Phenomena of physical sciences

The higher a topic appears in this list, the more it is apt to be significantly affected by place and may therefore need a double entry under the name of a locality, while the topics at the lower end of the scale seldom if ever need such double entries. For example, in a work on the preservation of wildlife in Africa, elephants in Kenya are discussed; instead of agonizing over whether to index under "elephants" or under "Kenya", it is best to make double entries, particularly if elephants in other parts of Africa or other Kenyan wildlife are also being dealt with:

elephants	Kenya
Kenya 58	antelopes 37
South Africa 62, 67	elephants 58
Zimbabwe 45	lions 13, 26

Obviously, in a work devoted entirely to the fauna of Kenya, only one index entry for "elephants" would be needed because the context would indicate the relationship.

Great care must be taken to avoid the mistake of multiplying the same subheadings (and even sub-subheadings) under double entries, e.g.,

lungs	cancer
blood vessels	bladder
cancer	lungs
chemotherapy	chemotherapy
diagnosis	diagnosis
surgery	surgery

Even worse is a set of subheadings under one main heading and a different set under a double heading:

lungs	cancer
cancer	lungs
diagnosis	chemotherapy
mortality rate	surgery

Such mistakes, which can easily be made during the compilation stage of an index, can only be caught in the final EDITING, when double entries with more than one subheading or any sub-subheadings must either be changed to *see* references or to new main headings and subheadings, especially if there is a proliferation of sub-subheadings. For the lung cancer examples above, *see* references may take one of the following forms (depending on the text and the resulting index entries):

cancer
  bladder
  lungs *see* lungs
  stomach

or even better (because shorter) if a number of different cancers is dealt with in the text:

cancer *see* names of organs

BS 3700: 5.5.1
ISO 999: 7.2.2.4
NISO Z39.4:

EDITING: THE 21 STEPS

Once the last page of a book or the last issue of a periodical has been indexed, the most important part of the job—editing the index—lies still ahead, whether or not the index was compiled the old-fashioned way—on cards or slips—or with the assistance of a computer and special indexing software. Although we are now in the age of computer-assisted indexing, there is unfortunately as yet only very little computer-assisted editing, and this arduous and time-consuming, yet absolutely crucial task must be undertaken by (admittedly fallible) human beings. Editing is almost entirely an intellectual task, and computers are simply not smart enough to do it.

The 21 Steps

All or most of the following steps must be implemented in order to produce a typescript, computerscript, or machine-readable medium from which an index can be generated either in print or electronically. An indexer whose product is intended for display in print, i.e., mainly book indexes or indexes to volumes of periodicals and other collective works, may have to make some editorial decisions that affect not only the intellectual content but also the layout and size as well as the legibility of an index. But decisions on the display of a database index in both printed and electronic (online) format or in the latter format only are not the responsibility of a database's indexers but that of its managers and technical specialists. Therefore, steps 1–16 pertain to the editing of all types of indexes, whether printed or intended for storage and display in electronic databases, while steps 17–21 are relevant for printed indexes only. Though it is possible to perform some of these tasks on screen, the physical limitations of screen displays make it often highly desirable to work from hard copy, especially for long entries. The steps which can be performed or assisted by a computer have been marked (C).

1. *Alphabetizing of main headings* (C). A first quick check of all main headings. If cards have been used, some of them may have been misplaced in the constant pulling and rearranging process. But even supposedly foolproof alphanumeric sorting programs that are not specially designed for computer-assisted indexing will occasionally misplace some entries, e.g., a heading enclosed in quotation marks may be arranged ahead of all other entries, and there may be other unpleasant surprises which must be corrected at this stage.

2. *Long multilevel headings: first round.* These are main headings followed by a large number of subheadings and often also sub-subheadings which would fill more than half a column and sometimes even an entire column or more on a printed page. It is good practice to skip these screens or to put the set of cards aside for the

time being, and to deal with them only after all other entries and headings have been edited. *See* step 13 below.

3. *Alphabetizing of subheadings* (C). The "raw" subheadings, as they accumulate under main headings on cards, are generally not in alphabetical order and must now be rearranged alphabetically. At the same time, they must also be edited for consistency, and perhaps be further subdivided if too many locators are listed under a single subheading. What has been said under (1) about alphanumeric sorting of headings by special programs applies, of course, here too, and the alphabetization of subheadings must also be checked for accuracy. This step can often be combined with the next one.

4. *Elimination of synonymous headings.* Synonymous (or nearly synonymous and quasi-synonymous) main headings must be eliminated and combined with the preferred term. Any subheadings under an eliminated term must then be transferred to the preferred term (*see* step 9 below). A THESAURUS for the specific field covered will be useful in deciding on a preferred term, especially when indexing periodicals in which different authors may use different but nearly synonymous terms for the same concept. *See* references must be made from all eliminated synonymous terms to the preferred term:

atomic weapons *see* nuclear weapons
coastal areas *see* littoral zones

5. *Elimination of headings.* Main headings or subheadings that are too specific (relative to the general level of specificity of the index) may have to be eliminated, especially if they have only one locator and are unlikely to be sought; an eliminated subheading may sometimes be subsumed under a more general heading that has already been established.

6. *Resolution of too many locators.* Generally, no more than five to seven locators should be listed after any heading. If there are more, specific subheadings should be made instead. For details *see* LOCATORS.

7. *Ambiguous headings.* All headings must be checked for potential ambiguity or lack of clarity. HOMOGRAPHS must be disambiguated by the addition of QUALIFIERS. Words with different meanings

in SINGULAR OR PLURAL (especially in legal indexes) must be given separate headings if this has not already been done.

8. *Subheadings.* Have all subheadings modifying a concept been listed under a single main heading? If synonymous main headings have been eliminated at step (4) their subheadings (if different) must be amalgamated with those already listed under the preferred term, and their proper alphabetical order ought to be checked again.

9. *Cross-references* (C). All CROSS-REFERENCES must be checked for referral to an actual heading. This is particularly important if headings have been eliminated or changed at step (4), so as to avoid "blind" or "circular" cross-references (*see* pages 131–132).

10. *Double entries* (C). Do they have the same locators? If not, the missing ones must be added. Does one (or both) have more than one subheading? If so, they ought to be changed; *see* DOUBLE ENTRIES.

11. *Spelling* (C). Misspellings and typos will inevitably occur on typed or handwritten cards and must be corrected. For computer-produced headings, software that includes a spelling checker will largely avoid or at least reduce misspellings, but many scientific and technical terms are not covered by such general-purpose devices, nor is there any automatic speller for names of persons and places (especially foreign ones) which may easily be misspelled or, even worse, be falsely "corrected" by the spelling checker.

CAPITALIZATION of main headings (if prescribed by the publisher's house style) must also be checked for consistency.

12. *Punctuation* (C). Since punctuation is kept to the barest minimum in modern indexes, it is only necessary to check for consistency in the few instances where it is used, especially when subheadings are displayed in run-in style. For details *see* PUNCTUATION.

13. *Long multilevel headings: second round.* Now the time has come to edit those headings previously skipped or set aside. Almost all of the tasks enumerated above may have to be performed on multilevel headings, albeit on a smaller scale, and some steps may have to be repeated several times until a multilevel heading can be whipped into its final shape. An effort should be made to reduce, if possible, the number of subheadings and sub-subheadings (if any) by consolidating, changing, or eliminating some of them. The methods of performing these tasks are discussed under "Length of multilevel headings", p. 147–149.

The following examples show an unedited long multilevel heading (for the sake of clarity, without sub-subheadings) and then the same heading in its final edited form:*

Multilevel heading before editing:

arithmetic assessment
    addition and subtraction 476–478
    addition calculation 465, 468
    conservation 425–426
    conservation task 475–476
    flexible interviewing 443–447
    interviewing 495–496
    goal of 415–417
    number facts 469–470, 483–486
    standardized measurement 441–443
    standardized tests 463–465, 491–495
    student's ability to learn 419–420
    student's learning potential 496
    subtraction 473
    thinking processes 485, 487
    thinking strategies 442–443, 447–456
    types of student thinking 418–419

Multilevel heading after editing:

arithmetic assessment
    addition 465, 468, 476–478
    conservation task 425–426, 475–476
    interviewing 443–447, 495–496
    goal of 415–417
    number facts 469–470, 483–486
    standardized tests 441–443, 463–465, 491–495
    subtraction 473
    thinking processes 418–419, 442–443, 447–456, 485, 487

During this editing operation, care must be taken to ensure correct alphabetization (especially if cards are being used). Indentions must also be carefully checked, especially in some scientific or legal indexes, in which sub-subheadings may be displayed not only on the third level, but even on a fourth or fifth one (beyond which no

*Reproduced from *Handbook of indexing techniques* (Fetters 1994), by permission.

modification of a heading should be carried). Each level must be indented deeper than the previous one:

1st level	main heading
2nd level	subheading
3rd level	sub-subheading
4th level	sub-sub-subheading
5th level	sub-sub-sub-subheading

Turnover lines, which will almost inevitably occur at the lower levels because of the shortness of lines, must be indented deeper than any other subheading (see Figure 16, p. 495). In addition, a decision may have to be made regarding a GROUPED ORDER of subheadings in biographies or historical works.

14. *Addition of entries.* Now is the last opportunity to add entries which for some reason were not made but need to be inserted into the index. This is often more difficult to do than eliminating redundant or superfluous headings, because the new headings may affect already existing main headings or subheadings, some of which may have to be changed or rearranged. For this reason, last-minute additions should be avoided as much as possible.

15. *Introductory note.* All decisions on alphabetization, display of subheadings, use of special typography, symbols, and layout, grouped subdivision of long entries, the indexing of footnotes, appendixes, etc. have now been made. All of these decisions may have to be conveyed to the prospective users of the index by means of an INTRODUCTORY NOTE. If there are MULTIPLE INDEXES, each of these may need such a note.

16. *Evaluation for user-friendliness.* At this point, the indexer should step back, as it were, and look at the index again from the point of view of the user. Is it really user-friendly? Three requirements should be met by an index in order for it to be considered user-friendly: first, it should be *cooperative,* assisting the user during the operation of searching; second, it should be *preventive,* anticipating that people are apt to make mistakes when searching and providing alternative routes of access; third, it should be *conducive,* that is, reliable, predictable, and assisting rather than controlling the user (Meads 1985). Although these requirements were formulated for interactive computerized information retrieval systems, they are

in principle and with only slight modifications equally applicable to printed indexes. Indexes have also been graded on a nine-point user-friendliness scale from a top "user-intimate" to "user-oriented" at midpoint and on to horrible "user-vicious" ones at the low end (Matthews & Williams 1984). So that an index may (ideally) qualify for the top grade of "user-intimate", it is very important to check and evaluate its major features with the needs and requirements of prospective users in mind:

Main headings. Are they relevant to the topics that will be searched? Are they neither too general nor too specific? Do they have more than five to seven locators? If so, provide subheadings.

Subheadings. Are they specific enough? Do they start with terms— nouns, adjectives, verbs—that are most likely to be searched? Do they start or end with PREPOSITIONS? If so, are they necessary for the clarification of the relationship between subheadings and main headings? If not, delete the prepositions. Do subheadings have more than five locators? If so, either break them down into sub-subheadings or convert them into main headings and subheadings.

Double entries. In most instances, COMPOUND HEADINGS should be listed under all their terms in order to provide access to the heading from each term. Do all double entries have the same locators?

Locators. Are they correct? Check several random samples for accuracy.

Cross-references. Do all *see* references lead to synonymous (or nearly synonymous) headings? Do all *see also* references lead to related entries?

Length. Is the LENGTH OF THE INDEX adequate—neither too long nor too short for the type of work indexed? If too long and complex—would it be more helpful for users to divide the index by type of entry (e.g., names/places/topics)? But *see also* Step 21 below!

17. *Generic coding* (C). Indexes prepared as computerscripts on disk must be tagged by generic codes to indicate typefaces other than roman (*italics*, SMALL CAPITALS, or **boldface**), special symbols or changes in type size. Most publishers demand the coding prescribed by the American National Standard NISO Z39.59 *Electronic manuscripts: Preparation and markup* (National Information Standards Organization 1988) which conforms to the International Stan-

dard ISO 8879 *Standard Generalized Markup Language (SGML)* (International Organization for Standardization 1986*a*).

The application of generic coding for computerscripts in general is treated in *Practical SGML* (Van Herwijnen 1994) and the specific use of these codes in the compilation of indexes is explained in *Generic markup of electronic index manuscripts* (Maddocks 1988). A clearinghouse for information on the application of NISO Z39.59 and its further development is the Electronic Publishing Special interest Group (EPSIC)* which publishes guides and a newsletter. Another set of generic codes (incompatible with NISO Z39.59 but required by some publishers) is the *Chicago guide to preparing electronic manuscripts for authors and publishers* (Chicago Guide 1987).

The various dedicated indexing software packages used by the majority of indexers are designed to insert the most commonly used generic codes automatically; only the relatively seldom used codes for DIACRITICS or mathematical and currency SYMBOLS will have to be inserted manually.

In typewritten index manuscripts (*see* step 18 below) the markings traditionally used by printers to indicate typefaces other than roman, namely: single underlining for italics, double underlining for small capitals, and wavy underlining for boldface, must be added manually.

18. *Printer's copy* (C). So far, everything is either still in the form of a somewhat raw computerscript or on cards. The index must now be put into the form in which either human typesetters or the printer's or publisher's computer will accept it in order to convert it to printed pages.

A computerscript on disk should already be in that form, provided that the disk and file formats as well as the generic coding prescribed by the publisher have been executed meticulously: all indentions have been properly set, the start and end of lines, typeface changes, and special characters or symbols have been correctly coded, and no gremlins or viruses have intervened. In practice, the ever-present gremlins will have done their nefarious work, and so even the supposedly last computerscript should be subjected to a final check before being sent to the publisher or printer, as detailed in step 19.

*c/o OCLC, 6565 Frantz Road, Dublin, OH 43017–3395

An index compiled on cards must always be retyped on $8\frac{1}{2}'' \times 11''$ (or A4) sheets, on one side of the paper only, double-spaced, and with ample margins ($1\frac{1}{2}-2''$ or 35–50 mm) on all sides. The line width specified by the publisher or a maximum length of 40 characters should be set. Only one column should be typed on each page. Indented lines should be moved two spaces to the right of the lines under which they are displayed. All pages should be numbered consecutively on the upper right-hand corner, because to rely only on the alphabetical sequence of headings is to invite disaster, since the pages may become mixed up on the typesetter's desk. Unfortunately, this retyping inevitably results in new mistakes and typos which can only be discovered at the next step.

19. *Final checking.* Everything is now in its proper format and place, but it is highly desirable to make one final check, preferably with the help of another person who has not been previously involved in the compilation and editing of the index. But why be so fussy about errors? Will not the printers make errors of their own which will have to be corrected, so that all corrections can be made at the same time? Well, printers will indeed make errors, but theirs will be corrected at no charge, while yours will cost a lot of money if they are on galleys and possibly even more if they are on page proofs, when a change or correction of even one line may upset the whole applecart (the layout of the page), and the indexer may have to reimburse the publisher for the cost of such alterations which can range from several dollars to dozens of dollars. Thus, even if several hours or perhaps even days have to be spent on the final checking of a large index, this will still be cheaper than the penalties that may be incurred for the resetting of faulty lines, adding a few locators that were forgotten or misplaced, or other calamities that show up in black and white in cold print.

The checked manuscript is now ready to be sent to the publisher for transmission to the printer. A machine-readable index is either submitted in the form of a disk or transmitted over telephone lines by means of a modem. In either case, it is also necessary to send the hard copy. Ideally, this should be the final form of the index manuscript, but it may happen that changes or corrections need to be made even at the last moment, just before mailing the index. Corrections that have not been made on disk must then be clearly marked on the hard copy using standard proof correction marks;

deletions should never be made by means of correcting fluid or by making the hard copy text illegible.

Whichever form the final printer's copy takes, the indexer must keep copies of the index typescript, computerscript, or machine-readable disk as a safety precaution in case of loss (both by mail and electronically) and also in order to be able to answer typesetters' queries, as well as for the proofreading step, though most publishers return the printer's copy with page proofs. When sending disks by mail, it is advisable to attach to the envelope a form, stipulating the conditions of use by the publisher (either in addition to conditions already included in the indexer's CONTRACT or as a separate document). Such conditions may include: a provision not to make more than one copy of the disk for production purposes; not to make the disk available to third parties (e.g., a database); and to edit the disk only for conformity to house style or for accuracy (Dorner 1992).

But wait—before putting the manuscript or the disk in an envelope addressed to the publisher, yet another step may have to be taken.

20. *Instructions to the printer.* Many publishers have a house style that governs the way a book and its index are being designed and printed. Large publishers have special index editors who see to it that the house style is properly applied to an index manuscript. If the publisher has provided specifications for index manuscripts in machine-readable form, and if the indexer has followed these instructions and has formatted the index on a disk, there is no need to worry about instructions to the printers, even though the house style may not produce what the indexer would have liked to see. (More on this under AUTHOR-PUBLISHER-INDEXER RELATIONSHIPS.) For example, a *(continued)* line may be required (if at all) only on top of the first column on a left-hand page but not elsewhere, and other such deviations from good indexing and printing practices may occur.

Smaller publishers, however, who use different printers for each job, may have to be provided with instructions on how to print a particular index, since not all typesetters and printers are familiar with the special layout and format of printed indexes. Such an instruction may take the following form:

Printer:
- a. Set all headings lc, except proper names.
- b. No commas at end of headings. No periods (full stops) after headings without locators, nor after last locator.
- c. Set subheadings line by line, indented 1 em, turnover lines indented 3 ems, sub-subheadings indented 2 ems:

main heading 30, 45
☐ subheading turnover ﹏
☐☐☐line 15, 36
☐☐ sub-subheading 57

If subheadings are to be displayed in run-in style, instruction c would have to be as follows:

- d. Set subheadings run-in, indented 1 em:

Main heading: subheading; sub-
☐ heading; subheading; sub-
☐ heading

- e. Set *see also* references 1 line beneath main heading, 2 ems indented, turnover lines 3 ems indented, subheadings 1 em indented:

main heading
☐☐ *see also* another﹏
☐☐☐heading
☐ subheading

- f. Page proofs: set (*cont.*) lines on top of every column for every main heading on a previous page or column that is followed by a subheading on the next column or page. If the subheading is also carried over, set (*cont.*) lines for both:

main heading (*cont.*)
☐ subheading (*cont.*)
☐☐ sub-subheading

The index typescript, computerscript, or disk and all instructions can now be sent to the publisher, but the editing process may still not be complete. A few weeks later, the indexer will receive either galleys or, more likely, page proofs, and the arduous task of PROOF-

READING will have to be undertaken. This may entail additional editorial work, such as adjustment of BAD BREAKS or the correction of improperly set indentions for cross-references and turnover lines for main headings and subheadings. Because of the differences between the uniform width of typewritten letters and the proportional one of printed letters, short turnover lines in the typescript or computerscript may appear as single lines on the printed page proofs, but, occasionally, the opposite may happen (a printed turnover line where there was none in the manuscript). Other mishaps may, of course, also have occurred during typesetting and must be corrected, but at this stage, no other editorial changes, additions or deletions may be made.

21. *Adjustment of length.* An editor may find that the index as printed is too long, and will ask the indexer to eliminate a certain number of lines so that it will fit into the pages allocated to it. And so, the very last step must be taken, the least agreeable one, namely, pruning the index to the required length. If only about a dozen lines or so have to be trimmed, this can be done relatively easily through elimination of some turnover lines by substituting shorter words for long ones or by lopping off superfluous prepositions, by elimination of a few entries for minor topics with only one locator, by scrapping some double entries, or by trimming the space left between each letter sequence to the absolute minimum of a single blank line (although the editor may have thought of that already, and the index is still too long).

But if the index is larger than the allocated space by, say, two to three pages, some more severe surgery must be undertaken, unless the publisher can be persuaded to provide the extra pages (which is unlikely, because it would mean the addition of at least eight pages, most of which would then remain blank). One way to achieve a sizable reduction in length is to change the display of subheadings from indented to run-in style, but this is not always acceptable, especially not for scientific and technical texts. Other than that, not very much can be done without some radical pruning which will often leave the index in a sadly truncated shape, to the sorrow of the indexer and author, and the detriment of the user.

To avoid such a calamity, it is desirable to ask the editor at the time when the index is commissioned how many pages will be allotted to the index, which type font and size will be used, and what will be the width of a column, so that at least an approximate idea can be formed about the permissible LENGTH OF AN INDEX. If a quick calculation (based on the average number of index entries per text page) shows that an index set in 8 point will probably exceed the number of allotted pages, the indexer may suggest to the editor a change to 7 point, which will be only slightly less legible yet may accommodate the index without any need for ultimate pruning. But "the best laid schemes o' mice and men gang aft a-gley" when last-minute addition of material such as pictures, maps, or a bibliography and end-notes larger than expected result in more text pages so that fewer pages remain for the index, the low man on the totem pole.

At this point, beginners in indexing may ask: are 21 steps really necessary to edit an index? And does this not take an inordinate amount of time? The answer is: yes, all or most of these steps must be taken, and not only that, but in the shortest possible time, because the publisher is anxiously waiting for the index, the last part of the book to be set in type so that it can finally be published. But not to despair: many editing steps can be performed simultaneously (they have been enumerated analytically only because each step pertains to a different aspect of the editing process). Using a computer and special indexing software during the compilation stage will either eliminate some of the editing steps or will at least cut down on the time needed to do them, even though such savings will seldom amount to more than about 5–10% of the editing process, compared with manual methods.

This brings us to the question of time spent on editing. Experienced indexers, working with the assistance of a computer and sophisticated indexing software estimate that, on the average, about 30–40% of the total time spent on indexing must be devoted to the editing process, and more than that if the index is very large and complex. The amount of time spent on editing an index will increase more rapidly than proportional to the length of an index. Thus, an index of, say, six pages may need two hours of editing, but an index of twice that length may need not four but six hours or more, depending on the type and topic of the indexed work. *See also* COSTING.

NISO Z39.59

EQUIPMENT

Computer-Assisted Indexing: Hardware

Anyone who intends to become an indexer will probably already own a personal computer or will at least be computer-literate to some extent. Since technical developments in the computing field are constantly changing, it would be futile to list here the desirable features of computer hardware that is primarily or exclusively to be used for indexing. Rather, having decided on a full-time or part-time career in indexing, the best course of action for a freelancer is to choose first of all one of the available dedicated indexing software packages, discussed below. Once a particular type of software has been chosen, the best hardware available and affordable should be acquired or the existing equipment be upgraded so that the capabilities offered by the software can be exploited to the fullest extent. On the other hand, bells and whistles that only make the hardware more complex and expensive without adding much or even anything to the quality of the finished product—well-designed indexes in machine-readable form and in hard copy—should be avoided.

Indexers employed in-house by a publisher or those working for a database producer will almost always have to work with their employers' specially designed hardware and software after undergoing training in the use of these facilities. Some of the automated indexing aids used by the major databases have been described by Hodge (1992).

Computer-Assisted Indexing: Dedicated Software

The first program specifically designed to assist in the compilation of indexes by performing all or most clerical and repetitive tasks was introduced in 1983. Since then, a range of dedicated indexing software packages has become available, varying in capabilities and price. The newsletters of the several SOCIETIES OF INDEXERS and the *Microindexer*, a specialized periodical published by the Society of Indexers in the U.K., carry regular reviews of new and upgraded

indexing software. The *Guide to indexing software* (Fetters 1986–)
published by the American Society of Indexers is being updated
about once a year. These publications should be consulted before
making a decision on a particular brand of indexing software. Most
software vendors will provide demonstration disks free or at low
cost.

Indexing software should be evaluated according to the following functions and capabilities:

1. Provision for at least 5,000 headings, but up to 20,000 or more
   may be desirable.
2. Provision for at least five lines of subheadings under each
   main heading, but preferably more.
3. Provision for up to four levels of subheadings and sub-
   subheadings.
4. Alphabetization of entries in word-by-word or letter-by-
   letter order; in both styles, sorting numerals in ascending
   arithmetical order before letters.
5. Formatting subheadings in either indented or run-in (paragraph) style.
6. Individual setting of column width and indentions.
7. Capability of ignoring nonsorting letters or words.
8. Cross-reference verification: checking for missing headings
   and locators or circular references.
9. Flipping of entries: changing an entry consisting of main
   heading and subheading to the opposite order.
10. Copying and duplicating any previously entered record.
11. Finding and replacing text anywhere in the index.
12. Suppression of repeated headings and subheadings.
13. Merging of locators in ascending numerical order.
14. Automatic punctuation for recurrent applications, e.g., com-
    mas between locators or semicolons between two or more *see
    also* references.
15. Printing either sequential or individual locators (e.g., "roses
    37–41" or "roses 37, 39, 40, 41".
16. Printing different typefaces (italics, boldface, small capitals),
    diacritics, symbols, sub- and superscripts.
17. Printing of the formatted index in two columns on the page.
18. Sorting of index entries in page number order.

19. On-screen editing of entries without the need to exit to a word processor.
20. Displaying the formatted index (all or parts of it) on-screen without having to print the file.
21. Conversion of the formatted index to a text file that can be edited by any word processor.

Several other desirable features of dedicated indexing software are listed in Fetters's *Guide* mentioned above, and in Mulvany (1994*b*, pp. 271–277).

"Embedded Indexing" Modules: Indexer Beware!

And now a word of warning against word-processing or page-layout software packages that include "automatic" and "embedded" indexing modules. Despite their names and the claims made for them, these devices cannot produce an index, that is, a key to concepts dealt within a text, and their relationships to other concepts in that text. They are designed by people whose idea of an index is an alphabetical list of words extracted from a text plus their locators.* Because machines can only extract and list words but cannot understand their meaning, none of the "indexing" modules can generate even the simplest multilevel heading, that is, one in which a heading is followed by one or more subheadings that modify it to indicate a relationship, e.g.,

lungs
  cancer
  tuberculosis

Neither can these modules provide prepositional or verb phrases that show the *kind* of relationship obtaining between a heading and its subheadings, e.g.,

lung cancer
  in coal miners
  smoking as a cause

*Compare Mr. Pountain's recipe for making an index, p. 217.

It is sometimes said that embedded indexing modules, while not producing indexes, do generate concordances, but even that is incorrect, because a concordance displays words and their location *in context*, i.e. surrounded by a few words before and after the displayed one. No embedded indexing module does that.

Embedded indexing modules, marketed under various brand names for word processing applications, are basically of two types.

a. *Computer-assisted.* These are subprograms within a word processing package. An operator may choose terms in the text or may add phrases to it; both are embedded in the electronic text file together with pointers to their places in the file. The "index" is then generated in a separate procedure by scanning for the embedded terms or phrases and their location in the text. This type of module is tedious and time-consuming to use because it needs a good deal of manual manipulation of index entries, and is thus not really "automatic".

b. *Fully automatic.* The software automatically selects and tags all words not on a stop list plus their place in the electronic text file without any human intervention. The tagged words and their locators can be displayed or printed in alphabetical order as a file separate from the text: "CLICK! You have just indexed an entire document", as advertised in large type on the box of one of these indexing modules.

The advantages claimed for embedded indexing modules are:

1. Writers of a text can tag index words as they go along without having to worry about locators (which will be added automatically).
2. When revisions of the text have to be made, only new words will have to be indexed, while previously indexed words will automatically get fitting locators as needed, and obsolete words will be eliminated.
3. An automatically generated index can be reused for subsequent editions.

All three claims are spurious and can easily be refuted:

1. Writing and indexing are two different intellectual activities, performed by using different skills. Few people possess both,

and even if they do, they cannot employ them simultaneously. Indexing, as defined above, can only be performed when a complete text is available, because only then are the relationships among concepts revealed.

2. Revisions of text will always result in changes affecting the context of at least some previously indexed terms, thus not only changing their locators but also their significance and relationships.

3. Reuse of an index is subject to the same limitations as revisions. If previously indexed entries are to be changed in any way, the necessary procedures are extremely time-consuming and tedious, often requiring five to eight keystrokes both before and after the "embedded" index term.

None of the "embedded" indexing modules is capable of performing any of the functions of dedicated indexing software listed above, with the sole exception of functions 4, 6, and 13; however, function 4, alphabetization, is almost always limited to unmodified ASCII sorting which is altogether unsuitable for sorting index entries (see p. 460). As noted above, they cannot automatically generate modifying subheadings, nor can they exercise synonym control by means of CROSS-REFERENCES.

What these indexing modules *will* do is: listing words indiscriminately in singular as well as plural form, depending on how they happen to appear in the text; and listing an unlimited number of locators, dutifully recording every occurrence of a word in the text.

The deficiencies, faults, and dangers of embedded indexing modules which are hawked by highly deceptive if not outright fraudulent slogans such as "With just a click of the mouse, you create back-of-the-book indexes!" or "Produce professional quality indexes at a rate of up to 50 pages per minute" have been exposed by Mulvany (1990, 1994a, 1994b, pp. 255–271), Wittmann (1991), and Mulvany & Milstead (1994). Lest it be thought that these are latter-day Luddites, anxious to preserve their turf and livelihood, here are the words of William Gallagher, a computer expert who tried to make indexes with the help of various embedded modules, as published in the section "Hands-on word processing" of *Personal Computer World* (March 1992, pp. 370–374):

Far from being the easiest and most numbingly uncreative part of writing [a] document, the index is a painstaking and difficult task. It's also impossible with the software that exists now. There isn't one piece of software that can do the job, so my only real recommendation must be: if you need an index, get an indexer (a human one) to do it.

Indexing with Cards

Cards as indexing tools are now almost entirely a thing of the past as far as professionals are concerned, although some oldtimers who switched to computers confessed publicly that it was more fun to shuffle and reshuffle cards than to stare for hours on end at screens with white, green, or yellow lines on a blue or black background. Be that as it may, using cards is now often called "manual indexing". This is an inept analogy to driving with a manual transmission compared to an automatic one, and it should be thrown into the dustbin of bad clichés. When using cards, indexers had to use their *minds* to the same extent as when using machines, whereas pounding a keyboard remains as much "manual" labor as was typing or handwriting on cards.

Indexers still working with cards generally use 3″ × 5″ (75 mm × 125 mm) cards, but some prefer 4″ × 6″ (100 mm × 150 mm) cards, especially when many large entries can be expected. Any format larger than that is, however, not suitable for indexing. For typing, the cards should be blank; for handwriting (which, when neat, is often quicker than typing), they should be ruled. A set of A to Z dividers, preferably with plastic reinforcement on tabs, is also needed. A shoebox or wooden tray about 1 foot (30 cm) long will hold about 1,000 cards, that is, 3,000–4,000 locators or more, which will be sufficient for most books of about 250–300 pages, except for scientific and technical works and for legal material, which often need a large number of headings per page. If a work needs MULTI-PLE INDEXES, a separate tray for each of them must be used; in this case, it is also advisable to use cards of different colors for each index so as to avoid accidental misfiling of a card in the wrong index. Both 3″ × 5″ cards and matching trays are now often available free of charge from libraries that have converted their card catalogs to online catalogs.

Typewriters. There is no law against writing entries on cards in neat handwriting or using a manual typewriter, as has been done for more than a hundred years, but these methods are now antiquated and too slow. Typed indexes should be produced on an electronic typewriter, most of which offer boldface typing, two or three choices of pitch, editing screens, spelling checkers, and other features that make neat and correct typing easier and faster. Even camera-ready copy can easily be produced on a good electronic typewriter.

Reference Works

An indispensable part of any indexer's equipment consists of REFERENCE WORKS, without which almost no index can be compiled successfully and cost-effectively. At the very least, one of each of the following should be at the indexer's elbow: an unabridged dictionary, an encyclopedia, a gazetteer, a biographical lexicon, and a guide to typographical practice, as well as one of the indexing standards listed on pp. xix–xx.

ERRORS

Errare humanum est—and since both the author and the indexer are human beings, errors may creep in at both ends. An author's errors may be discovered by the indexer during compilation: a misspelled name, a wrong date, a misplaced decimal, and the like. The indexer may wish to contact the author and ask for verification or correction. Most authors will either confirm that an unusual spelling is indeed the right one or be grateful for being made aware of an error, because book reviewers inevitably pounce on such mistakes and revile authors for their sloppiness.

An indexer's own errors—wrong or missing locators, misspelled names, missing subheadings, etc.—when detected right after the index manuscript has been sent to the printers, can sometimes still be corrected in the form of an "Errata" note if some space is available on the last index page or on any following blank pages. Alternatively, an errata slip can be inserted, though this is cumbersome and costly, so that publishers justifiably hate to do it, especially if it pertains to the index only and not also to the text. Nobody likes to draw attention to one's own errors, and it is questionable whether users will always notice corrections, much less whether they will enter them in the index at the appropriate place; but it is better for everybody involved—the author, the publisher, the indexer, and the user—to admit fallibility and to correct errors than to let them stand in the vain hope that nobody will detect them. An all-too-rare example of an errata slip for a major blunder had to be issued by Slavika Publishers of Columbus, Ohio; it ran as follows:

> Please note that due to an error all page numbers given in the index of Debrezeny and Lekman's *Chekhov's art of writing* are three too high. If the index says 70 you should read 67; if the index says 188, you should read 185, and so forth. Please put this slip into the book before page 193 (the first page of the index). We regret any inconvenience this may cause you.

EXHAUSTIVITY

Exhaustivity refers to the extent to which concepts and topics are made retrievable by means of index terms. At its lowest level it is no more than summarization by one or only a few terms, whereas high exhaustivity is the result of an analytical approach in which index terms are assigned to every name, event, object, method, action, agent or patient, location, or viewpoint that is deemed to be of interest to potential users. Thus, exhaustivity is a function of indexing *policy:* what an indexer decides to index, or what the manager of an indexing operation (such as a bibliographic database) decides to be an appropriate level for the type of material indexed.

The summarization approach is the one most often used in library catalogs of books, while detailed analytical indexing is generally the hallmark of good back-of-the-book indexes, especially for scientific, medical, and legal texts as well as for serial legal publications such as law reports, governmental regulations, and the like. The indexing of most PERIODICALS falls somewhere in between, since the average article seldom gets more than two or three index entries, although some scientific journals are much more exhaustive in their indexing.

The measure of exhaustivity is often thought to be the number of index terms assigned to a text, because summarization may result in no more than two or three terms, even for a large book, while highly analytical indexing may yield a dozen terms or more for a short article. But the topics discussed and the way they are treated also determine the possible and desirable level of exhaustivity, independent of the type or size of the text. Thus, two documents on the same broad topic, and of about equal length, may have to be indexed at different levels of exhaustivity, depending on whether one of them is a historical investigation containing many names of persons and places, while the other takes a philosophical or theoretical approach, perhaps needing fewer terms.

An example of various levels of exhaustivity in the indexing of the same document would be the following. Assume that a college-level textbook, *Elements of human anatomy and physiology* (Boolootian 1976), is to be indexed. When library catalogs were limited to cards, the book would have been indexed by the terms "anatomy, human" and "physiology, human" only (the inverted headings prescribed by the *Library of Congress subject headings*). Even in many current electronic library catalogs the same very low level of exhaustivity is still being offered to the public. In more sophisticated online catalogs a higher level of exhaustivity may be achieved by using some of the CHAPTER HEADINGS in the book, though not always in the form in which the author wrote them. The first chapter has the title "The organized individual"—a nice label for an introduction but hardly a meaningful index term. The second chapter is "Cell morphology and chemistry"; these are useful index terms, but they must be recast as "cells", followed by the subheadings "chemistry" and "morphology", with reciprocal entries under "morphology" and "chemistry", where "cells" will become subheadings, together with many other topics whose morphology or chemistry is being discussed. Other chapters, e.g., "The skeletal system" or "The muscular system", will simply become "skeleton" or "muscles", and so on.

The printed index of the book (which has 460 text pages) will provide a fairly high level of exhaustivity because an average of 5 index terms per page are listed, resulting in an index of more than 2,300 terms. Book indexes generally provide the highest level of exhaustivity per textual unit (normally a printed page).

High exhaustivity is particularly important for the indexing of journal articles by bibliographic databases in order to satisfy the information needs of general users as well as those of specialists. The following examples of two scientific articles* (one from the "soft" and the other from the "hard" sciences) demonstrate the average level of exhaustivity provided by databases for electronic post-coordinated searches.

In both cases, the indexing is based on the abstract accompanying each article (which is indeed the method frequently used by database indexers, provided that the abstract is well written and informative). Most of the indexing terms for Example A are from the *Thesaurus of psychological index terms* (American Psychological Association 1994) and those for Example B are from the 1993 edition of the *Inspec thesaurus* (1973–   ).

The indexing terms marked by an asterisk have been added by the indexer; they are not listed in the thesauri but appear in the abstracts and have been deemed to be sufficiently important for retrieval purposes. This, too, is a procedure commonly used by database indexers, as well as by experienced searchers who wish to achieve optimal retrieval results (Fidel 1992).

Example A:

Rules of language

Steven Pinker

Language and cognition have been explained as the products of a homogeneous associative memory structure or alternatively, of a set

---

*Both articles appeared in *Science* 253 (2 August 1991). The entries shown below for a printed periodical index are imaginary and do not appear in an index to *Science*.

of genetically determined computational modules in which rules manipulate symbolic representations. Intensive study of one phenomenon of English grammar and how it is processed and acquired suggests that both theories are partly right. Regular verbs (*walk-walked*) are computed by a suffixation rule in a neural system for grammatical processing; irregular verbs (*run-ran*) are retrieved from an associative memory.

Indexing terms: Associative processes. Cognitive processes. *English grammar. Grammar. Human information storage. Language. Memory. Neurolinguistics. *Suffixation. *Symbolic representation. Verbal memory. Verbs.

Example B:

Occurrence of earth-like bodies in planetary systems

George W. Wetherill

Present theories of terrestrial planet formation predict the rapid "runaway formation" of planetary embryos. The sizes of the embryos increase with heliocentric distance. These embryos then merge to form planets. In earlier Monte Carlo simulations of the merger of these embryos it was assumed that embryos did not form in the asteroid belt, but this assumption may not be valid. Simulations in which runaways were allowed to form in the asteroid belt show that, although the initial distributions of mass, energy, and angular momentum are different from those observed today, during the growth of the planets these distributions spontaneously evolve toward those observed, simply as a result of known solar system processes. Even when a large planet analogous to "Jupiter" does not form, an Earth-sized planet is almost always found near Earth's heliocentric distance. These results suggest that occurrence of Earth-like planets may be a common feature of planetary systems.

Indexing terms: Asteroids. Earth. *Earth-like bodies. Monte Carlo methods. *Planet growth. *Planetary embryos. *Planetary formation. Planets. Simulation. Solar system.

In a printed index to a volume of a periodical the same level of exhaustivity can be achieved, though the indexing terms may appear in a different format, similar to that of a book index, in which headings and subheadings are pre-coordinated. For Example A, the entries may be:

associative processes
cognitive processes
English grammar
    verbs
grammar *see also* English grammar
human information storage *see also* memory; verbal memory
language
    associative processes
    cognitive processes
    grammar
    suffixation
    symbolic representation
memory
        see also human information storage; verbal memory
    associative processes
    cognitive processes
suffixation
symbols
    representation in memory
verbal memory
verbs
        see also verbal memory
    irregular
    regular

For Example B, the entries may be:

asteroids
earth
earth-like bodies
    growth
formation of planets
growth of earth-like bodies
Monte Carlo methods *see also* simulation
planets
    embryos
    growth
simulation
        see also Monte Carlo methods
    growth of earth-like bodies
solar system
    asteroids

earth
planets

High exhaustivity will generally result in high recall: an exhaustive book index will allow the retrieval of all or most names mentioned and will reveal even minor facts or aspects of a topic, while an exhaustively indexed database will make possible the retrieval of all or most documents which have been indexed by particular terms. High exhaustivity may, however, also result in lower precision (that is, not only highly relevant documents but also marginally relevant ones will be retrieved) and it may even result in the retrieval of irrelevant information (fondly known as "false drops"). Thus, the Example B article may be retrieved in searches for Monte Carlo methods or simulation, although these topics are only subsidiary aspects in the article and would probably not furnish much information to a user interested in the two topics as such.

In certain indexing systems a limit is sometimes set for the number of index terms that may be assigned. Libraries did that in the past, often restricting the number of subject headings to no more than three because of the physical limitations of the card catalog; many of them still do so, though they now have online catalogs in which it matters little how many subject headings are assigned to a book. Limitations on the number of index terms have also been imposed by certain commercial indexing services covering journals. Such arbitrary restrictions are mostly counterproductive. The number of index terms assigned to a document should be governed solely by the amount of concepts and topics dealt with in a document, and the indexer should be free to assign as many terms as needed, because otherwise some information will not be retrievable or it may be distorted.

Now that you know the essentials of exhaustivity, look up also those of her twin sister, SPECIFICITY, without which there can be no DEPTH OF INDEXING.

BS 6529: 5.3
ISO 5963: 6.3
NISO Z39.4:

FICTION

Dr. Samuel Johnson, in a letter to his friend, the novelist Samuel Richardson, suggested to him the compilation of an index to his novel *Clarissa* so that "when the reader recollects any incident, he may easily find it". Moreover, such an index would be "occasionally consulted by the busy, the aged, and the studious" who would "want nothing to facilitate its [the novel's] use". Richardson followed Johnson's advice and compiled a combined index to his novels *Pamela, Clarissa,* and *Sir Charles Grandison* (1755), but his example was not widely followed, and novels have seldom been indexed. Only about a dozen or so indexes to fictional works are known to have been compiled from the mid-18th to the early 20th century, and indexes to contemporary literature can be counted on the fingers of one hand. Sir Walter Scott's *Waverley* novels were issued with very brief indexes in at least one of their many editions (but have now an extensive index running to 696 pages, compiled by Philip Bradley, the author of the survey discussed below); some of Jane Austen's novels were also indexed, but rather skimpily. A *Dickens index* (Bentley 1988), covering not only his novels but also his journalistic works and his life, fills a massive volume, and a *Guide to Proust* (Kilmartin 1984) similarly combines an index to *Remembrance of things past* with entries for the author's life and for real persons; the latter work was based on a French index to the original text. There is also another major French index to Balzac's *La comédie humaine,* consisting of four parts (characters, real and mythical persons, cities, and titles of works written by some characters) on 775 pages. Among modern novels, the busy James Joyce industry has produced several indexes and concordances to *Ulysses* and *Finnegans wake,* and George Orwell's *Nineteen eighty-four* has an extensive index of names and subjects in its Clarendon Press edition of 1984.

In the past, when people still read multivolume novels with complex plots and dozens if not hundreds of characters, the need for indexes of names and events may have been greater than now, when some of those same works are made into serialized TV dramas. Still, novels such as *Don Quixote, War and peace, The magic mountain, Gone with the wind,* and *Lord of the rings,* to name only a few mighty tomes with dozens or even hundreds of characters, places, and events, lack indexes, and many other classical as well as lesser known but voluminous and complex novels would also benefit from them. Long works of fiction are, after all, by no means a phenomenon of the days before TV: every year, many such works are written, published, and read (often in hundreds of thousands of copies), and many readers, particularly students who have to do assignments for literature courses, may wish to return to a passage in which a certain character appears, but find it difficult to do so for want of an index.

The blame lies, however, not entirely with publishers, most of which do not want to spend the extra money on an index to a novel whose fate in the highly competitive and turbulent literary marketplace is unsure. A survey on the need for fiction indexes, conducted among novelists, reviewers, members of literary societies, indexers, and plain readers of novels (Bradley 1989), revealed the surprising fact that there is relatively little interest in such indexes. The reluctance of publishers to provide indexes to novels is to a certain extent understandable though not entirely excusable, but when a novel becomes a best-seller and is being reprinted many times both in hardcover and in paperback, generating huge profits, it is difficult to understand why such works should remain indexless. The expense of indexing a best-selling novel would be a small fraction of its production costs. It could very well be that even more copies might be sold if the publisher would announce "John Wordsmith's superb and sexy spy thriller—now available with an index!"

Regarding novelists, most of them felt that novels were "not the sort of books that need to be indexed"; literary societies were only mildly interested; not even all indexers polled were enthusiastic about fiction indexes; and readers of fiction (including authors and reviewers) were about evenly divided between those who fervently pleaded for indexes and those who abhorred the idea.

Only one special type of index to fictional works is now being compiled more often than in the past, namely, concordances. Thanks to computer technology, it is now much easier to produce such word indexes once the text of a work is in machine-readable form. The first concordance to a literary work was, of course, one to the Bible, compiled by the Dominican Cardinal Hugo de Santo Caro (1200?–1263), who needed the help of five hundred monks even though his concordance listed only nouns, adjectives, and verbs. Later concordances were the work of single individuals, many of whom spent a lifetime listing every word in the Bible as well as in the works of Shakespeare, Dickens, Proust, Joyce, and other literary giants. The first machine-produced concordance was compiled in the early 1950s to the *Summa theologicae* of St. Thomas Aquinas, using a million or so 80-column IBM punched cards. This was soon followed by concordances to the Dead Sea Scrolls, Shakespeare, and classic or voluminous authors. By now, even relatively minor writers and works have been the subject of computer-produced concordances, listing every last word, including articles, conjunctions, prepositions, and sometimes even punctuation marks. Valuable as these word indexes are for literary criticism and historical research, they are of little use for the average reader of fictional works whose more mundane needs are still not being satisfied.

There is precious little that indexers can do to persuade authors and their publishers of the need and value of fiction indexes, seeing that even nonfiction works are often published without indexes, though they may be almost useless without such a finding aid. Only vigorous promotion of indexes by the SOCIETIES OF INDEXERS and by book critics of newspapers and literary reviews may perhaps ultimately succeed in convincing novelists, publishers, and even some members of the reading public that novels, too, need indexes.

The indexability of fiction and the problems faced by an indexer of modern fiction have been explored by Bell (1991*b*, 1992*c*).

FOOTNOTES

Genuine footnotes ought to be put on the list of endangered species and be protected from predators before they share the fate of the passenger pigeon. Computer typesetting, which in theory should have made it easier and quicker to put footnotes where they belong—at the foot of the page on which a reference is made to them—has made it more costly (though not more complex than in the days of Monotype and Linotype) to do so. Most publishers (with the honorable exception of a few university presses still publishing scholarly works with real footnotes) therefore relegate textual notes to the end of chapters or, even worse, to the end of books, just ahead of the index (if there is one). This forces the reader who wants to follow up such references to turn pages back and forth, thus interrupting the smooth flow of reading the text. Endnotes are not user-friendly; they are user-harassing.

But regardless of where they appear, should footnotes and endnotes be indexed? That depends on their nature and extent. If a note is, say, only the English translation of a phrase in a foreign language used in the text, or a similar brief annotation, it need not be indexed. But if in such a note the author of the quoted phrase and the work in which it appears are cited, that information ought to be indexed. Likewise, notes that contain (often quite lengthy) discussions, quotations, and citations which support an argument in the text must also be indexed if the user is not to be short-changed. Some authors, especially European scholars in the humanities, following a long-standing tradition, love to produce footnotes which sometimes cover almost an entire page, leaving only a few lines on top for the text itself, and spill over onto the next page. This certainly puts the cart before the horse and lends credibility to the opinion that footnotes ought not to be used at all because, if something is important enough to be discussed and cited, it could as well be integrated into the text, and if it is not that important, then why bother with a footnote at all? Yet, whatever the length of a discursive footnote or endnote, it ought to be indexed unless the editor, as sometimes happens, instructs the indexer not to index any footnotes.

In this book, footnotes have been used sparingly and, in general, for anecdotal matters only, which, if included in the discussion of a topic, would have unduly interrupted the flow of the exposition, while a busy reader choosing to skip such footnotes will not be deprived of essential information regarding the topic itself.

In legal texts, footnotes are of crucial importance, since they cite authorities or refer to statutes and precedent-setting cases. They must, therefore, be indexed very carefully and extensively. Names of authorities and the titles of their works are included in the general indexes to legal works, but cases and statutes are traditionally

indexed in the form of "Tables of cases" and "Tables of statutes",
which are displayed separately from the indexes to names, titles,
and topics.

A genuine footnote is indexed by adding the letter "n" to the
locator, e.g.,

Morison, Samuel E.   186n

which is unambiguous if there is only one footnote on a page. But
even if there are several footnotes on the same page (seldom more
than three), there is little risk of confusion.

Endnotes, on the other hand, may be quite numerous on a page,
especially if all notes are at the end of a book. If they are numbered
consecutively, those numbers may be given as subscripts to the
locator or following the letter "n", thus enabling a user to find a
specific endnote even among dozens on the same page, e.g.,

Smith, Mary 387_{18} *or*   Smith, Mary 387 n18

Things may, however, get more complex (both for the indexer and
the user of an index) when authors cite sources in the text only
implicitly, as in the following example:

Several studies[18] have found that the kiwi fruit is an excellent source
of vitamin C.

This sentence appears, say, on page 135 of the text. Endnote 18,
which appears on page 387 may be either a list of studies by Mary
Smith and others, but it may also be couched in narrative style, e.g.,

[18]Perhaps the most well-known study of the vitamin C content of
kiwi fruit is that of Mary Smith . . .

The problem in both cases is that Mary Smith is cited explicitly in
endnote 18 on page 387, but that she is also cited implicitly ("Several studies . . .") on p. 135; a user who is led by an index entry
"Smith, Mary 387n18" to the endnote has no clue to the text page to
which that endnote refers, namely page 135. A possible, though
somewhat cumbersome and space-consuming, solution is the enclosure of the locators for implicit citations of a reference in square
brackets, e.g.,

Smith, Mary 132, [135n 18], 147, 387n 18

where 132 and 147 refer to actual mentions of Smith's name, [135n 18] refers to the implicit citation, and 387n18 to the endnote. This practice, which is recommended in a slightly different form by the *Chicago manual of style* (1993, 17.28), must necessarily be explained in an INTRODUCTORY NOTE.*

The relegation of topical footnotes to the end of chapters or books has resulted in another custom that is highly user-unfriendly, namely, listing the bibliographic sources of notes only in endnotes instead of in the form of a bibliography arranged by authors' names or by subject. In index entries for this type of hidden bibliography, the locator for the first endnote citing a particular source is the most important one, because there the full bibliographic data of the source will be given, whereas the same source may be referred to in other endnotes only by the time-honored and space-saving, but again not very user-friendly, references "ibid." or "op. cit." When the first and only full citation of a source in a note is separated from subsequent citations of the same source by several other and quite unrelated notes, it becomes a tedious hide-and-seek game for the user to find the first note to which "op. cit." refers, because that note may not even be on the same page but on one of the previous pages, depending on where in the text the source was first cited. An index entry which pinpoints that crucial first note in which a source is identified can be a great time saver; unfortunately, such entries are seldom made because they would add a sometimes very large number of names to an index.

GREEK SCRIPT

The Greeks learned to write from the Phoenicians, whose consonantal alphabet—the first in the history of writing—they adopted, including the names of the letters. They adapted some letters for

---

*I am indebted to Nancy Mulvany who first drew my attention to this problem and formulated the example. See also Mulvany (1994*b*. pp. 96–97). H. H. W.

their vowels and added a few more for sounds not represented in the Semitic alphabet. The Greek alphabet was in turn used by the Etruscans, from whom the Romans took their—and our—alphabet. More than half of the 24 Greek capital letters are exactly the same as those we still use; only the lowercase letters look somewhat unfamiliar, though nine of them are also the same as Roman lowercase letters. The lowercase Greek letters are the ones predominantly used today in scientific terms and formulae, mainly in the fields of astronomy, biology, chemistry, mathematics, physics, and statistics.

Greek letters pose a problem in alphabetization, because, despite their common ancestry and close affinity to Roman letters, they cannot be arranged in the same alphanumeric sequence. There are three ways of dealing with the problem, depending on the discipline in which Greek letters are used.

1. *Disregarding Greek letters.* In biology and chemistry, Greek letters as prefixes or infixes of names or formulae are disregarded in alphabetization (as are also numerals, certain letters, and other prefixes) unless they constitute the only difference in a heading (*Scientific style and format: the CBE manual* 1994).

3-Ethyl-4-picoline
4-Ethyl-α-picoline
γFe_2O_3
Fe_3O_4
Gal$p$(β1–4)Glc (Lactose)
Glc$p$(α1–4)Glc (Maltose)

2. *Romanization.* In astronomy and physics, it is permissible to Romanize the name of a Greek letter in designations of stars or subatomic particles and radiation for the purpose of alphabetization:

Greek letter designation	*Romanization*
α Centauri	alpha Centauri
β rays	beta rays
γ rays	gamma rays
Λ hyperon	lambda hyperon
Ω^- hyperon	omega minus hyperon

3. *Arranging in a separate index.* All headings are alphabetized in the order of the Greek alphabet in an index separate from one in the Roman alphabet. This method is used in the humanities in order to

index Greek words, names, or phrases cited in the text in their original form, e.g., words or passages from the *Odyssey* or the New Testament.

Under no circumstances should headings written in Greek be intermingled with Roman-alphabet headings as if they had been Romanized. Nothing is being gained in terms of space by such a farrago, and users who know Greek may have some difficulty finding what they are looking for. Even though the Romanization of Greek is fairly standardized, the order of the letters in the Greek alphabet is different from that of the Roman one, so that some mental gymnastics is required to locate a Greek name or title among Roman script entries, e.g.,

> Phillips, Edward
> φίλον Ἰουδαῖοϛ*
> Phipps, James

(P is the 16th letter of the Roman alphabet, but φ, transliterated as ph, is the 21st letter of the Greek alphabet, close to its end.)

GROUPED ORDER

In indexes to large BIOGRAPHIES, collections of letters (*see* LETTERS AND DIARIES), or historical works on persons who were active in many different spheres of life and who may also have lived in several countries, many dozens or even hundreds of subheadings may be needed under the name of the person as main heading. Arranging them all in strictly alphabetical or chronological order, or (worst of all) in page number order, is clearly unhelpful.

An extremely bad example is the entry for Winston S. Churchill in the index to his own *The hinge of fate* (1950), volume 4 of *The Second World War*. It occupies six closely-packed columns on three pages, with more than 300 subheadings in page-order sequence—an exercise in futility and tedium which could have been relieved

---

*Philon Iudaios. The philosopher's name is better known in its Latin form Philo Judaeus.

by grouping the subheadings under, say, "As Prime Minister", "Military operations", "Relations with the United States", and a few others.

Thus, whenever the number of subheadings becomes so large that they fill more than one column, it is advisable to consider a grouped arrangement. Depending on the person and activities of a biographee, letter writer, or diarist, suitable paragraph headings may be chosen for personal matters, political, military, ecclesiastical, legislative, artistic, or literary activities, and so on. The number of subheadings under each group heading will then be much smaller and will neither intimidate nor confuse the user, as would an unbroken mass of subheadings stretching as far as the eye can see over several columns and pages.

A good example of such a grouping is the entry for Voltaire in the index of Will Durant's *The age of Voltaire* (1965). It occupies nearly three columns and is grouped as follows: "Early years in France"; "In France and in the Netherlands"; "In Germany"; "In Alsace and Lorraine"; "In Switzerland"; "At Fernay"; "Voltaire and science"; "Voltaire and social reform"; "Voltaire and the Jesuits"; "Voltaire and the war against Christianity"; "Voltaire, Diderot and Rousseau". All group headings are printed in small capitals, and each one forms a separate paragraph in run-in style, with individual subheadings arranged alphabetically.

Each paragraph in a grouped arrangement of subheadings must be clearly distinguished by an indention and a heading printed in a typeface different from that used for the sub-subheadings, e.g., small capitals or boldface, followed by the sub-subheadings in either alphabetical or chronological order. Each paragraph except the last one is to be punctuated at the end by a semicolon, but the last one remains without any punctuation after the last sub-subheading.

HOMOGRAPHS

Homographs are words having the same spelling but different meanings. They are often called *homonyms,* but that term, in the strictest sense, refers to words that may or may not be spelled differently but are pronounced the same way, which is not necessarily the case for homographs, as in *bow* (of a ship) and *bow* (a weapon). Since only the spelling of a word and its meaning are of importance in indexing, the term *homograph* is more appropriate.

Categories of Homographs

There are five major categories of homographs, each of which needs different QUALIFIERS. All qualifiers, except those for homographic forenames, are enclosed in parentheses (which are ignored in alphabetizing).

Personal names. Persons known by *forenames* only are qualified, in the case of popes and sovereign rulers, by Roman numbers followed by epithets, title, and / or name of the country; other persons known by forenames only are distinguished by place of origin, religious rank, occupation, epithet, or any other distinguishing term. Since numerals are arranged before letters, this results in a classified arrangement, because popes and rulers whose forenames are followed by a Roman number will automatically sort before the forenames of other people. If an index contains both forenames and surnames as homographs, the forenames are arranged before the surnames, which also entails classification (a feature otherwise to be avoided in an alphabetical arrangement). The resulting arrangement is, however, easily understood by users because it is the same as that found in library catalogs, bibliographies, and reference works. The following example is arranged strictly alphanumerically by the numbers and words following the homographic forenames in one sequence, followed by the homographic surnames in a second alphabetic sequence.

John
John I, East Roman Emperor
John I, King of Castile
John I, King of Portugal
John I, Pope
John III Sobieski, King of Poland
John IV, Pope
John IV, the Fortunate, King of Portugal

John V Paleologus, East Roman Emperor
John V, Pope
John VI Cantacuzene, East Roman Emperor
John, Archduke of Austria
John of Damascus
John, Saint
John the Baptist, Saint

John, Abigail
John, Thomas

This arrangement disperses the names of popes and those of rulers of the same country. If it is necessary or desirable to keep together the names of all popes and those of the sovereigns of each country who have the same forename, the arrangement would have to be first by number, then by title and country, transposing all other epithets of a sovereign to the end of the qualifier for the country, e.g., John IV, King of Portugal, the Fortunate.

Homographic *surnames* are normally distinguished by one or more forenames; if the forename is also a homograph, further distinguishing elements must be added: either dates of birth and death (or one of those if the other is not known), profession, or any other personal characteristic, e.g.,

Smith, Andrew
Smith, George (1789–1846)
Smith, George (1831–1895)
Smith, George Adam
Smith, George (anthropologist)
Smith, George (novelist)
Smith, George William

Corporate names. Homographic CORPORATE NAMES may be either those of different corporate bodies that happened to choose the same name (mostly in different countries) or those of the same organization working in different places in the same country or internationally. If they appear in the same index, they must be differentiated by place names, e.g.,

American Red Cross (Maryland)
American Red Cross (Virginia)

Labour Party (South Africa)
Labour Party (United Kingdom)

Place names. Homographic PLACE NAMES are differentiated by adding the name of the city, county, state, province, department, region, or a physical feature, such as lake, mountain, or river, as qualifiers; if necessary, two qualifiers may have to be combined, e.g.,

Don (river, England)
Don (river, U.S.S.R.)

Topical homographs. The different meanings of homographic terms for topics are indicated by qualifiers denoting the discipline, field of application, environment, or any other appropriate distinguishing characteristic, e.g.,

cells (biology)
cells (electricity)
cells (politics)
cells (prisons)

Titles. Identical titles of works are distinguished by the name of the author, e.g.,

Don Quixote (Cervantes)
Don Quixote (Strauss)

If the author's name is not known, the form of a work may serve as a qualifier, e.g.,

Abalone (poem)
Abalone (song)

Identical titles of periodicals are differentiated by place of publication, e.g.,

Natura (Amsterdam)
Natura (Milan)

Alphabetization of Homographs

Homographs in indexes to books and periodicals are no more difficult to alphabetize than any other headings because they are generally not very numerous, are distinguished by their qualifiers, and
are alphabetized by them, as shown in the examples above. Such is
not the case in large library catalogs, in which often dozens or even
hundreds of homographic personal, corporate, and place names, as
well as subject headings and titles, may have to be alphabetized.
The arrangement of all such homographs in one unbroken alphabetical sequence, governed only by the numbers and words following the homographic keyword, would disperse the various categories of homographs and would make it difficult if not impossible to
find all entries for, say, London as the name of the city, or all entries
for people with the surname London, or all corporate bodies whose
name begins with London, not to mention the titles of books beginning with London. For this reason, library rules for alphabetization
of catalog entries always prescribed a classified sequence for the
arrangement of homographs, although it is doubtful whether library users (other than librarians and filing clerks) were ever aware
of it or could make sense of the arcane and complex rules. Even the
post-1980 arrangement rules for libraries (except those of ALA)
prescribe certain classified sequences for the arrangement of homographs, but these are in most instances not suitable for the arrangement of homographs in indexes because, as mentioned above, the
relatively small number of homographs does not justify a classified
arrangement, nor would it be easy to explain to index users in what
kind of classified order the homographs are arranged.

The best way of alphabetizing homographs is to follow ALA rule
2.1, which stipulates that homographs should be arranged strictly
by the sequence of words following the homographic lead terms,
disregarding any punctuation (including parentheses or commas).*
The resulting arrangement will also be the one most easily understood by users.

---

*This is not the actual wording of the rule but a paraphrase of its text, together
with the provision of rule 1.2 on disregarding all punctuation.

Only in very long and complex indexes containing large numbers of homographic entries will it be necessary to resort to the classified arrangements prescribed by the other major arrangement rules namely BL, rule 4.3 and BS 1749, rule 7, both of which establish the following order:

personal names
   forenames
   surnames
corporate names/place names
subjects
titles

and LC, rule 4, which prescribes the following order:

forenames
surnames
place names
corporate names
subjects
titles

These rules specify further subdivisions which are, however, intended for bibliographic entries in library catalogs and will normally not be needed in indexes.

The following examples show the considerable differences between an alphabetical and a classified arrangement of different categories of homographs. In the alphabetical arrangement, Washington as a forename sorts before an identical topical heading, in accordance with ALA rule 2.2

Alphabetical arrangement	*Classified arrangement (LC rule 4)*
Washington [forename]	Washington [forename]
Washington [topical heading]	Washington, Booker T.
Washington Associates Ltd.	Washington, George
Washington, Booker T.	Washington, Martha
Washington, D.C.	Washington, Walter
Washington from above	Washington, D.C.
Washington Gas Light Co.	Washington (Indiana)
Washington, George	Washington, Lake
Washington (Indiana)	Washington Land

Washington, Lake	Washington (Missouri)
Washington Land	Washington (Pennsylvania)
Washington, Martha	Washington (State)
Washington (Missouri)	Washington Associates, Ltd.
Washington (Pennsylvania)	Washington Gas Light Co.
Washington (State)	Washington [topical heading]
Washington, Walter	*Washington from above*

Considering that, at last count, there were 1 capital city, 1 state, 1 monument, 1 bridge, 7 mountains, 8 rivers, 9 colleges, 10 lakes, 33 counties, and 121 cities, towns, and villages in the United States alone named after the first U.S. President, it is easy to see why a classified arrangement is preferred in gazetteers.

ALA: 2.1; 2.2
BL: 3.1; 4.3
BS 1749: 6; 7
BS 3700: 5.3.1.4
ISO 999: 7.2.1.3(c)
LC: 4; 5
NISO Z39.4:

HYPHENATION

All current arrangement rules prescribe that a hyphen is to be disregarded in alphabetization. This means that in word-by-word arrangement a hyphenated compound is treated as two words separated by a space. There are no exceptions to this rule, so that even hyphenated prefixes which cannot be used standing alone are arranged as if they were separate words. The prefixes

anti-, auto-, bi-, co-, hyper-, hypo-, infra-, inter-, intra-, macro-, micro-, non-, post-, pre-, pro-, pseudo-, quasi-, re-, self-, semi-, sub-, supra-, un-, tri-, vice-

and some others are generally written together with the following word without a hyphen in the United States, whereas they are often written with a hyphen in the U.K.

So-called "double-barrelled" PERSONAL NAMES, that is, those written with a hyphen between two (or more) parts of a surname, are also treated as two separate names and arranged under the first part; a cross-reference from the second part may be made if deemed necessary:

Badura-Skoda, Paul 59, 67, 92, 113, 147, 209, 260	Skoda, Paul Badura- *see* Badura-Skoda, Paul

Hyphenation of headings and subheadings at the end of index lines should be avoided as far as possible, and instructions to that effect should be given to the typesetters if the index is not delivered to the publisher in a machine-readable format from which misplaced hyphens have been eliminated.

Specialized software, named *Hyphenologist,* has been developed (McIntosh 1990). It hyphenates automatically in both American and British style, as well as in a number of other languages.

ALA: 1
BL: 1.2
BS 1749: 4.1
BS 3700: 6.2.1.2(a)
LC: 12
NISO Z39.4:

ILLUSTRATIONS

Illustrations—drawings, reproductions of artistic works, photographs, diagrams and other technical graphics, as well as MAPS— are accompanying a large and ever increasing number of verbal texts, both in books and in periodical articles. This development has no doubt been caused by the pervasive influence (not to mention competition) of television and video recordings as well as by modern reproduction and printing techniques which have made it possible to provide high-quality color illustrations in any type of publication at a reasonable price. It is not unusual to find articles consisting of one third of verbal text and two thirds of illustrations, especially in the life sciences, and even desktop publications are frequently illustrated in black and white or in color.

Unfortunately, illustrations are often much less thoroughly indexed than the verbal text to which they are attached. Even worse, illustrations are often not indexed at all, or if they are, their topic—*what* they show—is mostly subsumed under the heading for the person, object, or operation shown; that may indeed often be all that is needed, but details of a picture, style of presentation, or the mood conveyed to the viewer—*how* an illustration shows its subject—are seldom indexed. Yet those are just the aspects that are the reason for the old Chinese proverb "A picture is worth a thousand words", and Turgenev's similar remark "A picture shows me at a glance what it takes dozens of pages of a book to expound"* is even more apt in the context of indexing. For example, pictures in a biography should not merely be indexed by a string of locators under the name of the biographee but also specified as to what they show about the person's life at various stages and in different environments or occupations. In an index to an examination of an artist's work, recurring themes expressed in his or her pictures may be linked to their reproductions, e.g., anguish, fear, loneliness, sorrow, and death in the works of Edvard Munch. Such indexing of pictures by their meaning and emotional impact has been discussed by Krause (1988), Orbach (1990), and Shatford (1986, 1994).

The somewhat cursory indexing of illustrations or even the complete absence of index entries for them is, however, not always the fault of the indexer. When the text of a book is being submitted for indexing in the form of page proofs, the illustrations are seldom included, simply because they may not yet be ready. Even if they are, they may be handled by different editors and departments at the publishers, or they may be produced by a different printer, especially if they are not printed by letterpress but by another printing process. For economic as well as technical reasons, publishers often have the text of a book printed in one country (not necessarily

Fathers and sons, ch. 16.

their own) while the artwork is produced in another country. Small wonder, then, that the indexer of a book may not have any of its illustrations even though they may be referred to in the text. The indexer may not even have the benefit of a "List of illustrations", because such a list is part of the front matter, or "prelims", of a book (the part preceding the first text page) and is set in type only after all illustrations have been integrated with the text or placed near the pages referring to them on a "mechanical" or "paste-up" from which printing plates are prepared. It may even happen that a line drawing on a text page is at the last moment inserted or deleted, which may result in a change of pagination without anybody notifying the indexer of such a change—resulting in wrong locators for the topics dealt with on those pages, and the indexer being blamed for it. The indexer should, therefore, make an effort to obtain proofs of the paste-ups and to index the illustrations from them, even if that will entail last-minute additions or changes in the index manuscript.

In indexes to periodicals and newspapers this problem does not of course arise, because the indexer is working from actual issues in which all the illustrations are present. Likewise, for books consisting mainly of illustrations and relatively little or even no text at all except for the picture captions, such as art books, exhibition catalogs, photo essays, or popular picture books, the illustrations will be provided by the publishers when an index is being commissioned.

Two methods may be used to indicate the location of illustrations. One is the typographical differentiation of locators by printing them in italics or in boldface, or by adding an asterisk or enclosing them in square brackets. Although italicized numerals as locators for illustrations are widely used, they are often not easily discernible among a string of regular numerals for textual locators, so that users may have difficulties finding them. Boldface numerals are more conspicuous, but can then not be used for the indication of particularly important text passages. Asterisked or bracketed locators take up more space on a line, which may preclude their use if the number of illustrations is large. An illustration as frontispiece of a book must be identified by that term, since the page facing the title page is always unnumbered.

The second method of indexing illustrations is the use of a subheading which makes it possible to specify not only the place but also the type of picture:

Galilei, Galileo 13, 339–343
  Assayer, The 342
  portrait 355
  Sidereal messenger 341
    sketches of moon in 356
Golden Gate bridge
  cables 115
  construction 113–118
  photo: facing 120
  towers 117

This method is also the only possible one for a series of illustrations which is concentrated in one or more sections of a book between text pages but without any pagination, plate numbering, or numbers for individual pictures. In this case it is impossible to pinpoint the location of a particular picture, and the nearest substitute for a locator is the phrase "in section after x" where x is the number of the page preceding the picture section:

Watson, James Dewey
  double helix model of DNA 102–108, 112, 118
  Nobel prize 1962 20, 487
  photos in section after 198
  ribosome structure 494

BS 3700: 5.1.1.1
BS 6529: 4.2(e)
ISO 999: 7.1.1
NISO Z39.4:

INDEX: THE WORD, ITS HISTORY AND MEANINGS

If you are asked at a wine and cheese party what your profession or hobby is, and you answer proudly "I am an indexer", you may, depending on the background of your inquirer, be deemed to be a mathematician, a physicist concerned with optics, an anthropologist, a paleontologist, a geologist, an economist, a mechanical engineer, a forestry expert, or a computer scientist, possibly also a printer, a designer of playing cards, an employee of a motor vehicle licensing agency, or, of course, a person who tries to make the contents of books and journals retrievable by listing names and subjects in a predictable order, with an indication of their physical place in the source—in brief, an indexer of the kind that is most likely to read these lines. (Conversely, if you are applying for a credit card, stating your profession as "indexer", you may be rebuffed by a terse computer-printed note "No such occupation", as happened at one time to an indexer.)

It is, of course, not unusual that a common term assumes specialized meanings in various branches of science, technology, or business, but the word "index", which indexers tend to think of only or mostly in connection with their profession or hobby, has a particularly rich variety of applications. The reason for this is that the root of the word expresses a fundamental communicative action that transcends all languages and probably preceded them in the evolution of man: to show something to another human being by pointing to it with an outstretched forefinger.

Etymology: Where Does It Come From?

When looking up the word "index" in general English-language dictionaries that provide etymologies, or even in those specifically devoted to the history and genealogy of English words, such as the *Oxford dictionary of English etymology* (1966), *A comprehensive etymological dictionary of the English language* (Klein 1966–67), or *The Barnhart dictionary of etymology* (1987), one finds only that it is directly derived from the identical Latin word which originally meant "that which points out", hence "forefinger, pointer". To elicit more information, we must turn to large Latin dictionaries, where we may find that *index* also came to mean any kind of indicator, sign, token, or marker; a person who reveals or points out (from which developed the sense of one that betrays a secret, an informer, and a lookout man); the title slip of a scroll, and hence the title of a book; a summary or digest of a book or its table of contents; a list or catalog of books and their authors; and an inscription or caption. Many but not all of these shades of meanings have been preserved until our own time, and others have been added. The Latin noun, in turn, was derived from the stem of the verb *dicare*, which meant literally "to show", and the prefix *in-*, used to indicate the direction from a point outside to one within a limited distance, thus generating the verb *indicare*, which meant "to make known, point out, reveal, declare, give essential information" but also assumed the metaphorical (and more sinister) meanings of "to disclose, divulge, betray, give away, inform on" (the English verb "to indict" is related etymologically). Also closely related both in form and meaning is the verb *indicere* (*in* + *dicere*), which means "to give notice of, proclaim, announce, declare (war), impose, and inflict (e.g., punishment).

To revert now to the noun *index*, its ending *-ex* is the result of a simplified phonemic spelling, the *x* expressing the combined sounds of the final *c* of *dic-* (pronounced /k/) and the affix *-s*, which indicates the noun form. The *x* is used only in the singular *index*, whereas in the plural *indices* the *c* and *s* reappear. So far, we have traced *index* back to its Latin origins—but where did the Latin root come from?

When Latin became a written language it was already a highly developed and relatively late branch of the ancient and far-flung family of Indo-European languages. One of the remarkable features of the root of the word *index* is that, together with relatively few other roots, such as those for kinship terms (father, mother, brother, sister), it is not only found in most Indo-European languages, but is also preserved in its basic form from the most ancient languages of which we have documentary evidence down to the present form in various languages; moreover, these forms are easily recognizable even for someone not trained in comparative linguistics. Historical linguists assume that there once was a common Indo-European root *deik* (the asterisk indicates that the word is conjectural, i.e., not attested by actual written documents), meaning "to show, point out". It can be recognized in Sanskrit *didēṣṭi* "to show" and *diśā* "direction", as also in Avestan (the oldest known member of the Indo-Iranian branch of Indo-European, spoken in eastern Iran during the second millennium B.C.), which has *disyeiti*, and Hittite (an Indo-European-related language spoken in Anatolia between 2000 and 700 B.C.), which has *tekkušami* "I show", the first syllable of which is thought to be related to the Indo-European root. In classical Greek we find the verb *deiknunai* "to show" and the related *deixai* "to point out", from which the noun *deiktēs* "index, pointer" is derived, still being used also in modern Greek, although the word for book index is now *heuretērion*, derived from a root meaning "to find". (Both roots have found their way into English in the form of the adjectives *deictic* and *heuristic*.)

Turning now to the early medieval languages of northern Europe, we find Old English *taecan* "to show, instruct" (from which *teach* is derived) and also *tācn* "sign, mark" (our *token*). In Old High German there is *zeigon* "to point out" but also "to accuse" (from which comes the modern German *zeigen* "to show, point out" and the now somewhat obsolete *zeihen* "to accuse". In German as well as in many other Indo-European languages, including Latin, as we have seen, the word for "to show, point out" also assumed the meaning or was related to one that meant "to accuse, indict", evidently because the victim of or witness to a misdeed or crime pointed out its perpetrator to a judge, a practice still followed in our courts, where witnesses are asked to point out the person they are testifying about.

Since Latin was the language that rose to prominence and later to dominance during two millennia, giving birth to daughter languages spoken around the Mediterranean and beyond, both the verb and the noun *index* entered the vocabularies of the derivative languages and at a later date also that of the Germanic languages, whether by way of conquest or by cultural infiltration at a time when several vernaculars were spoken but only Latin (and to some extent Greek) was the language of worship and of learned discourse, both spoken and written. Thus, the word *index* has now become part of the vocabulary of every European language, including those of non-Indo-European origin, such as Finnish and Hungarian, although these languages have also developed their own words for the concept, namely, *hakemisto* (from *hakea* "to search") and *mutató* (from *mutatni* "to point out"), respectively. The meaning of the word is also fairly uniform across the languages of Europe, including those that were introduced into other parts of the world, as far as book indexes are concerned (with the major exceptions of German, which prefers *Register* (though *Index* is now also used), and Russian, which has *ukazatel'* (from *ukazyvat'*, "to point out").

The use of the term in the discipline of economics is also quite international. Yet, in addition to these translingually accepted meanings, the word *index* as used in English has acquired a plethora of meanings and denotations, some of which go far beyond its basic concept.

Grammar: Indices or Indexes?

The singular form of the word in English is *index*, but the plural may be written both in the traditional Latin form *indices* and in the Anglicized form *indexes*. The former is now generally thought to be obsolete and archaic, except in mathematics and occasionally in other scientific applications. The Anglicized plural *indexes* was commonly used already in Shakespeare's time, as witnessed by the often-quoted lines

And in such indexes (although small pricks
To their subsequent volumes) there is seen
The baby figure of the giant mass
Of things to come at large.

(*Troilus and Cressida*, I, iii, 343)

This was duly recognized in the late 19th century, when the fascicle of the *Oxford English dictionary* (*OED*) containing the word *index* was edited (it was published in 1900). The Latin plural should certainly not be used in the bibliographic sense; it would be incorrect and stilted to say "I compiled the indices to several books".

Semantics: What Does It Mean?

The various meanings in which the English word *index* and some of its derivations are used in different branches of scholarship and technology have been collected from the two most comprehensive and prestigious sources, namely, the *Oxford English dictionary* (*OED*) (1888–1933), including its *Supplement* (1972–86), and *Webster* (1961). The *OED* is the more exhaustive one, not only regarding the quotations on which the lexical meanings are based, but also regarding the number of such different or variant meanings. Webster offers, however, a few combinations of *index* with other words not found in the *OED,* and one additional combination was found in the *Dictionary of American English* (1936–44). Definitions of meanings and usages have been slightly adapted and shortened, and are not necessarily identical with those given in the respective sources. The year of the earliest recorded quotation for a particular sense is given below in parentheses after the definition, but it should be borne in mind that these dates indicate often not the very first written occurrence but only the earliest that came to the attention of the *OED* lexicographers. At any rate, words were always used orally as well as in private and ephemeral writing (e.g., in letters and notes) long before they found their way into more permanent documents, so that an *OED* date indicates only that a word has not been used for the first time later than that date. Since both the *OED* and *Webster* are held in many libraries, only a few quotations will be given here because they would take up too much space and can easily be found elsewhere.

Literal senses. The *OED* senses 1–3 might be called the literal senses of *index,* namely: forefinger, often, but not exclusively, when used in an anatomical context (1398); a piece of material that serves as a pointer, particularly on a graduated scale of an instrument (1594), and especially so on surveying instruments (1571); the hand of a clock or watch and the gnomon of a sundial (1594).

Metaphorical senses. *OED* sense 4 is the metaphorical use of *index,* meaning a guiding principle (1598) or a sign or token of something else (1607).

Figurative senses. The *OED* senses 5–10 may be called figurative or applied, in that the noun *index,* its combinations with other nouns, and its derivations *to index, indexing,* etc. are used for various devices, methods, or tools which in one way or another are linked to the basic concept of showing or pointing out, even though a few applications seem to be rather far-fetched and only tenuously connected with the basic sense.

Pragmatics: How Is It Used?

The following branches of learning and industry are listed here in the order in which their earliest use of the word *index* has been recorded in the *OED* or other sources.

Book indexes. Members of the societies of indexers may well take pride in the fact that this sense of *index* is indeed the oldest among the figurative or applied senses of the word, and that this specific usage (like the word itself) goes back to ancient Rome. There, when used in relation to literary works, the term *index* was used for the little slip attached to papyrus scrolls on which the title of the work (and sometimes also the name of the author) was written so that each scroll on the shelves could be easily identified without having to pull them out for inspection: "... ut [librarioli] sumant membranulam, ex qua indices fiant, quos vos Graeci ... sillybus appellatis" (so that [the copyists] may take some bits of parchment to make title slips from them, which you Greeks call sillybus) (Cicero, *Atticus*, 4.4a.1). From this developed the usage of *index* for the title of books: "Sunt duo libelli diverso titulo, alteri 'gladius', alteri 'pugio' index erat" (There are two books with different titles, one called "The sword", the other having the title "The dagger") (Suetonius, *Caligula*, 49.3). Those two books, by the way, were what we would call today "hit lists" of people whom Caligula wished to have assassinated shortly before that same fate befell him. At about the same time, in the first century A.D., the meaning of the word was extended from "title" to a table of contents or a list of chapters (sometimes with a brief abstract of their contents) and hence to a bibliographical list or catalog. Thus, Pliny the Younger (*Epistulae*, 3.5.2) writes to his friend Baebius Macer, who had asked for a list of books by Pliny the Elder, the author of *Historia naturalis:* "Fungar indicis partibus, atque etiam, quo sint ordine scripti [libri] notum tibi faciam" (I will provide for you a bibliography and arrange it in chronological order). Similarly, Seneca (*Epistulae*, 39) tells a certain Lucilius, who had asked him to suggest suitable sources for an introductory course in philosophy: "Sume in manus indicem philosophorum" (Pick up the list of philosophers), referring to a list of authors' names and the topics on which they had written.

However, indexes in the modern sense, giving exact locations of names and subjects in a book, were not compiled in antiquity, and only very few seem to have been made before the age of printing. There are several reasons for this. First, as long as books were written in the form of scrolls, there were neither page nor leaf numbers nor line counts (as we have them now for classical texts). Also, even had there been such numerical indicators, it would have been impractical to append an index giving exact references, because in order for a reader to consult the index, the scroll would have to be unrolled to the very end and then to be rolled back to the relevant page. (Whoever has had to read a book available only on microfilm, the modern successor of the papyrus scroll, will have experienced how difficult and inconvenient it is to go from the index to the text.) Second, even though popular works were written in many copies (sometimes up to several hundreds), no two of them would be exactly the same, so that an index could at best have been made to chapters or paragraphs, but not to exact pages. Yet such a division of texts was rarely done (the one we have now for classical texts is mostly the work of medieval and Renaissance scholars). Only the invention of printing around 1450 made it possible to produce identical copies of books in large numbers, so that soon afterwards the first indexes began to be compiled, especially those to books of reference, such as herbals (Wellisch 1978). The terms *index* and *table* were, however, applied somewhat indiscriminately to tables of contents (following the example of the ancients) and to indexes proper, i.e., those of names and subjects, the latter inserted either after the table of contents or, increasingly towards the middle of the 16th century, at the end of the book. Although the now-obsolete use of *index* for "Table of contents" preceded that of an alphabetical list of names and subjects, the *OED* lists the first reference to the latter in 1578, while the former is taken from Shakespeare's use of the word (1604), which in every instance refers to something preceding the main work (as is the case for a table of contents). For the alphabetical listing of names, subjects, and words, the more specific Latin terms *index nominum, index rerum,* and *index verborum,* respectively, were used in Latin as well as in some English and continental scholarly works until the end of the 19th century, but are now obsolete.

Index librorum prohibitorum (ILP). Closely related in time to the first modern indexes, the purpose of which was to make the finding of names and subjects in books easier, the infamous *ILP* was intended to identify books that good Catholics were not supposed to read at all. First published in 1564, it was soon followed in 1571 by the *Index expurgatorius,* which allowed people to read some of the books in the *ILP* provided that the offending passages had been deleted. (One of the most famous books listed in that *Index* was

Copernicus's *De revolutionibus* in which, amazingly, the heliocentric theory as such was not expurgated, but only those passages that openly contradicted the biblical account of cosmology.) The word *Index* in the title of these two works is of course Latin and thus has no direct connection with English usage, but they are so well known and have had such considerable influence that most dictionaries and encyclopedias list and explain these works together with the other uses of *index*.

Music. Here we encounter another obsolete use of the word *index*, namely, for a sign similar in appearance to a handwritten lowercase *w* which was used at the end of a stave to direct a player to the first note on the next stave (1597); it was therefore also called a *direct*.

Mathematics. In this field, an index or index number is a numeral or symbol written above or below, to the left or right of another numeral or symbol to indicate its position or an operation to be performed on a number or entity (1674). Thus, a_{23} means an element in the second row and third column of a matrix, and $\sqrt[3]{5}$ is shorthand for "cubic root of 5". Powers of a number are expressed by an *integral index*, e.g., x^2, roots by a *fractional index*, e.g., $x^{1/2}$, and reciprocals of a power by a negative index, e.g., $x^{-2} = \dfrac{1}{x^2}$ and there are other specifically named mathematical indices (here, as mentioned earlier, the Latin plural is still being used). There is also the *index set*, which is the set whose elements are used to indicate the order of elements of a series, e.g., $a_1, a_2, a_3 \ldots a_n$, where 1, 2, 3 . . . n are the members of the index set.

Printing. The sign of a hand ☞, formerly quite widely used, especially in advertising, is first mentioned in 1727 as an *index*, but the sign may of course be considerably older.

Scientific uses. It seems that *index*, either alone or in combination with other terms, found its way into scientific terminology towards the end of the 18th century, when increasing specialization and more exact measurements became the hallmark of modern science, which developed by then from the general pursuit of "natural philosophy". Again in the chronological sequence indicated by the earliest quotations, we encounter the *index glass* or *index mirror* (1773) as a part of astronomical and surveying instruments, the *index of refraction* in optics (1829), the *cephalic index* in anthropometry

(1866), *index maps* in cartography (1869), *index fossils* in paleontology (1900), *index forests* (1905), which are those that reach the highest density in a given locality, *index* and *index register* in computer science (1952), and *index horizons* in geology (1956); in addition, there are *index species* in biology and *index percent* in forestry (the increase in value of a tree or forest as an annual percentage of its present value), these terms being provided by Webster without indication of earliest use, but presumably sometime in the first half of this century.

Industry. The uses made of *index* and *indexing* in different branches of manufacturing are varied and not always obvious as far as their meaning is concerned. Thus, in the textile industry we find an *index machine* (1850), which was a kind of Jacquard loom, followed in mechanical engineering by a whole host of *index arms, bars, centers, circles, cranks, heads, pins, plates, spindles,* and *index tables* (1863–1950), most of which are used in the exact machining of parts that are being moved a certain distance between each operation, e.g., in the cutting of gear teeth. The word is now widely used in mechanical engineering and tool making in a sense rather far removed from what the layman (and the indexer!) would readily understand.

Since indexers of books use cards (though most have switched to microcomputers and word processors), it is only natural that the paper industry providing them with *index cards* uses the term *index board* (1937), also known as Bristol board, for the special sort of paper used to manufacture them. But, as we shall see in the "public administration" section, the same term had been used more than a hundred years earlier for a completely different purpose.

Economics. Rather surprisingly, the use of *index* and *indexing* in the sphere of economics seems to have escaped the notice of the *OED* lexicographers toiling under the stern direction of James A. H. Murray, although the words had by then long been in use in the senses only too well known to everybody today. Perhaps Frederick J. Furnivall and other members of the Early English Text Society who provided most of the original material for the compilation of the *OED* did not care too much for the writings of those engaged in the "dismal science" during a period which for them was the contemporary scene, namely, from the last three decades of the 19th century and on (and Adam Smith apparently had not used the word). Only the supplement to the *OED* revealed that the word had been used as early as 1875 to indicate variations in prices or values compared to a certain base period, from which later developed such things as the *cost-of-living index* (1913), the *Dow-Jones index* of stocks in the U.S. (1880's), and the *indexing* of wages, pensions, and taxes.

Public administration. An early and exclusively American use of *index board* (1830), recorded in the *DAE*, was as a term for street signs, but it seems that by the end of the 19th century it had gone out of fashion. The most recent combination of *index* with another word, and one probably limited to the U.K., is *index number* and *index plate* (1973), used instead of the more usual license number or plate of automobiles, motor cycles, and other motor vehicles. This, too, could be ambiguous, since there are also index plates in mechanical engineering and index numbers in mathematics, both with completely different meanings.

Derivations. All dictionaries treat the word *index* first in its capacity as a noun, although, as we have seen, it is itself derived from a verb. However, the verb *to index* is, at least in English, of more recent origin than the noun. The *OED* lists its first use in the sense "to furnish (a book etc.) with an index" in 1720, and "to enter (a word, name, etc.) in an index" in 1761. Ironically, the historic sense of the verb, namely, "to point out, to indicate", does not seem to appear in the literature before 1788, i.e., about half a century after its earliest use for listing purposes.

Needless to say, other derivations can easily be formed from the root *index*, such as *indexical* (1828), *indexer* (1856), *indexed* (1872), *indexing* (1887), *indexible* (or *-able*, take your choice, but the *OED* prefers *-ible*) (1951), *indexation* (1960), and, sad to say, *indexless* (which still too many books are), a situation first deplored by Carlyle, who coined the word in 1858.

All other senses of the noun have also been conferred on the verb, including the putting of a book on the *ILP* and the rotating of a piece of material that is to be machined through a certain part of a complete turn. Related to this is the indexing of microfilms, i.e., the various methods used to identify a certain frame for retrieval, especially in motorized microfilm readers.

Relationships to Other Concepts and Their Terms

Both the noun and the verb *index* are related to other words expressing cognate concepts, most of which have already been dealt with earlier under the various usages. The source for these and other relationships is, of course, *Roget's thesaurus*. In one of its latest editions the word *index* is shown to be related to the following, here given in the serial order in which they appear in that work: to relate (make a reference to, refer to, allude to, mention); to class (list, file, tabulate, alphabetize); numerical element (exponent, logarithm); list; finger; gauge; indicator; record (n: file, waiting list, card, microform; v: docket, file, catalog, archival store); edition (appendix, supplement), e.g., there may be an edition of a book with and without an index.

Odds and Ends

Inevitably the word *index* has been linked to other words in facetious, derogatory, and otherwise unclassifiable ways. The *OED* lists *index-hunting* (1699), followed by an *index-hunter* (Smollett 1751), *index-learning* (Pope 1728) and *index-rakers* (1876), none of which are complimentary. Then there are *index pips* (1899), which are the miniature indications of the denomination and value of playing cards printed in the corners. This and the outstretched index finger are the only illustrations of *index* in *Webster*.

Finally, if you as a reader or indexer discover an error in the index of a book or journal, do not lightly call it an *index error:* you might mislead a scientist who uses the same term for the error in the reading of an instrument whose scales are not carefully enough calibrated in relation to each other, thus resulting in erroneous measurements. In both cases, though, *errare humanum est,* which brings us right back to the Latin roots of *index*.

INDEXABLE MATTER

All indexes except complete concordances leave out something in the text they seek to make accessible for retrospective searching. Indexers are thus constantly making value judgments as they go through the pages of a work, deciding what to include and what to exclude from the index. That is what makes indexing an intellectual challenge without which it would be mere drudgery, and what makes it an art—at least as long as human beings will do it—and neither a mere technology nor a science. On the other hand, just this dependency on human value judgments and the inconsistencies, vagaries, and sheer follies of the resulting indexes are the reasons for attempts at automatic indexing, all of which rely in one way or another on the words of a text and are thus trying not to leave out anything except some function words (though these may often be just the ones that help to make sense of other words and avoid ambiguities).

The following guidelines are limited to book indexes and focus on certain parts of a text, because the criteria for inclusion or exclusion of topics or names from articles in PERIODICALS and NEWSPAPERS are discussed in those sections.

The first part of a book is the *title page*, which quite obviously is not to be indexed even if a quotation from some famous author should grace it, as was often the custom of authors in the more distant past.

A *dedication*, until the 18th century to a (generally high-born) sponsor or benefactor but now most often to a member of the author's family, may also safely be disregarded.

Next comes the *table of contents*, which today is not indexed but was itself labeled "Index" in the early days of printing and until about the mid-18th century because it listed not only chapter headings but often also contained summaries of each chapter and its subdivisions, as well as their locators.

The *preface* or *foreword* is at best a brief recommendation written by a good friend of the author or by a more or less well known authority in the field who could be persuaded to say a good word about the work and at worst just a piece of puffery. Generally, none of this should be indexed. A preface may also often serve as a vehicle for *acknowledgments*, or these may appear as a separately titled part. In any case, they are not to be indexed, even if famous persons may be among those thanked by the author.

The *introduction*, written by the author, is the first part of a book to be seriously considered by an indexer because it gives a general overview of the work, may discuss the contents chapter by chapter, and states the intended audience and purpose of the work—all invaluable for the indexer as general guidelines for the task ahead, and often providing the most important headings. But since these headings are certain to appear in the index, augmented by subheadings and cross-references, it is in most cases not absolutely necessary to include their locators in an introduction, unless the author mentions them in contexts other than those treated in the text of the book, or if any other circumstances seem to make it desirable to include them in the index. The decision to include or exclude topics mentioned in the introduction is in any case not a crucial one, because inclusion will only add one or a few locators to their headings.

The *chapters* of a text are of course what must be indexed. CHAPTER HEADINGS are sometimes a good source of appropriate index headings, and synopses of chapters (now only seldom found, but once very popular with authors and editors) may yield additional headings, subheadings, and cross-references. The general criteria for what should and should not be indexed in a work are discussed under THE INDEXING PROCESS. Deciding which topics to put *into* an index is relatively easy because important ones will be mentioned frequently, and may be discussed at length; it is the minor and ephemeral topics that need extensive and thorough knowledge of the field of study treated in a book in order to decide what to leave out, as inevitably some of the most minute ones will have to be left out for reasons of economy and clarity. If there is any serious doubt in the indexer's mind regarding inclusion or exclusion, the author or editor may have to be consulted, constraints of time permitting.

PERSONAL, CORPORATE, and PLACE NAMES must generally be indexed, but when they are mentioned only in passing and with no real connection with the general topic of the book or with the life of a biographee (e.g., people present at a meeting who are not otherwise important or mentioned elsewhere, artists and their works seen by someone in a museum, or authors read) they should be disregarded. The *Chicago manual of style* (1993, 17.73–74) has good examples of such intentional omissions from an index.

Quotations, which occur most frequently in biographical and historical texts, are generally too long to be included as entries in an index and must, therefore, be paraphrased when referring to a topic. But when a quotation is brief (not exceeding, say, one or at most two column lines) it can be given as an entry. For example, in the index to a biography of Louis XIV, his famous dictum "L'état c'est moi" may be a quoted entry.

Notes, either in the form of FOOTNOTES or endnotes after chapters and at the end of a book, are often treated as stepchildren, and older textbooks on indexing even recommended to disregard them altogether. They should, however, be indexed, particularly if they provide topical information and if they contain bibliographical references. The latter now often serve as "hidden" bibliographies instead of a real one arranged alphabetically by authors and titles. But even if such BIBLIOGRAPHIES AT ENDS OF BOOKS conclude a book, they are more often than not neglected in the index, although most entries for the names of authors and for titles will need only one additional locator which may make the task of finding bibliographic references in long lists much easier.

Glossaries are often included in books on topics whose terminology is still unstable or full of neologisms and specific usages of terms by the author. The presence of a glossary should be indexed, and the terms defined in it (which will almost inevitably be employed in the text and thus have index entries) should also be indexed, preferably by a subheading "defined", e.g.,

floppy disks
   applications 37, 42–45
   defined 126
   handling 32

APPENDIXES may or may not have to be indexed, as discussed in more detail in that section, depending on their content and form.

Advertisements and other extraneous matter in books should normally not be indexed, but those in PERIODICALS are sometimes indexed by the names of advertisers.

BS 3700: 5.1.1
Chicago manual of style: 17.73–74
ISO 999: 7.1.1
NISO Z39.4:

INDEXING LANGUAGES: NATURAL AND CONTROLLED

When people wish to communicate verbally, either in speech or in writing, they use natural language. This statement is somewhat akin to Monsieur Jourdain's revelation that he had "been speaking prose without knowing it for more than forty years".* Until the advent of computers there was hardly any need to make such a statement, although it was always tacitly understood that there also existed a universal language, namely mathematics—a *formal* and man-made language. Today, the curse of Babel has also struck formal languages, namely those used to program computers, and their number rivals that of the natural languages. These formal languages are of interest to indexing only insofar as some of them are being used to program computers that can assist the indexing process in various ways, from automatic alphabetization and spelling checkers to the formatting and printing of indexes.

Regarding the indexing of written documents, *natural* language—the way an author chooses words to compose a text—is often contrasted with *controlled* language—the one used to index the same text. What is a controlled language? It is any subset of a natural language whose vocabulary, syntax (the way words are put together to form sentences or phrases), semantics (the meaning of words), and pragmatics (the way words are being used) are limited. Of course, what people seldom realize is the inescapable fact that natural language, when used by a speaker or writer, is also controlled. A person's natural language is always a subset of the potential resources of a particular language. It is limited by that person's size of vocabulary, knowledge of meaning and use of words, syntactic patterns, and modes of expression and style that are appropriate to a particular communicative situation; it is also governed by the linguistic conventions and habits characteristic of different disciplines and fields.* No two persons will ever use the same controlled

---

*Molière, *Le bourgeois gentilhomme*, II, 4.

*It has been found that texts in science and technology differ significantly in their syntactic patterns and sentence structures from those in the social sciences (Bonzi 1990), and the same is probably true for the humanities.

subset of a natural language in the same way (a fact that has made it possible for computers to detect spurious passages in classic texts).

All *indexing* languages, being used for the purpose of rearranging the conceptual structure of natural-language texts in condensed and predictable form, are, by definition, controlled. The control they are subjected to is far more stringent than the one exercised by human beings over their natural language, because:

1. In their *vocabulary* they may use only certain classes of words: primarily nouns, adjectives, participles, and gerunds (but almost no other verb forms), a few prepositions and conjunctions, almost no adverbs or pronouns and no interjections.
2. In their *syntax* they may use those words only in certain limited constructions: no complete sentences of the pattern subject-verb-object and no dependent clauses may be employed; on the other hand, some indexing languages allow syntactic constructions that are illegal in natural language syntax, namely inverted phrases of the type "schools, elementary, curriculum of".
3. In their *semantics* words may be restricted in their meaning, or if that meaning is ambiguous it must be separately indicated by QUALIFIERS.
4. In their *pragmatics* words may be used only in their basic or primary sense, but not in a metaphorical, allegorical, or symbolic sense.

Who exercises this control? The indexer, when following the conventions and rules of indexing and observing the limitations on the use of words and terms set by the embodiment of a controlled indexing language, namely, a THESAURUS or subject heading list.

What actually happens when a text is being indexed is, therefore, the application of a more or less tightly controlled indexing language to a more loosely and *differently* controlled natural language, with the aim of making the large variety in wording, syntax, and style of a text amenable to retrospective searching.

As seen from this perspective, the question of natural vs. controlled indexing language seems to be moot: all indexing, irrespective of the content or form of a text, is essentially performed by means of a controlled indexing language.

However, the issue began to assume entirely different characteristics in the early 1980s when it became feasible to search the full text of documents online. The availability of every text word, mainly in periodical articles, statutes, court decisions, and other relatively short documents offered the possibility of AUTOMATIC INDEXING of their natural language as a cheaper and faster alternative to human indexing by means of a controlled vocabulary.

It must be stressed at this point that the indexing of booklength documents was virtually never the subject of a comparison between natural language and controlled indexing because no algorithm has ever been designed that could produce from full text the equivalent of a back-of-the-book index compiled by a human indexer. Attempts to produce book indexes automatically resulted inevitably in either incomplete, inadequate, or, in most cases, ridiculously flawed "indexes" of no conceivable use (Mulvany & Milstead 1994).

The advantages and disadvantages of natural versus controlled languages for indexing and information retrieval have long been debated in the professional literature. Many proponents of automatic indexing claimed that natural language gave the same or even better results than the use of a controlled vocabulary by human indexers. Their most conspicuous and prolific spokesman is Gerald Salton whose SMART system (Salton 1983) and dozens of articles and reports on various automatic indexing methods are well known.

However, as a result of research into the actual effectiveness of the two approaches to indexing and retrieval, it is now generally acknowledged that this is not an either-or proposition, and that the most successful retrieval strategy consists of the judicious blend of the two approaches, if both are available. In the words of an experienced searcher of patents (a field in which it is of crucial importance to find not just some but all relevant documents prior to filing a claim),

> It's silly to argue whether one should use natural language or controlled language. Both are needed, both play an important role. . . . A test search showed very clearly that natural language and API's controlled indexing vocabulary each made a significant [and] unique contribution to retrieval (Kaback 1992, p. 199).*

The issues and problems of natural and controlled languages for indexing and retrieval have been studied by many researchers, out-

*API = American Petroleum Institute

standing among whom are Calkins (1980), Carrow & Nugent (1981), Crystal (1984), Fidel (1991, 1992), Fugmann (1982), Lancaster (1986, 1991), Rothman (1983), Svenonius (1976, 1986), and Wall (1980). An historical survey of the debate and a summary of the state of the art as of 1993 is offered by Rowley (1994).

Tabular summaries of the advantages and disadvantages of natural versus controlled indexing languages have been provided by Feinberg (1983, p. 262) and by Aitchison & Gilchrist (1987, p. 4).

It may be appropriate to conclude this discussion, which opened with a quotation from Molière, with another one from a famous French author, Maître François Rabelais, who in the Third Book of his *Gargantua et Pantagruel* said, *"C'est abuse, dire que ayons langage naturel"* (It is a misuse to say that we have a natural language).

THE INDEXING PROCESS

The making of an index has in the past often been described in how-to-do-it publications aimed at authors who have to index their own works (including some guidelines issued by publishers) as a pretty straightforward and fairly simple affair: nothing much to it, just underline "important" words and names, write them on cards, add page numbers, then shuffle the cards in alphabetical order and type the resulting list of entries. Since the advent of personal computers, many simplistic schemes of this type, geared to the capabilities of a machine, have been added. A typical example, published in a well-known computer journal, distilled the principles of indexing into the following recipe for "instant indexing":

> To index a book, you need to perform these basic steps: 1. Atomize: remove all punctuation, capital letters, apostrophized endings, etc. and put each word in the book on a separate line. 2. Unique: remove all duplicate words. 3. Sort: sort the resulting list of words. 4. Boring: remove "boring" parts of speech like "and", "the", "but", etc. 5. Page: assign page numbers to the remaining words of interest (Pountain 1987).

The author may have been serious and even proud of having solved a seemingly difficult problem quite easily—no muss, no fuss! But his simplistic advice amounts to no more than a caricature of the indexing process, based on the premise that a computer can pick out significant words from a text (that is, all those not on a stop list of so-called "unimportant" words such as articles, prepositions, conjunctions, and adverbs), sort them alphabetically, add page numbers, and print the result. The problems of syntactic and semantic ambiguity, synonymity, homographs, variant word forms, the fact that just the "unimportant" words may be crucial for the indication of relationships, and the recognition of concepts only implicitly mentioned are blandly ignored by the proponents of such schemes, who have unfortunately been able not only to publish but even to sell their brainchilds. The results, when appended to desktop-published TECHNICAL MANUALS AND REPORTS and even to otherwise well-written books as "indexes", are nothing short of disastrous.

Indexing, far from being merely the alphabetically arranged concatenation of text words, is, first of all, a creative process. Though always, by definition, dependent on the work of another creative mind—that of a writer, artist, or compiler of data—it transforms the original text into a homologous but functionally different structure. In that structure, topics and names mentioned here and there in the text are arranged in an ordered and easily scannable sequence, indicating their place in the text. At the same time, both their explicit and implicit relationships are displayed in a way in which the original text does not or cannot reveal them.

Like other creative processes, such as literary writing, painting, or composing music, indexing relies on certain technical rules which can be learned by example, training, and experience. Yet the creative inspiration that will result in a good and useful index can neither be learned nor taught. Therefore, "Indexing is something you will either enjoy or detest; there is little middle ground" (Mulvany 1994b, p. vii). And if you enjoy it, you will become a good and successful indexer.

Beginning indexers often ask whether there is a theory of indexing. If by this is meant a coherent system of propositions explaining the mental activities involved in transforming a text into its index, the only honest answer is that we do not have such a thing. To be sure, whole books and numerous articles have been written, purporting to reveal an indexing theory, but these are either mere discussions of technical rules and their interpretation, or they are more or less conjectural speculations on what goes on in the mind of a person who is indexing a text.

All we know is that indexing is a highly complex intellectual process involving the use of language in a specific and somewhat artificial way, and that it is also to a considerable extent a matter of intuition, the workings of which cannot be reduced to fixed rules. It is "knowing what but not knowing how". In this respect, indexing is similar to other mental operations such as the recognition of faces and voices: we know that we can do it, but cannot describe in so many words how we do it, nor can we reduce it to a set of rules. At most, the observable facts of the indexing operation can be described (Farrow 1991).

However, all this does not mean that indexing is an arcane or mysterious craft. Its basic techniques can be learned and the tasks to be carried out can be specified.

Indexing Tasks

Despite of what has been said above on the lack of a theory and the impossibility of reducing the mental process of indexing to a fixed set of rules, there is general agreement on a number of essential tasks which an indexer should carry out in order to produce a useful index.

The function of an index is to provide its users with an effective and systematic means for locating information in documents. The indexer should perform the following tasks when indexing a verbal text.* (The indexing of nonverbal or only partially verbal texts, inasmuch as it is different from that of verbal texts, is discussed under NONPRINT MATERIALS.)

1. Identify and locate topics and features in the document which are relevant to the needs of the intended users.

*The wording of the tasks listed below is a condensed and partially paraphrased version of BS 3700, 3; NISO Z39.4; and ISO 999, 4.

2. Discriminate between such relevant information and merely passing mention of a topic.
3. Exclude passing mentions of topics that are of no apparent value for intended users.
4. Analyze concepts, topics, and features that have been identified in order to provide access to them by means of index entries.
5. Produce headings that employ as far as possible the terminology used in the document, while at the same time considering synonymous or equivalent terms that may be sought by potential users.
6. Ensure that the headings used are appropriate to the needs of prospective users in order to enable them (a) to retrieve quickly and accurately information on a remembered item in a document known to a user; (b) to establish quickly the presence or absence of information on a topic or feature in a document not previously known but thought to provide such information; or (c) to identify desired or needed documents in a collection.
7. Group together references to topics that are scattered in the text of the document.
8. Combine headings and subheadings into coherent multilevel headings.
9. Indicate relationships among concepts and topics.
10. Direct the user seeking information under terms not used to those that are being used by means of *see* references.
11. Draw the attention of users to related terms by means of *see also* references.
12. Arrange all headings in a systematic and helpful order (usually alphabetical).

Examining the Text

In order to perform these tasks, the text must first be examined. This does not necessarily mean that it must always be read from beginning to end before the actual indexing can be undertaken, but the indexer should be reasonably sure that no major topic or aspect of the work has been overlooked.

When the document to be indexed is a book, its overall or central topic may be expressed in the title (though many modern titles tend to hide rather than to reveal what the work is all about). Other clues to major or minor topics can often be found in the table of contents; an abstract or summary, if provided; the preface; the introduction, in which the author generally explains the scope and aim of the work and names its main topics; the opening paragraphs of chapters; section headings; captions of illustrations and tables; and the concluding statement.

Regarding articles, the indexer may be guided by the title (with the same reservation as for books); an abstract or string of KEY-WORDS (now often required to be supplied by authors, especially in scientific or technical journals); the opening statement; and the conclusion. For further details on the topical analysis of articles *see* PERIODICALS.

This first examination should provide the indexer with a fair assessment of the degree of EXHAUSTIVITY that will be needed and should prevent the twin mistakes of over-indexing and under-indexing. Over-indexing—the listing of too many names and topics which may be trivial and of no value for users—is the lesser of the two evils, because what may turn out to be of little or no importance once the index has been finished can always be eliminated or corrected at the EDITING stage. But under-indexing—the omission of indexable items—has two dysfunctional consequences: it will shortchange and annoy users of the index; and, if seemingly minor items have not been indexed in the early parts of a document but are found to be dealt with at length later on, the indexer must backtrack to complete the indexing of the earlier parts, thus wasting time. The level of exhaustivity is sometimes determined by the author or the editor who, for example, may instruct the indexer to use only one level of modifying subheadings.

After this first cursory examination, the indexer should have formed a general idea of the document. It must then be read again more carefully, analyzing the text, selecting indexable topics, and assigning index terms.

Aboutness and Selection of Topics

What, in the context of indexing, is a topic or, as most people are wont to say, a subject? The *Oxford English dictionary* lists 18 senses of the noun "subject", several of which pertain to the topics of books and other documents, most specifically sense 14: "The theme of a literary composition; what a book, poem, etc. is about". The last word of this definition is the root of the term "aboutness" of a document, coined in the early 1970s, and expounded by the British information scientist Robert A. Fairthorne.

Contrary to the still prevailing view that it is fairly easy to determine the "subject" of a document (particularly if it is a book and the indexing is done for a library catalog) and that it can be expressed by ready-made and standardized subject headings, Fairthorne distinguished between what a document "mentions" and what it is "about":

> What discourse speaks of,—that is, what it mentions by name or description—, are amongst its extensional properties. What discourse speaks on,—that is, what it is about—, is amongst its intensional properties. This, its topic, cannot be determined solely from what it mentions. For this, one must take into account extra-textual considerations, such as who is using it for what purpose, what purpose the author intended it to be used for, and for whom or for what the librarian, or other manager of messages, acquired it. . . . Topics are not the properties of text marks as such, but of discourse. . . . To create or assign topics to a text we must consider it in the wider context of what kind of person uses it for what, what other texts are used, and in what ways do these texts depend on each other (Fairthorne 1971).

The same ideas on the nature of aboutness have been expressed by F. W. Lancaster, one of the foremost researchers on indexing:

> Effective subject indexing involves deciding not only what a document is about but also why it is likely to be of interest to a particular group of users. . . . The same publication could be indexed rather differently in different information centers and should be indexed differently if the groups of users are interested in the item for different reasons (Lancaster 1991, p. 8).

Once the aboutness of a document has been established according to the two principal criteria—what does it mention and for whom is it intended—it may indeed be indexed for a library by assigning to it a few standardized subject headings for the catalog and a single class mark for shelving in the stacks, that is, at a rather low DEPTH OF INDEXING. But when indexing the same document analytically, as is the case for a back-of-the-book index or an article indexed for a bibliographic database, the indexer must ask for every textual item: Is this *relevant* to the aboutness of the document, and is it therefore *indexable?* And will this or that statement, fact, issue, problem, opinion or belief expressed in the text of the document be relevant also to prospective USERS OF INDEXES, that is, will it provide needed or wanted information, be worth knowing, or otherwise be of interest?

At this point it is necessary to stress the difference between the *relevance* and *pertinence* of a document as experienced by a prospective user. A document may be relevant for a user because it answers a specific question or relieves an uncertainty, that is, it generates new knowledge in the user's mind; it may also be deemed to be relevant to a certain degree because it is generally interesting or provides details and background to what the user already knows; or it may even be relevant if it stimulates the user's mind to work in a different direction or to make a new mental connection between seemingly unrelated concepts or facts (Wilson 1973). Pertinence, on the other hand, depends entirely on factors unrelated to a document's aboutness, such as a user's previous knowledge of the document ("I've seen this before"); the level of exposition ("That's too elementary"); the age of the document ("That's too old"); or its language ("I can't read Russian"). This means that any document, however well indexed and therefore being retrieved according to its potential relevance, may not be pertinent to a particular user.

Establishing a textual item's relevance and therefore its indexability is the initial step of the actual indexing process. The next step is to decide on an index term that would best describe the item (see below, p. 228) and on the SPECIFICITY of that term. In a third step, the indexer may have to consider whether it would be helpful to indicate that the indexable item is related to other items mentioned in the document, and if so, how. Obviously, the assessment of an item's relevance, the choice of index terms and their specificity, and the indication of its relationships to other items will always be subjective, not only because of the fallibility, inconsistency, and possible bias of human indexers, but also because of the difficulty of predicting the needs, wants, and interests of future users, not to mention their opinions and beliefs.

It is thus virtually always left to an indexer's knowledge, experience, and skill to select those topics that are essential and significant relative to the aboutness of a text and the message it is intended to convey. At the same time, there are certain more or less objectively determinable criteria and factors which, when applied during the analysis of a text, will help the indexer in arriving at reasonable and useful decisions on indexable items and topics. The following list of such criteria and factors is from the British Standard BS 6529, *Recommendations for examining documents, determining their subjects and selecting index terms* (British Standards Institution 1984), which provides also much other valuable advice on the indexing process.*

1. Does the document deal with a specific product, condition, or phenomenon?
2. Does the topic involve an action concept (e.g., an operation or process)?
3. Is the object or patient affected by the action identified?
4. Does the document deal with the agent of this action?
5. Does it refer to particular means for accomplishing the action (e.g., special instruments, techniques, or methods)?
6. Were these factors considered in the context of a particular location or environment?
7. Are any dependent or independent variables identified?
8. Was the topic considered from a special viewpoint not normally associated with that field of study (e.g., a sociological study of religion)?

These factors (except the last one) are mainly oriented toward the indexing of scientific and technical topics, where mention and aboutness often tend to coincide or nearly so, but they can be adapted or expanded to fit other fields of study such as those in the social sciences and psychology; however, they do not seem to work as well in the humanities (Tibbo 1992, 1994).

Needless to say, seldom if ever will all the factors have to be taken into consideration for the indexing of a particular document,

---

*The International Standard ISO 5963 (International Organization for Standardization 1985a) is virtually identical with BS 6529.

as shown in the following examples, one from the discipline of chemistry, the other from the field of education. (The analysis of factors is in these cases based on the title alone, which in reality would be quite insufficient and would result in poor and even faulty indexing.)

> *Example A:* "Resolving multiple overlapping calorimetric transitions by use of a microcomputer: studies on erythrocyte membranes."

Factor 1: calorimetric transitions
Factor 2: resolution
Factor 3: erythrocytes, membranes
Factor 4: (not identified in the title but probably mentioned in the text)
Factor 5: microcomputers
Factor 6: (not applicable)
Factor 7: (not identified in the title but probably mentioned in the text)
Factor 8: (not applicable)

> *Example B:* "Implications of teachers' cognitive style for implementation of computers in middle schools."

Factor 1: (not applicable)
Factor 2: implementation
Factor 3: computers
Factor 4: teachers
Factor 5: (not applicable)
Factor 6: middle schools
Factor 7: cognitive style
Factor 8: (not applicable)

Some of the potentially useful index terms could, of course, not be used as main headings because they would be nearly meaningless, e.g., "resolution" or "implementation", but they would become subheadings or parts of subheadings such as for

> *Example A:* calorimetric transitions
>   resolution of overlapping, by microcomputers
> *Example B:* computers
>   implementation in middle schools

Some of the best contributions to the discussion of aboutness, analysis of texts and the selection of indexable topics—the central issue in indexing—may be found in the anthology *Theory of subject analysis* (1985). Some later theoretical investigations are by Beghtol (1986), Blair (1986, 1990), and Hjørland (1992). A treatment of both theory and practice is *Subject analysis: principles and procedures* (Langridge 1989) which deals, however, only with topics in the humanities and social sciences. *Subject indexing: an introductory guide* (Bellardo 1991) is a concise manual, aimed at students and beginning indexers. *Indexing books* (Mulvany 1994*b*) is a practical textbook, covering book indexing with examples from almost all subject fields.

Types of Indexing

The indexing process as described so far is known by the technical term *assignment indexing*, because index terms are assigned to indexable items by an indexer, based not only on the terms of the text but also on their equivalent, broader or narrower terms (which may be taken from a THESAURUS or other sources), and on the indexer's own knowledge and judgment.

Other types of indexing are: *entity-oriented indexing* which emphasizes mainly or even exclusively the topics and features expressly mentioned in a document; and *mission-oriented indexing* which is not, as the term seems to imply, aimed at the conversion of heathens, but is focused strictly on the fulfillment of a mission or the attainment of a specific objective, so that only topics concerning the mission or objective are indexed, all others being disregarded. This latter approach is controversial and may even be counterproductive in the long run if the unindexed (and therefore unfindable) topics of a document turn out to be the important ones, long after the mission has been completed. An approach opposite to entity- or mission-oriented indexing is *request-oriented indexing* which is geared primarily to the terms used in inquiries by prospective users and their latent needs of information which may not necessarily be related to the overt topics of a document—a highly speculative approach, seeing that indexers cannot reasonably be expected to act as prophets or psychoanalysts. As emphasized before, effective assignment indexing should always be a judicious blend of entity- and request-oriented indexing, provided that the latter is meant to serve reasonably predictable information needs of prospective users (Dabney 1986*b*; Fidel 1994).

Lastly, in *derivative* or *extractive indexing*, only those terms actually occurring in the text of a document are selected for indexing, that is, primarily or exclusively the extraction of terms by machines, with little or no human intervention, hence *automatic indexing*.

Many attempts have been made since the 1950s to harness computers to the task of analysis and selection of topics from a text in order to eliminate the inconsistencies, idiosyncrasies and fallibility of human indexers, to speed up and streamline the process of indexing, and to lower its costs. However, the results have been meager, and it is unlikely that they will improve significantly in the foreseeable future. The mental activities resulting in the formulation of index entries cannot be observed and can therefore not be objectively described, measured or reduced to algorithms and fixed rules similar to those that govern the purely technical aspects of indexing such as alphabetization. That is the conclusion of a trenchant critique of attempts by various theoreticians of indexing to stipulate or to "discover" mental indexing rules purportedly guiding human indexing (Frohmann 1990). This conclusion is also supported by the arguments on the impossibility of algorithmic computation of mental processes by Penrose (1989, 1994), who refutes the exaggerated claims of "hard" artificial intelligence enthusiasts. Without such algorithms and fixed rules, computers cannot perform certain crucially important indexing tasks such as the recognition of implicit topics and relationships, or the indexing of anaphoric references which human beings can routinely execute without much difficulty. The mere listing of words and phrases that happen to be used in a text (which computers can do very well) is at best a poor substitute for effective indexing, as discussed in more detail in AUTOMATIC INDEXING and INDEXING LANGUAGES. The state of the art of automatic indexing has been critically reviewed by Korycinski and Newell (1990). Since then, scores of papers on this topic have been published (mostly by people with little or no experience in indexing), but no significant breakthrough replacing the work of human indexers has so far been reported (Milstead 1992*b*).

The matter has been stated succinctly by an experienced information retrieval specialist: "Subject identification is a messy and often indeterminate business. After everything else in bibliographic control has been programmed into a computer, this area will remain in the domain of human judgment" (Hagler 1991, p. 178).

Terminology and Synonym Control

Once a topic has been found to be indexable, the next step is to name it. When indexing a document written by one person, the terminology employed by the author should normally be followed because (a) the author probably knows best how to name the concepts dealt with in the work, and (b) because users who have read the work may remember, however vaguely, the terms of the text. Still, the SPELLING or usage of some terms must sometimes be checked in dictionaries and encyclopedias, and neologisms or new and unusual meanings assigned to existing words must be given special treatment, often by adding QUALIFIERS to index terms. For example, the word "virus" would have been understood as a biological term without any qualification before 1987 but may now have to be qualified as "virus (computers)" if used in that sense.

The major problem of terminology is the control of synonyms. The English language is particularly rich in synonyms and quasi-synonyms, partly because of the derivation of words from Anglo-Saxon as well as from Greek, Latin, and French roots, and partly because of the ease with which English is ready to accept words from other languages and integrate them into its vocabulary. Authors have, therefore, great freedom in the choice of terms and may use several words for the same concept, which may be admirable from the point of view of style, but would be disastrous when transferred unchanged to an index.

When a concept has more than one name, e.g., farming, agriculture, and husbandry, the indexer should choose the one most frequently used in the text or the one most appropriate to the needs of prospective users, while at the same time providing CROSS-REFERENCES for all unused synonyms of the preferred term. Users of an index may look up a concept that has more than one name under one of the synonyms not chosen by the indexer, but the cross-references will lead them from the unused terms to the preferred one under which all references to the sought concept will be found.

If the work to be indexed is a PERIODICAL, conference proceedings, or a monograph containing contributions by several authors, the problem of variant terminology and, therefore, the need for synonym control almost always arises. For example, in a journal on business management, the terms "pay", "wage", "salary", "compensation", and "emoluments" may have been used in the titles and text of various articles, all representing the concept "payment for work performed". On the whole, the problem is of lesser proportions in the natural sciences, where authors are more tightly bound to use accepted terminology, and it is probably at its worst in the social sciences, where authors are prone to use their special (and sometimes specious) jargon, coining terms known only to themselves and their students and followers.

The only proven way to ensure consistency in the indexing of collective works and periodicals is through the use of a controlled indexing language embodied in one of the many THESAURI which establish preferred terms for concepts that have several synonyms and display hierarchical and associative relationships (Feinberg, 1983; Booth 1987). Once a suitable thesaurus has been chosen as an authority to ensure consistency in the use of terms, it should as far as possible be strictly followed. Any decision regarding additions to or deviations from the terminology of the thesaurus should be carefully recorded for future guidance as well as for the benefit of other indexers who may collaborate in the indexing of a periodical or continue the work of a previous indexer.

The use of a thesaurus in indexing is shown schematically in the form of a flowchart in Figure 4. An earlier, more detailed version of such a flowchart is in Wellisch (1972).

Names of persons, places, events, and objects are relatively easy to deal with, though there may be many snags and problems, for which see PERSONAL NAMES, CORPORATE NAMES, and PLACE NAMES. The indexing of statements, propositions, assumptions, opinions, and abstract ideas is much more difficult and often demands not only specialized subject knowledge on the part of the indexer but even more the ability to paraphrase the wording of the text so that it can be cast into the form of terse index headings.

While authors are free to use all the resources of written language, the indexer is limited to nouns, adjectives, a very restricted range of verb forms, and a few prepositions—a more or less tightly con-

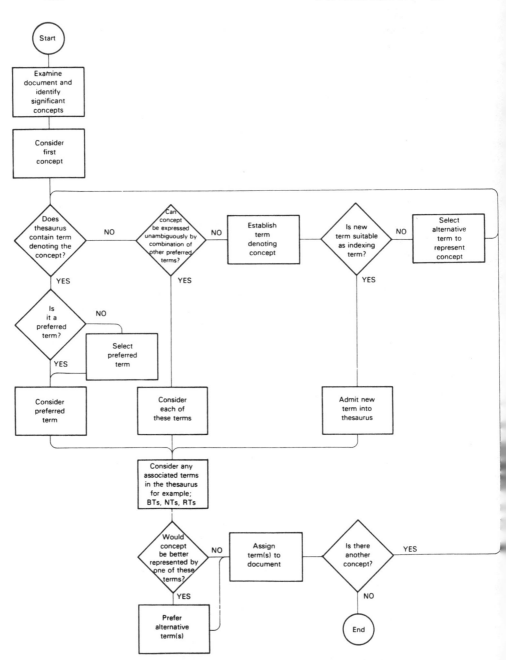

Figure 4. *Flowchart of the indexing operation using a thesaurus* Reproduced from ISO 5963: 1985 with the permission of the International Organization for Standardization, ISO. Copyright remains with ISO.

trolled and, therefore, somewhat artificial INDEXING LANGUAGE into which an author's natural language must be translated.

BS 3700
BS 6529
ISO 999
ISO 5963
NISO Z39.4

INDEXING TECHNIQUES

After the basic conceptual features of an index have been considered, and decisions have been made regarding the aboutness of a document, its indexability, and the terminology of headings, further decisions must be made concerning the design of the index—its format and layout.

Index Design

It might seem like putting the cart before the horse to consider the format and layout of an index after the formulation of index entries consisting of headings and subheadings. Should not the design of an index, like that of a building, be determined before the individual entries (the building blocks) are assembled? While this may be a logical approach, it cannot be applied to all types of indexes.

For indexes to books and other single documents, some design features can only be considered after all or most of the entries have been made and the indexer has become thoroughly familiar with the text. For example, whether to present the entries in a single alphabetical sequence, mixing names, topics, and titles, or to arrange them in MULTIPLE INDEXES can often be decided upon only after the number and type of the entries are known. Likewise, it may only be possible to decide on the DISPLAY OF SUBHEADINGS (indented, run-in, or hybrid) after their extent has been ascertained. These and most other design decisions will affect the LENGTH OF AN INDEX, and they will also determine the ease and speed by which users will be able to find entries in the index.

It must, however, be kept in mind that some design decisions for book indexes may be made by the editor according to the publisher's house style.

Indexes for PERIODICALS and bibliographic databases, on the other hand, must always be carefully designed in advance and in close collaboration with the management of the periodical or database, mainly based on decisions regarding indexing policy. Various design aspects and their impact on the quality and usefulness of an index have been explored in detail by Milstead (1984) and Mulvany (1994b) as well as by Thomas & Mulvany (1994) who deal particularly with periodical indexes.

In general, the structure of an index should follow a coherent and easily recognized pattern which can be grasped immediately by users without the need for any special instructions (although the use of symbols and typographical devices must always be explained in an INTRODUCTORY NOTE). The index should be well balanced: main headings, as far as possible, should not be overloaded with so many subheadings that they fill more than one column or even more than an entire page and sprout a large number of sub-subheadings; if that happens, at least some of the subheadings probably ought to be converted at the editing stage into main headings with their own (but less numerous) subheadings. CROSS-REFERENCES should be made where needed and be placed so that they will not be overlooked. At page or column breaks, headings should always be repeated and followed by (CONTINUED) LINES. PUNCTUATION should be used sparingly but consistently, especially when subheadings are displayed in run-in style. Sequential LOCATORS should be given in full to avoid ambiguities caused by the false economy of lopping off digits for hundreds or thousands. TYPOGRAPHY (an important detail over which indexers unfortunately have only little control) should be used to differentiate between types of headings, e.g., by using italics, boldface, or small capitals, and to distinguish between numerals indicating volumes, parts, and pages. These design characteristics are among the criteria by which critics and reviewers evaluate the quality of indexes.

Style Specifications

The publisher may have a particular house style in which all or most of the indexes to the firm's books are being presented. The house style may govern the system of alphabetization (word-by-word or letter-by-letter), the display of subheadings (indented or run-in), and their arrangement (alphanumerical or in the order of pages), the provision of a single index or of multiple indexes (author, title, subject), and other technical details. In the absence of such a house style, the indexer will have to decide on these and other design features.

Compilation Techniques

When the indexer has been commissioned to compile an index to a book (either by the author or by the publisher) the text will generally be supplied in the form of page proofs. For an index to a periodical, the indexer will work from the actual issues. The proofs or journal issues will often be sent with the publisher's instructions regarding technical data, format, and layout, from which the indexer can make an estimate of the size of the index.

Galleys

Galleys are now often dispensed with in book production, because generically marked-up computerscripts can directly be typeset as finished pages. But if galleys are available (often weeks before the page proofs will be ready), they provide an excellent opportunity to get acquainted with the text in good time before the rush job of actual indexing has to be undertaken. It is, however, not advisable to start indexing from galleys because LOCATORS cannot be assigned to headings, and changes (sometimes quite substantial ones) may still be made by the author, so that the final page proofs may be quite different from the galleys. Adding locators from page proofs to headings provisionally established from galleys is a time-consuming and error-prone procedure. For these reasons, galleys are only useful for a first reading of the text, but if so used they do save time and effort.

Page Proofs

The page proofs are, in most cases, the first opportunity to get acquainted with the text, which should be read through quickly in order to get a "feel" for what the author wishes to communicate and for what needs to be indexed, perhaps also at what depth to index. In principle, the page proofs should be the final form of the text from which headings and locators are to be derived; it happens, however, that the author is often making last-minute additions or changes when going over the page proofs at the same time that the indexer is working on the index. This may not only result in new or changed material to be indexed but will also almost certainly affect the pagination, which in turn may make it necessary to re-index parts of the text and to change locators.

Although time is always of the essence during the indexing process, a first quick reading (or at least browsing through the text), far from being a waste of time, will actually save the indexer time and effort, because it will avoid either over- or under-indexing in the early part of the text, something that may easily happen if indexing is started "cold turkey" without first getting acquainted with the entire work.

Indexable items are then identified during a second, very careful, reading of the text. Most indexers use highlighting pens to mark those terms and phrases that are deemed to be indexable, going through a book chapter by chapter, before keyboarding or writing the marked entries. This makes it easier to check pages for missed items, should this become necessary at a later stage, or when the text is being delivered to the indexer in installments, so that the indexing of later chapters makes it necessary to check chapters indexed earlier. Some indexers prefer to write or keyboard entries directly while reading each page. This is a matter of personal preference and working habits.

Making Entries

The results of an indexer's analysis of the text of a document are then keyboarded on a personal computer with the assistance of dedicated indexing software (*see* EQUIPMENT). A separate record

must be input for every main heading and each of its modifying
subheadings, e.g.,

calendars
  Babylonian 5–6, 14
calendars
  Christian
    Eastern Orthodox 8–10, 15
    Roman Catholic 9–10, 304
calendars
  Jewish 7–8, 567, 597
calendars
  Julian 7, 9–10, 303

The indexing software will then take care of most if not all technical
details and some EDITING tasks, such as the width of an index line
as specified by the publisher, the setting of indentions for subheadings and turnover lines, the alphabetization of headings and subheadings, the listing of locators in ascending order, etc., finally
producing the following multilevel heading:

calendars
  Babylonian 5–6, 14
  Christian
    Eastern Orthodox 8–10, 15
    Roman Catholic 9–10, 304
  Jewish 7–8, 567, 597
  Julian 7, 9–10, 303

Some brands of software will also arrange subheadings in run-in
format and in ascending page order instead of in alphabetical order,
as sometimes required for indexes to biographies, historical works,
and other topics in the humanities, resulting in the display:

calendars
  Babylonian 5–6, 14; Julian 7, 9–10, 303; Jewish 7–8, 567, 597;
  Eastern Orthodox 8–10, 15; Roman Catholic 9–10, 304

Note that the subheading "Christian" is left out, and the former
sub-subheadings become subheadings, because the run-in format
cannot accommodate sub-subheadings, as discussed on p. 146.

If entries are prepared on a word processor, the initial procedure of keyboarding separate headings and subheadings is the same; but since there is no software aid, each new subheading or additional locator must be entered manually by means of the search or find feature, which may become cumbersome and time-consuming, and is therefore not suitable for long indexes.

If entries are typed on cards, the width of an index line as specified by the publisher, and the depth of indentions (generally, two spaces for each level of subheadings or turnover lines) must be set on the typewriter. Then, the same separate heading/subheading records as shown above must be made and alphabetized under the main heading, ultimately to be combined, edited, and retyped as a multilevel heading in the index typescript.

Normally, the cards are kept in a tray in alphabetical order, although this will entail constant pulling of cards to which locators or subheadings have to be added, and then refiling them. This is a tedious and somewhat error-prone chore, but it has the advantage of keeping all entries in an easily retrievable order throughout the compilation stage, so that a term that first appeared on page 13 and is again encountered on page 45 can quickly be found and the second locator be added to the card. If the term has synonyms, not finding one of them may remind the indexer of the chosen term, and perhaps of the need for a *see* reference. Some indexers prefer to arrange cards in the order of pages indexed, every occurrence of a term being entered on a separate card. The cards are alphabetized only at the editing stage. The advantages of this system are that there is no need to pull and refile cards in alphabetical order during compilation and that the accuracy and completeness of the index can be easily checked by comparing the cards with the text after the last index entry has been made. Almost inevitably, gaps and omissions will then show up, and additional entries can be made. (Cards kept in alphabetical order do not afford such an opportunity for a final check.) The disadvantages of the system are that it may lead to the indexing of the same concept under several synonyms, often with different subheadings under each of them. It is also wasteful of cards, because a heading that has six locators will need six cards, five of which will have to be removed after alphabetization and editing (though the removed cards can often be reused).

Almost inevitably, some entries will pose problems which need clarification on the part of the author or verification of data that cannot be found in the indexer's own reference works (such as the correct SPELLING of names or the addition of forenames for persons mentioned in the text only by their surnames). Such entries should be kept apart from all others (either as separate printouts or in a separate card file) so that they can be discussed with the author or taken to a library with more extensive reference resources towards the end of the compilation process. This is much less time-consuming than trying to resolve such sticky problems one at a time.

When the entire text has been dealt with, including ILLUSTRA-TIONS or MAPS (which are generally not supplied with the page proofs, and must be asked for), the index is now in the form of a first draft which must still undergo the crucial operation of EDITING.

Concise descriptions of most basic indexing techniques and examples of their application can be found in the *Handbook of indexing techniques* (Fetters 1994).

BS 3700: 3
ISO 999: 4; 6.2; 7.2.1
NISO Z39.4:

INITIAL ARTICLES

Happy is the lot of an indexer of Latin, the Slavic languages, Chinese, Japanese, and some other tongues which do not have articles, whether definite or indefinite, initial or otherwise. They don't have to bother about their alphabetization, regarding or disregarding them, finding out whether they are in the nominative or any other grammatical case, whether to put them up front or to invert them. But an indexer who has to deal with titles or proper names, place names, or first lines of poems beginning with an article in English (or occasionally in other languages) must inevitably pay attention to those articles, because they are treated differently, depending on what type of heading they start, and which rules or standards are applied. That makes for a complex and sometimes confusing treatment of initial articles in an index—all with the laudable goal of making it easier for users to find headings beginning with an article. Needless to say, this goal is not always achieved.

Titles of Works

Because of the high frequency of initial articles in TITLES of works, it was for a long time the rule for indexes to transpose such articles to the end of the title, preceded by a comma, so that the title could be alphabetized by the (capitalized) word following the article, e.g.,

> *History of science, A*
> *Twelve Caesars, The*

This rule is prescribed by BS 3700, 5.3.4.2 and by ISO 999, 7.3.4.2 (in the latter for English indexes only). However, NISO Z39.4 prescribes that all titles be listed in the exact order of their words, including any initial articles, but to disregard that article in alphabetization, e.g.,

> *A history of science* [alphabetized at H]
> *The twelve Caesars* [alphabetized at T]

This is in accordance with the established practice in library catalogs, where titles beginning with an initial article have always been listed in this manner.* The rationale for this rule is that users who already know how to look up titles in library catalogs will be able to find them also in indexes, using the same search strategy.

Whether to follow the BS and ISO standard or the NISO standard and library practice will often depend on a publisher's house rules. Absent such rules, the indexer will have to decide which set of rules to apply. If it is decided to follow NISO Z39.4, there will be no

---

*In some online catalogs all initial articles in titles are now simply deleted. This abominable practice is a disservice to users.

problems—all titles are listed as given—but provisions must be made to disregard initial articles when alphabetizing headings. This is relatively easy for English titles (only *A* and *The* are involved), but when titles in foreign languages have to be indexed, the matter becomes more complex, and the disregarding of initial articles in alphabetization cannot simply be automated. The reason for this is that in foreign languages only articles in the *nominative* case are to be transposed in alphabetization. Most people who had to take French or German 101 will dimly remember that those pesky languages are inflected and distinguish between a number of cases for the noun, whereas English has shed all case endings except that of the possessive (or genitive) case, as in "the baker's house", where the final *'s* signifies the case but the article remains unaffected. What, then, is an article in the nominative case? In simple terms, it is one that precedes a noun which is the subject of a phrase or sentence. Any other articles in foreign languages, if they happen to be the first words of a title (which fortunately is very seldom the case), are treated as any other words and must be alphabetized.

To make matters worse, in many languages indefinite articles (a, an) may double as the word for the number one. If a title begins with an indefinite article, the article is disregarded, but if that word means "one", it is a word like any other and *is* to be regarded in alphabetization. For example, the title of one of Mozart's best-known works, *Eine kleine Nachtmusik* (A little night music), is to be filed under "Kleine", but the title *Eine von vielen* (One of many) is to be filed under "Eine", as shown in the comprehensive example on page 243.

How is a poor indexer to know what is an article in the nominative case and what is the word "one" when it looks the same as an indefinite article? Table 4 lists articles in the nominative case for some of the most commonly encountered languages, which should be sufficient for most purposes,* but, in order to distinguish between an indefinite article and the word "one", a knowledge of the respective language is necessary, and a mere table lookup will not be enough.

---

*A much more extensive list, arranged in alphabetical order by article, is the "List of initial articles" (1991) published by the Library of Congress.

Table 4. Articles in the Nominative Case in Some Foreign Languages
The articles are listed in the following order: singular—masculine, feminine, neuter; plural—same. An asterisk (*) before an indefinite article indicates that the same form is also used for the numeral one (which is to be regarded in alphabetization).

Language	Definite article	Indefinite article
Afrikaans	Die	'n
Arabic	al-, el-[1]	—
Catalan	El, En, L', La; Els, Les	*Un, *Una
Danish	Den, Det; De	*En, *Et
Dutch	De, Het, 't; De	*Een, Eene, 'n
Esperanto	La	—
French	Le, La, L'; Les	*Un, *Une
German	Der[2], Die, Das; Die	*Ein, *Eine
Greek (Classical)	Ho, Hē, To, Tō; Hoi, Hai, Ta	—
Greek (Modern)	Ho, Hē, To; Hoi, Hai, Ta	*Henas, *Mia, *Hena
Hawaiian	Ka, Ke, Na, O	He
Hebrew	ha-, he-[1]	—
Hungarian	A, Az	*Egy
Icelandic	Hinn, Hin, Hið; Hinir, Hinar, Hin	—
Italian	Il, Lo, L', La, Gli, Gl', I, Le	Un, *Uno, *Una, Un'
Norwegian (Bokmål)	Den, Det; De	*En, *Et
Norwegian (Nynorsk)	Den, Det; Dei	*Ein, *Ei, *Eit
Portuguese	O, A; Os, As	*Um, *Uma
Spanish	El, La, Lo; Los, Las	*Un, *Una
Swedish	Den, Det; De	*En, *Ett
Turkish	—	*Bir
Welsh	Y, Yr	—
Yiddish	Der, Di, Dos; Di	A, An, *Ein, *Eine

[1] In Arabic and Hebrew, the definite article, if joined to the next word by a hyphen, is to be disregarded in alphabetization. The Arabic article may also take the forms *ad-, ag-, an-, aq-, ar-, as-, at-, az-*.

[2] *Der* may also be the genitive feminine article (singular or plural) which, if used as the first word of a title, *is* to be regarded in alphabetization.

Personal and Place Names

Initial articles in PERSONAL NAMES or PLACE NAMES (which occur mostly in or are derived from the Romance or Semitic languages) form integral parts of such names, whether written separately or forming the first part of a string of letters. For this reason, initial articles in personal names (including nicknames, sobriquets, and phrases used as names, e.g., "An American") or in place names are neither transposed nor disregarded: they must be both written and considered in alphabetization. This rule applies also to English personal names derived from Romance languages, e.g., La Salle, Latrobe, Letelier, and to place names such as Las Vegas or Los Angeles, as also to English place names beginning with "The", according to NISO Z39.4.

This is a simplified version of ALA 4.2, BS 3700 5.3.3.2, ISO 999 7.3.3.2, and LC 13.1, all of which stipulate that initial articles in place names are to be retained if they are "integral parts" of such names (without, however, defining what is meant by this; presumably, they mean the official form used by governmental agencies). But they make an exception for English place names beginning with "The", such as The Hague in which the article is to be transposed. (Is the article in this case not an "integral part" of that name? And if not, why not?) Not content with this exception, a special rule governs place names in which the initial article is "not an integral part", e.g., Cevennes or Nile, although this is actually covered by the general rule for place names. It is anybody's guess which rule to apply in the case of "The Bronx", the borough of New York City invariably spoken and written about with the article but officially designated as Bronx.

There does not seem to be any reason for these exceptions and exceptions to exceptions, and since there are probably fewer than half a dozen English place names beginning with "The", it is far better to follow the consistent rule of NISO Z39.4 for indexing place names beginning with an article.

Corporate Names and Names of Objects

Initial articles in CORPORATE NAMES and in proper names of objects, such as ships, cars, airplanes, buildings, shops, etc. are neither omitted nor transposed but are disregarded in alphabetization, according to NISO Z39.4.

Examples:

The Church of God [congregation]	[alphabetized at C]
The Flying Dutchman [ship]	[alphabetized at F]
The H. W. Wilson Company [firm]	[alphabetized at H and optionally also at W]
The Spirit of St. Louis [airplane]	[alphabetized at S]
La Trattoria [restaurant]	[alphabetized at T]

However, BS 3700 5.3.2 and ISO 999 7.3.2 instruct in this case to omit such initial articles. This exceptional treatment of initial articles for just one category of names is probably confusing to users and does not seem to have any justification.

First-Line Indexes

Initial articles in first lines of poems (which may also be their titles) have always been printed and alphabetized as any other word in indexes to poetry, and should never be omitted or transposed.

Summary

Initial articles in titles of works, names of persons, corporate bodies, objects, place names, and first lines of poetry are *retained* in index headings and are neither omitted nor transposed. Those in personal and place names and in first lines of poetry are alphabetized as any other words in a heading, but those in titles of works and in corporate or object names are disregarded in alphabetization. These are the rules recommended in NISO Z39.4.

The relevant rules of the British and international indexing standards are inconsistent in their treatment of initial articles and contain several exceptions which complicate matters for the indexer without demonstrably benefitting users.

The following comprehensive examples show the alphabetization (word-by-word) and form of titles and personal, corporate, object, and place names beginning with initial articles, according to the American versus the British and international standard rules.

Form and alphabetization of headings beginning with an article

According to NISO Z39.4	*According to BS 3700 and ISO 999*
El-Abiad, Ahmed	El-Abiad, Ahmed
L'Africaine	*Africaine, L'*
An American in Paris	*American in Paris, An*
An American [pseudonym]	An American [pseudonym]
Anderson, James	Anderson, James
Un ballo in maschera	*Ballo in maschera, Un*
Al-Biruni, Abu Rayhan	Al-Biruni, Abu Rayhan
Die casting	*Die casting*
The Church of God	Church of God, The
Eine von vielen	*Eine von vielen*
El Dorado [city]	El Dorado [city]
El Greco	El Greco
Elburz mountains	Elburz mountains
Der Erlkönig	*Erlkönig, Der*
La forza del destino	*Forza del destino, La*
The H. W. Wilson Company	H. W. Wilson Company, The
Un homme	Hague, The
Das Kapital	*Homme, Un*
Klee, Paul	*Kapital, Das*
Eine kleine Nachtmusik	Klee, Paul
Kleist, Heinrich von	*Kleine Nachtmusik, Eine*
La Fontaine, Jean de	Kleist, Heinrich von
La Paz	La Fontaine, Jean de
Lafontaine, Jean	La Paz
Las Vegas	Lafontaine, Jean
Latrobe, Charles J.	Las Vegas
Le Bourget	Latrobe, Charles J.
Le Fèvre, Pierre	Le Bourget
Le Havre	Le Fèvre, Pierre
Lefèvre, Gaston	Le Havre
L'Enfant, Edouard	Lefèvre, Gaston
Los Angeles	L'Enfant, Edouard
Die Räuber	Los Angeles
The Spirit of St. Louis	*Räuber, Die*
The Tempest	*Spirit of St. Louis, The*
The Hague	*Tempest, The*
The Wash	Thebes
Thebes	*Trattoria, La*
La Trattoria	*Trovatore, Il*

Il trovatore	Un français [pseudonym]
Un français [pseudonym]	Unamuno, Miguel de
Unamuno, Miguel de	Wash, The
Washington, George	Washington, George
The Washington Post	*Washington Post, The*

ALA: 4
BS 3700: 5.3.1.5; 5.3.2; 5.3.3.2; 5.3.3.3; 5.3.4.2; 5.3.5
ISO 999: 7.3.2; 7.3.3.2; 7.3.3.3; 7.3.4.2; 7.3.5
LC: 13
NISO Z39.4:

INTRODUCTORY NOTES

Most indexes of moderate length and arranged in a single alphabetical sequence do not need any instructions or explanations; any users with a knowledge of the alphabet should be able to find what they are looking for.* Yet this ideal state of affairs can often not be achieved, either because of the length and complexity of the text, or the need for MULTIPLE INDEXES, or because of special features of the index which must be brought to the attention of users or which must be explained. Hence the need for introductory notes preceding the index entries themselves. To what extent such notes are actually read and appreciated by users of indexes is not known, and indexers have sometimes expressed doubts about the usefulness of these "sacred, unconsulted cows" (Bell 1989, p. 171). What is certain, however, is the fact that anything in an index other than straightforward alphabetical arrangement and normal locators referring to pages is not self-explanatory and will frustrate many users if not made explicit in an introductory note.

Some of the features of an index which may need to be explained or justified are:

*The fact that many users have only a rudimentary knowledge of the alphabet, and must recite it mentally to find the place of a letter beyond F or so, cannot be remedied by even the most beautifully written introductory note.

1. What is included or excluded (e.g., footnotes, appendixes, certain names).
2. The system of alphabetization (word-by-word or letter-by-letter).
3. The arrangement of NUMERALS (before or after all verbal headings, or as spelled out).
4. The arrangement of SYMBOLS.
5. The treatment of ABBREVIATIONS.
6. LOCATORS that do not refer to pages (e.g., paragraphs, sections).
7. LOCATORS for FOOTNOTES (indicated by n) and TABLES (indicated by t).
8. Typographic elements other than roman typeface: italics for ILLUSTRATIONS and TITLES, small capitals for names of persons, boldface for locators of particularly important references or for volume numbers, identification of columns as locators (a, b), division of pages into parts (a, b, c, d), etc.
9. Arrangement of subheadings (alphabetical, chronological).
10. The ROMANIZATION system used for names written in non-Roman scripts.

A separately published index, whether to a book, a single periodical, or a series of documents, must necessarily contain an introductory note in which the bibliographic data, such as author, title, edition, volume, section, or number of the indexed items, are clearly and comprehensively displayed.

If an introductory note is to achieve its intended purpose, it must be brief. Each feature that needs explanation should be presented in a tersely written separate paragraph. A note extending over a whole page or more will probably not be consulted or, even if read, will not be properly understood or remembered by users. Most lengthy introductory notes are a sure sign of an overly elaborate and complex index.

BS 3700: 5.1.1.2; 5.1.3; 5.4.2.1; 6.1; 6.2.2; 7.1.2; 7.1.5.2
ISO 999: 6.2(b); 7.1.1; 7.1.3; 7.2.2.4; 7.4.2.1; 8.4; 8.6; 9.2
NISO Z39.4:

ITALICS

When people are asked "What are italics?" the answers may range from "Something that has to do with Italy" to "Sloping letters". While both answers are right to some extent, and the latter is closer to the truth than the former, it is by no means the full answer. For that, we must go back to Venice and one of the most famous early printers, Teobaldo Mannucci (1450–1515), who latinized his name in the manner of all Renaissance humanists to Aldus Manutius. Aldus, as he is generally known, conceived of the idea to print the Latin classics in carefully edited but small and inexpensive books instead of in heavy and expensive folio tomes (as was the custom of other printers) and to print them in large numbers–the forerunners of today's pocket books. For that purpose he needed a typeface that would allow him to cram as much text as possible onto a small page without impairing legibility. The typefaces then generally used by printers in Italy, which were modelled on ancient Roman monumental inscriptions, were preferred by the humanists for the printing of Latin texts and were known as *antiqua* types (a term still used by European printers); they have come to be called *roman* in English. But their upright and somewhat expansive style, though beautiful and much more legible than the German "gothic" types, did not fit the aims of Aldus, who wanted a condensed and narrow typeface. He therefore commissioned Francesco Griffo, a Bolognese scribe, to design such a typeface. Griffo based his new type on the handwriting style then employed for informal writing by the papal chancery, the *cancellaresca cursiva*, which was also widely used by Italian humanists. This elegant and legible type became the companion of the more formal *"antiqua"* or roman type. Griffo's type font was first used by Aldus in one of his highly successful new pocket editions, containing the works of Vergil, published in 1501. The type was further refined by the Roman printer Lodovico degli Arrighi in the 1520s. Soon, the graceful letters designed by Italians were widely employed by printers throughout Western Europe and became known as "italics". They were first used in England by Wynkyn de Worde in 1524, who thus departed from the ugly and almost illegible gothic type used by his former master, William Caxton (the first English printer).

Our contemporary italic type fonts are the direct descendants of Arrighi's types, but they are not just roman letters written at a slant: the italic letters *a, e, f,* and *g* have shapes that differ considerably from that of their roman counterparts, and italics initially had no capitals—only lowercase letters. Later, italic capitals were also cut, but they are, indeed, only slanted versions of roman capitals.

Italics are now no longer used for printing whole texts, with occasional exceptions for poetry. They have been largely relegated to the limited functions of emphasizing words and phrases and indicating titles and proper names of ships, aircraft, and other vehicles, as well as the command terms in cross-references; in the words of a writer on printing, "italics are forever doomed to be no more than servants and handmaids to roman" (Jennett 1967, p. 208).

While that may be true for the printing of continuous texts, italics play a much more important role in indexing. In a text, it is possible to identify a title or a proper name simply by the use of a brief phrase and without necessarily having to use italics: "The title of Shaw's play is Saint Joan" or "The name of the ill-fated space shuttle was Challenger". No ambiguity here. But in an index it must be made clear to the user in the most concise form that a page reference to *Saint Joan* means the title of a work, or that *Challenger* is a proper name. The typographical device of printing titles and proper names in a distinct typeface serves that purpose very well and without any need for further explanation. Regarding cross-references, the italicized words *see* and *see also* are unambiguously set off from whatever terms follow them, thus enhancing their role as semantic signposts.

Italic numerals are often used as locators for ILLUSTRATIONS, but since they differ only very slightly from regular numerals they are easily overlooked by users who seldom bother to read the relevant instructions in an introductory note. It is therefore better to use other typographical devices, such as asterisks or square brackets, for locators of illustrations, even though they take up a little more space.

KEYWORDS

The term "keyword" is used in indexing in two quite different senses: (1) the first word of a heading; and (2) a significant word taken from the title or the text of a document and used in a heading (but not necessarily as the first word in it). Since these two senses of the term are quite different, it is important to distinguish clearly between them. Keywords in the first sense are now generally called LEAD TERMS, while the second sense is currently the best known one for "keyword".

Keywords in Titles or Texts

Keywords in the current sense, that is, significant words in the title, chapter and section headings, and text, have always been the primary candidates for index headings, even though in the final index synonyms may be the better choice, or keywords need to be modified in various ways. But books have long since ceased to be the primary sources of information. Since the mid-19th century, articles in journals have assumed that role. In the 1950s, when the ever-increasing number of articles, reports, patents, and other documents, both printed and in nonprint forms, threatened to overwhelm users of information (especially in science and technology), the growing problem of information storage and retrieval coincided with the first nonnumerical applications of computers. An engineer with IBM, Hans Peter Luhn, proposed to extract all significant words from the titles of articles and reports, to put them on punched cards (then the only known input device), and to sort these so that the printout would show every word, arranged alphabetically down a column in the middle of a page and surrounded left and right by all or most other title words, with an indication of the document number or any other physical retrieval tag (Figure 5). This could be done without any human intervention save the initial keypunching of title words, and the resulting alphabetical display of keywords would constitute a subject index to the documents derived from their titles. Luhn, who first published the successful application of his idea in 1958, called his method KWIC (*Key Word In* Context), and it became, indeed, the first and to this day the only

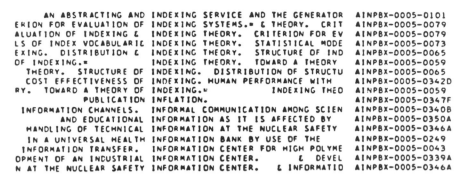

```
        AN ABSTRACTING AND  INDEXING SERVICE AND THE GENERATOR    AINPBX-0005-0101
ERION FOR EVALUATION OF  INDEXING SYSTEMS.■ & THEORY.  CRIT      AINPBX-0005-0079
ALUATION OF INDEXING &   INDEXING THEORY.  CRITERION FOR EV     AINPBX-0005-0079
LS OF INDEX VOCABULARI&   INDEXING THEORY.   STATISTICAL MODE    AINPBX-0005-0073
EXING.  DISTRIBUTION &    INDEXING THEORY.  STRUCTURE OF IND     AINPBX-0005-0065
OF INDEXING.■            INDEXING THEORY.  TOWARD A THEORY       AINPBX-0005-0059
    THEORY.  STRUCTURE OF  INDEXING.  DISTRIBUTION OF STRUCTU    AINPBX-0005-0065
   COST EFFECTIVENESS OF  INDEXING. HUMAN PERFORMANCE WITH       AINPBX-0005-0342D
RY.  TOWARD A THEORY OF   INDEXING.ᵛ           INDEXING THEO     AINPBX-0005-0059
            PUBLICATION  INFLATION.                              AINPBX-0005-0347F
 INFORMATION CHANNELS.   INFORMAL COMMUNICATION AMONG SCIEN      AINPBX-0005-0340B
          AND EDUCATIONAL INFORMATION AS IT IS AFFECTED BY       AINPBX-0005-0350A
 HANDLING OF TECHNICAL   INFORMATION AT THE NUCLEAR SAFETY       AINPBX-0005-0346A
  IN A UNIVERSAL HEALTH   INFORMATION BANK BY USE OF THE         AINPBX-0005-0249
 INFORMATION TRANSFER.   INFORMATION CENTER FOR HIGH POLYME      AINPBX-0005-0043
OPMENT OF AN INDUSTRIAL   INFORMATION CENTER.      & DEVEL       AINPBX-0005-0339A
N AT THE NUCLEAR SAFETY   INFORMATION CENTER.   & INFORMATIO     AINPBX-0005-0346A
```

Figure 5. *Example of a KWIC index.* From the subject index to the *Proceedings of the American Society for Information Science Annual Meeting. Vol. 5. Information transfer. Columbus, Ohio, Oct. 20–24, 1968.* New York: Greenwood Publishing, 1968. The locators refer to: the CODEN (a unique identification code for serials) of the publication; the volume number; and the page number (letters indicate abstracts, of which there are several on a page). Reproduced by permission of the publisher.

fully automatic indexing method. As so often in the history of science and technology, Luhn's idea was actually not new. A British librarian of Italian descent, Andrea Crestadoro, proposed in 1858 virtually the same idea for the compilation of a subject catalog of books in the British Museum, which would complement the alphabetical author catalog then being compiled by his fellow Italian, the famous Antonio Panizzi, Keeper of Printed Books at the British Museum. Crestadoro's proposal remained, however, on paper, because, despite its inherent simplicity, it would still have been very labor-intensive, and there were as yet no machines to perform such tasks automatically.

The Three Stooges: KWIC, KWAC, and KWOC

One dictionary definition of "stooge" is "a subordinate who does routine work". It is probably not stretching a metaphor too far if the title of the famous comedy series is applied to the products that grew out of Luhn's proposal. Despite the pun in its name, a KWIC index is actually neither an index nor is it quick to use (though it is admittedly quick and cheap to produce). It is not a real index because title words alone seldom if ever express the entire subject matter of a document, and sometimes do not express it at all, as in the title of Lenin's famous pamphlet *What is to be done?*, published in 1902, which laid the groundwork for the Russian Revolution in 1917. A KWIC index is thus no more than a display of words which an author happened to choose for a title. And it is not quick to *use* because scanning long columns of keywords (mostly printed in all uppercase letters which are hard on the eyes) and correlating them with the surrounding remnants of the title is a tedious and time-consuming business. Soon after the first KWIC indexes had been produced, it was recognized that the so-called "unimportant" words—articles, conjunctions, and prepositions, as well as some adverbs which had been put on "stop lists" so that they were not listed in the column of significant keywords—were not quite as unimportant as some people had thought. Thus, the elimination of the indefinite article *a* made it impossible to search for "vitamin A", and the absence of "very" impeded a search for "very high frequency". The automatic and arbitrary truncation of words at the end of a line and their "wraparound" at the beginning of the same line led occasionally to hilarious results, as in

EROTIC TENDENCIES OF TRAPPIST MONKS. ATHEROSCL

an entry which once adorned a KWIC index of articles on cardiovascular diseases. Even worse was the elimination of words from long titles which took up more space than just the width of one line, leaving the user to guess what may have been the full title, as can be seen in Figures 5 and 6.

INDEX	WEEKLY SUBJECT INDEX AS A POST-COORDINATE INDEX	29	1	47
INDEX	LTR-TO-ED THE JASIS KWCC INDEX: EDITOR'S REPLY	29	5	260
INDEX	LTR-TO-ED THE JASIS KWCC INDEX	29	5	260
INDEXES	INFORMATION FROM CITATION INDEXES BE SIMPLIFIED?	29	6	308
INDEXING	AUTOMATIC INDEXING CF PATHOLOGY DATA	29	2	81
INDEXING	INDEXING DOCUMENTS BY GEDANKEN EXPERIMENTATION	29	3	107
INDICATORS	INFORMATION AND TEXT AS INDICATORS OF RELEVANCE	29	1	15
INFORMATION	THE DEVELOPMENT OF AN INFORMATION SYSTEMS TYPOLOGY	29	5	256
INFORMATION	CATALOG INFORMATION AND TEXT AS INDICATORS OF	29	1	15
INFORMATION	EVALUATION OF INFORMATION RETRIEVAL SYSTEMS: A DEC	29	1	31
INFORMATION	GROWTH DYNAMICS OF INFORMATION SEARCH SERVICES	29	2	67
INFORMATION	EDUCATION FOR INFORMATION SCIENCE AS A PROFESSION	29	3	148
INFORMATION	TOWARD A LIBRARY AND INFORMATION POLICY, BY WILSON	29	3	167
INFORMATION	SCIENCE AND THE PHENOMENON OF INFORMATION	29	4	210
INFORMATION	LTR-TO-ED INFORMATION SCIENCE AND THE PHENOMENON C	29	4	210

Figure 6. *Example of a KWOC index.* The locators refer to volume, issue, and page numbers. From the subject index to the *Journal of the American Society for Information Science,* vol. 29, 1978, copyright John Wiley & Sons, by permission of the publisher.

To overcome, at least partially, such shortcomings of KWIC indexes, KWOC (*Key Word Out of Context*) indexes were soon invented, displaying the keyword flush left instead of in the middle of the page, followed by the full or truncated title, as shown in Figure 6. (Thus, the two senses of "keyword" were here conflated so that a keyword serving as an index term was at the same time also used as a lead term.) This made it easier for users to scan such an index but could do nothing to improve the "indexing" itself, which still amounted to a mere display of title words. Moreover, it had the disadvantage that pairs of adjacent words were not preserved, so that meaningful phrases in a title such as "information retrieval" could not be looked up directly, except when the second word happened by chance to be the first word in the rest of the title after the KWOC. As a further refinement, the KWOC technique was also applied to permuted indexes (another form of fully automatic indexing of titles) in which all keywords are alphabetically listed as subheadings under each keyword in KWOC position (thus resembling multilevel headings in conventional indexes). This allows the user to scan word pairs, although obviously not all combinations will always be meaningful. The full title on which a permuted index is based must be displayed in a separate file. For example, the title "Development of an industrial information center" (last but one line in Fig. 5) would generate the following permuted KWOC displays:

INFORMATION	CENTER	DEVELOPMENT	INDUSTRIAL
CENTER	DEVELOPMENT	CENTER	CENTER
DEVELOPMENT	INDUSTRIAL	INDUSTRIAL	DEVELOPMENT
INDUSTRIAL	INFORMATION	INFORMATION	INFORMATION

The word pairs DEVELOPMENT CENTER, DEVELOPMENT INFORMATION, INDUSTRIAL CENTER, INDUSTRIAL DEVELOPMENT, and INFORMATION DEVELOPMENT are either meaningless or misleading.

Finally, someone came up with KWAC (*Key Word Alongside Context*), which was used for the production of library catalogs, showing also bibliographic data alongside the title keywords, but that was really only a variation on KWOC.

Despite their crudeness and the lack of actual subject indication, KWIC indexes and their KWOC and KWAC cousins are still being used as rough-and-ready substitutes for the real thing because they do not need skilled personnel, are cheap to produce, and can indeed claim to be fully automatic, provided that titles of documents are available in machine-readable form or can easily be put in such a form.

Attempts have also been made to overcome the most obvious shortcoming of KWIC indexes, namely, that title words do not always express even the most important topics dealt with in a document, by "enhancing" titles with keywords taken from the text by an indexer. This means that the indexing is no longer performed fully automatically, and needs the skills of a human being, thus going back to square one. Such "enhanced" KWIC or KWOC indexes were, therefore, only seldom compiled and soon went out of fashion.

Keywords in Online Searching

With the advent of modern computer technology, which allows scanning of texts at speeds of up to 12 million characters (the equivalent of 12 average novels) per second (!), the words used by authors are now increasingly serving as substitutes for index terms assigned to documents by human beings. Full-text searching of online databases relies exclusively on the retrieval of keywords from texts, with the important difference from primitive earlier automatic retrieval tools that it is possible to search not only for individual words but also for adjacent ones, words within a specified distance from a keyword, left and right truncation, and other refinements. Yet even such more sophisticated methods of keyword searching without any indexing whatsoever are still hampered by their inability to overcome the problems of synonyms and homographs, especially when a search is being conducted across several different databases in which authors are apt to use different terms for the same concepts because of traditional usages in a field or because they have been encouraged to employ terms prescribed by a particular thesaurus.

Assigned Keywords

With an eye on the pitfalls of full-text retrieval, editors of professional journals often demand that authors or in-house indexers assign keywords to articles, preferably taken from a thesaurus, to ensure consistency and uniformity and to improve the effectiveness of retrieval, whether online or in personal indexes kept by users. Such keywords, intended to complement and enhance full-text searching, are then not just those found in titles or texts of articles but also those found in abstracts (which are often required to accompany articles) or chosen by authors or indexers as supplements to the terms that occur in the text. Many retrieval tests have shown that searching for keywords in the natural language text of a document, combined with the use of assigned keywords from a controlled indexing language, is the most effective way of information retrieval from bibliographic databases (Fugmann 1982; Fidel 1992). Thus, keywords have come a long way from their rather primitive and indiscriminate computerized listing in KWIC indexes to their sophisticated use as searching aids, albeit with some help from human beings—authors and indexers. *See also* STRING INDEXES.

LATIN TERMS

Latin is often called a "dead" language because it is no longer spoken by people, either in Rome or elsewhere, in their daily lives, but it is very much alive and well in the disciplines of biology, medicine, and law as also in Roman Catholic theology, where Latin terms and phrases are frequently used. When indexing Latin expressions, certain conventions must be observed.

Spelling

The alphabet of classical Latin had only 23 letters. The letter *i* was used to express also the sound of consonantal *y* (as in *yes*), and *v* was used to write also the sound of *u*. The letters *j*, *u*, and *w* were added in the Middle Ages and first appeared in print in the late 16th century, in order to distinguish between *i* and *j* (the latter representing consonantal *y*), and between *u* and *v*, while *w* was added to express sounds in English, German, and some other lan-

guages for which there were no Latin equivalent letters. Consequently, words and names in which *i* has the sound of consonantal
y are often spelled with a *j*, e.g., *Julius* or *Ursa major* (the Great Bear
or Big Dipper), and only purists would write *Iulius* or *Ursa maior*.
But, as these examples show, even purists do not write *Ivlivs* or *Vrsa
maior*, as the Romans did. If, however, Latin titles of old books are
cited, the spelling of the title page is often followed exactly, especially in bibliographic works, and index entries should then follow
the usage of the text:

Epistola ad Gvilielmvm Tvrnervm, theologvm & medicvm excellentissimvm

Classical Latin also used the digraphs (pairs of joined letters
expressing a single sound) *æ* and *œ*, which in English spelling are
rendered either as *ae* and *oe* or are sometimes simplified to *e* (for
both). In all of these instances, the usage of the author should be
followed, except when the "house style" of a publisher prescribes
one particular form or when the same word or name is spelled
differently by various authors, as may be the case in a collective
work or in a periodical; the indexer must then decide on the preferred form. Cross-references should be made from any form not
used, e.g.,

haemophilus see *hemophilus*
oesophagus see *esophagus*

Capitalization

The ancient Romans had only one kind of letter: the majestic script
engraved on their monuments and tombstones which became the
model, in virtually unchanged form, for our capital letters or majus-
cules (literally "the slightly larger ones"). Lowercase letters or mi-
nuscules ("the slightly smaller ones") evolved only in the early
Middle Ages, around the fifth century, from a cursive style of writing capitals with a pen on parchment. Thus, the Romans did not
have to worry about capitalization, but in our time almost all Latin
expressions are written in lowercase letters. As far as indexing is
concerned, Latin words and names are capitalized in two instances
only, namely:

1. Proper names and adjectives (with an important exception in taxonomy, discussed below).

Caesar, Gaius Julius
Scipio Africanus

2. The first word of a title (but never any other word in a title, as is the custom of American printers for English titles):

De revolutionibus orbium coelestium (Copernicus)

Scientific Names of Plants and Animals

The Swedish scientist Carl von Linné (1707–1778), who, following the custom of his time, latinized his name to Carolus Linnaeus, under which he is best known, invented the system of plant and animal classification that is essentially still in use, at least as far as the construction of scientific names is concerned. Every living organism is given a name derived from Latin or Greek (or a hybrid of both), the first part (a noun) indicates the genus and the second (an adjective) the species.* The noun part of a binomial taxonomic term is always capitalized, the adjective never, even if it is derived from the proper name of a person or place. All taxonomic terms are traditionally italicized and are written according to the rules of Latin spelling, that is, no double consonants are used, and the letter *y* in modern names, when pronounced as a short *i* (as in *bit*), is written *i* (*see* the second example below) but in names derived from Latin or Greek roots originally written with a Y it is retained (*see* the third example below):

Campanula portenschlagiana (a species of bellflower)
Cassia marilandica (Wild senna)
Pteretis pensylvanica (Ostrich fern)

When more than one species of a genus is to be indexed, as in gardening books or in field guides to animals, their names are often listed in run-in style, e.g.,

*A third adjective may be added to indicate a subspecies.

Rosa 67–69; *alba* 73; *centifolia* 71; *chinensis* 83, 85;
foetida 92; *rugosa* 75

Translation

Latin terms and phrases should not be translated in an index but
listed exactly as given in the text. For example, in LEGAL TEXTS
Latin expressions such as *alieni juris, certiorari, nolo contendere, ratio
decidendi,* and many others are frequently used and may have to be
indexed if their meaning is discussed in the text. If the text contains
both a Latin expression and its English equivalent or translation,
e.g., the common as well as the scientific name of a plant, both need
to be indexed in their proper place, and no *see* reference needs to be
made:

buyer beware 52	*caveat emptor* 52
Moss rose 173	*Portulaca grandiflora* 173

But if there are many subheadings under either the Latin form or
the English translation of a heading, only one of them should display all subheadings, and a *see* reference be made from the other in
order to save space. Which form to choose for the full display of
subheadings will depend on the nature of the work and the needs
or habits of prospective users, e.g., in a legal work most users will
probably look up the Latin rather than the English term, but in a
work on gardening the English term will be preferred by most
people.

Latin Abbreviations

Abbreviations of Latin terms can still be found in indexes, especially those to scholarly works in the humanities. They are the last
survivors from a time when Latin was thought to be the only language fit for scholarly discourse. However, such abbreviations do
not have any justification in indexes intended for English-speaking
people and in which all other words are in English. Though some of
the Latin abbreviations are a tad shorter than their plain English
equivalents, the saving in space on a line is minimal, whereas those

not familiar with the abbreviations—and that is today the majority of users—are baffled as to what they mean. The following abbreviations should, therefore, not be used anywhere in a modern index:

Abbreviation	Full form	Translation
cf.	*confer*	compare
et seq.	*et sequens*	and the following [pages or items]
f.	*folio*	[and] on the [following] page
ff.	*foliis*	[and] on the [following] pages
q.v.	*quod vide*	which see

To these should be added the word *passim*, which means "here and there" (on consecutive pages). A locator followed by the abbreviation "et seq." or "ff." is particularly unhelpful because it leaves the user in the dark as to how many of the following pages deal with a topic—two, three, six, or more? And "123–131 *passim*" does not do much more than what the two locators already tell the user: that a topic is dealt with on eight consecutive pages.

Typography

Most Latin terms and phrases are printed in italics, both in texts and in indexes. CROSS-REFERENCES between two Latin terms are then printed in roman type so as to make them stand out among the italicized terms:

dementia praecox see also *schizophrenosis*

Some Latin expressions commonly used in English, such as ad hoc, de facto, quid pro quo, and status quo, are not italicized, since they are now considered to be part of the English vocabulary; but they are, in any case, unlikely to be used as index headings.

LEAD TERMS

The choice of the first word of a heading, its *lead term*, is of utmost importance for the usefulness of an index, since users will find desired information only if the first word of a heading leads them to it. Lead terms should, therefore, always be terms that are likely to be sought by users. No one will quarrel with this statement, but to translate it into actual index headings is another kettle of fish because of the richness and vagaries of human language. For topics that can be named by single nouns, the difficulty lies in making choices among synonyms and in distinguishing HOMOGRAPHS. But topics that can only be expressed by COMPOUND HEADINGS, that is, noun phrases (most often consisting of an adjective and a noun), have always been a vexing problem in indexing: should they be given in natural language order or should they be inverted? Since the 1960s, natural language order has been the preferred way of formulating a compound heading, on both theoretical and practical grounds, although many traditional subject heading lists and indexes continue to exhibit inverted headings. When the noun in a compound heading is not the lead term but is relegated to the second or third place in the string of words forming a heading, CROSS-REFERENCES must be made to take care of expected alternative approaches by users.

LEGAL TEXTS

Legal indexers can look back on a long tradition, beginning in the Middle Ages, when manuscript indexes to the immense tomes of Roman and Canon law were compiled. These were continued in printed form soon after the invention of the art, the earliest surviving one being the index to Nicholas Statham's *Abridgement of the laws of England,* published in 1490, though there may have been earlier printed legal indexes of which nothing remained because they were so often used that both they and the texts to which they referred disintegrated and were discarded.

The necessity of providing keys and guides to the ever more complex field of law (deemed by the satirist John Arbuthnot to be "a bottomless pit" in 1712) contributed substantially to the evolution and refinement of techniques that are used today in all kinds of indexes.

This discussion of indexing techniques is primarily devoted to legal texts in book form. The indexing of articles on legal matters is now to a large extent the domain of databases—either those that do not depend on human indexing but provide electronic free-text searching of full-text files or those in both printed and electronic format, such as *Index to legal periodicals* or *Current law index*, which employ teams of indexers, and train them in the use of their in-house indexing rules and thesauri. Most of the discussion on the indexing of PERIODICALS applies necessarily also to that of articles on legal matters.

Legal Literature

Law books fall into several categories. The first five of those listed below are about equal regarding the complexity and size of their indexes; the degree of detailed subject knowledge required of their indexers; and the time needed for their compilation.

(1) collections of statutes; (2) collections of case law (judicial decisions), known as *Reporters* in the U.S. and as *Reports* in the U.K.; (3) collections of administrative law (decisions of administrative boards); (4) treatises on specific branches and topics of law; (5) legal reference works; (6) textbooks for undergraduate and graduate students; (7) works on legal aspects of commercial or professional topics for practitioners in those fields; (8) popular accounts of legal matters for the general public.* Books in categories 1–3 are sometimes issued as LOOSE-LEAF PUBLICATIONS which makes their indexing more challenging and complex.

What Makes Legal Indexing Different?

Legal indexing is often thought to be difficult and arduous by those who have never tried it but have seen specimens of legal indexes that may at first sight look forbidding, both regarding their structure and their size. However, only a few of the indexing techniques

---

*Digests of case law are not listed because they are themselves indexes.

used for legal texts differ substantially from those applied to most other indexing, while the basic rules of all indexing remain valid also for this specialty.

Laws and legal principles are essentially abstract ideas that exist only in the mind. They have no physical substance save that expressed by written words ("written" used here in its widest sense as encompassing all forms of recorded information). It has therefore been said that law is "a profession of words". In no other field or discipline are words used in such a precise manner to convey a distinct and closely circumscribed meaning that leaves (at least in theory) nothing or as little as possible to individual interpretation. This does not mean, however, that the wording of statutes is always unambiguous (Corbett 1992).

At the same time, law suits involve the parties in quite concrete issues such as car accidents, stolen property or zoning permits. Thus, the terminology of things to which the law pertains is as much subject to ambiguity, change, and misinterpretation as any other wording of texts. The indexer of legal materials must therefore be familiar both with the precise and authorized meaning of legal terms as well as with the much looser and shifting terminology of the issues at stake in legal proceedings.

The precise meaning of legal terms is the cause of several characteristics of the language (and eo ipso also of the indexing) of legal texts:

1. *Specialized terminology.* This is, of course, a trait shared with any other special field, but it is particularly conspicuous in legal texts whose language is often largely incomprehensible to anyone not trained in the law.*

2. *Old and new terminology.* Anglo-American law, based on the ancient principle of *stare decisis* (literally: "to stand by what has been decided", that is, abide by decisions reached in prior cases) uses phraseology hundreds of years old—discussed below—but must also use the most recent neologisms describing things and actions pertinent to legislation or litigation.

---

*"It is likewise to be observed that this society [of lawyers] hath a particular chant and jargon of their own, that no other mortal can understand, and wherein all their laws are written, which they take special care to multiply" Jonathan Swift, *Gulliver's travels.*

3. *Latin and French terms.* The roots of Anglo-American legal practice are more than a thousand years old. Phrases couched in medieval Latin or French (which was the language of English courts until 1731) have survived to this day and are frequently used in modern legal texts. Examples are: *alieni juris, caveat emptor, ex parte, habeas corpus, in re, nolo contendere, profit à prendre, pur autre vie, res judicata, voir dire.* Such phrases are always indexed as given in the text and should never be translated or split into their constituent parts.

4. *No paraphrases.* Words, phrases, and sentences used in legal texts should virtually never be paraphrased by an indexer. While it is often necessary in other types of indexing (particularly in the humanities and social sciences) to index concepts and ideas that are mentioned only implicitly in the text, this is seldom the case in legal indexes.

5. *Synonyms.* In indexes to statutes and cases, synonymous terms should as far as possible be listed as cross-references only if *legal* definitions (as distinct from dictionary definitions) have established their equivalent meaning. For example, whereas in general indexing the terms "home" and "marital residence" could very well be considered as synonyms (with a cross-reference, say, from the second, less usual, and longer one to the commonly known and shorter first one) in legal usage there is an important difference between the meaning of the two terms, and they can therefore not be treated as synonyms. Synonyms and quasi-synonyms that do not pertain to strictly legal terms, but to the issues dealt with in cases, may be cross-referenced more conventionally and without regard to minor differences of meaning, e.g.,

pistols *see* handguns   *or*   pistols *see also* revolvers

as the case may be.

Which of two or more terms with legally equivalent meanings to choose as the principal heading will depend on the intended audience (lawyers or general public) and, other things being equal, on the length of terms, as in the example above; a shorter term will be easier to read and will allow more locators on the same line, e.g.,

wills 87, 324, 348, 567–573
testamentary dispositions *see* wills

Specialized sources of synonyms in legal texts are *Legal thesaurus* (Burton 1992) for American terms, and *A legal thesaurus* (Smith & Miskin 1987) for British terms. Both works list a number of equivalent or quasi-synonymous terms under alphabetically arranged headings, but without distinguishing between hierarchically and otherwise related terms or broader and narrower terms; they are therefore, despite their titles, not indexing thesauri in the modern sense, but rather more like alphabetized editions of *Roget's thesaurus*.

6. *Citations.* References to statutes and cases, known as citations, are essentially a special type of LOCATORS, although they may look unfamiliar, convoluted and even cryptic to the uninitiated. However, this is a purely technical matter, the details of which can be mastered relatively easily because legal citations follow fixed patterns. In the United States, federal and state statutes are cited according to *The bluebook: a uniform system of citation* (1991), while citations of British statutes and cases follow the *Manual of legal citations* (1960).

A problem is posed by many statutes that are better known by their popular titles than by their official ones, e.g., the G.I. Bill of Rights = Servicemen's Readjustment Act of 1944; the Taft-Hartley Act = Labor-Management Relations Act of 1947; Lord Campbell's Act = Duties in American Colonies Act, 1765; Statutes of Fraud = 1677 (29 Car.2, c.3). In the U.S., *Shepard's acts and cases by popular names* (1968–   ) helps to sort out this problem, but in the U.K. no equivalent guide has so far been compiled (Noel-Todd 1989). A brief guide to citations of Act of Parliament has been offered by Haig-Brown (1979).

7. *Definitions.* Since, as mentioned above, the legal definition of a word or phrase is of crucial importance, such definitions are often collected separately in indexes to legal texts; it is also not unusual to find a term listed both as legally *defined* or as merely *described* when the two meanings differ from each other in some respect. Sources for such definitions are listed at the end of this section.

8. *Tables of statutes and cases.* These, too, are compiled according to traditionally set patterns with which all lawyers are familiar, and which must therefore be followed meticulously. Such tables form essentially parts of MULTIPLE INDEXES, but are physically separated from topical indexes, sometimes appearing in the front part of

monographs on specific topics, and not in the back as other indexes
to the same works.

Similarities with General Indexing

The basic rules and principles of indexing must often be followed
more rigorously in legal indexing, or minor deviations from the
norms of general indexing may be necessary to achieve the desired
results: clarity of entries and ease of finding them.

Single terms. All significant and meaningful single terms used in
legal texts must be carefully indexed, with modifying subheadings
for any related terms. What would be deemed to be "over-
indexing" or disparaged as "mere word indexing" in other types of
index is just what is needed by lawyers who are always in a hurry
to find a particular statute or case, looking for the exact terms or
phrases that are pertinent to the issue at hand.

Phrases. It has been found that, on the whole, PHRASES occur in
legal texts about twice as often as single words (Moys 1992). This
means that legal indexes will contain a large number of COMPOUND
HEADINGS. These fall into two distinct categories: (1) fixed phrases
with legally defined precise meanings, and (2) phrases constructed
ad hoc (as in any other texts), to express facts, actions, situations,
circumstances, etc. pertaining to a case, ranging from brief and
concise, e.g., "custody of grandchild" to long and complex, e.g.,
"adult rocking gently in swing reserved for children", or "action by
claimants against workers' compensation, insurers alleging negli-
gent safety inspection of workplace".

Phrases of category (1) are either *adjectival* noun phrases, e.g.,
"circumstantial evidence", "contributory negligence", "false pre-
tenses", "larcenous intent", "personal property", etc., or *prepositional* noun phrases, in which a preposition is interposed between a
modifier and the principal noun, e.g., "accessory after the fact",
"breach of contract", "estate by entirety", "interests in land", "tenant at will", etc.

All such fixed phrases must first of all be indexed in their natural
syntactic form, that is, without any inversions, because that is the
form in which lawyers wish to find them. In an index to a legal
work aimed at the general public, however, it may be desirable to

make DOUBLE ENTRIES for the principal noun of such phrases and
to display the modifier as a subheading (especially if there are also
other modifying subheadings), e.g.,

> negligence
>   actionable
>   contributory
>   criminal
>   hazardous
>   willful

or to make a general CROSS-REFERENCE, e.g.,

> negligence *see also* actionable, contributory,
>   criminal, hazardous, willful negligence

Phrases of category (2) containing PREPOSITIONS, i.e., those constructed ad hoc, need to be indexed differently when factored into a
main heading and one or more subheadings, depending on whether the subheadings precede the main heading syntactically or follow it.

When a subheading *precedes* its main heading syntactically, e.g.,

> minors
>   testimony

(which is actually read as "testimony by minors") prepositions after
the subheading, such as *by, for, in, of,* are superfluous because the
meaning is clear. Prepositions at the end of subheadings should be
used only when the meaning would otherwise be ambiguous, e.g.,

> grandchildren
>   custody by
>   custody of

(where the first subheading refers to the rare but possible case that a
grandchild has custody of an incapacitated grandparent). No comma should be written before a preposition, e.g., "custody, of" which
is illogical, because one would not write "custody, of grand-
children" when writing the full phrase.

However, when a subheading *follows* its main heading syntactically, e.g.,

custody
    for minority

an initial preposition always serves to clarify the meaning and must therefore be retained. This is particularly important when the same main heading may be followed by subheadings beginning with different prepositions, the meanings of which must be carefully distinguished from each other, e.g.,

custody
    by grandchildren
    for minority
    of grandchildren
    to grandparents

Two writers on this issue (Moys 1992; Moys et al. 1993; Thomas 1983) suggest even to highlight the prepositions typographically when more than one subheading appears under each of them, e.g.,

custody
    by
       grandchildren
       guardians
    for
       minority
       six months only
    of
       grandchildren
       stepchildren
       twins
    to
       grandparents
       stepfathers

This practice, which is wasteful of space, would generally not be followed in other types of indexes, but it is said to be appreciated by busy lawyers because it makes articulated entries easier and quicker to scan.

A third type of fixed phrases in which two nouns are joined by the conjunction *AND* also occurs frequently in legal texts, e.g., "husband and wife", "landlord and tenant", "master and servant".

These, too, must be left in the fixed form in which they are most familiar to lawyers, without changing singular to plural or vice versa, but with suitable cross-references to the second term linked by "and" to the first one, e.g.,

wives *see also* husband and wife

Grammatical form of headings. This issue, discussed in SINGULAR OR PLURAL? is of particular importance in legal indexing, because a number of terms frequently encountered in legal texts have entirely different meanings when used in the singular or plural, e.g., cost / costs, damage / damages, security / securities. The two forms, if present in the same text must therefore be indexed by two separate entries.

Depth of indexing. As already mentioned above regarding single words, legal indexing must strive for the highest degree of EXHAUSTIVITY, not omitting any significant term in a text. At the same time, a very high degree of SPECIFICITY is also required, which finds its expression in the terminology of subheadings as well as in their successive levels. While in general indexing three levels of sub- and sub-subheadings would normally be considered as the limit, some legal indexes may sport four, five, and more levels, each one properly indented under the previous one, and each also provided with (CONTINUED) LINES when subheadings are carried over from page to page or from column to column, as shown in Figure 7. The reason for this is, again, the ease and speed with which indented subheadings can be scanned by lawyers for whom time is of the essence. Needless to say, the run-in style of subheadings is almost never used in legal indexes.

The Legal Indexer

As in every special field or discipline, the indexer must be familiar with the language of its practitioners. As noted above, the terminology of law has always seemed to be particularly opaque and puzzling to outsiders, and in order to understand and to index it, it would be desirable to have studied as well as practiced law, but this

	SECTION	VOL.	PAGE
Building Code — (Continued)			
Plumbing and gas piping — (Continued)			
Fixtures — (Continued)			
Overflows	**§C26App. RS16-P104.3**	**4**	**181**
Physically handicapped	**§C26App. RS16-P104.1(c)**	**4**	**180**
Pools	**§C26App. RS16-P116.1**	**4**	**261**
Required	**§C26-1600.6(1)**	**3**	**775**
Separate	**§C26App. RS16-P104.1(b)**	**4**	**180**
Showers	**§C26App. RS16-P104.9**	**4**	**187**
Sinks	**§C26App. RS16-P104.10**	**4**	**187**
Strainers	**§C26App. RS16-P104.15**	**4**	**188**
Traps			
Domestic dishwashers	**§C26App. RS16-P105.1(a)(4)**	**4**	**190**
Prohibited	**§C26App. RS16-P105.1(c)**	**4**	**190**
Sizes	**§C26App. RS16-P105.1(b)**	**4**	**190**
Separate, and exceptions	**§C26App. RS16-P105.1(a)**	**4**	**189**
Urinals	**§C26App. RS16-P104.5**	**4**	**185**
Vents	**§C26App. RS16-P109.8**	**4**	**228**
Wall-hung	**§C26App. RS16-P109.8**	**4**	**228**
Water			
Closets	**§C26App. RS16-P104.4**	**4**	**181**
Supply protection	**§C26App. RS16-P104.2(e)**	**4**	**180**
Flanges, floor, materials	**§C26App. RS16-P102.4(e)(9)**	**4**	**175**

Figure 7. *A five-level index.* Note that all headings, subheadings, and sub-subheadings carried over from previous pages have been marked with —(Continued), and that indentions at the fourth and fifth level are generous (4 ems and 3 ems respectively), in order to make rapid scanning easier. The locators are typical for a legal index, showing sections, volumes, and pages for each building code. (Source: *New York City charter & administrative code.* New York, 1974, 1977.)

is not an absolute necessity.* It is a fact that paralegals, law librarians, and legal secretaries are able to master the intricacies of

*In one of the earliest articles on legal indexing, Sir Henry Thring, an eminent British lawyer, urged that only experienced lawyers should index statutes (Thring 1877). But today, few if any practicing lawyers would wish to become indexers, because even at the highest current rate for this type of work, the remuneration would constitute only a fraction of what they could earn in their chosen profession.

legal language, and they are indeed often the indexers of legal texts, not to forget, of course, retired lawyers (as was the founder of the Society of Indexers in the U.K., C. Norman Knight). It ought not to be impossible for an intelligent and well-read person to acquire the necessary skills if one wishes to devote oneself to legal indexing.

Beginners should perhaps first try to index legal works aimed at the general public, such as popular explanations of business law for small business owners, or the making of a will. Having gained some experience, an indexer may then be ready to try textbooks for students before tackling compilations of statutes and case law, or deciding to specialize in one of the subfields of legal literature such as patent law or constitutional law.

Reference Works

Black's law dictionary. Rev. 6th ed. St. Paul, MN: West Publishing Co., 1990.
The bluebook: a uniform system of citation. 15th ed. Cambridge, MA: Harvard Law Review Association, 1991.
Burton, William C. *Legal thesaurus.* 2nd ed. New York: Macmillan, 1992.
Dictionary of English law. 2nd ed. London: Sweet & Maxwell, 1977.
Manual of legal citations. London: University of London, 1960.
The Sloane-Dorland annotated medical-legal dictionary. St. Paul, MN: West Publishing Co., 1987.
Smith, Nigel; Miskin, Christine. *A legal thesaurus.* Hebden Bridge (UK): Legal Information Resources, 1988.
Words and phrases. St. Paul, MN: West Publishing Co., 1940– . Updated annually by "pocket parts".
Words and phrases legally defined. 3rd ed. London: Butterworth, 1988–89.

LENGTH OF AN INDEX

A long index is not necessarily also a good index, although a short index is almost always deficient in some respect. "Long" and "short" are, of course, relative terms, referring to the ratio of index pages to text pages. Many "long" indexes are so big because they contain unnecessary entries—the result of overindexing—while at the same time they may lack some rather obvious and necessary entries, especially for synonyms and related terms which do not actually appear in the text but may well be sought by users. On the other hand, in certain disciplines, particularly in law as well as to some extent in the biomedical and chemical fields, large indexes almost approaching concordances are a necessity (or at least so the lawyers claim).

The length of an index depends, in descending order of importance, on the following factors.

Space and Time Allotted by the Publisher

The publisher will, in most instances, decide on the number of pages that are allotted to the index and will also stipulate a deadline for the submission of the index manuscript. Often there is little if any leeway to negotiate either of these two crucial elements, and the length of the index will therefore be fixed in advance: there can be only so many entries on an index page. If the index is to be compiled over the weekend (even allowing for "several extra days at either end" as the *Chicago manual of style* [1993, 17.24] wryly remarks), the number of entries will necessarily be smaller (and the number of potential omissions and errors larger) than that which would have resulted had the indexer been given more time. But if the publisher's restrictions are unreasonable (such as a requirement to index no more than about one entry per page) the job should be rejected, because the shoddy index that would result would violate professional ethics and could only reflect adversely on the indexer's reputation.

Technical Data

The data needed to make an approximate computation regarding the length of an index are:

1. The size of a page.
2. The number of pages allotted to the index.

3. The number of columns per page (generally two, but sometimes three or four).
4. The type size to be used (most often 8 point).
5. The number of lines on an index page.
6. The maximum width of a column line, measured in picas (1/6 of an inch, a printers' measure) or in "units" (each letter, space, or punctuation counting as a "unit").

These data will enable the indexer to compute the maximum number of lines that can be accommodated in the available space. For example: the page size of a book is $6\frac{1}{8}'' \times 9\frac{1}{4}''$ (156 × 234 mm). There are 345 indexable pages and the index has been allotted 10 pages, to be set in two columns in 8 point Times Roman, 34 units per column line. Table 5 shows that this will result in 136 lines per page, or a theoretical maximum of 1,360 lines. From this number must be subtracted 80 lines (2 × 15 = 30 lines to accommodate the title and an INTRODUCTORY NOTE and another 50 lines for the 2-line spaces between alphabetic groups of entries), which leaves 1,280 lines for index entries. About 20% of that number may have to be subtracted for turnover lines of long headings, so that the actually available number of lines will be 1,280 − 256 = 1,024. Dividing the number of available lines by the number of indexable text pages will yield the average number of 1-line index entries per page, in this case 1,024 ÷ 345 = 2.97, or about three entries per page. The approximate computation of index entries per page may alert the indexer to the possibility that the number of pages allotted to the index is insufficient and that either a few more pages or a smaller type size (or both) are needed for an adequate index; this would have to be discussed with the editor.

The number of available lines is, however, by no means the limit of possible indexed items. Many headings will have more than one locator, so that the actual number of indexed items, assuming an average of three locators per heading, may be closer to 2,000 or even more—quite sufficient for a popular introduction to a subject or a travelogue, but perhaps too little for a biography or a historical work containing many names and events. If the type size can now be changed to 7 point Times Roman (still quite legible), this will yield 154 lines per page for a theoretical maximum of 1,540 lines. Subtracting again 80 lines leaves 1,460 lines; subtracting 20% for

Table 5. Number of Index Lines per Page in Common Page Sizes

| Trimmed size[a] | | 7 point type Columns | | | 8 point type Columns | | |
U.K. mm	U.S. inches	Single	Double	Triple[b]	Single	Double	Triple[b]
219 × 276	8½ × 11	93	186	279	81	162	243
201 × 258	7 × 10	75	150	225	85	170	255
156 × 234	6⅛ × 9¼	77	154	231	68	136	204
138 × 216	5½ × 8¼	70	140		61	122	
	5⅜ × 8	67	134		58	116	
111 × 178	4⅛ × 7	58	116		51	102	
	4⅛ × 6¾	51	102		45	90	

The number of column lines per page does not take into consideration space for the "sinkage" (the blank space required for the word "Index" and an introductory note as needed on the first page) or 2 blank lines between alphabetic groups of entries.

Find the number of index lines per page for the given trim size, type size, and number of columns. Multiply by the number of pages allotted to the index, which will result in the maximum possible number of index lines. Subtract 50 lines for the 2 blank lines between alphabetic groups of entries (in most indexes the letters X and Y form one group or are not used at all); subtract also the number of lines for the sinkage (5 to 15 lines, depending on the book designer's specifications). Subtract further from this number between 20% and 50% for turnover lines and unforeseen additions, depending on the nature of the text: an index of names only may have few or no turnovers, while a biomedical or chemical text, containing many polysyllabic terms, may generate a large number of turnover lines. The result will be an estimate of index lines actually available on the pages allotted to the index.

[a]Metric sizes are those stated in the British Standard BS 1413:1989 *Page sizes of books;* they are not the exact metric equivalents of U.S. paper formats measured in inches, except for the format 6⅛ × 9¼.

[b]The number of triple column lines for sizes narrower than 6" (152 mm) is not given because the lines would be too short (see Figure 15, p. 493).

turnovers results in 1,460 − 292 = 1,168 lines, a net increase of 144 lines, or the equivalent of about one additional page, which may make the difference between a skimpy index and an adequate one.

Occasionally an indexer may be given an open-ended assignment: to compile an index that is adequate for the work to be indexed, no matter what size it may be or how long it may take to finish the work. This may happen when a publisher or editor has developed a long-standing relationship with an indexer and knows that the indexer will not try to "stretch" the index beyond a reasonable length, yet will produce an adequate index and will deliver it within an acceptable time. Open-ended index assignments are also customary for cumulative indexes to periodicals and large bibliographies, and generally for any unusually complex or large indexes whose size cannot easily be estimated in advance. For the latter type of index, a sophisticated method of estimating the length as well as the time needed for completion of the work (at least approximately) has been described by Boodson (1975).

Nature of the Text

Travelogues, popular expositions of factual topics, textbooks for elementary schools, and children's books will generally need rather brief indexes, ranging from 1–3% of text pages. At the other end of the scale, highly specialized monographs on scientific and technical topics may need as much as 15% or more of index vs. text pages. History, biography, and high school to undergraduate textbooks fall somewhere in the middle with 5–8%, though biographies may range from no or very skimpy indexes to 10% or more (not always depending on the fame and stature of the biographee). Works of reference, such as handbooks, encyclopedias, and directories, need very extensive indexes which may amount to 10–15% of the text pages.

In a quantitative study of 433 book indexes by Bishop et al. (1991) the average ratio of index to text pages was 3.3. In a study of cross-references in indexes by Diodato (1991), based on 376 books, it was found that the mean ratio of index to text pages was 3.12. However, books in LC classes A and Z (which include many encyclopedias and other reference works) had a ratio of almost 10 index to text pages. In another study of indexes by Diodato & Gandt (1991), based on a sample of only 64 books, the average length of an index was found to be 9 pages, and the number of index pages per 100 pages of text was 3, that is, virtually the same ratios as those in the other studies. Diodato & Gandt also found that indexes compiled by indexers who were not the authors of the books were significantly larger than those prepared by authors: the average ratio for the length of indexer-compiled indexes to author-compiled ones was 4:3. Authors of articles also tend to assign fewer and less specific index terms than professionals indexing the same articles (Rasheed 1989).

Number of Names

The number of names of persons and places (and sometimes also the titles of works cited) will affect the length of an index to a considerable extent, the more so if many of the persons need also extensive subheadings for their activities, works, travels, or meetings with other people. Thus, a biographical, historical, or geographical work may need an index that is much longer than one for a work of comparable size in which persons or places are only occasionally mentioned.

Subheadings

Many works, even some technical or scientific ones, can be adequately indexed by one-line entries with no or only a few subheadings without impairing the quality of the index. But both names and topical headings often need an extensive DISPLAY OF SUBHEADINGS. When subheadings are displayed in indented style (as is the custom for indexes to technical and scientific texts) it will add considerable length to an index. If space for the index is limited but a large number of subheadings is anticipated due to the nature of the text, it is better to decide in advance on the space-saving display in run-in style rather than having to redesign the index when the allotted space is exceeded. Such redesign will entail not just a mechanical reshuffling of the subheadings (which can pretty easily be done on a computer but will mean complete retyping of the index manuscript without one!); in most cases, it will also result in the elimination or rephrasing of sub-subentries (if any) as well as in changes of punctuation, all of which is time-consuming and costly. For other methods of trimming the length of an index so as to fit into a given space see EDITING, step 21.

Length of the Text

Contrary to a popular notion, a long text is the least important factor affecting the size of an index. Even a very long text does not necessarily need an index that is more extensive than the average ratio for the type of work concerned. A historical work of, say, 800 pages indexed at the 5% level will have an index of some 40 pages, which may seem to be "large" yet is actually not more voluminous than what is par for the course.

The issue of the length of an index has been treated by Mulvany (1994*b*, pp. 63–67), including a table of estimated index length for various types and categories of books. The matter has been nicely summarized by John L. Thornton, an expert on legal indexing: "The indexer must submit the size of index the publisher requests—and deserves!" (*Training in indexing* 1969, p. 143).

BS 3700: 4.3
Chicago manual of style: 17.65–67
ISO 999: 6.2
NISO Z39.4:

LETTERS AND DIARIES

Collections of letters and diaries need detailed indexing perhaps more than any other text of narrative prose, but, sad to say, they seldom get it. Some publishers of letters and diaries seem to be under the impression that such collections will be read from cover to cover like a novel and, therefore, need no index, which is patently absurd. Rather, biographers, historians, literary critics, and just about anybody interested in a letter writer or diarist will wish to pinpoint what occupied his or her mind at a particular time or in a certain place, whether any letter was addressed to certain other persons, or whether the letter writer had an opinion on a particular subject or event which was discussed informally in correspondence with friends and acquaintances. Rare is the letter writer whose every epistle is a small literary gem, so that a straightforward perusal of the collection would be a pleasurable and useful experience, and, even if that were the case, the need for an index to a large number of items mentioned in letters or diaries would still remain.

A good index to a collection of letters or to a diary will, therefore, have to provide access to at least the following topics:

1. The letter writer or diarist him- or herself.
2. The persons to whom the letters were addressed.
3. Other persons mentioned, including authors of books read or plays seen.
4. Places in which the letter writer lived or which he or she visited.
5. Subjects and events discussed.

Other topics or details may have to be added to the indexable items, depending on the special characteristics of the collection of letters or the diary.

Such a variety of topics, and the need to provide easy and accurate access to them, may suggest that MULTIPLE INDEXES (at least for persons, places, and subjects) are called for. Two exemplary indexes to this type of text (both of which happen to be for letters and a diary from the 17th and 18th centuries) show that a multiple as well as a single index can be an excellent finding tool. The index to the collection of Dr. Samuel Johnson's *Letters* (1952), edited and indexed by R. W. Chapman, occupies almost all of the third volume and is divided into seven parts: (1) Samuel Johnson himself; (2) Other persons; (3) Authors of books (not listed in part 2); (4) Places; (5) Subjects; (6) Johnson's works; and (7) Johnson's English, that is, obsolete or deprecating words, and innovations coined by him. This must be one of the most extensive multiple indexes in existence, adding considerably to the value of the collection by providing information pertaining to the letters which otherwise would have to be given in footnotes and commentaries.

On the other hand, the index to the definitive edition of *The diary of Samuel Pepys* (Pepys 1983), compiled by Robert Latham, one of the work's two editors, lists names of persons, places, events, and subjects in a single alphabetical sequence, occupying the last volume of the 11-volume set. Despite a somewhat idiosyncratic structure made necessary by the peculiar nature of the diary, this unified index provides easy access to the myriad of issues dealt with by Pepys and was justly awarded the Wheatley medal for the best British index of 1983.

A grave mistake often made by inexperienced indexers of diaries and collections of letters is the accumulation of dozens and even hundreds of undifferentiated LOCATORS for the diarist or for frequent correspondents of the letter writer. A horrible but by no means unusual example is shown in Figure 8, p. 280 and should serve as a warning for diary indexers.

Only a few indexers have given accounts of the problems encountered in the indexing of large or unusual collections of letters. The indexing of Dickens's letters has been described by Thornton (1965), and that of a collection available only on microfiche has been discussed by Meltzer (1981); a particularly difficult indexing project concerning a large collection of partially illegible letters has been reported by Bruner (1984).

LOCATORS

The term, as now used to denote the indication of the place at which an indexed item will be found, is a fairly recent coinage in indexing terminology. Though, according to the *Oxford English dictionary*, it has been part of the language since about 1600, it meant until recently a *person* who finds or locates something, especially one who "determines the boundaries of land", which is still the only definition in the *Random House dictionary of the English language* (1987). But the *Supplement* to the *OED* (1987) adds the definition "something which locates; a device for indicating the position . . . of something" and traces it in the sense in which indexers now use it to 1971. It seems, however, that the term appeared in the literature of indexing only about a decade later. Before 1980 writers on indexing invariably used the term "references" or "page references", although it was well known that this term was ambiguous or even incorrect: "reference" has several different meanings depending on the context*, and not all index "references" are to pages. The

---

*In the index to *Indexers on indexing* (1978) the entry "Reference(s)" has four subheadings—only one of which is about locators, while three others are on cross-references—and a *see also* reference to citation indexing and cross-references. Confusion worse confounded!

term "locator" avoids such ambiguity and impreciseness. It made its official appearance in 1984 in the American National Standard ANSI Z39.4, the predecessor of NISO Z39.4, and has now become firmly established in the U.S. as well as in the U.K. (though BS 3700: 1988 still uses "location reference", a somewhat cumbersome hybrid); it is also used in ISO 999 which ought to give it worldwide currency.

Locators for Single Printed Works

Most locators for books, pamphlets, and other single printed materials are to page or column numbers or (nowadays rather seldom) to folio (leaf) numbers if the item is printed on one side of a leaf only. But other kinds of locators may be more appropriate or useful even if the work itself is paginated: item numbers are used for entries in bibliographies or in collections of abstracts; passages from plays are indicated by act, scene, and line numbers in specific editions; citations from Scripture have locators consisting of book, chapter, and verse. In official documents, reports, and legal works the locators often refer to paragraphs or to a combination of these with volume and page numbers, e.g.,

	SECTION	VOL.	PAGE
Common show license violation	§B32-44.0	4	924
Compliance failure, rent and housing			
maintenance department	§D26-52.01	4	482
Concrete testing laboratory license . . .	§B26-1.9	3	365

Sequential locators. If a topic is treated continuously or frequently throughout a sequence of pages or other numbered parts, the first and last numbers of the sequence should be given, separated by an en dash* without spacing at either end, e.g.,

elephants 597–599
whales 1039–1043

This seemingly simple and straightforward matter has been the subject of many debates and quasi-learned disquisitions regarding

*An en dash is half as long as an em dash, thus slightly longer than a hyphen.

the form of the second locator, particularly when the numbering of locators reaches three or four digits. Should the final locator be abbreviated, and if so, by how much? Should it not be given at all, but only implied by adding *f*, *ff*, or *et seq.* to the first locator, meaning one, two, or several pages respectively? Or should it always be shown in full? The advocates of abbreviation, that is, lopping off one or two digits if this can be done without ambiguity, are not of one mind regarding the extent of abbreviation. More or less elaborate schemes have been proposed, such as not to abbreviate any locator below 100, to omit only the first digit from three-digit numbers (e.g., 183–95) and two digits from four-digit numbers, (e.g., 1293–95) but not 197–02 for 197–202 or 1293–07 for 1293–1307, and several other variations on this theme. It is, however, doubtful whether the saving of one or two digits is worth the potential confusion of users, especially since the various abbreviation "rules" are often not applied consistently. BS 3700, 5.4.3.1, ISO 999, 7.4.3.1, and NISO Z39.4 do not permit any abbreviation of locators indicating a sequence of pages, columns, or any other alphanumeric sequence, except for very long final numbers exceeding 5 digits, for which only the last 2 or 3 digits may be given if space is limited, e.g., 100327–34 instead of 100327–100334. Not abbreviating any locators is indeed the simplest, easiest and most user-friendly way of dealing with this matter. On the related issue of indicating a sequence of pages by adding *f.*, *ff.*, or *et seq.* after the first locator, the same sections of the three indexing standards deprecate the use of these LATIN TERMS, and the *Chicago manual of style* (1993, 17.9) warns "never" to use them, because they are imprecise (how many pages or items after the first one—two, six, ten?).

When a topic is mentioned briefly here and there (but not continuously) in a sequence of pages, this should be indicated by listing the locators for the relevant pages, e.g.,

pesticides 14, 16, 17, 19

rather than in the form 14–19 or 14–19 *passim,* another vague Latin term meaning "here and there", which adds nothing to a user's understanding of the exact places in which pesticides are mentioned but may actually take up more space on a line than the listing of the relevant locators; the use of *passim* is also deprecated by BS

3700, 5.4.3.1, and NISO Z39.4, while the *Chicago manual of style* (1993, 17.9) allows its use "if passing references to the subject over a long sequence of pages are actually important enough to index".

For documents which are paginated in sections or by chapters (as is often the case in TECHNICAL MANUALS AND REPORTS) sequential locators should be given in the form

A-26 to A-31 *or* 6.35 to 6.38

(not A-26–A-31, 6.35–38 or other combinations of hyphens or dashes) in order to avoid ambiguity, even though this may lengthen the locators somewhat.

Number of locators for a heading. One of the worst mistakes made by inexperienced indexers is the indiscriminate listing of dozens or even several hundreds of locators after a heading. Examples of this abomination can be found in old indexes as well as in quite recent ones, particularly in those to bibliographies, collections of abstracts, and the like, in which sometimes hundreds of locators are listed for a single heading, all duly compiled by a computer. Surfeits of locators are found not just in indexes of works published by small and obscure publishers, but—as the following examples show—large and prestigious presses (whose editors ought to know better) are often equally guilty of this offense against the right of users not only to know where a particular item of information can be found but also to find it easily and quickly and labeled as specifically as possible. The mindless accumulation of locators is of no use to man or beast, since nobody will wish to look up, say, some 150 places in which the term "indexing" is mentioned in a collection of abstracts or 420 undifferentiated locators for Mr. John Forster (see Figure 8), nor will anyone have the patience, energy, and perseverance to do so.

Human beings are normally capable of dealing simultaneously with about seven items or "chunks" of information, plus or minus two, as has been shown in a classic paper by George A. Miller. He found that "the span of immediate memory imposes severe limitations on the amount of information that we are able to receive, process, and remember" (Miller 1956, p. 95). Seven plus or minus two may also be the most sensible limit to the number of locators listed against any single heading. NISO Z39.4 recommends the low-

Fontenai, M., i. 273
Foote, Mr., i. 188
Forbes, Captain, i. 486, 508, 509; ii. 136, 245
Foreign Quarterly Review, The, ii. 78, 192
Forester, Cecil, ii. 186
Fornesari, ii. 207, 217
Forrest, Edwin, i. xii, 349, 350, 351, 352, 353, 354, 359, 360, 361, 362, 364, 365, 366, 384, 389, 396, 432, 440; ii. 224, 225, 226, 228, 229, 231, 232, 233, 237, 242, 264, 272, 274, 285, 289, 291, 302, 313, 326, 327, 328, 329, 330, 331, 334, 348, 349, 404, 405, 406, 407, 409 *n.*, 410, 411, 412, 413, 414, 415, 417, 421, 422, 430, 443, 451, 462, 467, 470, 483, 486
Forrest, Mrs., ii. 225, 275, 290, 483, 486
Forster, John, i. 36, 69, 71, 72, 73, 77, 79, 83, 85, 86, 88, 90, 91, 92, 96, 97, 99, 109, 113, 115, 117, 118, 123, 124, 126, 128, 133, 135, 139, 140, 145, 155, 157, 159, 161, 168, 172, 184, 187, 194, 199, 209, 216, 219, 221, 223, 227, 230, 232, 234, 238, 239, 243, 248, 251, 254, 255, 257, 258, 259, 261, 262, 263, 264, 267, 272, 273, 275, 276, 277, 278, 279, 281, 294, 295, 299, 301, 303, 304, 305, 309, 312, 313, 314, 315, 317, 318, 319, 320, 321, 322, 323, 324, 326, 328, 329, 333, 335, 339, 340, 347, 348, 350, 351, 352, 353, 355, 356, 357, 358, 359, 363, 364, 366, 369, 370, 371, 373, 374, 380, 381, 382, 383, 384, 385, 386, 387, 388, 389, 390, 391, 392, 394, 397, 400, 401, 402, 404, 411, 413, 415, 417, 419, 420, 422, 423, 424, 426, 427, 428, 429, 430, 432, 433, 435, 439, 440, 443, 444, 445, 447, 450, 451, 452 *n.*, 453, 454, 455, 456, 458, 459, 462, 465, 466, 467, 469, 473, 475, 476, 477, 478, 479, 481, 483, 484, 486, 492, 494, 495, 496, 498, 499, 500, 501, 503, 504, 505, 506, 510, 511; ii. 2, 3, 4, 5, 6, 7, 9, 12, 14, 16, 20, 21, 22, 23, 24, 25, 26, 27, 29, 33, 34, 35, 43, 44, 45, 53, 55, 57, 60, 63, 64, 67, 69, 70, 71, 72, 73, 74, 75, 76, 79, 80, 81, 82, 83, 84, 85, 86, 87, 88, 89, 91, 92, 94, 95, 97, 98, 102, 103, 104, 105, 106, 107, 108, 109, 110, 112, 114, 115, 117, 120, 121, 122, 123, 125, 126, 128, 130, 132, 134, 135, 137, 139, 140, 142, 143, 144, 145, 146, 147, 149, 151, 155, 157, 158, 159, 162, 164, 165, 166, 168, 169, 171, 175, 178, 179, 185, 186, 188, 189, 191, 192, 196, 198, 203, 205, 207, 208, 209, 211, 213, 214, 215, 218, 219, 220, 238, 244, 277, 288, 289, 295, 296, 297, 299, 300, 301, 302, 304, 305, 306, 307, 308, 310, 315, 316, 317, 318, 320, 322, 323, 325, 333, 334, 336, 338, 339, 340, 341, 347, 348, 349, 351, 353, 357, 359, 360, 361, 362, 365, 366, 367, 369, 370, 372, 374, 375, 376, 377, 378, 380, 382, 383, 385, 387, 388, 391, 392, 395, 397, 398, 399, 403, 419, 434, 435, 437, 441, 447, 449, 452, 454, 455, 457, 458, 461, 464, 465, 466, 467, 468, 469, 471, 472, 474, 475, 476, 477, 478, 479, 480, 481, 482, 483, 484, 485, 486, 487, 488, 489, 490, 491, 492, 493, 495, 497, 498

516

Forster, Major, i. 197, 245
Forster, Mrs., i. 197, 245
"Forster, the butcher-boy," i. 427
Fortescue, Earl, ii. 136
Fortescue, Miss, ii. 140, 145, 146, 147, 149, 150, 151, 152, 160, 200, 318
Fortunio, ii. 211
Fosbrooke, Mrs., i. 117, 199
Foscari (Byron's), i. 124, 233, 410, 447
Foscolo, Ugo, i. 277 *n.*
Fourrier, ii. 372
Fowler, Mr. i. 87
Fox, Colonel, ii. 16, 118
Fox, Miss, ii. 20, 349
Fox, Rev. William, i. 264
Fox, William Johnson, i. 122, 141, 148, 153, 215, 216, 304, 325, 462, 465, 481, 482, 492, 508, 511; ii. 15, 21, 23, 24, 54, 69, 76, 102, 126, 128, 144, 171, 180, 189, 200, 205, 209, 218, 295, 299, 300, 307, 316, 321, 360, 374, 383, 437, 474, 482, 483
Foxhow, ii. 330
Foy, Judge, ii. 240
Fra Diavolo, i. 425
Fra Rupert, ii. 110
Francis, Dr., ii. 242
Franciscus, Mr., ii. 267
Franklin, Sir John, i. 244; ii. 483
Fraser (of Birmingham), i. 40
Fraser (an actor), i. 471 *n.*
Fraser's Magazine, i. 69 *n.*, 77, 239 *n.*, 248, 262, 311; ii. 266 *n.*
Fraudulent Marriage, The, i. 435
Frederick II, Life of, i. 5
Freeman (a playwright), i. 361
Freeman's Journal, The, i. 111; ii. 313
Freemason's Tavern, ii. 15, 136
French, S. (M.P.), i. 235, 282, 449; ii. 78
French Revolution, The (Carlyle's), ii. 34

Figure 8. *From the chamber of horrors: undifferentiated locators.* Reproduced from *The diaries of William Charles Macready.* London: Chapman & Hall, 1912.

er limit of five locators, an ideal that may not always be attainable in practice; both BS 3700, 5.2.3.4 and ISO 999, 7.2.3.5 state only that undifferentiated locators "should be avoided".

If more than about seven locators accumulate for one heading during the compilation stage of an index, this should be a signal for the indexer to start making modifying subheadings, to each of which in turn no more than seven locators should be assigned. It will only very seldom be the case that a topic is dealt with at the same level and without any modification in more than about seven places, except for the names of prolific authors listed in a bibliography, in which case more than a dozen locators may be needed. But few if any serious authors produce more than one work per month, and, if the bibliography covers more than one year, the locators can be broken down by dates of publication. An experienced indexer will almost always be able to make appropriate subheadings for a heading with too many locators, thus breaking up an otherwise unmanageably long string of undifferentiated numbers, as shown in the following example culled from the index to *A history of the Jewish people* (1976), published by Harvard University Press, no less.

Not this	*But this*
Jerusalem 19–22, 37, 41, 50, 56–59, 96–100, 104–107, 111, 113, 115, 116, 118, 127, 131, 134, 138, 141–56, 159, 163, 166–81, 191–9, 203, 204, 208–18, 223–6, 229, 231, 232, 237, 241–71, 275, 276, 279, 281, 284, 285, 291–4, 297, 303, 314–26, 330–2, 334, 338, 342, 350, 352–4, 357, 362, 363, 393, 395, 403, 414, 449, 451, 532, 571–3, 617, 634, 635, 665, 695, 788, 907, 915–8, 921, 925, 926, 991, 998, 1012, 1050, 1052, 1053, 1056, 1057, 1060–2, 1078, 1079, 1084	Jerusalem under Egyptian rule 19–22; mentioned in El Amarna letters 19–20, 37; conquered by Joshua 50; conquered by David 96; under King Solomon 96–100, 104–107; as capital of Judah 111–118; (etc.)

The index shown at right corresponds to only the first three lines of the bad example on the left and would, of course, take up more space, even though it is printed in run-in style. The bad example contains, however, many locators for trivial mentionings of Jerusalem which do not add an iota to information on the history of the city but only make the long string of numbers more bulky.

If too many locators accumulate under a subheading, there are two possible ways of breaking up a long string of numbers. One is to further modify the subheading by sub-subheadings. If this cannot be done because the subheadings are displayed in run-in style, or may not be done (if the editor decided that the index may only have subheadings but no sub-subheadings), the other (and generally better) possibility is to convert the subheading into a main heading which can then be further modified by subheadings. The following example shows both methods.

Not this

Copernicus 56, 67, 71, 110, 119, 151, 152
   conservatism of 29, 36–46
   Dante and 29–35
   heliocentric theory 34, 68–72,
      78–81, 84, 96, 119–120, 138,
      153

But either this *(Sub-subheadings)*	*Or this* *(Conversion to main heading)*

Copernicus 56, 67, 71, 110, 119,
    151, 152
    and Ptolemaic system 34
    conservatism of 29, 36–46
    Dante and 29–35
    heliocentric theory 138, 153
       Bacon on 119–120
       Galileo on 78–81
       Mersenne on 84, 96
       religious objections to 68–72
	heliocentric theory
	    and Ptolemaic system 34
	    Bacon on 119–120
	    Copernican 138, 153
	    Galileo on 78–81
	    Mersenne on 84, 96
	    religious objections to 68–72

Locators after modified main headings. The examples above illustrate another issue on which opinions among indexers differ:

should locators be listed after a main heading that is modified by subheadings, and if so, what do they mean to users? Are the locators after "Copernicus" in the top and left-hand examples the most important references to his life and work, or are they those minor references that could not be adequately characterized by subheadings? There is no good way to indicate either one of those alternatives to users, unless no modified main heading is followed by locators and only the modifying subheadings will lead users to specific topics. This is the practice exemplified in the right-hand example, where the locators 138, 153 for "heliocentric theory" in the left-hand example have been converted to "Copernican" (a term that is only implied in the left-hand example by the subordination of "heliocentric theory" to "Copernicus"). In this case, the conversion of the "overloaded" subheading into a new main heading also happens to solve the problem of inherently ambiguous locators after a main heading.

In general, it is preferable not to list any locators after main headings which are modified by subheadings so as not to mislead users into thinking that these are the most important references, whereas they are in most instances just those for which no suitable subheadings could be constructed because they were too brief or trivial. They could, of course, be left out entirely, but even brief references to a name or topic should not go entirely unnoticed in a good index. One way of dealing with this problem is to list all minor locators under a collective subheading "alluded to", "also mentioned", or "other references" and to relegate it to the end of all other subheadings. This method assures that users will not be led to think that the unspecified locators after a main heading are the most important ones; and it can also be used when some minor subheadings with only one locator each have to be eliminated during editing in order to save space and those locators have to be subsumed under the subheading "other references". The method has, however, two drawbacks: (a) a subheading "also mentioned" (or similar ones) will in most cases not be in its proper alphabetical place among other subheadings; and (b) it is fairly long and, when followed by more than a few locators, will spill over into one or more turnover lines.

In the index to this book, the introductory note explains the nature of locators following a main heading, but the use of such professional jargon in other indexes would probably be lost on readers who are not indexers.

Another method—not recommended here—has been used in a brilliant spoof on indexes in Peter Schickele's *The definitive biography of P.D.Q. Bach* (1976), whose index is preceded by the following introductory note:

> Important references are given in boldface. Italicized numbers indicate fleeting references, whereas numbers in parentheses refer to mere implications or unwarranted extrapolations. Asterisks are used to identify particularly distasteful passages.

The index has no boldface locators (at least none visible to the naked eye), and a typical entry is

Bach, J. S., vii, (ix), (xiii), 3*, 4–5, 6, 11, 15–18, . . .

and so on and on for a total of some 30 locators. But perhaps Schickele has a point here?

Locators for parts of a page. The very first printed indexes were in this respect more sophisticated than most modern ones, because they cited not only the number of the leaf (later of the page) but also the position of an indexed item on the page. This was done by means of a sometimes rather elaborate system of dividing a leaf or page into sections which were labeled in the margin by letters (Wellisch 1986). This system of pinpointing items on a page in indexes was still widely used during the 16th century and was recommended by Conrad Gessner, the "Father of bibliography", who wrote the first known instructions on the compilation of indexes in the introduction to his *Pandectarum . . . libri XXI* (1548) (Wellisch 1981). The method was used by Gessner himself in many of the elaborate indexes he compiled for his own works and was also used by the historian Polydore Vergil in his *Anglicae historiae libri XXVI* (1534), where he indicated both page numbers and line numbers of indexed items.

The practice is still in use today in a few indexes, e.g., in the *Facts on file yearbook* (1941-), which uses the letters A to G in the margins of its three-column text pages, each letter covering about 12 lines; a locator 84B3 identifies an item on page 84 at B (about two inches from the top), third column. But in most modern indexes the more or less precise indication of items on a page is limited to one of four methods: (a) reference to paragraph or section numbers, provided that a text is so organized; (b) sequential numbering of items on each page, e.g., in *The Oxford dictionary of quotations* (1992); (c) the labeling of columns by *a* and *b* (for unnumbered columns on a numbered page), e.g., in *Bartlett's familiar quotations* (1992); or (d) dividing a page into four quarters labeled *a*, *b*, *c*, *d*,

a	c
b	d

so that an item in the lower left-hand quarter of page 25 would get the locator 25b. Bibliographies in which items are not numbered are sometimes indexed by this method: for example, the page number 0342D in figure 5 (p. 249) indicates that the reference is to the fourth abstract printed on page 342—a return to 15th century methods while using the automated KWIC indexing!

Line numbers. While the various types of locators discussed above provide only an approximate indication of terms or phrases on a page, line numbers can pinpoint their exact location. Line numbers are most often used in very densely printed documents, for example in certain LEGAL TEXTS. They may accompany a text from beginning to end, thus serving as direct locators instead of page or paragraph numbers. They may also be employed for each chapter or section of a document, in which case the chapter or section number must precede the line number, e.g.,

water pipes 4: 537, 648, 1023   *or*   stop valves B: 42, 128, 365

where the first number or the letter indicate the chapter and the numbers after the colon indicate the lines on which the topic is mentioned. Sometimes, line numbers cover only the text on a single page, so that the page number must precede the line number, similar to the example above.

Typography. Numerals in locators must be in the same style as those used in the text. If there is anything to be indexed in Roman-numbered prelims (the initial pages of a book preceding the text itself, which may contain a preface or introduction) or in any other section of a book paginated by Roman numbers, lowercase Roman numerals must be used in the locators; all Arabic-numbered pages or columns are of course so indicated. Pages numbered by combinations of letters and numerals, e.g., B 34 or any other unusual method of pagination, must also be indicated exactly as given.

Locators for particularly important or extensive passages, such as entire chapters, may be distinguished from other, less important ones by printing them in boldface, e.g.,

tuberculosis 27, 34, **41–58**, 56, 63

but the listing of such emphasized locators at the beginning of a sequence, that is, **41–58**, 27, 34, 56, 63, would be confusing to most users and should not be used.

For a long time it was the universal custom to set off a heading from its first locator by a comma, and this is still recommended by the *Chicago manual of style* (1993, 17.57), whereas BS 3700, 7.1.4.1 recommends no comma but only a space, and both NISO Z39.4 and ISO 999, 7.4.5 permit the use of a comma, other punctuation marks as needed, or two spaces; NISO Z39.4 has the same provision. Leaving two (typed) spaces or 1 em space in print instead of a comma is more logical because the locators follow a heading as an integral part of an entry, whereas a comma seems to imply that there is a break between the heading and its locators. Both BS 3700 and NISO Z39.4 recommend, however, to put a colon after a heading that ends with a numeral so as to avoid possible confusion, e.g.,

Catch 22: 23, 27
vitamin B2: 3, 5

All typographical devices other than plain numerical locators must be explained in an INTRODUCTORY NOTE to an index, but since users pay only scant attention to such notes or ignore them altogether, they may not know the meaning of different types of locators, so that it seems best not to make too extensive use of italics, boldface, or other typographical variants of locators. Under no circumstances should the same typographical device be used for different purposes in the same index, e.g., boldface to indicate important passages and to distinguish volume numbers from part or page numbers.

Locators for Articles in Periodicals

Locators for articles take different forms depending on the way a PERIODICAL is structured and numbered. Locators must distinguish clearly and unambiguously among the various parts of a periodical, all or most of which are numbered.

In its fullest form, a locator for a periodical article consists of the following elements:

Title of periodical
Year
Volume number
Issue number (or verbal designation, e.g., Spring)
Part of issue
Pagination

This order of elements is prescribed by the International Standard ISO 690 *Bibliographic references—content, form and structure* (International Organization for Standardization 1987*b*). It is in descending order from the most general to the most specific data. The number of elements needed depends on the type of index: the fullest form must be used in references to articles in an index covering a number of different periodicals, while an index to one volume of a single periodical intended to be bound with all issues in the volume needs only page numbers as locators.

Title abbreviations. Periodical titles are often quite long and may, therefore, be abbreviated in locators in order to save space. An abbreviation should follow the rules prescribed in the International Standard ISO 4 *Documentation: Rules for the abbreviation of title words and titles of publications* (International Organization for Standardization 1984, revised 1994) which is almost identical with the British Standard BS 4148 (British Standards Institution 1985) and with NISO Z39.5 *Abbreviations of titles of periodicals* (National Information Standards Organization 199x). These rules are so designed that the same abbreviation is not used for two or more words beginning with the same sequence of letters, e.g., "Int." is to be used for "International" but not for "Internal", whose abbreviation is "Intern." Titles consisting of only one word (exclusive of an article) should never be abbreviated. "Home-made" abbreviations designed ad hoc should not be used, nor should titles be condensed into acronyms or initialisms such as JAMA or BASOR, because these may be unintelligible to most people not familiar with a title, including reference librarians, who are often baffled by requests for a periodical identified only by a mysterious code. While medical workers in the U.S. will probably recognize JAMA as an acronym for the *Journal of the American Medical Association,* other people may not, and BASOR may be an enigma for anyone who is not an archaeologist specializing in the Middle East (the acronym stands for *Bulletin of the American Schools of Oriental Research* and is often found in references to archaeological literature).

Generally, all articles, conjunctions, and prepositions are omitted from title abbreviations. Thus, when properly abbreviated, the two periodical titles just cited would look as follows:

Bull. Am. Sch. Orient. Res.
J. Am. Med. Assoc.

If, however, prepositions are needed to distinguish between similarly abbreviated titles, they must be retained, though they may also be abbreviated:

Archiv für Philosophie abbreviated to *Arch. f. Phil.*
Archives of Philosophy   "   "   *Arch. of Phil.*

Numerical elements. Since all or most of the elements in a locator for a periodical article are expressed by numbers, it is of the utmost importance to distinguish among the various elements either typographically or by punctuation marks or by both methods. PUNCTUATION between elements should be distinctive, unambiguous, and uniform throughout the same index. Various national standards on bibliographic references prescribe different kinds of punctuation for each element. The American National Standard ANSI Z39.29 *Bibliographic references* (American National Standards Institute 1977)* prescribes in section 4.6 parentheses for issue-identification data, colons for "location extent", and semicolons before dates. The British Standard BS 1629 *Recommendations for references to published materials* (British Standards Institution 1989c) has no specific rules on punc-

---

*This standard is currently being revised and may be published as NISO Z39.29 in 1995.

tuation and its examples show various punctuation for different elements, whereas BS 3700, 5.4.4.2 uses only colons in its examples to distinguish between different elements of locators. Other national standards also vary regarding punctuation of bibliographic references. For this reason, the International Standard ISO 690, 6.4 states that "A consistent system of punctuation shall be used for all references . . ."; a note to that section states: "In order to emphasize the importance of consistency, a uniform scheme of punctuation and typographic distinction has been used in the examples. . . . The scheme is only intended to be illustrative, however . . .". The punctuation used consists almost entirely of commas. However, the related International Standard ISO 9115 *Bibliographic identification (biblid) of contributions in serials and books* (International Organization for Standardization 1987*a*) and the identical British Standard BS 7187 *Specification for code for bibliographic identification (biblid) of contributions in serials and books* (British Standards Institution 1989*d*) prescribe in section 4.2 a punctuation scheme whose relevant parts are shown in Table 6. This style of punctuation is probably the most useful one, because it is simple and unambiguous. Moreover, it is now internationally acknowledged and used.

Dates (the day, the month or season and the year) are enclosed in parentheses; days must be indicated for periodicals issued more

Table 6. Punctuation of Bibliographic References According to ISO 9115

Punctuation Mark	Purpose	Example
( )	To enclose the year of publication	(1987)
:	To separate the first order of division in the issue designation from the next, e.g., volume 10: issue 10	10:10
;	To separate the second order division in the issue designation from lower orders other than pagination, e.g., issue 7; part 4	7;4
–	To separate the first and the last page, where the pagination is continuous	p. 76–81
/	To separate the first and the last page, where the pagination is not continuous	p. 101/226
,	To separate the abbreviation for "page(s)" from the preceding part, e.g., vol. 2, issue 4, page 7	2:4, p. 7
.	To indicate the abbreviation of "page(s)"	p. or pp.

than once a month, i.e., weeklies and biweeklies; names of months and seasons should be uniformly abbreviated by three letters (except for "Fall"). Although the names of some months and seasons can be abbreviated using only one or two letters, the saving of space is minimal, while three-letter abbreviations are unambiguous and uniform. If no ambiguity will result, the digits indicating the century may be omitted from the date.

Volume numbers may be printed in boldface to distinguish them from issue numbers (which normally follow them); Roman numerals used as volume numbers are always converted to Arabic numerals because they tend to take up much space, e.g., XXXVIII, and most people cannot figure out that, say, CXLVII is 147. If a volume is either a part of or subdivided into series, the series number or designation is either given in full or suitably abbreviated, e.g., "Ser. 2" or "New ser".

Issue numbers are separated from volume numbers by a colon. When an issue is further divided into numbered parts, a semicolon separates issue from part number.

Page numbers must indicate the full extent of an article: the first and last page, or those pages on which the text appears if article pages are interspersed with advertising pages or other extraneous matter. Under no circumstances should only the first page of an article be listed in an index, because users want to know how long or short an article is (although this is by no means an indication of its value) or for the purpose of ordering a photocopy. A single page number should always indicate that an article is contained on just one page.

The complete reference to an article in a periodical index would be:

Svenonius, Elaine. Unanswered questions in the
design of controlled vocabularies. *J. Amer. Soc.
Inform. Sci.* (Sept. 86) 37:5, pp. 331–340.

Locators for Graphic Materials

Locators for ILLUSTRATIONS are often indicated by printing page numbers in italics, but this practice is not very effective, because italic numerals are often difficult to distinguish from regular numerals printed in roman type when the locators for illustrations are interspersed with those for textual references. Asterisks or square brackets enclosing illustration locators are more conspicuous, though they take up a little more space. Verbal extensions of locators may also be used, for example, when a plate is inserted between text pages, which can be indexed as

Franklin, Benjamin 32, 67
    portrait facing 54

If locators for pictures are to be distinguished from other illustrations or nontextual items such as MAPS or charts, letters may be added to page numbers, e.g., *m* for maps and *p* for pictures. But since this may confuse users rather than help them to find specific items, it is preferable to convert such locators into subheadings which are much clearer, even though they do take up more space:

Yukon Territory 17, 54
    history 23–25
    map facing 18
    minerals 68, 72
    photos 45, 57, 63
    wildlife 62–65

For the indication of features on the face of graphic materials, such as places on maps or details on charts, drawings, or graphs, a grid system like that on most maps may be used, so that in the entry "Anytown C2", the locator refers to the grid:

	A	B	C	
1				
2			Anytown o	
3				

If a grid locator is not appropriate or feasible, the indexer must design a system of locators specially geared to the graphic material to be indexed.

Locators for Nonprint Materials

Locators for NONPRINT MATERIALS may pose problems, because the mode of recording information often does not lend itself to an exact way of pinpointing the place of a particular item.

If a nonprint material consists of items that are or can be numbered sequentially, the principles governing the listing of locators for printed materials may be applicable, though they may have to be suitably adapted to the nature of the medium. Photos, pictures, slides, sound recordings, movies, video cassettes or tapes, and optical disks, taken as individual units of a collection, can be numbered. Any of these may, however, contain more than one indexable item. Thus, if a specific piece of recorded sound contained on a long-playing record, a compact disk, or on magnetic tape is to be indexed, one must resort to relative location, such as playing time from a particular point in addition to the serial number of the medium itself. The same method may be used for specific scenes on film, video tape, or videodisk.

For multi-media materials, more than one system of locators will be necessary, e.g., playing time for one piece on a video cassette and page numbers for an accompanying printed manual.

BS 3700: 5.4
ISO 4 ≡ BS 4148
ISO 690: 3.3; 10
ISO 999: 7.4
NISO Z39.4:
NISO Z39.5

LOOSE-LEAF PUBLICATIONS

A loose-leaf publication is a work originally published in one or more sturdy ring binders, pages of which are from time to time added or withdrawn in order to keep the work constantly up to date. They are published primarily in two fields: (a) comprehensive collections of laws, statutes, and regulations; and (b) service manuals for all kinds of appliances or vehicles from dishwashers to jumbo jets. Since many loose-leaf publications comprise thousands of pages, they need very detailed indexes in order to be usable. LOCATORS are practically always paragraph or section numbers, though the pages themselves may also be numbered and may occasionally be used as locators.

Publishers of loose-leaf publications provide a main index with the original set of binders, but when new batches of replacement pages are issued, they are often accompanied by an interim index which refers only to the additions, changes, or deletions that have been made, while a complete new main index is published only once a year or at even longer intervals.

Indexing loose-leaf publications is, therefore, comparable to the labors of Sisyphus: just when the indexer thought that the index to the latest batch of updating pages had been finished, along comes a new batch, and the work has to be started again, sometimes from scratch, that is, when a new main index has to be compiled. On the other hand, an indexer of a large loose-leaf publication is virtually assured of steady long-time employment, whether as an in-house indexer at the publishers' or as a freelancer.

The addition of new material poses relatively few problems, although care must be taken to use terminology for subheadings and cross-references consistent with that used for related previous items. Changes in the wording of items are more difficult to deal with, since the new terms must be reconciled with those already used for the same topic before the change was made. It also happens, particularly in the legal field, that a section which was deleted in an earlier batch of pages is not only revived or re-enacted but is also moved to a different place, which affects the locators of the relevant headings. Deletions of items will affect not only the main headings referring to them but also a large number of subheadings under other, still valid, headings.

All of this must be incorporated into each supplementary index accompanying a new batch or replacement pages, and users must also be reminded to cancel the headings in their main index which have been deleted.

In order to make the required changes when compiling a supplementary index, the indexer must be able to find each heading and all of its subheadings by locator in the main index and in previous supplementary indexes. It is, therefore, necessary to have constant and rapid access not only to the alphabetical sequence of entries but also to a "reverse index" arranged by paragraph or section numbers, for which purpose a computer with a sufficiently large memory and sophisticated indexing software are virtually indispensable.

MAC

What will go down in history as "The Big Mac Battle" was not a fight among competing fast-food chains over the best, largest, or juiciest hamburger but one over the proper alphabetization of Scottish and Irish names beginning with the patronymic Mac or its variant spellings Mc or M'. All arrangement rules before the start of that great battle in 1980 prescribed intermingling of all such names "as if" they were all spelled Mac-. (That was only one of dozens of such rules for alphabetizing not what was clearly written but what was to be arranged "as if" it had been written differently or not at all—never mind that users of alphabetical lists so arranged were not privy to such arcane rules and therefore could not find what they were looking for.)

Since computers invariably work according to the wysiwyg principle ("what you see is what you get"), the "as if" arrangement of Mac, Mc, and M' could not (and still cannot) be automated, quite apart from the fact that Africans such as M'Bengui or M'Bow are now also appearing as authors in indexes and other alphabetical lists, and their names cannot be treated "as if" the M' stood for Mac. In Queen Victoria's time (during which the "file-as-if-Mac" rule was probably invented) there were of course no such African names to compete with Scottish ones.

When new arrangement rules were published in 1980 by the American Library Association and by the Library of Congress, followed in 1985 by the British Standards Association, the inexorable necessity of making the arrangement of words, including family names, almost entirely automatic was recognized. All "arrange as if" rules were virtually eliminated, and that was also the end of the rule to alphabetize Mc and M' as Mac. While ALA and LC rules do not even mention the Mac/Mc/M' issue, and allow no exceptions, the British alphabetizing and indexing standards (BS 1749:1985 and BS 3700:1988, respectively), anticipating the wrath of warriors from the North, are straddling the fence; they state that "Mac and its contractions should be filed as given unless the nature, purpose, or tradition of a list requires arrangement as if spelt out in full". Similarly, the *Chicago manual of style* (1993, 17.109) prefers the alphabetizing of names beginning with M', Mac, and Mc "as they appear" but allows also arrangement as if the two short forms were spelled Mac. Incidentally, the Scottish Record Office prefers to spell all pre-1750 names as Mc-, even if written in other forms, that is, the exact opposite of what later filing rules prescribed until 1980—so much for consistency in this matter!

Notwithstanding the compromise solution offered in the British filing and indexing standards, the Scots did not let this assault on their hallowed traditions go unchallenged. Great lengths of typewriter ribbon, many squirts of ink jets, and even plain old ink were spent on written diatribes against this outrage, and fiery oratory from Scottish pulpits was heard at gatherings of British indexers, defending the "file-as-if-Mac forever" doctrine, solemnly swearing never to submit to the unconscionable demands of the Sassenachs and their soulless machines.

The rationale behind the old rule was that users could not be sure whether the name they were looking for was spelled Mac-, Mc-, or M'-, and would therefore have an easier time finding a Scottish or Irish name quickly if only the part of the name following the patronymic had to be searched. There may be some kernel of truth to this reasoning when it comes to phone books, genealogical lists, and other long listings of names, but it does not necessarily pertain to indexes of books and periodicals. People who have read a book and wish to find a particular MacSo-and-so may often remember the spelling of that name; also, in one book there will in any case not be a tremendous number of Scottish names (unless, of course, the book deals exclusively with Scotland and things Scottish), so that it will be easy to find a particular one in the index even without any

artificial intermingling of different spellings. In indexes to periodicals, a larger number of names beginning with Mac, Mc, or M' may
occur, especially in cumulative indexes covering more than one
year, but searches in such indexes are in most cases triggered by a
citation, so that the particular spelling of a name will be known in
advance (barring some printing error in the source).

Needless to say, in electronic bibliographic databases and in their
printed versions produced from the machine-readable record, no
"file as if" rule can be applied, since all sorting is done exclusively
by computer. Such databases have now been with us for a long
time, and while users complain loudly about various difficulties in
searching, no such complaint has been heard so far about not being
able to find Scottish or Irish names beginning with Mac, nor have
any protests been lodged against American phone books, which for
many years have listed such names exactly as written, omitting
even cross-references from Mac to Mc or M' and vice versa (the
latter omission not being good practice).

It is perhaps useful to remind the adherents of the old "file-as-if-
Mac" rule that other countries and languages have similar problems
with variously spelled names without having to resort to "as
if" arrangement. In German, the very common names Maier /
Mayer / Mayr / Meier / Meyer are all pronounced the same but are
not merged in phone books or indexes. In the Scandinavian countries there are many dozens of patronymic names, each of which
may be spelled in several different ways, e.g.,

Petersen
Peterson
Peterssen
Petersson
Pettersen
Petterson
Petterssen
Pettersson

Although in some Scandinavian phone books such names may be
listed together under the heading "Petersen" with cross-references
from other spellings, no such practice is followed in book or periodical indexes, and the Danes, Norwegians, and Swedes can live
with that.

Because the post-1980 "arrange-as-written" rules have now been in force and in use for a long time and are not likely to be withdrawn or substantially changed any time soon, it is best to follow them also for alphabetizing Scottish and Irish names beginning with Mac, Mc, or M' in all indexes and lists, however distasteful this may be to the good people living north of Hadrian's Wall who in this as in other matters spiritual and temporal will probably continue to follow their own traditions.

The following examples show that the pre-1980 rules will in any case not keep all such names together in one unbroken sequence but will make it more difficult to find other names beginning with the letter sequence Mac- or African names beginning with M':

Scottish and Irish names arranged as if all spelled Mac	All names arranged as written
MacAdam, John	MacAdam, John
McAlister, Mary	Maccobi, Daniel
Maccoby, Daniel	Mach, Ernst
McCrank, Lawrence	Machiavelli, Niccolò
McDonald, Angus	Machinery Design Co.
Mach, Ernst	Machlup, Fritz
Machiavelli, Niccolò	Mack, Diane
Machinery Design Co.	MacKay, Donald
Machlup, Fritz	Macpherson, Thomas
Mack, Diane	MacRae, Richard
MacKay, Donald	Mazzini, Giuseppe
McPartland, Alan	M'Bow, Amadou
McPhee, Alice	McAlister, Mary
Macpherson, Thomas	McCrank, Lawrence
M'Quade, William	McDonald, Angus
MacRae, Richard	McPartland, Alan
Mazzini, Giuseppe	McPhee, Alice
M'Bow, Amadou	Mozart, Wolfgang Amadeus
Mozart, Wolfgang Amadeus	M'Quade, William

ALA: 6
BS 1749: 5.3.4
BS 3700: 6.2.1.5
LC: 15

MAPS

Maps are indexed in three quite different and unrelated ways. One is the indexing of maps in books and periodicals; another is the indexing of individually published maps and that of atlases; and a third is the indexing of map collections.

Although maps printed together with textual matter are technically illustrations, it is not good practice to index them simply like any other pictures or diagrams, e.g., only by italicized or otherwise specially marked LOCATORS. Maps convey unique visual information, clarifying and amplifying the verbal description of a region, journey, military campaign, and the like, so that their presence and location should be separately indexed. In most cases, no more than a brief indication in the form of a subheading for the area or place is needed:

> Mount St. Helens
>   eruption 36–39
>   geology 25
>   map facing 34
>   reforestation 41

Unfortunately, maps are often inserted into the text of a book at the very last moment, especially if they are printed as separate plates, and neither they nor the accompanying captions nor their location may be shown on the page proofs; for that reason, maps are often not included in an index, and the indexer is then blamed for the omission. An indexer working on a book that by its very nature may include maps should ask the editor to supply at least their captions, which will in most instances contain sufficient information to index the maps under appropriate headings.

Indexing a map, that is, all named features on it (of which there may be more than a thousand on a single sheet), and even more the indexing of an atlas are among the more complex and time-consuming indexing tasks. Virtually all map indexes are the work of experienced in-house indexers at cartographic publishers who compile such indexes in close cooperation with cartographers (Burneston 1994). Anyone who has ever used a road map knows that a named feature—a city or town, a river, mountain, or monument, streets and buildings—is indexed by a grid system marked on the margins by letters and numbers, the intersections of which identify a rectangle or trapezium serving as an approximate locator (*see* illustration on p. 291). Sometimes, the latitude and longitude are used instead of letters and numbers or in addition to them, which has the advantage of pinpointing a place on the map exactly and not only somewhere on a grid unit. Much care must be exercised not to omit even a single named place or feature on a map and to list also all those that straddle more than one grid unit, such as mountain ranges, rivers, or long streets. Difficulties may arise in gazetteers regarding the alphabetization of PLACE NAMES, many of which may be HOMOGRAPHS, e.g., places named Washington in the United States, as a look at the relevant section of a gazetteer to any large and comprehensive atlas will show. The indexers and editors of gazetteers sometimes devise special arrangement rules in order to cope with the problems of alphabetizing homographic place names; such rules must be made known to users in an INTRODUCTORY NOTE to the gazetteer. The complexities of arranging homographic place names can be avoided to a large extent by dividing a gazetteer into separate indexes for each state, province, or district, as is often done in road atlases for motorists.

The indexing of map collections is generally descriptive only, because its purpose is the retrieval of a particular map out of a large number stored. Each map must be identified by several characteristics, such as country or area, scale, language and script, provenance, and other features, depending on the character, size, and prospective use of the collection. Details on descriptive indexing of maps are listed under NONPRINT MATERIALS on page 337.

MEDICAL TEXTS

The medical profession shares with that of lawyers the honor of having produced not only the earliest written records of remedies for illnesses and of laws respectively, starting with Egyptian papyri some 4,000 years ago, but also of indexes to those compilations. For medical works, these can be traced to the late Middle Ages, followed by some of the earliest printed indexes, beginning with the *Gart der Gesundtheit* (The garden of health), published in 1485. That "index to find out quickly about all diseases of human beings", as it was advertised, was designed for the do-it-yourself patient, and was divided into a subject index, arranged by diseases "from head to foot", and a bilingual index of plant names in Latin and German. The indexes were placed after the text which consisted of descriptions of medicinal plants, and served as a model of indexes for later medical and other scientific works well into the next century (Wellisch, 1978).

The indexing of modern medical works, like that of other specialized fields, must first of all follow the basic rules set forth under THE INDEXING PROCESS and INDEXING TECHNIQUES, but the special topics of the field and the information needs of its practitioners and other professional users, as well as those of the general public, make it necessary to observe some additional rules and features that are characteristic for medical indexes.

This discussion pertains to all forms of medical literature but the emphasis is on the indexing of books which generally form the bulk of a medical indexer's work. Periodical articles from all over the world are extensively indexed by the large biomedical databases such as BIOSIS, MEDLINE, Excerpta Medica, and others which set their own rules and train their in-house teams of indexers in the use of a thesaurus developed by the database. In addition, many medical PERIODICALS provide their readers with annual volume indexes which may be commissioned from professional indexers.

The Medical Literature

The medical literature can be divided into four broad categories:

1. Works on clinical practice;
2. Works on scientific medical research;
3. Works on allied health fields (nutrition, optometry, physical therapy, podiatry, radiological technology, speech pathology, etc.);

4. Works on paramedical techniques (acupuncture, chiropractic).

Within each category, there are several types of works, aimed at different audiences, in ascending order of specialization and difficulty of comprehension:

a. works for non-medical readers;
b. elementary textbooks for students;
c. works for nurses and allied health practitioners;
d. comprehensive textbooks on specific branches of medicine or on specific diseases and disorders;
e. reference works: medical atlases, dictionaries, encyclopedias;
f. advanced treatises on specialized topics (often in the form of symposia or conference proceedings).

The increasing level of difficulty of these types of works may result in increasingly complex levels of indexing. On the other hand, this does not necessarily mean that a medical book written for a general audience is always easier to index than an advanced treatise; as usual, much depends on the style and writing skill of the author.

The various types of works listed above may be focused on one or more of the following main topics:

a. History and epidemiology of a disease or disorder;
b. Anatomic site (organs and organ systems);
c. Etiology and pathology;
d. Physiology;
e. Procedures and techniques (diagnostic, therapeutic, surgical, laboratory, experimental);
f. Drugs and biochemical substances;
g. Prognosis and results;
h. Appliances and instruments.

Indexable Matter

The decision on *what* to index is generally not too difficult because most medical works are written in a straightforward style, in brief paragraphs, and with a systematic pattern of exposition. But *how* to

choose main headings and subheadings will to a large extent depend on which of the main topics is the focus of a medical text. If it
is about one specific disease, condition or procedure, its name may
not appear at all in the index as a main heading, or it may be used
for only a few very general entries. Rather, the headings will reflect
the wording of CHAPTER HEADINGS and the headings of sections
and subsections, e.g., the pathology, therapy, surgical procedures (if
any), and other aspects of a disease, while the subheadings may
cover conditions, effects, complications, and other related matters.
If the work is devoted to a particular anatomic site or organ system,
say, the gastrointestinal tract and its diseases, the main headings
will primarily include the names of the diseases with subheadings
for their etiology, pathology, and physiology, while other main
headings may be for therapies (drugs, diets, etc.) and surgical procedures, each with subheadings for the names of individual anatomic sites, and for conditions, effects, and other aspects.

   Multiple entries are usually necessary in order to provide quick
and easy access to every aspect of a topic, tailored to the needs of
different users. At the same time, care must be taken not to scatter
information in an unhelpful manner, as discussed in DOUBLE EN-
TRIES. Some publishers have a policy that limits the amount of
multiple entries for headings with many subheadings.

Depth of Indexing

Medical indexing must be performed at a high level of EX-
HAUSTIVITY, including not only all significant terms in a text that
pertain to diseases, their symptoms, treatment and therapy, techniques and procedures but also terms for items shown and labeled
in ILLUSTRATIONS and TABLES, especially if these are not expressly
mentioned in the text. The need for high exhaustivity which may
yield a dozen or even many more entries per page in highly advanced and specialized texts results in long indexes that are fairly
typical for the medical literature. Occasionally, authors or editors
may consider some minor topic as not worth indexing because in
their opinion "no one will wish to look that up", not taking into
account that, first, even a medical specialist may have to search for a
term that is common in a different medical specialty; and second,

students and other less well trained people may occasionally use the index to an advanced work and will then need access to terms that are familiar to the specialist.

The same reasoning applies to SPECIFICITY of medical indexing which in virtually all instances should be as high as the text allows, following as far as possible the terminology of the text, but also employing preferred descriptors, broader, narrower, and related terms from sources that are well known and widely used by the medical profession. The principal source of authorized medical terms is the *Metathesaurus* (1990–), the central vocabulary tool of the Unified Medical Language System (UMLS), developed by the U.S. National Library of Medicine (NLM). This annually updated thesaurus combines terms from NLM's *Medical subject headings (MeSH)*, the College of American Pathologists' *Systematic nomenclature of medicine (SNOMED)*, the *International classification of diseases, 9th ed., clinical modification (ICD-9-CM)*, and selected *MeSH* terms (Schuyler 1993). The *Metathesaurus* is available on CD-ROM only, and is intended to be used in large biomedical information retrieval systems. It is thus not a tool for the individual medical indexer, among whose best friends are *MeSH*, *Grateful Med* (NLM's online thesaurus), Excerpta Medica's *MALIMET* (Master List of Medical Terms), or any of the printed or online thesauri covering specialized medical fields.

An appropriate DEPTH OF INDEXING may result in multilevel headings with several levels of modification (main heading, sub-headings, and sub-subheadings), especially for advanced treatises and textbooks, but more than three levels of modification should be avoided, because they tend to become confusing, as in the following example:

```
polycythemia
  blood pressure in
    decreases
      at sea level
    increases
      at high altitude
      during exercise
```

This can be simplified to

polycythemia
  blood pressure in
    altitude effects
    exercise effects

with additional entries for

altitude levels
  effects on blood pressure
    in polycythemia

blood pressure
       see also hypertension; hypotension
  altitude effects
    in polycythemia

exercise
  effects on blood pressure
    in polycythemia

hypertension
  in polycythemia
    altitude effects
    exercise effects

hypotension
  in polycythemia
    altitude effects
    exercise effects

Some of these entries may have to be changed or eliminated in the final EDITING. Note also that the subheading "altitude effects" may serve for both high and low [sea level], but neither that subheading nor "exercise effects" may be needed if no other mention of these factors is made in the text because that would constitute over-indexing. It may even be possible to reduce the entries to

polycythemia   *and*   blood pressure
  blood pressure in   in polycythemia

depending on the level and complexity of the text.

Terminology

Medical terms differ from other specialized vocabularies in several ways:

a. *Size.* The medical vocabulary is very large and is constantly growing. Its size is exceeded only by that of lists of chemical compounds whose terms are often also used in medical contexts, especially for drugs.

b. *Etymology.* More than three quarters of all medical terms are derived from Greek and Latin roots, both of which may be combined to form a single hybrid term, e.g., gastrointestinal (from Greek *gastēr* [stomach], Latin *intestinum,* and the English suffix -al). Consequently, many terms are exceedingly long, being formed from concatenations of several Greek and Latin roots, e.g., cerebellorubrospinal, cholecystogastrostomy, or erythroleukothrombocythemia.

c. *Changing terms.* While many terms, especially anatomical ones, have been in continuous and often unchanged use for more than two millennia, terms for diseases, therapies, genes, enzymes, proteins, and many other biomedical matters are frequently changed as more is being learned about their nature. For example, what was once called consumption is now pulmonary tuberculosis, and what was once known as mongolism and later (erroneously) as chromosome 21 syndrome, is now called Down syndrome. In every instance, CROSS-REFERENCES from the unused or obsolete terms to the current one must be made.

d. *Eponyms.* Many medical terms are eponymous, that is, they are named for the person who first described a disease or performed a technique, e.g., Alzheimer's syndrome, Wassermann test. Most eponyms are internationally known but some are used only nationally or regionally, e.g., hyperthyroidism is known in Central Europe as Basedow's syndrome, but has also been called elsewhere Flajani's, Graves's, or Perry's syndrome.

e. *Synonyms.* Many medical terms are synonyms which may be used interchangeably by different authors, e.g., mortinatality vs. natimortality. This phenomenon is frequently encountered in collective works such as multi-author textbooks, conference proceedings or international symposia, particularly in papers by authors whose native language is not English. The indexer must make sure that two or three different terms (including eponyms) are indeed synonymous; if so, one term must be chosen as the preferred one, all others being referred to it by cross-references.

In order to resolve problems posed by changing terms, eponyms, synonyms, and other terminological pitfalls, the indexer must have recourse to current medical dictionaries, glossaries, and thesauri, some of which are accessible online and are being updated continuously (see list on p. 313).

f. *Neologisms.* The sources just mentioned are, however, of little or no use for newly invented terms and specialist jargon often found in conference proceedings, symposia on the latest advances in a particular area, and in literature reviews of research. Neologisms are particularly difficult to deal with because their exact meaning is not always made clear when they are first used, the inventors assuming that their peers would know what they mean. In the absence of an explication the indexer may have to contact the author or editor or, if all else fails, must make an educated guess.

A particularly bothersome type of neologism, known as "medicant", is the substitution of euphemisms and circumlocutions for unpleasant or embarrassing aspects of medical practice, such as "negative patient care outcome" as a description of a patient's death, or "decreased propensity for cell replication" for the process of aging. Such tortuous expressions should preferably not find their way into an index, but should be translated into the terms of their commonly understood meaning, possibly with cross-references from the euphemistic medicant to plain English.

Binomial Terms

Many medical terms consist of a noun and an adjective, and are therefore known as binomial terms. They are either derived from Greek or Latin (or from both), or form hybrids of English and Greek or Latin roots. There are three types of medical binomial terms which must be treated differently in indexing.

1. *Taxonomic terms* for plants and animals (which medicine shares with biology) always follow the Latin grammatical pattern noun + adjective, the noun indicating the genus and the adjective

the species, sometimes followed by an additional adjective for sub-species. The two parts of taxonomic binomials should never be separated in indexing but should always be listed as a unit, e.g.,

Correct	Incorrect
Digitalis lanata	*Digitalis*
Digitalis purpurea	*lanata*
Escherichia coli	*purpurea*
Escherichia freundii	*Escherichia*
	coli
	freundii

Taxonomic terms are always italicized, and the noun is capitalized but not the adjective, even if derived from a proper name (as in the last example above).

2. *Anatomical binomials* occur mostly in English form (adjective + noun), e.g., femoral artery, transverse colon, though Latin terms, in noun + adjective form, e.g., vena cava, are also frequently used. These binomials, too, must always be given in their standard form, and must neither be inverted nor split into main and subheading. Latin anatomical binomials are neither italicized nor capitalized.

3. *Binomial terms of diseases.* These are to be treated as COM-POUND TERMS in which the noun component is the name of the disease and a modifying adjective indicates either

a. its anatomic site, e.g., glandular carcinoma; pulmonary tuberculosis;
b. its diagnostic or histological description, e.g., rheumatoid arthritis; sebaceous nevus;
c. its etiology or pathogenic factor, e.g., malignant hypertension; viral pneumonia.

These binomials should preferably not be inverted, but should be split (factored) into a main heading for the noun component and modifying subheadings for the adjectival components; if the latter pertain to an anatomical site, they should also appear as separate entries in noun form. Cross-references may be made to facilitate retrieval of other adjectival components.

Examples:

binomial terms in text	*index entries*
melanotic carcinoma	carcinoma
pulmonary	melanotic
carcinoma	pulmonary
	lungs
	carcinoma
intestinal tuberculosis	intestines
open tuberculosis	tuberculosis
viral tuberculosis	open tuberculosis *see* tuberculosis: open
	tuberculosis
	intestinal
	open
	viral

The same Latin nouns in binomial terms of diseases may be modified either by Latin adjectives, e.g., nevus anemicus, or by English ones, e.g., blue nevus. Latin binomials should always be treated as an indivisible term, that is, they should not be split into a main heading and subheading; hybrid English-Latin binomials, however, may be split (as in the examples above). For example, the term "nevus", when modified by both Latin and English adjectives, should first be listed as a main heading with the English adjectives as subheadings in indented style, then followed by the Latin terms, e.g.,

nevus
   amelanotic 102
   blue 138
   stellar 136
   white 129
nevus anemicus 129
nevus fibrosus 141
nevus maternus 122
nevus vinosus 138

Mixing Latin and English-Latin binomials in run-in style, e.g.,

nevus
   amelanotic 102, anemicus 129,
   blue 138, fibrosus 141, maternus 122,
   stellar 136, vinosus 138, white 129

should not be used in a medical or other scientific index, unless space is at a premium.

Under no circumstances should the adjectival part of any binomial term be used as a main heading, with the noun parts forming subheadings, e.g.,

spinal
  anesthesia 388
  cord 85
  nerve 286

Instead, compound headings, e.g., spinal anesthesia, spinal cord, spinal nerve, should be used in this instance, with double entries for the nouns as required.

Drug Names

The indexing of drugs mentioned in medical and biochemical texts is made difficult by the fact that all drugs are known by at least two synonymous appellations: the brand name invented by the manufacturer and the verbally expressed chemical composition, both displayed on the label of the container. But virtually all currently available drugs have additional names and identifiers: the U.S. Adopted Name (USAN), the molecular formula and weight, the CAS registry number, the graphic formula, and they may also have an International Non-proprietary name (INN), assigned by the World Health Organization. After the expiration of the patent and the copyright for the manufacturer's brand name, other firms may produce and market the same drug under various other names, one example being acetylsalicylic acid ($C_9H_8C_4$), originally named Aspirin, and now marketed under more than 80 different brand names around the world (Snow 1992).

Any of these names may be used by medical writers, sometimes in the same work, particularly if it is a symposium devoted to a new drug or to a therapy using a particular drug, to which authors from different countries contribute papers. Even if all authors use English, they may use different spellings (sulfate/sulphate) for the same name, and if the editor of such a multi-author work has not taken care to standardize the nomenclature and spelling of drug

names (as is unfortunately all too often the case in conference proceedings and symposia), the indexer must decide on the name and
its spelling, often with the aid of a medical dictionary. Preferably,
references should be made from trade names to the generic chemical name, e.g.,

>   Advil *see* ibuprofen

or, if only one or two locators are involved, a double entry may save
the reader's time:

>   Advil (ibuprofen) 34, 46   ibuprofen 34, 46

Spelling

Not only the names of drugs may occur in various different spellings, but many other medical terms have alternative forms, e.g.,
fetus/foetus, nevus/naevus. The major medical dictionaries are
not always of one mind about the preferred SPELLING of a term.
The house style of a medical publisher is generally based on a
particular dictionary and will, therefore, govern the choice of
spelling, but authors' preferences should be followed, particularly
in the case of neologisms, until a spelling has become generally
accepted or authorized. A case in point was reported by a major
publisher: an author had used the word "jugulomohyoid", a concatenation of "jugulo-" (which means in or of the jugular region)
and "omohyoid" (which means pertaining to the scapula and the
hyoid bone). This raised two editorial questions: (a) should the
term be accepted though it was not in any dictionary? and (b)
since the first component of the terms ends in an *o* and the second
one begins with an *o*, should there be one or two *o*'s in the middle? Because similar concatenations are listed in medical dictionaries with two *o*'s, it was decided to (a) accept the term and (b)
spell it "juguloomohyoid". An indexer, who is not privy to such a
decision, should, therefore, in case of doubt refer to the editor of
the text.

Acronyms

The medical and biochemical literature employs an abundance of acronyms, probably more than are found in the texts of any other field or discipline, with the possible exception of the military. The indexing of acronyms is discussed under ABBREVIATIONS, but medical acronyms often pose additional problems for the indexer. It is only natural for medical writers to prefer acronyms to the sometimes enormously long names of drugs, chemical compounds, syndromes, therapies, and organizations, but not all authors take care to spell out an acronym the first time it is being used in a text, nor is a list of acronyms always provided. Some authors do not spell out acronyms because they assume that "everybody knows" what is meant, which may be true for that author's collaborators and colleagues, but not for the rest of the profession, much less for general readers.

Many frequently used medical acronyms have become so well known that even people who are not medically trained know their full form or at least their meaning, e.g., AIDS (acquired immunodeficiency syndrome), ECG (electrocardiogram), or ENT (ear, nose and throat), but even these should preferably be indexed first of all as main headings in their full form, and as acronyms only in subheadings (in order to save space) and in cross-references. This practice obviates the need to make awkward decisions on which acronyms are "well known" and may therefore be indexed without further explication, and which are not.

When an acronym is not spelled out anywhere in a text, the indexer may find it in one of the specialized dictionaries of medical abbreviations and acronyms which are published in updated editions every few years so as to keep pace with the rapidly growing number of abbreviated terms.

The Medical Indexer

The indexing of medical works, just as that of any other specialized subject field, should preferably be performed by a person who has had some medical background and is familiar with the common terminology of the medical profession, such as nurses, allied health personnel, medical secretaries, administrative hospital personnel, and of course by retired physicians, if they are so inclined. Contrary to the myth that authors are also the best indexers of their books, physicians who write books will seldom have the time, desire, and—most important—the skills necessary for quality indexing, nor would the fees earned by indexers be likely to appeal to them.

Although it would be nice if the indexes to specialized medical monographs, conference proceedings, and symposia could be compiled by indexers who also specialize in the relevant topics, in practice this cannot be expected to happen. A surgeon may choose to be a specialist in, say, orthopedic surgery with emphasis on hip replacement techniques, (and may write on this topic) but an indexer similarly specializing would soon starve to death. Rather, a broad knowledge of medical terminology, its characteristics and problems, together with a "feel" for the style of indexing appropriate for each work are the necessary prerequisites. Unfortunately, such a "feel"—a skill that all successful indexers in specialized fields tend to develop over time—cannot be taught.

Indexers who have already gained some experience in indexing general works but wish to specialize in medical texts might try their hand at health-related works for the general public such as the popular one-volume compendia on the most common diseases and their treatment, written "for the whole family", or works describing the symptoms, etiology, and therapy of a particular disease, say diabetes, for non-medical readers. Another good source for beginners (and even for experienced indexers who are unfamiliar with medical terminology) are basic texts for medical students; such textbooks are generally well organized and clearly written, and medical terms are explained and exemplified in text and illustrations. As familiarity with medical topics increases and medical indexing skills improve, clinical texts for general practitioners and nurses can be tackled and these may in due course lead to the indexing of specialized monographs and major treatises, for the indexing of which higher fees can be expected.

Medical indexers who prefer steady work (and income!) to the vagaries of freelancing may become employees of one of the large biomedical database producers who provide training in the use of their specialized thesauri and the particular kind of indexing they prefer. One of the incentives for this type of work is the indexer's constant exposure to the latest advances in the biomedical field, which may to some extent compensate for the less enjoyable aspects of the work, such as the high speed and large output generally required of indexers by the management of biomedical databases.

Reference Works

Dictionaries:

Butterworth's medical dictionary. 2nd ed. London: Butterworth, 1978.
Davies, P. M. *Medical terminology: a guide to current usage.* 5th ed. London: Butterworth-Heinemann, 1991.
Dorland's illustrated medical dictionary. 27th ed. Philadelphia: Saunders, 1988.
Dorland's medical abbreviations. Philadelphia: Saunders, 1992.
Jablonski, S. *Jablonski's dictionary of syndromes & eponymic diseases.* 2nd ed. Malabar, FL: Krieger, 1991.
The Sloane-Dorland annotated medical-legal dictionary. St. Paul, MN: West Publishing Co., 1987.
Stedman's medical dictionary. 25th ed. Baltimore: Williams & Wilkins, 1990. Also available in WordPerfect ® versions for IBM and MAC PCs.
Taber's cyclopedic medical dictionary. 17th ed. Philadelphia: F. A. Davis, 1993.

Drug names:

British national formulary. London: British Medical Association and The Pharmaceutical Society of Great Britain. Thrice annually.
USAN and the USP dictionary of drug names. Rockville, MD: United States Pharmacopeal Convention. Annual.

Style manuals:

American Medical Association manual of style. 8th ed. Baltimore: Williams & Wilkins, 1989.
Scientific style and format: the CBE manual for authors, editors, and publishers. 6th edition. New York: Cambridge University Press, 1994.
Units, symbols, and abbreviations: a guide for biological and medical editors and authors. 5th ed., edited by D. N. Baron. London: Royal Society of Medicine Press, 1994. (Contains also a selection of British Standard proof correction marks.)

MULTIPLE INDEXES

One index or several? That question has been hotly debated among indexers for a long time. Early indexes to learned works in Latin published in the 16th and early 17th centuries were generally divided into an *index nominum* (name index) and an *index rerum* (subject index), but most later indexes to English books and periodicals from the second half of the 17th century onward combined entries for names and subjects in one single alphabetical sequence. Single indexes dominated until the end of the 19th century and well beyond, when Henry B. Wheatley (1838–1917), a prolific indexer, author of the first modern textbooks on indexing, and one of the founders as well as Secretary of the Index Society, argued time and again for "the index, one and indivisible". Well, the world in Wheatley's days and the books written about it were simpler than a hundred years later, and even then there were quite a few books that could not usefully be indexed by a single string of entries from A to Z. Robert Collison (1914–1989), an eminent indexer and influential writer on indexing, was another champion of single indexes who claimed that "intelligent use of typography" could solve virtually any problem encountered in combining entries for persons, places, subjects, and titles (Collison 1972, pp. 86–87). A single index is, however, neither always the only possible one nor is it necessarily the most useful one. Other writers on this issue, while also preferring single indexes for most books, have admitted that works on scientific subjects, law, theology, and classical literature often need multiple indexes.

Nevertheless, matters can be taken too far, as in the case of a 16th century Chinese pharmacopoeia whose translators announced that it was to have "a Chinese index, a Japanese index, a set of indexes for the other Asian languages, a clinical index, General Index, and an index of botanical synonyms . . . posing some most interesting problems".*

The Indexer (Spring 1962) 3:1, p. 46.

Single Versus Multiple Indexes for Books

Single indexes have one undeniable advantage over multiple indexes: users need to look in one place only and do not run the risk of missing an entry because they were looking in the wrong index. Books written for the general public, from travelogues and biographies to popular science, do-it-yourself advice, and cookbooks, are indeed best served by a single index. But neither the extent of a work nor its genre or subject are necessarily valid criteria when a choice has to be made between compiling one index or several indexes. No foolproof guidelines on this issue can be formulated, and being stubbornly dogmatic about it will be of little help. The most important considerations must always be the usefulness of an index and the ease with which entries can be found.

The following factors may govern the decision on single or multiple indexes:

1. The publisher's (and sometimes the author's) preferences. A publisher's house style may prescribe single indexes for all books regardless of subject, and the indexer will generally be unable to change a long-standing policy, however unsuitable it may be for a particular book.
2. The ratio of names to topical entries. If the index will contain a large number of names but only relatively few topics, it may be preferable to compile separate name and subject indexes, because the topical entries may become "lost" among the many names and "appear almost as a disruption of the even course of the basic alphabetical arrangement" (Hunnisett 1972, p. 91), especially when the topical headings have many subdivisions.
3. Name indexes may themselves have to be divided into personal and place names, but this should be done only if the amount of either type of name is so large that two separate name indexes are decidedly more advantageous, e.g., in geographical treatises.
4. The presence of special features which are either difficult or even impossible to integrate into a single alphabetical sequence. Some of these are: lengthy lists of taxonomic names of

plants or animals; chemical formulae; statutes and cases cited in legal works; Scriptural citations, especially when given in the original Hebrew or Greek; names or titles in those and other non-Roman scripts which, when written in the original, should not under any circumstances be intermingled with entries in the Roman alphabet; quotations from classical literature, cited by line or verse in standard editions; and any other features that are both numerous and of such a nature that they cannot, or cannot easily, be integrated into a single index or into name and topical indexes.

5. Anthologies of POETRY almost invariably need several indexes for authors, titles, sources, and first lines. Most classified BIBLIOGRAPHIES IN BOOK FORM should have separate author and topical indexes, and some TECHNICAL MANUALS AND REPORTS may also need more than one index.

6. Official bilingual documents, e.g., Canadian English/French governmental publications, must be provided with separate indexes in both languages.

Typography

Collison's suggestion to use different typographical devices in order to distinguish between various types of entry in single indexes is valid and useful, but it must be applied with discretion. Titles of literary works and names of ships and other vehicles or objects are traditionally printed in italics; names of persons may be printed in small capitals, which make them stand out among the topical entries printed in lowercase roman; foreign phrases and quotations may be distinguished by printing them between quotation marks and in italics, and boldface may occasionally also be used, as shown in Figure 13, p. 490. But too much of such typographical variety may give an index a ragged appearance and may actually render it less legible than the use of just a single font for all entries except italicized titles.

If a book has multiple indexes, each one must not only have its own title, e.g., "Author index", "Subject index", but the title of the index must also appear as a running head on top of each index page in order to alert users to the fact that there is more than one index and to make it easier for them to find a particular one. Book designers provide running heads as a matter of routine, but desktop publishers are not always aware of this seemingly minor but important typographical detail.

Periodicals

Most periodical indexes contain a large number of names: authors of articles, authors of books reviewed, names of reviewers, and names of persons who write letters to the editor or replies to critics. For this reason, names and subjects are mostly separated in periodical indexes, but there may also be separate title indexes, book review indexes, and indexes of advertisers. Legal periodicals often have separate indexes of cases and statutes.

BS 3700: 5.1.4
ISO 999: 7.1.4; 9.4.2
NISO Z39.4:

NARRATIVE INDEXES

Scientific, technical, and instructional texts are virtually always indexed in a straightforward, factual manner: each heading is a term, identifying the name of a person, organization, place, object, operation, or procedure, modified, if necessary, by equally factual subheadings. "Just the facts, Ma'am"—no explanations, interpretations, or other embellishments added by the indexer, save occasional QUALIFIERS for ambiguous headings.

Not so in indexes to works in the humanities and the social sciences, or in BIOGRAPHIES and general and popular works, which tend to be indexed in a narrative style aimed at providing the user with the context of an indexed item. Such narrative indexes have been compiled ever since the 13th century, when itinerant Francis-

can and Dominican friars from Oxford used handy pocket indexes
to find suitable citations from Scripture and the Church Fathers for
the sermons they preached to the laity. These manuscript forerunners of modern citation indexes and concordances were known as a
vademecum (literally: "go with me"). The tradition of compiling such
indexes continued unbroken until the appearance of the first
printed index in 1467, which was appended to a tract by St. Au-
gustine, *De arte praedicandi* (On the art of preaching). The work was
very popular among 15th century preachers and was reprinted several times (Wellisch 1986). Unfortunately, the name of the indexer
has not come down to us (then, as now, indexers were seldom given
credit), but he stated in his preface that buyers "will have in the
back of the little book a most extensive alphabetical index which
has been compiled with great care. . . . And . . . they will benefit
mightily from the many labors I have bestowed on it during a long
time." The index contained entries such as:

> Goodwill of listeners, gaining of
> Listeners, how to teach them
> Study of the art of preaching, not to be neglected

Regarding format and style, such entries might very well have been
written today.

The narrative style of indexing has always enjoyed great popu-
larity among indexers, to judge from the examples that have come
down to us through the ages, and they were probably much appreciated by users who wanted to know not only the exact place in a
text at which an issue was being dealt with but also in which context, why, where, and how. Occasionally, this was carried a bit too
far, as in the following partial (!) excerpt from an index entry in
William Prynne's *Histrio-mastix: the players scourge,* a monstrous
and, in the judgement of Thomas Carlyle, unreadable diatribe
against theatrical performances, published in 1633:

> Women-Actors notorious whores . . . and dare any Christian women
> be so more than whorishly impudent as to act, to speake publikely on
> a stage perchance in man's apparell and cut haire here proved sinful
> and abominable in the presence of sundry men and women? . . . O
> let such presidents of imprudency, of impiety be never heard of or
> suffered among Christians, 385

The author-indexer, a Puritan lawyer, was later severely punished by having his ears cut off, was put in the pillory, and had to pay a fine of £5,000 (though not for his prolix writing and indexing, but for incurring the wrath of Queen Henrietta Maria, who acted in plays performed at court), as reported by Knight (1968).

The earliest known index to a work of fiction, Samuel Richardson's combined index to his novels *Clarissa*, *Pamela* and *Sir Charles Grandison*, contained the following specimen:

> *Aged* persons should study to promote in young people those innocent pleasures which they themselves were fond of in youth, VI, 859. *See* Mrs. Shirley.

Narrative indexes of the 19th and early 20th centuries, while not as excessive as those just quoted, also strike us today as quaint and overly elaborate, though perhaps fitting for the Victorian drawing room with its heavy gold-tasseled draperies, velvet- and plush-upholstered chairs with anti-macassars, potted palms, and crystal chandeliers. The following entries, excerpted and culled from the feature "Indexes past" of *The Indexer*, give the flavor of narrative indexing as it was sometimes practiced (though, to be fair, there were also many better indexes). All locators have been replaced by a dash, and the dates are publication dates of the works indexed.

1776	Canadian, the remarkable behaviour of one—
	Sex, female, the character and conduct of, vindicated—
1850	Black broth, Lacedaemonian, was it coffee?—
	Duke, no one in England so well lodged and tended as our prisoner-scoundrels—
	Premier, mad methods of choosing a—; a more unbeautiful class never raked out of the ooze—
1862	Inverness, the ancient capital of the Picts, supposed to have been near—
	Style, new, of reckoning time introduced—
1873	Oliver, W., a viper catcher at Bath, discovered salad oil to be a cure for the viper's bite—
1895	Army, the English, according to Mr. Grant Duff, of no use—
	Capital, the small importance of, to industry—; Mr. Mill's mode of increasing—; is properly represented by the general type of carpenter's plane, and must not therefore be borrowed—

1897   Servants, England the paradise of household—
       Toothache, that terrific curse—
1900   Knowledge, diffusion of, injurious to the vulgar?—
       Man, a, lessened by another acquiring, equal knowledge—
1909   Chaintry, posting station of, Royal Family recognised at, in
          flight to Varennes—
       Spain, greatness of, in sixteenth century, difficulty of
          understanding today—

It should not go unnoticed that the two 1897 examples were contained in an index compiled by no less an expert than H. B. Wheatley himself, who is considered to be the "Father of modern indexing" and in whose honor the annual Wheatley Medal is bestowed on the past year's best British book index. Will our contemporary indexes look equally silly a hundred years from now?

What all this shows is that in indexing, as in all human activities, there are fashions that come and go. At present, no doubt under the influence of more factual indexing of scientific and technical works, and also because modern readers have less time than their forefathers, indexes to biographical, historical, and general works—the types of text most often indexed narratively—tend to be less flowery and elaborate without any apparent loss of clarity. A study of award-winning modern indexes to such works showed that the average length of their subheadings was no more than five words (Wittmann 1990). The index to *The diary of Samuel Pepys,* compiled by R. C. Latham, one of the editors of the diary, and deservedly honored by the Wheatley Medal for 1983, is an outstanding example of a modern narrative index that manages to provide the necessary context for every indexed item with a minimum of verbiage, partially achieved through the use of symbols, e.g., one asterisk under "books" indicates that Pepys has seen a book, two asterisks mean that he comments on it. The following are typical excerpts from this index:

BAGWELL—; wife of William: her good looks—; P plans to seduce—; visits—; finds her virtuous—; and modest—; asks P for place for husband—; P kisses—; she grows affectionate—; he caresses—; she visits him—; her resistance collapses in alehouse—; amorous encounters with: at her house—[more than a dozen locators!]
CANTERBURY, Kent: King visits—; P visits cathedral—; remains of

Becket's tomb—; list of archbishops in—; alluded to—
CARNEGIE, Anne, Countess of Southesk: Duke of York's mistress—;
gives him pox—; at theatre—

The elaborate and ponderous style of narrative indexing still indulged in by some contemporary indexers has been ridiculed by several authors whose satirical indexes are quoted in Knight (1979, pp. 178–181); two entries from the index to *The stuffed owl; an anthology of bad verse* (Lewis & Lee 1948) may suffice to convey the flavor:

Angels, not immune from curiosity, 31, 162; give Mr. Purcell a
flying lesson, 37; patrol the British sky, 47; invited to take up
permanent quarters at Whitehall, 50; and Britons, mixed choir
of, ibid.
Italy, not recommended to tourists, 125; examples of what goes on
there, 204, 219, 221

A recent spoof of narrative indexing is Sidney Wolfe Cohen's hilarious index to the equally funny *The experts speak* (Cerf & Navasky 1984), a collection of cocksure statements concerning the future made by well-known authorities on diverse subjects who were sadly mistaken in their self-assumed role of prophets. Here are some typical entries:

automobiles, foreign: U.S. not to worry about—; horse not to be
replaced by—
computers, home, no reason seen for—
germs, as fictitious—; heat generated by kisses as destructive of—
Pickering, William Henry: on fallacy of expecting airplanes to
reach speed of trains and cars—; on uselessness of airplanes in
war—; on visionary notion of transatlantic passenger flights—

This index was justly honored by The H. W. Wilson Company Award for Excellence in Indexing for the year 1984.

Another fault sometimes found in narrative indexes is bias on the part of the indexer, be it positive or negative. Authors who index their works understandably tend to be biased in favor of their own opinions or statements and seek to emphasize them in index entries, even repeating entire phrases from the text just to make sure the reader is getting the point. On the other hand, indexers who happen to disagree with an author's opinion, yet have to index a work nevertheless, may show their negative bias in subtle (and occasionally not so very subtle) ways by using pejorative rather than neutral terms in their narrative descriptions of issues and features, or they may altogether fail to index certain items that they deem to be objectionable or unimportant, thereby making it impossible or at least very difficult to find such items. Such neglectfulness on the part of an indexer (which may not be limited to narrative indexes) has rightly been condemned as an instance of censorship (Intner 1984). Bias in indexing, whether narrative or straightforward factual, favorable or unfavorable, must be avoided as being unprofessional and unethical. The issue has been explored in more detail, citing examples, by Bell (1991).

Narrative indexing is undoubtedly needed and useful for certain texts in the humanities and the social sciences, as well as for many popular works, but it should be employed sparingly rather than lavishly. The indexer should not try to tell users every last detail that they will find when turning to the indexed item on a particular page. Nothing is easier than writing rambling phrases, more or less copying what the author has already stated. Rather, good narrative indexing provides an opportunity for the indexer to be creative in paraphrasing the text, using concise and terse formulations taking up a minimum of space yet conveying the necessary context for the benefit of users. Here, as elsewhere in stylistics, Goethe's words "In der Beschränkung erst zeigt sich der Meister" (Just in limitation does the master show himself) should be the narrative indexer's guiding light.

NEWSPAPERS

The following is not aimed at those who index the London *Times*, the *New York Times*, the *Washington Post*, the *Toronto Globe and Mail*, or other national or major regional papers. Rather, it is intended for the person who undertakes to index a local paper for a public library or historical society, a high school paper or the newsletter of a society or congregation. Indexing a local paper does not need a team of a dozen indexers and highly sophisticated hardware and software. It is suitable for someone who can devote one or two hours every day (more for a Sunday edition) to such a task, and the fact that only one person does the job will assure a certain measure of consistency and continuity. It is, however, amazing how often the indexing of a local paper is performed by volunteers with lots of good intentions and maybe also ample free time but no or very little experience in indexing, apparently on the assumption that anybody who can read a newspaper (and loves to do so) can also index it. Nevertheless, while it is true that the indexing of a newspaper, whether national or local, benefits from an experienced and skilled indexer, sometimes the only person available for the job is the inexperienced volunteer, to whose needs this section is addressed.

What To Index (and Not To Index)

The first order of business is to decide on a policy governing what is and is not to be included in the index. The big national and regional papers index almost every story because their indexes—whether kept as in-house tools for their own journalists or published for the benefit of the general public—must make it possible to find even small and seemingly unimportant and trivial items which at some later time may become part of big stories or may be sought by people interested in the details of a person's life or an organization's development for the purpose of writing a biography or a historical account of people and events.

Not so for the indexing of a local newspaper, which must necessarily be done selectively. World and national news may safely be omitted, since it can always be found in the published indexes of the big papers, most of which are now also available online. Weather reports, announcements of meetings, routine crime reports, whimsical human interest stories, fashion, food, gossip, and sobsister columns, a well as gardening and interior decoration tips, should also be disregarded—unless, of course, the latest storm devastated a whole neighborhood, Mr. Cooper managed to grow a super-jumbo pumpkin (complete with picture of same), or Mrs. Jones won a prize for her carrot cake in a national competition.

Some (but practically never all) of the following items may be covered in a local newspaper index.

1. *Persons.* Nothing is more important to people than other people. Not only celebrities, politicians, screen and stage stars, sports heroes, and notorious criminals—again, these will mostly be covered by national news indexes—but also whoever is mentioned in the local paper, be it the mayor or a newsboy (who may in due course become the mayor).
2. *Obituaries.* They are often the only source of personal data for future inquiries on persons.
3. *Places.* Next to other persons, people are interested in buildings and areas, their history and development, especially in this age of nostalgia and powerful preservation movements. Road projects and other changes in the man-made environment may also have to be indexed for future reference.
4. *Local politics.* The lifeblood of a local paper.
5. *Sports events.* Only those in which a local team or athlete is prominently involved.
6. *Entertainment.* Local theater, ballet, or musical performances and their reviews; stories of the local girl or boy, now famous in Hollywood, who won an Oscar.
7. *First and last events.* First woman sheriff. Last trolley car.
8. *Crime.* Only if major, unusual, and of more than local importance.
9. *Social trends.* Rise or fall of population figures, changes in ethnic composition of the city or county, etc.
10. *Economic news.*
11. *Editorials.* Selectively indexed by events and persons discussed.
12. *Letters to the editor.* Very selectively indexed on issues that are also indexed under topical headings, and also if written by well-known personalities.

Indexing Techniques

The indexing of newspapers is based on the same principles as that of books or periodicals—discussed under THE INDEXING PROCESS and INDEXING TECHNIQUES—but there are important technical differences in the way in which indexed items are recorded, whether this is done with the aid of a computer or on cards. If the index, as is very often the case, serves also as a retrieval tool for a collection of clippings, at least two copies of the paper must be available, because an item clipped from page 3 often carries on its back part of another item on page 4. A third copy may have to be retained for permanent storage in bound form, although even small newspapers now prefer microfilming for archival storage because of the rapid deterioration of newsprint and the enormous bulk and weight of bound volumes.

Items to be indexed are marked by the indexer, using a colored marking pen; some indexers recommend using different colors for names and events. Each index entry should have a more or less uniform layout consisting of five parts: heading, subheading, locator line, by-line (which may be omitted), and related stories line.

Headings

These will normally consist of the name of a person or organization, or a term indicating an event, composed of a noun or a noun phrase. PERSONAL NAMES should virtually always be qualified by indicating dates, occupation, place of residence, place of employment, or place with which identified in a news story, such as a street or building; if necessary, some of these QUALIFIERS may have to be combined to distinguish between HOMOGRAPHS, e.g.,

Jones, Charles (attorney)
Jones, Charles (clerk, Marks & Spencer)
Jones, Charles (clerk, Woolworth)
Jones, Charles (Walnut Street)

CORPORATE NAMES must also be qualified if they are homographic, e.g.,

Stamp Collecting Club (Licksville)
Stamp Collecting Club (Tweezefield)

Terms for topics and events are, as in all indexing, the biggest problem. Easily foreseeable and recurring topics such as

Airplanes
Fires
Health
Public finance
Roads
Schools

and dozens of other such common and general headings can readily be taken from long-established news indexes, such as those of the
New York Times, *The Times*, and other large national or regional
papers, and in the United States also from the *National Newspaper
Index* (1979–) and from the indexes of *NewsBank* (1970–), the latter
specializing in the coverage of local papers from more than a hundred cities. These sources will also provide cross-references from
synonyms which are not to be used, though they are by no means of
one mind in this respect: what is a heading in index A may be an
unused synonym in index B, and yet another synonym in index C.

Under general headings, hundreds of entries may quickly accumulate even if the index covers only one year, which makes searching time-consuming and tedious. To avoid this, two methods can be
used, often simultaneously:

1. General headings may be subdivided by commonly recurring
subdivisions such as

Accidents
Agriculture
Finance
History
Law
Personnel
Prices

and some others, all of which may also be used as general headings.

2. Indexing stories under specific headings rather than general
ones, if at all possible. For example, a story on one of the local high
schools should be indexed under its name, "Booker T. Washington
high school", not under "Schools" or "High schools".

Although some textbooks recommend them, lists of subject headings for library catalogs, such as the *Library of Congress subject headings*
(1989–) and its derivatives, are largely unsuitable as sources of
headings because (a) they are designed for books on more or less

well-established topics, not for fast-breaking news; (b) their terminology is often outmoded, quaint, and sometimes offensive to some people, and it always lags behind current usage; and (c) they use lots of dreadful inverted headings, such as "Education, elementary" or "Gas, natural", which are utterly unsuitable for a newspaper index and should be avoided at all costs.* Needless to say, pre-cooked subject heading lists cannot cope with unforeseeable events, which may become known under names that have little to do with the events themselves, such as "Watergate" (initially indexed by the *New York Times* under "Robberies and theft" and "Democratic National Committee").

For such stories that cannot usefully be indexed under general and standardized headings, new headings must be devised. When formulating a new heading two aspects must be considered: (a) what is the best way to express this topic in terms that are as concise as possible yet easy to comprehend; and (b) how will the new heading relate to those already in use: is it more specific or more general? Is it the same or nearly the same as an existing heading but in new terms? For a new heading, it is best to employ the terminology used by the headline writer, provided of course that the headline is factual and not just eye-catching, such as the famous *New York Daily News* banner line FORD TO CITY: DROP DEAD (on the decision by President Ford not to bail out the nearly bankrupt city). If no usable heading can be fashioned from a headline, the first or second paragraph of a story will normally yield suitable terms, and the caption of a picture may also be a good source for a heading.

A list of headings, whether chosen from an existing source or newly coined, should be listed in the format that is now customary for THESAURI, that is, with strict synonym control and indication of broader terms (BT), narrower terms (NT), and related terms (RT).

Subheadings

These should tell the user as succinctly as possible what, when, where, and how something happened (the "who" having been taken

---

*The indexers of the *Atlanta Constitution* ruefully stated that "We rather slavishly adhered to the LC guidelines but probably wouldn't do so if given a second chance" (Thaxton & Redus 1975, p. 226).

care of mostly in the heading). The subheading should complete the sentence introduced by nouns and adjectives in the heading by using a verb describing the action, quite similar to a secondary headline of a news story. The use of "now" or "soon", even if used in a headline, should be avoided because by the time the index will be consulted the adverbs will have lost their meaning. If a story continues for several days or even weeks, the subheadings are arranged chronologically by adding them successively under the heading.

Locator Line

The locator line for each story should always appear in the same position, namely, immediately after the subheading. It must contain all data that identify an item accurately and completely. The following data (some of which may not be applicable to all newspapers) are included in a locator line.

Length of story: indicated by the well-known abbreviations for clothes sizes, S (less than 6″); M (6″–18″); L (more than 18″).

Source: only if more than one newspaper is covered by a single index.

Date: day and month, expressed in numerals, separated by slashes; year is omitted if the index covers only one year.

Edition: if the newspaper has more than one edition (e.g., a city edition and suburban editions, or early and final editions), the edition in which a story is carried must be indicated by a suitable abbreviation.

Section: indicated by section letter.

Pages: indicated after section letter without punctuation.

Column: starting column of the story, separated from the page number by a colon; if the story is continued on a different page, the first locator ends with a semicolon, followed by the locator of the continuation.

Illustrations: indicated by abbreviations such as px or p for pictures, gr or g for graphs, tb or t for tables; no indication of columns is normally needed for pictures, graphs, and tables because these are almost always in or near one of the text columns, but pictures without an accompanying story must be identified by page and column.

The aim of the locator line is to convey a maximum of information in a minimum of space, yet unambiguously and with as few abbreviations as possible.

By-Line

This line, too, should be placed in a fixed position, namely, after the locator line; it records the name of the journalist who wrote the story, and a separate entry may have to be made for that person if it is desirable that all articles by the same journalist can be quickly identified.

Related Stories Line

If an event is covered by more than one story in the same issue of a newspaper, the last line, labeled *Related*, indicates other locators (but not the headings) in the same style as in the locator line.

Examples

Typical examples of newspaper index entries, containing a heading, subheading, locator line, by-line, and related stories line are:

> O'Connor, Patrick
>   Sworn in as police chief
>   L 5/8/87 C3:5 px; C8:1
>   By Fred Johnson
>   *Rel:* A1:3 px

Line 3 indicates that the O'Connor story was published on May 8, 1987 in section C, page 3, column 5, accompanied by a picture, and that it was continued on the same day in section C, page 8, column 1. The last line records that a related story was published in section A, page 1, column 3, also with a picture.

> Washington Monument
>   Stone from Okinawa added
>   M 8/5/89 B1:1; B7:3 px
>   By Nancy Callahan
> Water sports—Accidents
>   2 youngsters drown in
>   Indian Creek as canoe capsizes
>   M 7/13/87 C3:3

City curtails water sport
    program after canoe accident
S 7/15/87 B2:6
By John Miller

Cross-References

Both name and topical headings must often be cross-referenced. For example, the O'Connor item must be linked to the heading "Police", the Washington Monument to "Okinawa", and the canoe accident to "Indian Creek" and perhaps also to the names of the victims. *See also* CROSS-REFERENCES.

Much useful information on the indexing of local newspapers, with examples of techniques and excerpts from the indexes, will be found in the surveys by Sandlin et al. (1985) for U.S. papers and by Beare (1989) for U.K. papers. The problems of indexing large newspapers have been discussed by Milstead (1983) and by Peterson (1994).

NONALPHABETICAL ORDER

The normal arrangement of index headings is alphabetical. There are, however, instances when arrangement by other methods is necessary, such as for headings beginning with NUMERALS or SYMBOLS. Other alternative arrangements of headings which on occasion may be more useful than straight alphabetical order are:

1. CHRONOLOGICAL ORDER, which is often used for subheadings in BIOGRAPHIES or historical works, and for serially occurring events such as annual meetings or reports.
2. GROUPED ORDER, which may also be called for in biographies.
3. *Evolutionary order*, which may be helpful in works on geology, mineralogy, paleontology, and related fields, e.g.,

conifers
    Tertiary 57, 59
    Cretaceous 61, 63
    Triassic 78
    Permian 81–83

4. *Canonical order,* which may be employed for the arrangement of texts on Scripture and classical literature with a fixed order of parts, chapters, or other subdivisions, e.g.,

    Divine Comedy (Dante)
    Hell 48
    Purgatory 51
    Paradise 55

5. CLASSIFIED ORDER, which should be avoided unless it is supported by a numerical or alphanumerical notation indicating the classified sequence or hierarchy. (The Dewey Decimal Classification, well-known to users of most public libraries, is a classified index to the shelf arrangement of books, its decimal number notation serving as an indicator of the classified order.)

Without a notation, the system on which a classification is based will almost never be obvious or known in advance by users. Classified order without notation may only be employed when it is self-explanatory and unambiguous, as in the explication of cartographic symbols in the legend of a map which serves as an index to recurring features on a map. In the following example, the graphic representation of various kinds of roads from the largest and best-paved to the smallest and unpaved (actually also a notation) creates a classified hierarchy that is easy to understand and is well-known to users of maps:

    ━━━━━━━ interstate highways
    ═════ state roads
    ────── local roads and streets
    -------------- unpaved roads

However, such instances of self-evident classifications are very rare.

Any nonalphabetical arrangement should only be resorted to when definitely more helpful to prospective users than the conventional alphabetical order. The indexer should always keep in mind that other people learn early in their lives only two basic systems of order: the alphabet from A to Z (about which many people are not too sure) and the set of positive integers 1, 2, 3. . . . Any other arrangement, however "logical" or "self-evident" it may seem to be, will in most instances only confuse people, particularly if it is intermingled with an alphabetical arrangement.

BS 3700: 6.3
ISO 999: 8.4
NISO Z39.4:

NONPRINT MATERIALS

Images, sounds, and objects are means of expression and communication which transcend language and words. Nevertheless, their physical embodiments in stone or metal and on wood, canvas, paper and film, as well as in video and sound recordings, need indexing if they are to be retrieved from stores of hundreds or even tens of thousands of physically similar media. This contradictory relationship between visual, aural, or three-dimensional expression and its reduction to written symbols is the principal one of five basic differences between the indexing of texts and that of nonprint materials (NPM).

The first difference is that many NPM cannot be indexed by their "aboutness" (Svenonius 1994). A text—be it a book, a periodical, or a single article—can be indexed not only by names of persons, places, or events (real or fictional) but also by its aboutness, the ideas and topics discussed, explained, or refuted. Plato's *Crito* is about Socrates, his friends, his ideas on justice, ethics, and religion, his execution, and also on the sacrifice of a cock to Asclepius. Kurt Vonnegut's *Slaughterhouse five* is about Dresden, World War II, bombing raids, the futility of war, and many other things. *Othello* is about a black soldier of that name, his wife Desdemona, and his enemy Iago, and also about the intangible ideas of love, hate, and jealousy, not to mention a handkerchief. Some or all of this can be indexed by names and words. But can Michelangelo's *David* or one of Jackson Pollock's abstract canvases, Mahler's Ninth symphony or Gershwin's *Rhapsody in blue* be indexed by what those images and sounds convey to the viewer and listener in terms of emotions, feelings, or reactions? The answer is no. All one can do is to index the merest identifying data: the name of the author or artist, the title (if any) of a work, and perhaps some other purely physical marks of recognition, including those pertaining to the reproduction of a work in print or as a replica, or the recording of its sounds.

A second difference concerns the physical relationship between an item and its index. The index of a book or a periodical is virtually always an integral part of its physical embodiment, and it is irrelevant whether or not the item is part of a collection of similar items (as, for example, in a library) or only a single item in the hands of a user. Not so for NPM: the index is always quite separate physically from the indexed item itself, and the recorded images, sounds, or data are almost always part of a *collection*—be it a small or private one, such as an album of photos or a shelf of video cassettes in somebody's home, or a large public or institutional collection, such as a film archive or a library collection of sound recordings or slides.

A corollary of NPM's virtually always being part of a collection is the fact that individual items are best identified by serial numbers that indicate their places within a collection of physically similar items and thus serve as LOCATORS. For continuously recorded media such as movies, videos, and sound recordings it is often necessary to assign two locators: one for the entire recording medium, e.g., a reel of film, a video cassette, or a compact disk, and another one for an individual frame on a film, a certain scene in a video recording, or a particular piece of music on a disk.

A third difference lies in the fact that the indexing of texts is normally not concerned with the physical medium and its appearance or quality, such as paper, printing, typography, and binding, whereas the indexing of NPM must almost always include, in addition to data on the work itself, the details of the physical medium in which it is presented or recorded.

The fourth difference pertains to the relationship between the user and the medium. Print media can be used in the form in which they are presented. They do not need any intermediary mechanical, electrical, or electronic implements in order to be used and to be useful—only light and, for many people, eyeglasses. NPM, with the exception of original works of visual art and their reproductions in printed form, can only be used with the help of machines. The details and specific properties of NPM in relation to these machines must also be indexed before the user of NPM can make a decision on whether or not to choose a particular item from a collection for pleasure, training, instruction, research, or any other purpose. For example, a teacher of English literature who wants to discuss *Hamlet* can assign the reading of the play, and virtually any of the countless editions of Shakespeare's plays will do for this purpose. But if scenes from a video recording of the play as staged at the Royal Shakespeare Theater in Stratford are to be shown to the students, the index entry, in addition to the Bard's name, the title of the play, the names of the performing company and maybe of its chief players, and perhaps a summary of the plot, must also carry information on whether the recording is in VHS format or on optical disk. Depending on the availability of the proper playback equipment, it may or may not be possible to show the video recording.

The fifth and final difference concerns indexing technique. While a text—whether a book or an article in a periodical—must be read (or at least scanned) from beginning to end so as not to miss any indexable items in it, it is not always feasible or even necessary to examine a NPM from start to finish. For example, a movie or video does not have to be watched for an hour and a half, nor does a computer program have to be run in order to be properly indexed. Indexing may be carried out by relying, in the case of movies and videos, on the first (and sometimes also the last) frames, which contain the title, credits, and other identifying data, and on written synopses that may accompany them; in the case of a computer program, the written documentation that comes with it will provide the necessary indexing data.

This means that the indexing of NPM will almost always include data and particulars which are actually in the domain of what in library practice is known as descriptive cataloging. The multiplicity of data that must be indexed for NPM makes it necessary to provide for the retrieval of these data in any desired combination in order to satisfy requests such as, "Is there a recording of Benjamino Gigli singing 'La donna è mobile' in Giuseppe Verdi's *Rigoletto*, and, if so, is it the original monaural recording or an electronically produced stereophonic one?" Formerly, such requests could be successfully answered only by making copious cross-references on cards, and some major record and movie archives did, indeed, keep indexes on millions of cards. All this can now be done much easier, more comprehensively, and much more economically by constructing a database with the aid of a computer, making it possible to correlate or combine any indexed data and to retrieve any desired item from a collection. This can be done either by using one of the many commercially available database management systems (DBMS) or by custom-designing one for a particular collection of NPM. Some works on the design, construction, and maintenance of DBMS, written specifically for databases of indexing data, are by Hlava (1984), Fidel (1987), McCarthy (1988), and Tenopir & Lundeen (1988).

When indexing visual art objects or graphic materials it is advisable to use the terms of the *Art & architecture thesaurus* (1994) and to apply them according to its *Guide to indexing* (1994).

The data which may need to be indexed for each of the most commonly used NPM are listed below. They are based on the cataloging rules for NPM in AACR2. The amount of detail will, of course, vary for each collection, depending on the needs of prospective users and the purposes for which an individual piece or part of a collection is to be used. Data which ought always to be indexed, if available and applicable, are marked with a dot (•). Examples are listed in parentheses. Explanatory notes, detailed contents lists (e.g., for a slide show), summaries or synopses (for movies and videos), and entries for the topic(s) dealt with should be added as needed.

Graphic Materials

Although some graphic materials are produced by a printing process, they are listed here because their indexing is similar to that of other NPM and quite different from that of books or periodicals.

Art originals: paintings, drawings, prints, sculptures
- Name of artist
- Original title
  Translated title

- Date
  Period (baroque; renaissance)
  Genre (still life; landscape)
  School (impressionist; dadaist)
- Medium (oil on canvas; chalk on paper; marble)
- Dimensions

Art reproductions

As for "Art originals" above, except for "medium", for which substitute:

- Reproduction method (photogravure; lithograph)

Additional data:

- Color (b&w [black and white]; colored)
- Dimensions of reproduction
  Dimensions of original
  Place of original (Louvre, Paris)
- Place of publication
- Publisher or distributor
- Date of publication
- Locator (Portfolio M 23, no. 7)

Photographs

- Name of photographer
- Original title
  Translated title
- Date
- Positive or negative
  Method of printing (collotype)
- Color (b&w; colored; tinted)
  Dimensions
- Locator (Album 12, page 7)

If there is no title, add a brief description of what is shown. *See also* ILLUSTRATIONS.

Slides and transparencies

As for "Photographs", above, except for "Method of printing", and add:

- Place of publication
- Publisher or distributor
- Date of publication

If accompanied by a sound recording, add data as listed below under "Sound recordings—Music—Recording data".

Technical drawings

- Title and / or serial number
  Name of person or organization responsible
- Date
  Type of material (blueprint; mylar)
  Dimensions
- Locator (File 6, drawer 7, no. 12)

Maps

- Title or other indication of area
- Scale
- Place of publication
- Publisher
- Date
  Language and script (Russian; Cyrillic script)
  Color
- Dimensions
- Locator (Europe file, Denmark 27b)

See also MAPS.

Sound Recordings

Music

CONTENT DATA (the first eight are also applicable to printed music)

- Name of composer
- Original title of entire work
  Translated title
- Title of part (aria; chorus)
- Key
- Opus number
- Form (concerto; sonata)

- Instrument(s) or orchestra
  Name of conductor
  Names of soloists or performers

RECORDING DATA   (the first three are also applicable to printed music)

- Place of publication
- Publisher or distributor
- Date
- Type of recording (cassette; compact disk; disk; tape)
  Playing speed ($33\frac{1}{3}$ rpm [revolutions per minute]; $3\frac{3}{4}$ ips [inches per second])
- Monophonic or stereophonic sound
  Dimensions
- Side and band (side 2, band 4)
- Accompanying material (text of oratorio)
- Manufacturer's number of recording
- Locator (Jazz, no. 1875)

Speech and drama

CONTENT DATA

- Name of author
  - Original title of entire work
    Translated title
  - Title or number of part (poem; scene)
    Name of speaker or performers
    Place and name of theater, stage, or event

RECORDING DATA

As for "Sound recordings—Music—Recording data".

Animal sounds

CONTENT DATA

- Name of animal (bird; insect)
  - Location
  - Date

RECORDING DATA

As for "Sound recordings—Music—Recording data".

Other sounds

CONTENT DATA

* Object generating the sound (hammer; locomotive)
  * Frequency (constant; intermittent)
  * Pitch (high; low)
  * Type (knocks; whistles)

RECORDING DATA

As for "Sound recordings—Music—Recording data".

Movies and Video Recordings

CONTENT DATA

* Original title
  Translated title
  Name of director, producer, photographer, composer of soundtrack, etc.
  Names of actors
  Names of other persons shown
  * Location (Tanzania, Serengeti National Park)
  * Date of production or event

RECORDING DATA

* Place of publication or release
* Publisher, manufacturer, or distributor
* Date of release
* Number and form of recording (3 film reels; 1 videocassette)
* Type of recording (Beta; VHS; optical disk)
  Playing time
  Sound or silent
  Original language
  Language of subtitles

- Color (b&w; colored)
- Dimensions (16 mm; 35 mm; $\frac{1}{2}''$)
  Length in feet or meters
- Accompanying material (study guide)
- Locator (No. 567, min. 14–17)

NOTES

For feature films or videos: summary of the plot. For events: description of the event (Richard Nixon and Nikita Khrushchev debating at American kitchen display in Moscow exhibition). If the film or the video contains several different events, indicate for each the footage or time from the start of the recording as locator, e.g., 14–17 minutes in the example above.

Microforms

Virtually all microforms are reproductions of printed materials, and their indexing is therefore in principle not different from that of eye-legible texts (except that the indexer will have to toil at a reading machine and will not be able to mark passages to be indexed, not to mention the resulting eye strain). The physical data to be indexed are:

- Number and type (3 microfiches; 1 microfilm cassette)
- Positive or negative
- Dimensions (16 mm; 35 mm; frames 5–12)
  Material (silver halide; diazo)
- Locator (MF Periodicals, *Time*)

Computer Files

Computer files fall into two categories (a) *data files,* which may be numeric, text, or graphic files; and (b) *program files,* which contain the instructions directing a computer to perform certain operations on a data file. Both categories may be combined in a single file.

- Title
- Name of person(s) or organization responsible for the creation of the file

- Edition or version (version 3.0)
  Number of files and number of records or bytes (1 file, 200 records)
- Place of publication
- Producer, manufacturer, or distributor
- Date
  Physical description (2 computer disks; 1 computer cassette)
  Sound
  Language
  Color
  Sides used
  Density
- Dimensions
- Manufacturer's number
- System requirements (IBM PC, 64 K RAM, 2 disk drives)
- Accompanying material (teacher's guide; codebook)
- Notes: (a) what the file is or does (game; spread sheet; word processor); (b) description of the contents (a biology program simulating fish tagging procedures in a lake); (c) any other pertinent information.
- Locator (Programs, no. 47)

Electronic Text and Images

Hypertext is the electronic storage and presentation of text (in the widest sense of this term, that is, not only written but also pictorial and aural) that permits both authors and users to work in nonlinear sequences. The "nodes" of hypertext (the terms, phrases, or themes of the text) constitute the items of information which can be connected freely and at the discretion of the user to other nodes by means of "links". Some of these links may be built into the hypertext by its author, while others can be generated interactively as the need arises. In effect, these links are playing the roles of conventional *see* and *see also* cross-references in print indexes. "In many ways, the task of organizing hypertext is strikingly similar to traditional indexing. It can be argued that hypertext links and index terms have much in common. Links provide meaning and structure to hypertext" (Liebscher 1994, p. 103).

It has also been suggested that authors of hypertext ought to start with a conceptual structure that specifies the relationships (links) between the nodes in order to provide users with a variety of approaches by which information may be sought (Marchionini 1994).

While the field of hypertext is still in its developmental stage, and further expansion of its potential as an information retrieval medium can be expected, it is safe to assume that the experience gained in compiling print indexes will be valuable also in the design of hypertext links.

Electronically stored images—paintings, photos, graphs, maps, and images of three-dimensional objects—can essentially be indexed in the same way as art originals and graphic materials, out lined above. The important difference is that the various characteristics indexed can not only be retrieved in any desired combination, but related information in books, periodical articles, or other sources can also be accessed if the material is organized in the form of hypertext. This may serve the specific information needs of historians, art historians, curators, architects, illustrators, and picture researchers which are difficult if not impossible to satisfy by means of conventional indexes.

Collections of Objects

People collect not only the traditional stamps, coins, and butterflies but just about anything under the sun, from postcards to key rings, porcelain dolls, and antique fountain pens. If such collections are to be useful and manageable, they must be indexed. The indexing data that are necessary for the successful identification and retrieval of individual items from a collection must in most cases be tailor-made for each type of collected object. Some data will be obvious, such as country and city or place for postcards and either scientific or common names for butterflies, while identifying data for key rings, dolls, and fountain pens may be more difficult and elusive; sometimes only the owners of a collection of unusual objects can provide indexing data which will allow an indexer to get a handle on their ever-growing accumulation of collectibles.

BS 3700: 5.4.2.3
BS 6529: 4.3
ISO 999: 7.4.2.3
NISO Z39.4:

NUMERALS

A lot of people seem to have difficulty distinguishing between numerals and numbers, and think that these are just different names for the entities by which things are counted. This misconception (against which even the editors of the ALA and LC *Filing rules,* sad to say, were not immune) is caused by the derivation of both terms from the Latin word *numerus* for "number". But the relationship between numeral and number is the same as that between letter and word: a numeral is a graphic symbol or *grapheme* by which a *number*—a member of the set of positive integers or other sets of mathematical objects derived from them, such as fractions or complex numbers—can be written. Thus, in the decimal system there are only 10 numerals, 0 to 9, which are used to express an infinity of numbers. These 10 graphemes, universally but incorrectly known as Arabic numerals, were actually invented by Indian mathematicians; they became known to and were adopted by Arabic mathematicians in the 8th century and reached Europe in translations of Arabic works in the 12th century, slowly supplanting the cumbersome Roman numerals (or rather, letters serving as numerals) which had been in use for more than a millennium. (Ironically, the numerals used today in the Arabic script are quite different from our "Arabic" numerals.)

The problem caused by numerals in indexing is their arrangement within an otherwise alphabetical sequence, especially when they constitute the first element of an index term, most often a title such as *007 James Bond* or *60 American painters* but also in chemical nomenclature, e.g., 1,2-dithiolenes, or within a string of letters or words, such as B-52 bomber. The solution of this problem, now

uniformly embodied in British, American, and international indexing standards is the arrangement of all numbers written in numerals (that is, not spelled out) in ascending arithmetical order after
spaces, punctuation marks, and other symbols, and before any
heading beginning with a letter.

Before 1980, all arrangement rules recommended treating numbers written in numerals as if spelled out in the language of the text.
This attempt to amalgamate two incompatible ordering systems by
forcing one into the mold of the other led to many difficulties and
yielded incongruous results when followed literally, e.g., in the
arrangement of names followed by Roman numerals:

Henry VIII
Henry V
Henry I
Henry IV
Henry IX

which practice "it would be madness to use" (*Training in indexing*
1969, p. 44). It did not occur to the makers of the old rules that the
"arrange as spelled out" rule was sheer madness to begin with,
since in English there is sometimes more than one way of spelling a
number. Is 007 to be spelled double-oh-seven, oh-oh-seven, zero-
zero-seven, or nought-nought-seven? Is 1066 to be arranged under
T as ten-sixty-six, or under *O* as one thousand and sixty-six? Moreover, when designations of serially numbered objects such as airplanes were indexed "as if spelled out" the resulting sequence, e.g.,

F-15
F-14
F-16
F-13

confused most users, who naturally expected to find the designations in ascending numerical order.

The post-1980 arrangement rules and standards eliminated all
these inconsistencies and ambiguities, besides making it possible to
automate the sorting of headings consisting of strings of numerals
or letters or both. These rules should be strictly followed in the
alphanumeric arrangement of all indexes. Only the *Chicago manual*

of style (1993, 17.102) still allows numerals to be "alphabetized as though spelled out, especially when there are few such entries", but then admits that arranging numerals before letters is "particularly useful when there are many such entries or when the numbers are complicated".

Dates

Dates may have to be used as QUALIFIERS for PERSONAL NAMES which are HOMOGRAPHS. They are arranged in chronological order. Centuries expressed only by the first two digits and the word "century" or its abbreviation, e.g., "16th cent.", are arranged as if written from the first to the last year, e.g., 1500–1599 (which is technically incorrect because a century begins with year 1, but most people tend to think that a century starts with the year ending in -00).

Qualification of dates, such as b. (born), d. (died), fl. (flourished), or a question mark (for a date that is uncertain), are disregarded in the chronological arrangement of dates (ALA, 8.7.1; LC, 16.7.2); e.g.,

Smith, John, fl. 16th cent.
Smith, John, 1619–1654
Smith, John, 1619?–1678
Smith, John, b. 1705
Smith, John, 1705–1767
Smith, John, d. 1808
Smith, John, 1934–
Smith, John Henry, 1841–1902

Roman Numbers

As far as the arrangement of index terms and headings is concerned, the letters employed by the ancient Romans to write numbers are today used only to distinguish between homographic names of popes and secular rulers, and sometimes for the designation of centuries (the latter especially in the Romance languages, where it is apparently felt that the traditions of the common ancestor should be honored). For arrangement purposes, Roman numbers must be mentally converted to their Arabic equivalents and be arranged in their arithmetical sequence, e.g.,

Charles
Charles II, King of Great Britain
Charles III, King of Navarre
Charles XIV, King of Sweden and Norway
Charles, fl. 15th century
Charles Albert, King of Sardinia

This is a feat which computers cannot perform, unless the Roman numbers are specially coded and then sorted by an algorithm designed for that purpose. When only a small number of Roman numbers in names is involved, it is quicker and easier to sort them manually in a computer-produced index manuscript.

Roman numbers indicating volumes, chapters, parts, or pages will normally appear only in locators and will not cause any difficulties.

Subscript and Superscript Numerals

These occur mostly in chemical formulae or other scientific notations and are arranged as "on-the-line" numerals, e.g.,

Notation	*Arranged as if written*
H_2SO_4	H2SO4

A mixture of Arabic and Roman numerals is treated the same way:

$$Pb^{II}_2Pb^{IV}O_4 \qquad Pb22Pb4O4$$

If deemed necessary for the sake of clarity, a verbal double entry may be made; for the formula above, it would be "dilead(II)lead(IV)oxide".

Fractions

A fraction is unlikely to appear as the first element of a topical heading, but titles of books or poems beginning with a fraction are known to exist, and they must be arranged in title or first line indexes. Numerals in common fractions are arranged in the following order: numerator, line (horizontal or diagonal, treated as a space), denominator:

⅓ *of an inch*
2½ minute talk treasury
³⁄₁₀ for the ladies
3:10 to Yuma
3 and 30 watchbirds

Note that the fractions are not arranged by their numerical value as less than 1, but by the individual digits, spaces and slashes or lines (the equivalents of spaces): ⅓ is arranged as 1-space-3, and both ³⁄₁₀ and 3:10 are arranged as 3-space-10, subarranged by the words following the numerals.

Numerals in decimal fractions are arranged digit by digit from left to right; those not combined with zero or an integer (e.g., .45) are treated as if written after a zero and arranged before the integer 1:

.300 Vickers machine gun
.303-inch machine guns and small arms
1, 2, buckle my shoe
3-D scale drawing
3 point 2 and what goes with it
The 3 Rs and the new religion
3.1416 and all that
3.8 Kilometer nach Berlin

ALA: 1; 8
BL: 1.2.3
BS 1749: 4.1
BS 3700: 6.2.1.2(c); 6.2.1.4
Chicago manual of style: 17.102
ISO 999: 8.3
LC: 1.2; 16
NISO Z39.4:

PERIODICALS

Periodicals are the most numerous and ubiquitous types of publications that constitute the large family of *serials* which are defined in

AACR2 as follows: "A publication in any medium issued in successive parts bearing numerical or chronological designations and intended to be continued indefinitely". This definition covers not only journals, magazines, bulletins, and newsletters (collectively known as periodicals) but also publications issued only once a year or even less frequently (such as yearbooks, almanacs, annual reports, and the proceedings of regularly held annual meetings or conferences). NEWSPAPERS (which technically also qualify) are, however, not considered in the following discussion, and their indexing is treated separately.

Differences Between Book and Periodical Indexing

The basic principles of indexing—the analysis of a text, the identification and naming of relevant concepts, and the indication of their relationships—apply equally to books and periodicals. But in several technical respects, periodical indexing is quite different from back-of-the-book indexing. *See also* THE CONTINUUM OF VERBAL TEXTS.

The most obvious difference is that a book index is compiled only once, within a relatively short time. Periodical indexing, on the other hand, is a continuous process, more often performed by a team of indexers than by a single person and lasting for an extended period (often as long as a periodical is being published), normally resulting in a series of self-contained indexes at the end of each volume.

Another difference pertains to the text. A book generally deals with a more or less well-defined central topic that is treated at a certain set level of specialization (popular, for the educated layman, or for the specialist). Periodical articles deal with a great variety of topics at varying levels of sophistication, even in a highly specialized scientific, technical, or professional journal.

Closely related to this is the difference in the use of terminology. For a book index it is normally not necessary to establish a list of terms in advance; the indexing terms are almost always derived from the text, that is, they are those used by the author, although synonymous terms must also be provided for, most often by cross-references. In a periodical index, it would be disastrous to index articles just by employing the terminology of authors, who may use a variety of synonyms to describe the same topic, e.g., "cancer", "carcinosis", "neoplasms", "oncosis", or "tumors". The terminology of a periodical index must, above all, be consistent, not only in the annual index to one volume but also, as far as possible, for several years, so that retrospective searches can be undertaken with reasonable certainty that a topic sought under a particular term will be found in at least the indexes for the past three to five years. (Terms should also remain stable for the foreseeable future, but the gift of prophecy is as rare in indexers as it is in humankind in general.) To ensure such consistency, it is absolutely necessary to use standardized and accepted terms established by a THESAURUS or subject heading list.

In book indexes, the SPECIFICITY of terms is largely governed by that of the text itself and by the needs of its intended audience. In a periodical index, the terms may be prescribed by a thesaurus, but their level of specificity may be lower than that of a book index because the terms must fit a variety of articles on the same topic written with different degrees of specificity.

Differences pertain also to indexing techniques. While a book indexer must read (and sometimes re-read) every single page, periodical indexers generally do not read every article from beginning to end. Instead, they scan them for indexable items or may rely on an abstract or a summary (if available), because each article must be indexed within a rather short time.

There are also differences regarding the physical form and use. A book index is virtually always bound with the indexed text, and the user, having found a reference to a topic or item in the index, can turn to the desired information immediately in the same physical object. The index to a periodical, however, is in most instances compiled seriatim as each issue appears during a year, thus leaving users without an index to individual issues until the index is cumulated and printed when the volume is complete (and even then there may be a considerable time lag between the publication of the last volume issue and that of the annual index). A printed indexing service covering many periodicals must necessarily lag behind the publication of its sources (time lags vary from as little as one to three months to as much as two years or more), and the index is in this case physically removed from the indexed items, serving only as a pointer to the sources, which must be found elsewhere.

Finally, the difference that is perhaps most significant yet not readily perceived: in a book, virtually the entire text is subject to indexing, and no part or almost none is excluded. But a periodical index cannot be started before a number of policy decisions have been made regarding what and how to index. To bring order into the chaotic conglomeration of ideas, arguments, assertions, and opinions, as well as their refutations and rejections which may appear in the articles of a periodical, and to achieve this order by means of an annual index, it is of the utmost importance to ensure consistency in every respect. Though this is an admirable and necessary quality of any index, a book index may occasionally contain some minor inconsistencies without being much the worse for it. A periodical index, in order to be useful at all, must be consistent in its indexing policy regarding indexable items, the indexing language used, and its design and format. This is true whether the periodical index is to a newsletter or small journal carrying only a few articles in each issue which can easily be indexed by one person, or is a database covering either a single periodical or a large number of journals, produced by a team of indexers.

Indexing Policy

First, it must be decided what constitutes an indexable item. Articles are, of course, the most obvious candidates. But what is an article? Most index editors decide that it is a contribution that has a title, is signed by one or more authors, and is at least one page long (irrespective of page size). Editorials, though generally less than one page long, are, nevertheless, often also treated the same way as articles. What remains are smaller and often anonymous pieces, such as news items, personal news (nominations to office, awards and prizes won, obituaries), book reviews, letters to the editor, and question-and-answer columns, any of which may or may not qualify as indexable, depending on the nature of the periodical, the needs of its readership in tracking down information through the index, and the maximum size of the index, which, in turn, is a corollary of the financial means available to produce it. Most periodical indexes do not cover items like gossip columns, human interest stories, food, restaurant and game columns, and other trivia (unless, of course, a periodical is devoted solely to any of these topics). Advertisements are also excluded, although individual issues of a journal may have an index of advertisers. No two index editors will make the same decisions, even for the same periodical; but, once a policy on inclusion or exclusion of items has been set, it should be followed consistently for at least several years so that users are not confronted with a different choice of indexed items in each annual index. New developments will, of course, from time to time necessitate changes in indexing policy.

Having decided what (and what not) to index, the next policy decision concerns how to index: the choice of an indexing language. To ensure consistency of indexing terms, a suitable thesaurus or other form of a controlled indexing language must be chosen. Hundreds of THESAURI exist today for almost every discipline, field, or specialty, and sometimes it may even become difficult to decide on the most suitable one. Having chosen an authoritative source of indexing terms and synonym control, further decisions must be made: should the chosen thesaurus be followed strictly (which is the best but not always the most feasible course) or should it be adapted for the specific needs of an index, and if so, in which way? Is the level of its SPECIFICITY too high, sufficient, or too low and in need of further refinement? Revisions and additions to a chosen thesaurus must be made before any indexing is performed, and further changes will always have to be made in light of what the indexing process itself will reveal, especially when new topics and issues are treated in articles and must be indexed by new terms not yet in the thesaurus. The operation of indexing with a thesaurus is shown schematically in Figure 4, p. 230.

Additional indexing terms may be suggested by authors of articles who are often asked by their periodical editor to supply potentially useful terms. Such encouragement should, however, not become coercion, as is unfortunately the practice of some professional journals which compound their error by limiting authors to no more than a fixed number of terms, say, 10. Authors of articles are for the most part not trained in indexing, and may fail to grasp the essentials of what other people (including their colleagues) are looking for when searching the periodical literature. A study comparing indexing terms assigned by authors of medical articles with terms chosen for the same articles by professional indexers at the MEDLINE database found that the terms assigned by indexers were more specific and more numerous than those suggested by authors (Rasheed 1989).

Finally, decisions must be made regarding the form of an index. Most periodical indexes other than those for very small journals, newsletters, and the like are in the form of MULTIPLE INDEXES. Division into an author or name index and a subject index is the most common one, but separate indexes for book reviews or special features (e.g., statutes and cases in legal journals or taxonomic indexes in biological periodicals) are sometimes also compiled.

Specific Indexing Techniques

Names of persons. It used to be axiomatic that all authors and coauthors of articles are to be listed in a periodical index. There is, however, a growing trend in science and technology to list the names of dozens and even hundreds of coauthors*, which in turn led to a decision by some major abstracting and indexing databases to limit the number of named and indexed coauthors to no more than ten, even though this may do an injustice to young scientists who are members of a large team working on a problem or project, since their names may not be indexed and will therefore not be cited in references. Regarding the latter, it is now virtually impossible as a practical matter to list in a periodical index the names of all cited authors (not to mention their numerous coauthors). But persons honored by awards or prizes and those eulogized in obituaries should always be indexed, because this is just the type of information often sought in periodical indexes.

Articles. Ideally, every article should be indexed under all topics and issues dealt with. The publishers or editors may, however, impose limitations on the number of topical headings that may be assigned to an article; limits as low as three indexing terms are

---

*A Japanese paper submitted to a scientific conference in 1986 sported no fewer than 257 coauthors; an American paper published in *Physical Review* had 108 coauthors from 14 universities. These data were reported in *Science* 242 (25 Nov. 1988), p. 1130.

sometimes set for indexes of popular and trade journals, but this is not good indexing practice and is a remnant from the times when all indexes were not only produced on cards but were often also available only in this form. Such limitations on EXHAUSTIVITY are generally not found in the indexes to scientific and technical periodicals, where the number of headings for a single article may reach a dozen or more, e.g., when an article deals with many chemical compounds, methods, and applications, or with a large number of different species of plants or animals.

Titles of articles do not need to be indexed separately, because they are seldom if ever remembered by users. They are, however, sometimes included in author indexes, where they are listed under the first author's name; the names of coauthors are then linked to that of the first author by cross-references:

> Tzeng, Ovid J. L.; Daisy L. Hung; Linda Garro. "Reading the
>   Chinese characters" 287–305
> Hung, Daisy L. *see* Tzeng, O. J. L.
> Garro, Linda *see* Tzeng, O. J. L.

Editorials should be indexed under their topics as any other article but differentiated from the latter by the addition of (Ed.) or (E.). If an editorial is signed, the name of the author should be included in the author index. The titles of editorials may be indexed as subheadings under a collective heading "Editorials" or "Leaders", e.g.,

> Editorials
>   "The engineering of species" 37
>   "Reliability of electric service" 85
>   "Synthetic membranes" 422

Letters to the editor often contain important information and should, if considered indexable, be indexed by topic, not under a caption that may have been assigned by the editor. Whether or not to index also the names of letter writers depends on the nature of the periodical and its readership; it is advisable to index at least the names of persons who commented on or criticized an article as well as the author's response, e.g.,

> Doe, John. "Effect of magnetic fields" 37–43; errors (H. Smith) 75;
>   correction 185 [index entry for author]

Smith, Henry. "Effect of magnetic fields" (John Doe, pp. 37–43):
    errors 75 [index entry for letter writer]

Book reviews are indexed by the title of the book, followed by the
name of the author, the locator, and the designation (R), e.g.,

Guide to reference books, 10th ed. (Sheehy) 68 (R)

unless all book reviews are listed under the class heading "Book
reviews" or in a separate index.

The name of the reviewer should be included in the author or
name index, the locator likewise being followed by (R) to distinguish it from locators for articles written by the same person, e.g.,

Dixon, Geoffrey 68 (R), 92–96, 123

Introductory Note

An INTRODUCTORY NOTE is virtually always needed in a periodical
index in order to explain its structure and its parts (if more than
one), what has been included or excluded, and which symbols or
special typography have been used.

The problems of management and pricing of large periodical
indexes covering several years have been described by Thomas &
Mulvany (1994).

BS 3700: 5.5.3
ISO 999: 7.5.3
NISO Z39.4:

PERSONAL NAMES

Names of persons are among the easiest as well as the trickiest
items an indexer may encounter. They are easy to spot: names

seem to jump out from a printed page because they are invariably capitalized (*pace* e e cummings), and, at least for texts dealing largely or exclusively with contemporary issues and Western-style names, the name of a person can easily and quickly be set down following the well-known pattern of surname, comma, forename(s). But even among European languages there are two—Hungarian and Icelandic—in which names do not fit this pattern, and many African and Asian languages have entirely different patterns for the proper entry of indigenous names.

Generally, no agonizing decisions have to be made on whether or not to include names in an index, though it would be folly to index every single name appearing on a page without regard to the context. In a biography, for example, the author may relate the story that the famous hero read Homer, Virgil, Shakespeare, and Milton at the tender age of 10, but if no further mention is made of these literary giants their names should not appear in the index at all. For entirely different reasons, a limit is sometimes set for the listing of multiple coauthors' names in indexes to PERIODICALS. So much for the easy part. And now for sticky problems that the indexer of personal names may be confronted with.

Rules for Entry of Personal Names

For most problems regarding the entry of personal names an indexer need not invent solutions, because for virtually all of these problems there are now standardized and authoritative rules which have been developed for the purpose of library cataloging and which are equally valid for indexing. Nevertheless, since some of these rules are "flexible" or allow for different interpretations, an indexer must often decide on the best or most useful way of entering personal names in an index. The following rules are based on those in two codes: one is AACR2, chapter 22, "Headings for persons", which is followed not only in American, British, Canadian, and other English-speaking libraries but also in many other countries; the other one is *Names of persons: national usages for entry in catalogues* (1977), published by the International Federation of Library Associations and Institutions (IFLA) and referred to in the following as the "IFLA manual", which details the way in which libraries in more than 80 countries record the names of their citizens in almost 150 languages.

Since these rules are primarily intended for large research libraries and international use, and are admittedly sometimes quirky and illogical (though this is mainly caused by traditional national preferences, not the whim of catalogers), the question may well be asked why indexers should follow these rules. The answer is that a user who encountered a name in a text should be able to find additional information on the bearer of that name in a library catalog without undue trouble, although the ideal agreement between the form of a name in a text, in an index, and in a library catalog is, unfortunately, often far from being achieved. An example of this phenomenon is the name of the famous British philosopher, mathematician, and polemicist Bertrand Russell, which may be found in various catalogs, bibliographies, indexes, and reference books in no fewer than eight different forms, namely

Form of name	Source
Russell, Bertrand Arthur William, 3rd Earl Russell, Viscount Amberley	20th century authors
Russell, 3rd Earl, Bertrand Arthur William Russell	Who's Who (U.K.)
Russell, Bertrand Arthur William Russell, 3rd earl	Cumulative book index (until 1980)
Russell (Bertrand Arthur William) Earl Russell	British Library
Russell (Bertrand Arthur William)	Bibliothèque Nationale
Russell, Bertrand Russell, 3rd earl	Library of Congress
Russell, Bertrand, Earl Russell	Who's Who in America
Russell, Bertrand (According to AACR 2, 22.6A)	Books in print British books in print British national bibliography Cumulative book index 1981–

This shows that the advice in AACR2, 22.2A "If a person is known by more than one name, choose the name . . . that appears most frequently in reference sources" may create more problems than it solves.

Forms of Names

Problems that frequently arise even for seemingly straightforward names are caused by their form. Names may be known or written in various degrees of fullness; forenames may have been omitted in the text; names may be differently spelled; and the same person may be known by variant names in different languages. In back-of-the-book indexes, the forms of names used in the text should, as far as possible, be followed even if sometimes they are not quite compatible with standard forms, because users are likely to remember names in the form in which they have read them in the text. CROSS-REFERENCES from a standard form to the form used in the text may have to be made. In PERIODICAL indexes, however, consistency is the overriding consideration, and only the form of the name that conforms with widely accepted norms should be used if authors of articles name the same person in different ways.

Fullness of Names

Authors often mention famous persons by their surnames only, on the (not always justified) assumption that "everybody knows" who is meant. In this case, the indexer should add forenames, which may be found in biographical dictionaries or other reference works, or may have to be elicited from the author. But not all names need to be listed in an index in their fullest form, because that form may not even have been used by the person. For example, if the text mentions Montesquieu, his name need not be entered as

Montesquieu, Charles Louis de Secondat, Baron de la Brède et de

because an index cannot and should not serve as a substitute for a biographical dictionary. It would be quite sufficient to enter the name as

Montesquieu, Charles Secondat, Baron de

or even simply as

Montesquieu, Charles

(but not just "Montesquieu"). Neither should Mozart be entered as

Mozart, Johann Chrysostom Wolfgang Amadeus

a form in which, to its everlasting shame, the Library of Congress insisted on cataloging the composer's name before 1980 because it was so entered in the baptismal register of Salzburg!* Another notorious case of overly punctilious listing of a name is that of Winston S. Churchill, who always signed his name in this form, which did not prevent *Debrett's peerage* from listing him under the "correct" form Spencer-Churchill, Sir Winston, though the great man thoroughly resented it. The last two examples simply confirm the old adage "Against stupidity even the gods struggle in vain".

The opposite phenomenon—indexing names only by surname and initials, although the full name is displayed in the text—is now often found in indexes to periodicals and abstract journals, ostensibly in order to save keystrokes or possibly some space. While it may save a small amount of space to pare down an author's name to surname and initials in that part of an abstracting and indexing service in which the abstracts appear, in the monthly or annual author index, where each author's name appears only once and occupies normally only one line (even if there are several contributions by the same person), there is no justification for not listing at least the first forename and middle initial. The "initials only" form of names often makes it impossible to distinguish between two or more entries for Brown, C. H. or Smith, J. A. and similar common surnames in other languages. Users are badly served by such parsimonious indexing.

The name of a person may also be given in the same text in various degrees of fullness, ranging from initials through nicknames and pet names to the full name and anaphora (the substitution of a pronoun or noun for a name mentioned earlier). Thus, the name of the 26th president of the United States may appear as TR, Teddy, Theodore Roosevelt, "he", and "the president", all or most of which need locators in an index under Roosevelt, Theodore.

---

*Mozart's last given name was actually Theophilus, which he later changed to its Latin equivalent Amadeus.

Language

A person may be known in several languages by different forms of name, but only one of these may be chosen for entry in an index, with cross-references from other forms if needed. Christopher Columbus (a curious hybrid of an Anglicized Latin forename and a Latinized Italian surname) never knew this form of his name but was in his lifetime variously known as the Genoese Christoforo Colombo and later in Spanish as Cristóbal Colón. Many other foreign names, particularly those of ancient Romans, royalty, saints, and popes, have traditionally been Anglicized, so that Titus Livius became Livy, Marcus Tullius Cicero became a simple Tully (though this somewhat frivolous-sounding form is now no longer used), and Gaius Plinius Secundus became Pliny the Elder; Friedrich II of Prussia and Karl XII of Sweden are always written about in English as Frederick and Charles. Commoners, however, seem to have largely escaped such enforced Anglification, so that we are spared reading about Frederick Schiller, Louis van Beethoven or Joseph Verdi.

Spelling

The name of the same person may be spelled in different forms, especially for people living before the 18th century, when SPELLING was a matter of caprice, and authors or scribes spelled words and names any way they saw fit. But even today, members of the same family may choose to spell their names differently, to the great exasperation of genealogists and indexers of family histories, who may have a hard time sorting out Feasey, Pheasey, and Veasey, or Jewet, Jewett, Jewit, Jewitt, and Juet.

The names of persons originally written in a non-Roman script, e.g., Arabic, Chinese, or Cyrillic, may appear in various different ROMANIZATIONS, such as Petr Il'ich Tchaikovsky, Peter Iljych Tschaikovskij, Pjotr Iljič Čajkovskij and many other renderings, and Mao Tse-tung is now mostly referred to as Mao Zedong. In a book written by a single author, the usage of the author should normally be respected unless it is quite at variance with commonly used forms as found in newspapers and reference works. But when the same name is variously spelled in the same document (e.g., in badly edited conference proceedings in which a number of authors use various Romanizations of the same name) the indexer must rely on the spelling most commonly found in reference works or else use a systematic Romanization according to the *ALA-LC Romanization tables* (1991).

Changes of Names

People change their names for many reasons. They may migrate from their country of birth to another country, become naturalized citizens, and choose a new name more in tune with their new language: Teodor Josef Konrad Korzeniowski thus became Joseph Conrad. They may enter holy orders and become monks or nuns; they may be elected to the papacy, whereupon Cardinal Angelo Giuseppe Roncalli became Joannes Papa XXIII, or Pope John XXIII for the English-speaking world. During the Renaissance, scholars translated their vernacular names into more prestigious Latin or Greek ones, so that Fisher became Piscator, Smith became Faber, and Philipp Schwarzerd became Philipp Melanchthon. Some people change their name for reasons best known to themselves such as Ford Madox Ford, whose original name was Hueffer. Finally, in Western society, a married woman generally takes her husband's name and in the U.S. and U.K. formerly often lost her forename too, a Miss Jane Doe after marrying Mr. John Blow being known and addressed only as Mrs. John Blow; well, women's liberation put an end to much of that, and none too soon, although it led to a considerable increase in double-barrelled names (on which more below).

Indexing changed names is relatively straightforward. If the text deals with a person only after a name change, perhaps mentioning the former name only in passing, the new (or last) name only need to be indexed. But if a person was well-known also under a previous name, cross-references from and to the changed name should be made, e.g.,

Karol Wojtyła *see also* John Paul II, Pope
John Paul II, Pope *see also* Karol Wojtyła

because before his election to the papacy he wrote plays, poems, and secular essays which, if treated in a text, must be indexed under his former name. The same treatment applies to married women who became well-known under their maiden names and continued to create literary or artistic works or became otherwise known also under their married names. A woman who married more than once is normally entered under the name of her latest husband, but the likes of Zsa Zsa Gabor or Elizabeth Taylor are best indexed under their maiden names or show business names, which are well-known to the public. Finally, an unusual but notorious case (not likely to recur any time soon) is that of the controversial member of the British royal family who had to be indexed at various times as Wales, Edward, Prince of; Edward VIII, King of Great Britain and Northern Ireland; and Windsor, Duke of.

Pseudonyms

Before 1980, most library catalogs listed pseudonymous authors under their real names even when it was well known that the author had never published under that name, the prime example being Mark Twain, whose works could be found in catalogs only under Clemens, Samuel Langhorne (with a single cross-reference "Twain, Mark *see* Clemens, Samuel Langhorne"). Such arrant nonsense is now mercifully a thing of the past, and catalogers as well as indexers may normally list names in the form appearing on a title page or in a text, even for authors who use several pseudonyms or pseudonyms *and* their real names, e.g., John Creasey, who masquerades also as Gordon Ashe, Michael Halliday, J. J. Maric, Anthony Morton, and Jeremy York. Cross-references from a real name (whether actually used or not) to a pseudonym may be made but are not mandatory.

Pseudonyms beginning with an INITIAL ARTICLE, such as "An Observer" or "The Rambler" are alphabetized by the article which forms an inseparable part of such fictitious names.

Compound Surnames

These fall into two categories: those written with a hyphen (also fondly known as double-barrelled names) and those that are not.

The first category is easily dealt with: a name of the pattern A B-C is always entered under B-C, A, with a cross-reference from C, A B-, e.g. Cecil Day-Lewis is entered as Day-Lewis, Cecil with a cross-reference from Lewis, Cecil Day-. Bearers of very common German names sometimes add the name of their birthplace or hometown to their surnames as a distinguishing element, e.g.,

Fischer-Dieskau, Dietrich
Müller-Breslau, Heinrich

but in these cases, a cross-reference from the place name is not needed.

Compound names without a hyphen are more intricate because the middle part of a tripartite name may be part of the surname or it may not, depending on national usage or the wishes or whims of the bearer of such names. For example, Harriet Beecher Stowe, though an emancipated woman by 19th-century standards, had to use her husband's name, Stowe, on the title page of *Uncle Tom's cabin*, but she retained her maiden name, under which she had published stories before her marriage, as a middle or second surname. This is now also what many modern women are doing, with or without a hyphen between the two surnames. Henry Cabot Lodge is entered as Lodge, Henry Cabot (the Cabot part honoring his ancestor, a 15th-century explorer named Giovanni Caboto, who changed his name to John Cabot), but Ralph Vaughn Williams is to be entered as Vaughn Williams, Ralph. Thus, the only guideline for the correct entry of such compound names is a person's preference regarding the structure and composition of a surname. How can an indexer know? For famous people, reference works should be followed (although these do not always agree among themselves); for lesser known or unknown people, if the author of the text does not know, it is best to index under the last part of a name without any reference from the middle part, which is then treated as a forename.

Prefixes

Probably no other detail of personal names generates as many headaches as the treatment of names with prefixes—an article, a preposition, a combination of both, or a word indicating filial or paternal relationship. Should the name be entered so that the prefix precedes the main part of the name or should the prefix follow the forename after inversion? And if the name, as is sometimes the case in Romance languages, consists of several parts with and without prefixes or conjunctions, which one is the surname to be entered as the first element of the name in an index? In vain does an indexer look for any rational system that can be applied across the board, because every nation in whose language surnames may begin with a separately written prefix seems to have contrived different rules for entering prefixes either before or after the main part of a surname.

The following is a summary of the rules for names with prefixes in some major languages, assuming always that a person is or was either a speaker or writer of that language. (No rule can ever cope with the names of people who move from country to country and write in more than one language, such as the Dutch historian and novelist Hendrik van Loon, who wrote in Dutch in his homeland, then emigrated to the United States and continued to write in English; such cases must be decided on an ad hoc basis, taking into account, where possible, the practice of national libraries.) For details, see AACR2, rule 22.5D and the IFLA manual. Other reference works, such as biographical dictionaries, are notoriously unreliable in their treatment of prefixed names and should be used only if no official rules are available.

Before trying to penetrate the thicket of various national usages for entering prefixed names in catalogs and indexes, two pieces of good news: one is that prefixes that are written together with the main part of a name as a single word are uniformly entered under the prefix in all languages, e.g., Delacroix, Descartes, Delmonte, Lafayette, Lebrun, or Vandenberg are all entered as single surnames, and no cross-references from the original forms, e.g., De la Croix ("of the cross") or Van den Berg ("of the mountain"), are needed unless the index contains the names of two persons, spelled, say, Lafayette and La Fayette, in which case reciprocal *see also* cross-references should be made if word-by-word alphabetization is used. (In letter-by-letter alphabetization the two forms of the name would be arranged in a single sequence, and no cross-reference would be needed.)

The other piece of good news is that prefixed names of people who are or were citizens of, or lived and worked mainly in, an English-speaking country are invariably entered under the prefix, e.g.,

De la Mare, Walter
De Morgan, Augustus
Du Maurier, Daphne
L'Enfant, Pierre Charles
Van Buren, Martin
Van Loon, Hendrik

The same rule applies to Afrikaans, modern Italian names (but not to medieval or Renaissance names, for which reference works and catalogs should be consulted), and Romanian names, except for those beginning with *de*.

And now for the "bad" news, the rather complex rules followed by some other nations and language communities. Dutch, French, German, and Portuguese names with prefixes are entered under the main part of the name and the prefix follows the inverted fore-name(s) as the last element, e.g.,

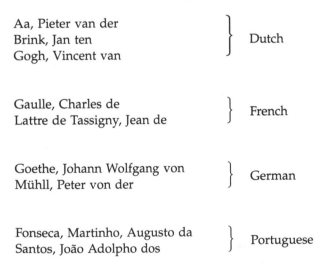

Aa, Pieter van der
Brink, Jan ten   } Dutch
Gogh, Vincent van

Gaulle, Charles de
Lattre de Tassigny, Jean de   } French

Goethe, Johann Wolfgang von
Mühll, Peter von der   } German

Fonseca, Martinho, Augusto da
Santos, João Adolpho dos   } Portuguese

Spanish names with prefixes are treated the same way, except for those prefixes that consist of an article only which are entered under the article, e.g.,

Casas, Bartolomé de las   *but*   Las Heras, Manuel Antonio
Figueroa, Francisco de
Río, Antonio del

There are other important exceptions: in French, the articles *la, le,* and *les* and their contraction with the prepositions *des* and *du* in prefixed names are entered under the prefix, but *De la* is split into *La* before and *de* after the name, e.g.,

Des Prés, Josquin
Du Barry, Marie Jeanne
La Fontaine, Jean de
Le Rouge, Gustave

In German, the contractions of prepositions and articles *am* (an dem), *im* (in dem), *vom* (von dem), *zum* (zu dem), and *zur* (zu der) in a prefixed name are entered under the prefix, but such names are rather seldom encountered:

Am Thym, August
Vom Ende, Erich
Zur Linde, Otto

Danish, Norwegian, and Swedish are straddling the fence: if a prefix is of Scandinavian or German origin (*af* or *von*), the main part of the name becomes the entry word; but if it is of Romance (mostly French) origin, the name is entered under the prefix:

Ekeberg, Anita af   *but*   De Geer, Gerard
Linné, Carl von   De la Gardie, Magnus Gabriel

Finally, some languages use patronymics as prefixes, e.g., Arabic *Bin* (or *Ben*) and *Ibn* (Ben Bella, Ibn Saud), English *Fitz* (Fitz Alan), Hebrew *Bar* or *Ben* (Bar Ilan, Ben Gurion), and Welsh* *Ab* or *Ap* (Ab Ifor, Ap Rhys). Arabic also has the teknonyms *Abu* and *Umm* (indicating, respectively, father or mother of someone) as well as the words *Abd-al* (or *Abdul*) (servant of) as prefixes (Abu Said, Umm Kulthum, Abd-al-Nasir). All such names are entered under the prefix.

*The complexities of indexing Welsh patronymics have been explored in detail by Moore (1990).

The problems caused by the features of personal names discussed so far have been documented with many examples in a
classic paper by Blanken (1971) and by Piternick (1992).

Homographic Names

Persons having the same surname and forename must be distinguished in an index by the addition of QUALIFIERS such as dates of
birth and/or death, occupation, professional title, term of address,
or epithet, e.g.,

> Smith, John 1863–1891
> Smith, John (architect)
> Smith, John, Dr.
> Smith, John, Reverend

Names of numerous members of the same family, often for several
generations, should not only be distinguished by their forenames or
nicknames but also by their kinship; the name of a biographee or
other person to whom the family members are related is generally
abbreviated to initials in order to save space. For the same reason,
their forenames may be indented under the surname of the first
person listed instead of repeating the surname for each person. The
following example is from a biography of Mozart:

> Mozart, Anna Maria, née Pertl (WA's mother)
>   Constanze, née Weber (WA's wife)
>   Franz Aloys (WA's uncle)
>   Franz Xaver Wolfgang (WA's son)
>   Johann Georg (WA's grandfather)
>   Joseph Ignaz (WA's uncle)
>   Karl Thomas (WA's son)
>   Leopold (WA's father)
>   Maria Anna (WA's sister, called Nannerl)
>   Maria Anna Thekla (WA's cousin, called Bäsle)
>   Wolfgang Amadeus (WA)

For details on the arrangement of homonymous names *see* HOMO-
GRAPHS.

Forenames

Persons known only by their forenames (which, when listed in an
index, often become HOMOGRAPHS) fall into two categories regarding their distinction in indexes: one is the exclusive club of popes,
emperors, kings, queens, and other sovereign rulers, who are distinguished by adding Roman numbers (and sometimes epithets) to
their names; the second category is that of all other persons known
by their forenames only, mainly those who lived in antiquity or in
the Middle Ages, who are distinguished by place of origin, occupation, religious rank, or some other epithet, e.g.,

> Abraham (Bishop of Nisibis)
> Abraham (King of Axum)
> Abraham (Patriarch)
> Abraham (Rabbi of Beja)

If the distinguishing term has become an integral part of the name,
no comma or parentheses are used, e.g.,

> Abraham a Santa Clara
> Erasmus of Rotterdam
> John of Salisbury
> Leonardo da Vinci
> Walther von der Vogelweide

A special case of forename entry is that of Icelandic names (see
below, p. 370).

Royalty

Emperors, kings, dukes, and princes and their female counterparts
are traditionally entered under their forenames, distinguished, if
necessary, by Roman numbers and by their titles; if they are also
known by epithets, these should preferably not be used in an index,
but the official name should be given and a cross-reference from the
epithet to the official name should be made, e.g.,

Charles the Bold *see* Charles, Duke of Burgundy
Ivan the Terrible *see* Ivan IV, Tsar of Russia

Children of royalty are entered by name and title, e.g.,

Anne, Princess

(for the daughter of Elizabeth II, Queen of Great Britain and Northern Ireland).

British Nobility*

This is another area where not only angels but even experienced indexers fear to tread. While most nobles of other European nations have names with one or more prefixes and titles such as Fürst, Duc, Herzog, Marquis, Baron, Ritter, or Graf (or Greve, Grof) which stay pretty stable throughout their lives, British nobility has traditionally had the choice of using either their family name or their title when writing books or otherwise making themselves known. Authorities on the listing of noblemen's names are hopelessly divided, so no help can be expected from the *Dictionary of national biography* or the catalog of the British Library, both of which enter nobility under their family names, or from Burke's or Debrett's *Peerage,* which prefer titles of nobility as entry terms, as does also AACR2, 22.6A. Indexing noblemen and -women under their family name has the advantage of keeping all members of the same family together and separating different families, members of which may have had the same title (e.g., there are no fewer than fifteen Earls of Essex who belonged to eight different families). But it seems that British indexers (and both British and American catalogers) prefer to enter noblemen under their title unless the person definitely wishes to be known by family name. Adding to these ambiguities, British noblemen may sometimes choose to renounce their title of nobility in order to pursue a political career, as did the 14th Earl of Home (entered as Home, 14th Earl of), who as Prime Minister became Sir Alec Douglas-Home (entered as Douglas-Home, Sir Alec).

*For this section, the exposition in Knight (1979, pp. 71–73) has been partially followed. A more detailed treatment of problems in the indexing of British nobility is by Lee (1991).

Persons who were ennobled late in life but are better known by their former names should be indexed under their surnames, e.g., Benjamin Disraeli, who became Lord Beaconsfield, should be entered as Disraeli, Benjamin, Earl of Beaconsfield. In such cases, cross-references for any names not used as main headings should be made.

The titles of honor *Sir, Dame, Lord,* and *Lady* are always placed before the forename when such names are arranged by surname, e.g.,

Beecham, Sir Thomas
Gordon, Lord George
Stanhope, Lady Hester
Thorndike, Dame Sybil

Religious Appellations and Titles

These are capitalized and given after the person's forename in inverted name style, preceded by a comma, e.g.,

Angelico, Fra
Ehrenpreis, Marcus, Chief Rabbi of Sweden
Spellman, Francis Joseph, Cardinal
Temple, William, Archbishop of Canterbury

Optionally, cross-references may be made from an earlier (secular) name or from the appellation, e.g.,

Bojaxhiu, Agnes Gonxha *see* Theresa, Mother
Mother Theresa *see* Theresa, Mother

Saints

Saints are traditionally entered under their forenames (in English form if there is one), followed by a comma, the word "Saint" (which is *not* abbreviated to St.), and any additional epithets, e.g.,

Stephen, Saint
Stephen, Saint, King of Hungary

If the text deals with a person who had a family name during his or her lifetime as well as with that person's sainthood, a cross-reference should be made, e.g.,

More, Sir Thomas
Thomas More, Saint *see* More, Sir Thomas

Hungarian Names

In Hungarian, a person is always addressed or written about in the form surname-forename (in writing, *without* a comma between the two parts), e.g.,

Bartók Béla

Outside of Hungary, a comma is inserted in the usual way between surname and forename for the sake of uniformity in indexing personal names, i.e.,

Bartók, Béla

Icelandic Names

Old Norse, the tongue of the Vikings, is to a large extent still the language of modern Iceland, and the Viking custom of naming children as sons and daughters of their father still prevails. Thus, Icelandic names consist of a forename and a patronymic which, however, is not the equivalent of a surname because it changes with each generation: if, for example, Gunnar Olafsson has a son Stefan, his name will be Stefan Gunnarsson, and Stefan's son Thorsteinn will be Thorsteinn Stefansson. Icelandic names are therefore entered under forename followed by patronymic without a comma in between, e.g.,

Bjarni Benediktsson
Steinunn Sigurðardottir

Since most people are not familiar with Icelandic names, a cross-reference from the patronymic should be made, e.g.,

Benediktsson, Bjarni *see* Bjarni Benediktsson

Russian Names

Russian names consist of three elements: forename, patronymic, and family name. Forenames ending in -*a* are feminine, all others are masculine, but many masculine nicknames and diminutives (which are very common) also end in -*a*, e.g., Kolya for Nikolai. Patronymics for men always end in -*ovich* or -*evich* and those for women in -*ovna* or -*evna*, e.g., Petrovich = son of Petr, Petrovna = daughter of Petr. The standard form of address is the forename and patronymic but not the family name. Thus, Ivan Petrovich Smirnov is addressed as Ivan Petrovich; if this form appears in a text, its second element should not be mistaken for a family name and indexed as Petrovich, Ivan, and an effort must be made to ascertain the family name (which may also end in -*ovich* or -*evich*).

Since the patronymic is a term of respect, Russians generally do not use it when referring to themselves, e.g., the bearer of the name cited above will sign himself as Ivan Smirnov, Ivan P. Smirnov, or I. P. Smirnov, the last form being the most common one in indicating authorship of an article, both in the by-line and when cited in Soviet bibliographies and indexes.

Russian names, originally written in Cyrillic, must be rendered in Roman script indexes by means of ROMANIZATION, preferably according to the American National Standard ANSI Z39.24 *System for the Romanization of Slavic Cyrillic characters* (1976) or the British Standard BS 2979:1959 *Transliteration of Cyrillic* and *Greek characters* (1958). But if a different Romanization scheme is used in the text, it should be followed in the index, provided that it is not too idiosyncratic, e.g., the name of the Russian poet Evtushenko, Evgenii (strict Romanization) may be indexed in the more popular and well-known form Yevtushenko, Yevgeny (a practice sanctioned since 1980 also for American library catalogs).

In indexing, Russian names are treated as other Western names, i.e., family name, comma, given name, and patronymic (if known), e.g.,

Smirnov, Ivan Petrovich

Non-Western Names

The structure of names and the choice of entry word in African and Asian languages are often quite different from those of Western names, although many citizens of African and Asian countries have westernized their names in this century. Specific rules for Arabic, Burmese, Chinese, Hebrew, Indic, Indonesian, Japanese, Malay, and Thai names are given in AACR2, 22.21–28 and in the *Chicago manual of style* (1993, 17.114–126). Names in these and many other African and Asian languages are treated in the IFLA manual.

Arabic, Hebrew, Vietnamese, and East Asian names are briefly treated here because they are frequently encountered in the literature and in the mass media but are not dealt with (except for Arabic and Hebrew) in AACR2 and only partially in the *Chicago manual of style*.

Arabic Names

Contemporary Arabic names follow mostly the Western pattern of forename and surname, and are therefore inverted, e.g.,

> Arafat, Yasser
> Ashrawi, Hanan
> Sadat, Anwar

The INITIAL ARTICLE *Al-* (or *El-*), joined to a name by a hyphen, is a part of that name and is not transposed but is disregarded in alphabetization (and is therefore in some Romanizations spelled in lowercase) however, the prefixes *Abd, Abu, Bin* (*Ben*) and *Ibn* are integral parts of surnames and may neither be transposed nor disregarded in alphabetization, e.g.,

> Abd-al-Nasir, Jamal
> Abu Bakr, Hasan
> el-Baz, Faruq
> Ben Bella, Ahmed
> Ibn Said, Muhammad
> Al-Sheniti, Mahmud

The rendering of names of persons living before the 19th century and written in Arabic script (mainly Arabs, Jews, and Persians) is complex and cannot be reduced to fixed rules, as discussed by Houissa (1991) and exemplified in AACR2, 22.22. It needs an intimate knowledge of the Arabic language and access to special reference works (which often do not agree on forms of entry and on ROMANIZATION of a name). An additional difficulty is that many famous medieval authors bearing Arabic names are better known in the West by their Latinized names which are, however, often garbled and resemble only remotely the Arabic names, e.g., Averroës, whose name was Muhammad ibn Rushd or Avicenna (Abu Ali ibn Sina).

Hebrew Names

Hebrew names of Jews living in Palestine since about 1880 and in Israel since 1948 generally consist of one or two forenames followed by a surname and are treated like Western names, e.g.,

Agnon, Shemuel Yosef
Meron, Hana

Problems in indexing Hebrew names are mainly caused by various forms of ROMANIZATION used by authors who rely on different traditions of rendering names in Roman script or who invent their own system. For example, the same Hebrew surname may be found in the spellings Misrachi, Misrahi, Mizrahy, and other variations.

The patronymic prefixes *Bar, Bath* and *Ben* as well as the definitive article *Ha-* in modern Hebrew names are integral parts of surnames, whether or not they are written as separate elements, joined to the rest of the name by a hyphen or written together with it, e.g.,

Bar Ilan, Meir
Bath-Miriam, Yokheved
Ben Aharon, Yitshaq
Hakohen, David

Hebrew names of Jews who lived before the early 19th century have almost always the pattern: forename(s), followed either by a patronymic or by an epithet or both; they are indexed by forename, e.g.,

> Akiba ben Joseph
> Benjamin of Tudela

The form of pre-19th century Hebrew forenames, when cited in English texts, is virtually always that of the Authorized Version of the Bible, which in many cases differs substantially from the rendering of the same names for contemporary bearers, e.g.,

	Hebrew names
Anglicized form	*Romanized systematically*
Isaac	Yitshaq
Jacob	Ya'akov
Rebecca	Rivka
Solomon	Shelomo

The patronymic names of some medieval Jewish authors are most familiar to Western readers in a Grecized form (though they never wrote anything in Greek), e.g., Maimonides, whose Hebrew name was Moshe ben Maimon (both forms meaning "Son of Maimon"). The name of at least one medieval Jewish poet and philosopher, Shelomo ibn Gabirol, suffered (like those of his Arabic contemporaries) from pidgin-Latin mutilation, becoming Avicebron in the Latin translation of one of his philosophical works.

The form of an Arabic or Hebrew name in an index will, of course, virtually always follow the usage of the text, but if that is inconsistent (e.g., in a periodical or in a collective monograph) cross-references from a chosen form to variants will be necessary.

Vietnamese Names

These consist of a family name and a given name in two parts, the last one usually being the one by which a person is known and addressed. Entry is, however, by family name followed by the given name without a comma in between, e.g.,

> Ngo Dinh Diem

East Asian Names

The three major East Asian languages—Chinese, Japanese, and Korean—are or were written in Chinese characters. Japanese uses in addition to Chinese characters (*kanji*) two forms of a syllabary (*katakana* and *hiragana*). Korean was written in Chinese characters until about the first half of the 20th century, but is now almost exclusively written in an indigenous alphabet, *Han'gul*. Names in these three languages must be rendered by transcription, conveying to English-speaking readers a rough approximation of their pronunciation. See ROMANIZATION for details on transcription systems.

Chinese Names

Chinese names consist of two elements, a family name and a given name. When Romanized, they are written in this order and without a comma between the two elements. The family name is most often a single syllable, although two and three syllables may form the family name of Chinese in countries outside mainland China. Given names consist of two syllables; in Wade-Giles Romanization, a hyphen is written between the first and second part of a given name, whereas in Pinyin Romanization the two parts of a given name are written together, e.g.,

Wade-Giles	*Pinyin*
Chou En-lai	Zhou Enlai

As this example shows, the differences between the two Romanization schemes affect, in many cases, the alphabetization of personal names.

Japanese Names

Japanese names also consist of two elements, a family name and a given name, traditionally used in this order and, when Romanized, without a comma in between. However, many modern Japanese, particularly those in frequent contact with Western people, now prefer to write their names in Western style, putting their given names first, but in Japan only the traditional style is used. That style is also exclusively employed for all Japanese names in use before the Meiji Restoration in 1868. Thus, the name of Lady Murasaki, the author of the famous 11th-century romance *Genji monogatari* (The tale of Genji), whose given name was Shikibu, must be entered in the form Murasaki Shikibu. But the name of the Nobel prize-winning modern author Yasunari Kawabata must be inverted in an index to Kawabata, Yasunari as if it were a Western name.

Korean Names

Korean names, similar to Chinese ones, consist of a family name followed by a given name consisting of one or two syllables, and are so entered, e.g.,

Kim Pu-sik
Namgung Pyok
Park Chung Hee

No comma is written between family name and given name, but if the given name is a Christian one, Korean names are often treated as if they were Western names, e.g.,

Park, Thomas R.

Obscure Names

Persons mentioned briefly by surname or forename only but otherwise not known should be further identified by occupation, position, or activity, as derived from the context; a date may be added, if it can be readily ascertained, e.g.,

Barbara (Mrs. Smith's friend)
Choglokov (Russian officer, 1768)

Names of animals may also be treated this way, e.g.,

Secretariat (American racehorse)

AACR2: chapter 22
BS 3700: 5.3.1
Chicago manual of style: 17.75–89
ISO 999: 5.3
NISO Z39.4:

PHRASES

Prepositional phrases, which are often used as chapter headings and as section headings, e.g., "cars for handicapped persons", "graphs in statistics", and "climate of planets", were in the past frequently indexed either in that form or inverted to "planets, climate of", etc., because of the pervasive influence of the *Library of Congress subject headings* in which such phrases, sometimes in direct form and sometimes inverted, are legion. Even worse, prepositional phrases are sometimes chopped up into the dreadful form "Persons, handicapped, cars for". These three practices are now considered unsuitable for a well-designed index, though, regrettably, they are still employed by some indexers.

Phrases in which the PREPOSITIONS *for, in, of,* and others are used to indicate a relationship between two or more concepts should seldom if ever be used as main headings but should be split (or "factored") into their components, as discussed under COMPOUND HEADINGS.

Other expressions which are technically prepositional phrases but have simply become common terms (and are often hyphenated), e.g., "cost of living", "Sergeant-at-arms", "Lady-in-waiting", "mother-of-pearl", should not be split and do not need any cross-references from the second part of the phrase. The same applies to set expressions used in many scientific, technical, and professional fields, e.g., "strength of materials" (engineering), "goodness of fit" (statistics), "balance of payments" (finance), or "notice of motion" (law).

Phrases in foreign languages, occasionally used by (somewhat pretentious) authors, e.g., *sauve qui peut, se non è vero è ben trovato,* and *Sturm und Drang,* seldom need index entries, but if such a phrase is deemed to be indexable in a particular context, it should be left untranslated—*dictum sapienti sat est**.

Phrases are sometimes used as names of real or mythical persons, especially by writers who prefer pseudonyms to their real names, e.g.,

> An American
> Father Time
> Mr. Fixit
> Poor Richard

Phrases are also employed for the identification of persons (mostly artists) whose real names remain unknown, e.g.,

> Author of Early Impressions
> Master of Moulins

Phrases used as names should not be inverted but should be indexed as they stand; if deemed necessary, cross-references may be made, e.g.,

> Jemima, Aunt *see* Aunt Jemima

PLACE NAMES

Most place names are easily indexed if the text deals with a brief period of time and if places do not play a significant role relative to

---

*Plautus, *Persa* 729 and Terence, *Phormio III, iii.*

the main topic. But in historical, biographical, geographical, and some scientific texts, the indexing of place names may present problems. Foremost among these are forms of place names, especially the Romanization of geographic names in countries using non-Roman scripts; different names for the same place in various languages; and a few other, relatively minor, problems.

Rules for Entry of Place Names

All sovereign countries have official names, and many, especially those that do not use the Roman alphabet, have also Romanized or English versions of their names. These can be found in the annually updated *Statesman's yearbook.* The International Federation of Library Associations and Institutions (IFLA) published a guide (*Names of states,* 1981) to official names of sovereign states and autonomous overseas territories and dependencies (but not names of cantons, states, or republics of federal systems) as of 1980; the names are listed in vernacular form as well as in English, French, German, Russian, and Spanish. In the United States, the U.S. Board on Geographic Names (BGN)* is the authority on the official English form of place names, including those that must be Romanized; in the U.K., the Permanent Committee on Geographic Names (PCGN) has the same task. The Library of Congress generally employs the forms of names designated by the BGN so that its catalogs constitute an official reference source for the form of many place names, with the exception of places in the former U.S.S.R. and China (a problem discussed below under Romanization). To some extent, the rules of AACR2, chapter 23, "Geographic names", are also applicable to the indexing of place names.

English Versus Vernacular Place Names

Many places are traditionally known by their English names, which are sometimes close to the vernacular form, e.g., Florence / Firenze or Brittany, which is Bretagne in French and Breiz in the Breton

---

*c/o Defense Mapping Agency, 8613 Lee Highway A-20, Fairfax, VA 22031.

language. But, more often, an English place name is quite different from the vernacular one, e.g., Albania/Shqiperia, Dublin/Baile Átha Cliath, Lake Constance/Bodensee, and Yellow River/Huang Ho. The usage of the text should be followed, but if the vernacular form is not mentioned, no cross-reference is needed.

In countries where two or more official languages are used, the same place often has quite different names, none of which has an English equivalent, e.g., in Finland (whose vernacular name is Suomi) the city called Turku in Finnish is known as Åbo in Swedish. Here, too, an author's usage should be followed, but if two or more forms are used, as may happen in a periodical, one must be chosen as index entry and CROSS-REFERENCES from all others must be made.

Changes of Name

Most places, large and small, do indeed stay in place—though entire continents and everything on them, according to the plate tectonics theory, are in constant movement, and cities devastated by natural disasters have sometimes been moved to a different location, retaining their former names. But rulers or owners of places change in the course of centuries or even within a decade or less, and many of them decide to change the name of a country, a territory, or a city, not to mention changes of street names and the names of buildings. The latter half of the 20th century has probably seen more such changes than any other period in the history of mankind, particularly in Africa and Asia and in the former U.S.S.R. Northern Rhodesia is now Zambia, Southern Rhodesia became Zimbabwe; East Bengal, formerly a part of India, became East Pakistan and is now Bangladesh; Saigon became Ho Chi Minh City; and the city of Tsaritsyn became Stalingrad but is now Volgograd, and Leningrad reverted to St. Petersburg.

In these and hundreds of other such cases, a back-of-the-book index will have to follow the usage of the text, and no cross-references will be necessary unless another form of a place name is also mentioned. Sometimes, separate entries for two different names of the same place need to be made in historical works covering a long period, e.g., in a history of Australia, both Van Diemen's

Land and Tasmania may be used repeatedly, and separate entries for the two names of the island would be necessary.

In periodical indexes a policy decision must be made in order to maintain consistency. Three rules have been found useful for this purpose, namely,

1. If the change of name does not involve territorial change (or only minor ones), enter under the new name as soon as it has become firmly established, e.g., Thailand instead of Siam.

2. If a territory has been split into two parts, enter under the two new names with a cross-reference from the former name with the date of change, e.g.,

> Federal Republic of Germany
>   *see also* Germany for events before 1949 and after 1990
> German Democratic Republic
>   *see also* Germany for events before 1949 and after 1990
> Germany
>   *see also* Federal Republic of Germany and
>   German Democratic Republic for events
>   from 1949 to 1990

Cross-references from the popular names of the two states, West Germany and East Germany, respectively, would also have to be made.

3. If two territories unite to form a single one, enter under the new name as soon as it has become firmly established, e.g., the former Tanganyika and Zanzibar have been united as Tanzania since 1964.

These three rules will not cover all eventualities but will help to ensure consistency in most cases.

Homographs

Places which have the same name but are in different geographic regions must be distinguished by adding the name of the country, province, state, or other jurisdiction if both are mentioned in a text, e.g.,

London (England)   York (County)
London (Ontario)   York (Diocese)
                        York (Province)
                        York (Yorkshire)

Topographic Features

Many topographic features such as mountain ranges, plateaus, lakes, deserts or national parks lie across political boundaries, yet are often described in works on countries, states or other political entities. If it may be expected that users will wish to find both the geographical and the political aspects of the topographical feature, DOUBLE ENTRIES should be made. For example, a work describing the hydrography and water resources of Lake Victoria, which is in Kenya, Tanzania and Uganda, will need an entry under its English name, or its African equivalent Victoria Nyanza, as well as cross-references to the names of the three countries. But a description of the Sese Islands, which are in the Ugandan part of the lake, need only an entry under their name and perhaps under Victoria Nyanza and Uganda, e.g.,

Sese Islands
  fauna 34
  flora 42
  population 27

Uganda
  agriculture 63–72
  fisheries 68
  population 25–28
  Sese Islands 27, 34, 42
  Victoria Nyanza 17
  White Nile 18, 56–59, 102
  wildlife 93

Victoria Nyanza
  see also Kenya; Tanzania; Uganda
  discovery by Europeans 17
  fisheries 68
  flood control 123–135, 153, 169–172

Initial Terms Indicating Jurisdiction

Terms indicating jurisdiction, when forming the first part of the official name of a place, are disregarded and only the proper name is entered, e.g., the Irish County Kerry is entered as Kerry, the German Kreis Alfeld as Alfeld, the French Département Seine-et-Marne as Seine-et-Marne, and the Italian Provincia di Milano as Milano; in the last example, it may be necessary to distinguish between Milano (city) and Milano (province). But if a jurisdictional term is an integral part of a place name, it is so entered, e.g.,

Città di Castello
Ciudad Bolivar
Mexico City

Geographical Terms as First Element

If a term denoting a geographical feature, e.g., Bay, Cape, Gulf, Lake, Mount, or Sea, forms the first element of a place name but the place is not a bay, cape, etc., the term is written as given in the place name and is neither inverted nor treated as a qualifier, e.g.,

Bay City (a town)
Cape Town (a city)
Lake Placid (a town)
Mount Vernon (an estate)
Sea Cliff (a town)

If, however, one of the English words Bay, Cape, Gulf, Lake, Mount, or Sea forms the first part of the name of a place that actually is a bay, cape, gulf, lake, mountain, or sea, those terms are customarily inverted in most dictionaries, encyclopedias, and gazetteers, and therefore also in most indexes. There is no good reason for this procedure other than perhaps to avoid an accumulation of too many entries beginning with the same word, and it is probably due to the practice of inversion of many COMPOUND TERMS in a misguided attempt to bring the "more important" term to the fore. Since, however, geographical terms in foreign languages, such as Golfe, Lac, Lago, Mare, Mont, or Monte, are never inverted, the practice of inversion in English place names is quite incongruous and inconsistent (is the Isle of Man to be so entered or is the name to be inverted to Man, Isle of?). The following examples show that the listing of all place names having geographical features as their initial elements, whether English or foreign, in their natural word order is not only simpler but will keep the names of such places together, which may be of more importance to many users than the inversion of some (but not all) such place names.

Place names beginning with English geographical terms inverted	*All place names entered as written*
Bay City	Bay City
Bothnia, Gulf of	Bay of Fundy
Everest, Mount	Cape Farewell
Farewell, Cape	Cape of Good Hope
Fundy, Bay of	Golfe du Lion
Golfe du Lion	Gulf of Bothnia
Good Hope, Cape of	Gulf Stream
Gulf Stream	Lago Maggiore
Lago Maggiore	Lake Placid
Lake Placid	Lake Superior
Mont Blanc	Mont Blanc
Mount Vernon	Mount Everest
Okhotsk, Sea of	Mount Vernon
Sea Island	Mount Washington
Superior, Lake	Sea Island
Washington, Mount	Sea of Okhotsk

Initial Articles

If the first element of a place name is an article, the name is entered under it, without inversion (*see also* INITIAL ARTICLES), e.g.,

La Paz
Las Vegas
Le Havre
Los Angeles
The Hague
The Vale

Romanization

The rendering of place names written in non-Roman scripts has always been a major headache for geographers and cartographers, but it is now a relatively minor one for indexers because the American BGN and the British PCGN (mentioned on p. 379) jointly designed Romanization schemes for the major non-Roman scripts (U.S. Board on Geographic Names 1994). An earlier version of these schemes was recommended in 1972 by the United Nations Conference on the Standardization of Geographic Names and has been adopted by virtually all English-speaking countries and their national or major libraries, with the exception of the Library of Congress, which uses its own transliteration for places in the former Soviet Union and enters Chinese place names in the old Wade-Giles Romanization. Most libraries outside of the U.S. employ now the official Pinyin Romanization system used by the People's Republic of China. The difference between the two systems may affect the alphabetization of a name, e.g., Peking vs. Beijing. In a back-of-the-book index, the Romanization of the text should be followed (if it is not too idiosyncratic), but in periodical indexes a consistent policy must be established regarding the Romanization of Chinese place names. For place names in the People's Republic of China it is best to use the Pinyin system, which has been in official use since 1958 and is not likely to be changed; for place names in the Republic of China (Taiwan), however, the Wade-Giles Romanization may be the only one available, since it is the one officially used in Taiwan.

AACR2: chapter 23
BS 3700: 5.3.3
Chicago manual of style: 17.69; 17.128–130
ISO 999: 7.3.3
NISO Z39.4:

POETRY

Poems have virtually never been indexed individually, though some very long ones, such as Milton's *Paradise lost*, Byron's *Childe Harold* or *Don Juan*, and Ezra Pound's *Cantos* would seem to need indexes to the many characters, events, allegories, and allusions that abound in them. Since these and other long poems are the objects of literary criticism and linguistic or historical research, the task of providing keys and finding aids to such poems (mostly in the form of computer-produced concordances) may safely be left to the scholars whose province they are.

Poems of all kinds and ages are, however, often indexed by their first lines in anthologies, compendia of quotations, and other reference works on poetry. Such first-line indexes are relatively easy to compile once the selection of poems has been made, and many such indexes are now produced automatically if the text is available in machine-readable form. Every word in the first line of a poem, including INITIAL ARTICLES (which are otherwise disregarded or transposed in indexing), must be listed in its alphabetical place. Care must be taken, however, in determining the truncation point for a citation, and this should definitely not be left to the tender mercies of a computer but needs human editing. Any arbitrary decision to truncate a citation after a certain number of words or at the end of a printed line may result in unintelligible lines or may sometimes result in unintentionally humorous entries, such as those cited by Knight (1979, p. 183), taken from old first-line indexes to hymn books: "O Lord what boots" (the beginning of "O Lord what boots it to recall / The hours of anguish spent . . .") and "There is a land mine" (for "There is a land mine eyes have seen . . ."). These inanities were, however, perpetrated by human indexers long before the advent of computers (and in the case of the "land mine" before these lethal devices had been invented).

Anthologies of poetry, in addition to their self-evident author and title indexes, are sometimes also indexed by broad categories of topics and issues addressed in the poems, as well as by the titles and dates of the literary journals or collections of poems in which they were first published. Such indexes are so different in their content and format that they are most often arranged in separate sequences: author, title, first line, subject, and source indexes. This shows clearly that a single combined index is neither always the most useful one, nor is it invariably the best form of presentation, as discussed in more detail under MULTIPLE INDEXES.

There are indexes to poetry, but is there "Poetry in indexes"? Indeed, says Dena N. Sher (1994) in an article in which she compares indexers to poets, and asserts that

> [T]he indexer and the poet both weave a net of words and phrases in the exercise of their craft. In this process, relationships of facts, ideas, concepts, or impressions are revealed which may appear as new to the user of the index as to the reader of the poem.

PREPOSITIONS

Experienced cooks know that hot spices and strong seasonings such as red pepper and garlic should be used sparingly, and only where they will enhance the natural flavor of a dish. The same is true for the use of prepositions in subheadings. All indexing textbooks, style manuals, and standards agree on the desirability of keeping the use of *as, at, by, for, in, of, on* and a few other prepositions to a minimum. A study of the characteristics of award-winning indexes to historical works showed that about 85% of their subheadings did not start or end with prepositions (Wittmann 1990). Although physically subheadings follow a main heading which they modify, most of them *precede* it in word order to form a phrase in which the relationship of the two parts is quite clear even without any prepositions, as in the following examples, shown with and without prepositions:

with prepositions	*without prepositions*
Philadelphia	Philadelphia
industry in 26–30	industry 26–30

population of 11, 12   population 11, 12
rivers at 3, 4   rivers 3, 4
universities in 29   universities 29

Probably no one looking at the right-hand entry will be in doubt that the subheadings indicate topics at, in, or of the city of Philadelphia.

Prepositions must, however, be used in two instances: one pertains to subheadings whose word order *follows* that of the main heading, because without a preposition the meaning of the resulting phrase would not be clear, e.g.,

bowel movement
  after childbirth 248
  in pregnancy 239
  of babies 266
  of elderly persons 271

The other instance of subheadings that need prepositions has to do with the clear indication of relationships which would otherwise remain ambiguous, e.g.,

bibliographies
  indexing of 28–31
  of indexing 105

evaluation
  of students by teachers 76
  of teachers by peers 57, 61
  of teachers by students 58

If all subheadings start with the same preposition (and that preposition is indeed necessary in order to avoid ambiguity, as in the example above) it is also possible to add the preposition to the main heading, thus shortening the subheadings and making it easier to scan them, e.g.,

evaluation of
  students by teachers 76
  teachers by peers 57, 61
  teachers by students 58

On another issue pertaining to prepositions, textbooks (especially older ones), and style manuals are often at variance with each other and with national and international standards, namely, the alphabetization of prepositions as the first words of subheadings. The *Chicago manual of style* (1993, 17.54) states that "subentries should ordinarily be arranged alphabetically according to the first important word . . ." (without defining what is meant by "important" or how importance is to be assessed). In section 17.104 the *Manual* tries to justify this practice, claiming that it "is based on the assumption that a reader scanning a long list of subheadings is looking for key terms and will find them most readily if they are in alphabetical order". This assumption is essentially correct, but it is a convincing argument for starting subheadings, if at all possible, with meaningful LEAD TERMS instead of prepositions, not for disregarding prepositions in alphabetization. The section continues:

> If subheadings are alphabetized according to *and, in, of* and the like, the reader has to outguess the indexer, so to speak, while searching for terms: the choice of one such introductory word over another is often pretty arbitrary.

This is actually untenable. As shown above, initial prepositions, far from being "unimportant", are crucial for a correct understanding of the meaning of the terms that follow them in a subheading, as demonstrated by legal indexing practice which not only alphabetizes initial prepositions but sometimes even highlights them typographically, as shown by the example in LEGAL TEXTS, p. 265. Most prepositions have indeed a unique function, that is, they are *not* arbitrarily interchangeable: *as* indicates in which capacity someone or something is related to the topic of a main heading; *at* indicates a location; *by* indicates an agent or action; *for* indicates a purpose; and so on. Only *in* and *of*, when indicating a possessive relationship are sometimes interchangeable, i.e., in the "bowel movement" example on p. 388 the last two subheadings could as well have been

in babies
in elderly persons

However, the "principal" or "important" words following the prepositions are not unique. Quite to the contrary, the enormous richness of the English vocabulary that contains synonyms or near-synonyms for almost any concept results in a high degree of uncertainty on the part of users regarding the terms that follow a preposition in a subheading, as discussed in INDEXING LANGUAGES: NATURAL AND CONTROLLED, p. 214. Thus, the example on p. 388 could have been formulated in any of the following variations (synonymous alternatives are separated by slashes):

    bowel movement / defecating
      after childbirth / delivery / parturition
      in / during gestation / maternity / pregnancy
      in / of babies / infants / young children
      in / of aged / aging / elderly / old people / senescents

Although some of these terms are less likely to be used than others, they are all legitimate and possible substitutes for each other, whereas only *in* and *of* and the less often used *during* are interchangeable in this context.

While there is much that is not yet known about the use made of indexes, it is well known that most people are somewhat vague about the order of the alphabet beyond its first five or seven letters, and that most users have enough to do to sort out even strictly alphabetically arranged sequences of headings and subheadings without having to jump, as it were, back and forth between the left margin of the graphic display and whatever shifting point to the right at which the actually sought "important" word is to be found. Research on eye movements during reading and scanning of lists has shown that any disturbance of expected visual arrangement tends to be confusing and slows down the sequential scanning of entries. Thus, contrary to the bland assumption of some unknown indexer of a bygone age, a pseudo-alphabetical arrangement of index entries, skipping initial conjunctions and prepositions, is counterproductive. Many editors, however, still consider the rules of the *Chicago manual* to be the revealed truth, and some stretch them to inordinate lengths, excluding from alphabetization even prepositions relatively seldom used in subheadings, such as *among, between, under,* and *over.* The following (partial) example from the index of Borko and Bernier's *Indexing concepts and methods* (1978)

shows that the normal alphabetical sequence of lead terms is seriously disturbed by the disregarding of initial prepositions and
conjunctions:

> cross-references
> > between adjacent . . . headings
> > application on first survey
> > blind, in index evaluation
> > in KWIC concordances
> > making and use in or out of index
> > from multiword headings to inverted headings
> > protection against being discarded
> > among synonyms
> > in thesauri

Most normal users, expecting all subheadings to be alphabetized by
their first words, would probably not find the sequence b-a-b-i-m-f-
p-a-i to be quite what they thought of as alphabetical order. The
matter has been neatly summarized in an apt metaphor by a legal
indexer: "Prepositions leading entries and excluded from the alphabetical order are like rocks strewn in a sprinter's path slowing the
speed and wrecking the rhythm" (Thomas 1983, p. 171).

In contradistinction to the textbooks and style manuals which
advocate skipping prepositions and other "unimportant" words in
alphabetization, all current national and international indexing and
arrangement standards are uniformly based on the principle that
every word in a heading or subheading should be alphabetized
without any exception, because the notion of "important" versus
"unimportant" words flies in the face of everything that linguists
know about human language. Clearly, strict alphabetization of every word in a heading or subheading, long or short, "important" or
"unimportant", is the only sensible procedure, and indexers should
insist on it (even though a struggle over this issue with ossified
editors may, alas, often end in defeat).

BS 3700: 6.2.2
ISO 999: 7.2.2.5; 7.3.3.2; 7.3.3.3; 7.3.4.3; 8.6
NISO Z39.4:

PROFESSIONAL INDEXING

The art of indexing, like that of the closely related one of printing,

> if it be followed faithfully, is hard work—full of detail, full of petty
> restrictions, full of drudgery. . . . But . . . it is as interesting a work as
> exists—a broad and humanizing employment which can indeed be
> followed merely as a trade, but which if perfected into an art, or even
> broadened into a profession, will perpetually open new horizons to
> our eyes and opportunities to our hands.*

Yet indexing is neither the best nor the easiest way to become rich
and famous. The monetary rewards are moderate at best, and fame
eludes the indexer, whose name is seldom mentioned on the first
index page, and even less often acknowledged by the author of a
book. Why, then, are people doing it?

Full-Time Freelancers

Freelance indexers who choose indexing as a full-time occupation
and a business are people who want to do things their own way,
free from supervision by a boss and free to spend their time as they
see fit. They also cherish the opportunity to do intellectually stimu-
lating and variegated work which even allows them, within certain
limits, to be creative and inventive. The feeling of being one's own
boss and being free to choose one's working hours is, of course,
somewhat illusory. Authors or publishers who commission indexes
become the real bosses, because a freelancer's bread and butter
comes from indexing books or other book-length documents. Authors and editors may often force indexers to meet sometimes very
tight deadlines. At the same time, several jobs may pile up simultaneously, demanding long work days and even weeks without
respite. Such hectic periods may then alternate with slack ones
when no jobs are coming in and both the indexer and his or her
expensive equipment are sitting idly. Still, the advantages of working out of one's own home, often in a quiet, pleasant, and inexpen-

---

*From the concluding statement in *Printing types* (Updike 1962, v. 2, p. 276)

sive place far from the hustle and bustle of a big city, with no need to commute to work in crowded trains or on equally crowded highways, appeal to many people who want to have their own small business without almost any of the hassles of other commercial ventures. However, some freelancers have found that an office at a separate location can be more convenient and cost-effective than one at home (Cohen & Nickerson 1995).

Setting up the business. Before hanging out, as it were, his or her shingle "Indexes made to order. Inquire inside", a prospective full-time freelancer must make preparations for conducting the business in a businesslike manner. Trying to get organized while the first indexing jobs are undertaken will almost inevitably result in a waste of time—and time is the most precious commodity an indexer has, especially in the beginning. Some of the necessary steps to be taken are the following.

1. Register with the city or county as a business owner, if this is required. Check whether conducting a business out of your home is permitted by local or community regulations.

2. Designate a room such as a spare bedroom or a den as your workplace where you can do your indexing with a minimum of disturbance. (This may also be important for tax purposes.) In the past, indexers were often working at a dining table on which stacks of 3" × 5" cards could conveniently be spread out, shuffled and reshuffled before being put into trays. Those days are long gone, and the personal computer or word processor have taken the place of the typewriter and cards. Choose a desk that is large enough to hold not only a computer and printer, but also the material to be indexed, which may sometimes be bulky. Treat yourself and your backbone to the best ergonomic chair you can find and afford—you will spend many long hours on it. In sum, the efficient conduct of the business of full-time freelancing needs "a room of one's own".

3. Set up separate checking and savings accounts; the latter may be convenient for setting aside amounts to be paid quarterly as estimated tax.

4. Install a separate phone line, an answering machine (a must) and a fax machine (desirable).

5. Get a supply of well-designed stationery and business cards. Though many people may think that this is a trivial issue, it should be given serious attention. It matters little whether the card simply

shows the freelancer's name and an indication of the services or type of specialization offered, or whether the card shows a snappy business name such as "Alpha Beta Editorial & Indexing Services". What does matter is the typographic design, which should be simple and elegant, yet eye-catching without being overly "aggressive". Color printing, raised lettering, colored card stock, and a distinctive logo will make a business card stand out among plain black-and-white ones in the file of a customer. It is therefore advisable to have stationery (business cards, letterhead, billing statements, and other necessary forms) designed by a professional graphic artist rather than having it printed in one of the humdrum styles offered by office supply printers.

6. Set up a bookkeeping method. A one-person business can initially use simple methods and ready-made forms and ledgers. Until the indexing business grows to considerable proportions, there is probably no need for elaborate spreadsheets and other sophisticated bookkeeping software (Oliver 1993). The help of a certified accountant may also be considered, especially at tax time.

7. Set up a work schedule that fits your personal habits and requirements. Indexing is not a nine-to-five job. Your working hours must be flexible in order to cope with rush jobs as well as with slack periods. Do your indexing during your best working hours, whether early mornings, late afternoon and evenings or even at night—but set aside more or less fixed periods for relaxation, exercise, shopping, housework, and social activities. Leave also time for networking with other indexers, which is an important part of your business: you will gain valuable experience by exchanging views with other indexers, and you may even be put in touch with prospective clients through indexers whose schedule is full and who may recommend you for the job they cannot take on.

8. Select electronic EQUIPMENT which has all the features necessary for the effective use of dedicated indexing software and the production of first-class hard copy, but without any bells and whistles that may never be used, but which may add to the price.

Getting started. A beginning freelancer may first try a local publisher, or a firm, society or organization that may need indexes for their publications, such as TECHNICAL MANUALS AND REPORTS. But in this age of fax machines and computers that generate and transmit written material almost instantaneously across continents, indexing is not limited to local availability of either indexers or their customers. Thus, even beginning freelancers should seek to establish contacts with publishers outside their own area, and those specializing in a certain field such as LEGAL TEXTS or MEDICAL TEXTS may also find it useful to get in touch with publishers in their specialty wherever they may be. Publishers in the U.S. and Canada are listed in the manual *Literary market place (LMP)* and those in the UK can be found in *Publishers in the United Kingdom;* these and other national and regional directories of editors and publishers are available in many public libraries. Advertisements for a freelancer's business can be placed most effectively in the *Publisher's Weekly resource directory.*

For many would-be indexers, the first hurdle that must be overcome when trying to establish themselves in the business is their shyness and initial reluctance to knock on the doors of publishers (literally or by mail and phone) or to talk to their representatives at book fairs or at commercial exhibits. Contrary to what beginners often fear, most editors or publishers' representatives are quite nice and urbane people who will not slam their door in the face of a poor freelancer or hang up on them when contacted over the phone. They will in most instances listen to a serious person who is politely offering a service that they may need—if not right away, perhaps in the near future. After all, there is always some turnover in a publisher's pool of freelance indexers—people choosing other occupations, moving to Hawaii or other nice but distant places, or retiring—so that editors are frequently on the lookout for new indexers.

Public and academic libraries are also valuable contact points. Authors, including college professors (who have to write books in order to earn their bread) frequently ask their librarians when in need of an indexer for a book they have just completed; they are often particularly happy to find one on the local scene (notwithstanding what has been said above on indexing no longer being tied to physical proximity). Reference librarians, being themselves vitally dependent on indexes of all kinds, will be glad to furnish the names of local freelancers who have left a supply of their business cards with them, not only to writers and professors but also to members of literary clubs, local newsletter editors, and others who may occasionally need the services of an indexer.

Freelancers should also join their respective SOCIETIES OF IN-
DEXERS and related professional societies in the publishing and
information fields in order to get their publications and to attend
their meetings where informal contacts with prospective clients can
often be made. They may also subscribe to electronic bulletin
boards that specialize in featuring indexing problems, queries and
business opportunities. Many professional, commercial, and governmental organizations in need of indexers, either on a permanent
basis or for a special job, advertise in the papers and in professional
journals; the latter are also one of the most suitable outlets for a
freelancer's own ads, offering his or her specialized indexing
services.

When following up one of these leads to a potential indexing job,
it is necessary to provide a well-written résumé highlighting the
freelancer's special skills or qualifications that may be applicable to
the successful execution of the advertised job; samples or excerpts
from indexes compiled should accompany any application. While
the going may be tough in the beginning, it has been the experience
of most freelancers that competent and reliable work will lead in a
relatively short time to a more or less steady flow of indexing jobs
offered by publishers or organizations on a regular basis, thus keeping the indexer busy "full time" or nearly so.

A full-time freelancer must, of course, make efforts to really keep
the business going full time, soliciting indexing jobs so as to minimize idle periods while on the other hand trying to avoid backlogs,
so as not to substantiate Robert Benchley's definition of a freelancer
as "One who gets paid per word, per piece, or perhaps" (Thurber
1981, p. 121). Both slack or idle periods and backlogs may badly
affect the viability of an indexing business. While a temporary lack
of work will only result in a diminished cash flow that will normally not be disastrous, it is vitally important to clear up a menac-
ing backlog as quickly as possible, even at the risk of having to
decline a new job. An editor who is being told that the offered job
cannot be accepted because of previous commitments will almost
always appreciate the indexer's candidness and may return with
other job offers at some other time, but one whose deadline is being
badly missed may never offer another indexing job.

Indexers with several years' experience will generally have established good contacts with potential customers: publishers of
books and periodicals; organizations that need indexing at specified

periods, e.g., for annual reports, updated in-house manuals or occasional publications; and database producers who are farming out some or all of their abstracting and indexing needs. Useful hints for getting (and keeping) clients are offered by Spence (1983).

Part-Time Freelancers

Many people work as part-time indexing freelancers, ranging from housewives and young mothers who want to put their education to good use while having to care for small children, to retired professionals such as lawyers, doctors, nurses, chemists, engineers, and so on. Professional people no longer active full time because of retirement or a physical handicap may have intimate knowledge of facts and details in highly specialized fields and can combine this asset with the skill of indexing, often having been intensive users of indexes themselves when still working in their profession. All of them, and those in between—that is, anyone who for some reason decides, or is being asked, to compile an index—appreciate the opportunity to make a little money on the side while enjoying an interesting biography or travelogue, or keeping up with what is going on in a scientific, technical, or professional field by getting to read books or articles long before any of their still-active colleagues will see them. Part-time indexers may sometimes undertake the indexing of a book written by a good friend, a local newspaper, a congregation's newsletter, and the like as a labor of love, which may be laudable as an act of friendship or good citizenship. However, if this is done by a person without any training in indexing it may yield deplorable results and constitutes in any case unfair competition with competent and professional indexers.

Various professional and business aspects of freelancing are dealt with in *Starting an indexing business* (1994) which contains papers, panel discussions, and survey results culled from the proceedings of annual meetings of the American Society of Indexers between 1989 and 1992.

Salaried Indexers

Lastly, there are salaried indexers, working for a publishing firm or for producers of databases, either as members of a team or from their home. Compared to the sometimes precarious financial situation, the fluctuating work load, and the tight deadlines that are the occupational hazards of freelancers they enjoy the advantages of a steady income, fringe benefits and an even work flow. Indexers employed by governmental or commercial database producers are primarily engaged in indexing legal, administrative, or technical documents and articles. In most instances, their work is supported by automated indexing aids for vocabulary control, thesaurus look-up, and the execution of clerical tasks, so that they can concentrate on the intellectual work of indexing. In return, they are expected to fulfill fairly high daily output quotas, ranging from 40 to 70 articles in general interest journals which are indexed at a relatively low level of EXHAUSTIVITY and SPECIFICITY. Scientific, technical, and scholarly articles are indexed at higher levels of exhaustivity and specificity, depending on their difficulty and specialization, resulting in lower daily output quotas.

Other salaried indexers may be experts in the indexing of encyclopedias or other large reference works, or in the highly specialized indexing of periodically updated legal publications in book or looseleaf format. Whatever their specific tasks within the framework of a commercial or governmental organization, salaried indexers, far from having to perform only dull routine work, for the most part enjoy their work no less than their self-employed colleagues, because particularly in specialized fields, an indexer will often be confronted with intellectual challenges and will have opportunities to solve indexing problems in a creative way. Last but not least, proficient indexers who are also subject experts may expect a good salary, especially if they have an academic degree in their field.

The prospects and opportunities of a career in indexing, whether as a freelancer or as a salaried employee, have been summarized in the brief but highly informative *Guide to careers in abstracting and indexing* (Cunningham & Wicks 1992).

Personality and Skills of Indexers

Anyone with a well-rounded education and a broad range of interests can become an indexer after having undergone some TRAIN-

ING IN INDEXING. But successful indexing does not result from a knowledge of basic rules and techniques alone; it also needs a certain flair for the task, as well as intuition, and these cannot be learned but must be traits of an indexer's personality. And, as in all creative vocations, truly outstanding indexers are born not made.

Among the desirable personality traits of a good indexer are the following:

- Being a rapid yet attentive reader of texts, including occasional boring or trivial parts.
- Being keen on organizing and arranging things in neat and logical order.
- Being a stickler for accuracy.
- Having a good memory for small details.
- Being capable of grasping relationships and connections, especially those not explicitly mentioned in the text but only implied.
- Being able to work alone for long periods.
- Being prepared to work long hours if necessary to meet a deadline, even if sick, exhausted, or troubled by personal problems. The spirit of "Damn the torpedos! Full speed ahead!"

Among the necessary skills are:

- A thorough familiarity with the topic, field, or discipline of the text to be indexed, preferably gained by several years of active involvement. (Many people turn to indexing in middle age or after retirement from a professional career. This does not necessarily mean that a young person cannot become a successful indexer, but thorough experience in a field is an asset that can be acquired only after many years of work.)
- An above average breadth and depth of knowledge.
- The ability to keep track of details and facts (and checking them for accuracy) while at the same time paying heed to general themes and ideas discussed in a text.
- A sense for the proper use of language—grammar, style, and orthography—without being pedantic or schoolmarmish.
- The ability to express complex concepts in concise terms.
- Familiarity with prospective users' viewpoints and requests.

It is not for nothing that indexing has been called an art. Not everybody can or should do it. Yet those who engage in it and do it well, whether as a full-time or a part-time occupation, as the work of a salaried employee, or even as a hobby, derive from it a deeply felt satisfaction. It provides them with a sense of being, as it were, collaborators or coworkers of those whose creative minds produce texts, and of being intermediaries for those who want or need to use, enjoy, or learn from those texts, but who require signposts and guides to names, facts, thoughts and opinions that are not easy to find in them.

And that is why people do indexing.

PROOFREADING

Some time after the index manuscript has been sent to the publisher, the indexer may expect to see the index, transformed from its typewritten or word-processed shape or from a disk, as lines of print which must be proofread. These lines will appear either on *galleys*—elongated sheets of paper showing only a single column without pagination—or on *page proofs*, which show the layout of columns as they will appear on pages but lack as yet (CON-TINUED) LINES. Unfortunately, not all publishers submit proofs to their indexers, claiming that too much time is lost in sending galleys and page proofs back and forth, relying instead on their own in-house proofreaders. But to the same extent that proofs are sent to the author of a book, so also the proofs of its index should be submitted to the indexer. Proofreading an index involves more than just correcting mistakes, particularly when it comes to page proofs, where BAD BREAKS must often be adjusted and (*continued*) lines must be provided; this, in turn, may need the elimination or adjustment of a line or two by shortening the wording of a heading or the cancellation of a minor subheading with only one locator—tasks which a professional proofreader is not trained to do. Indexers should therefore insist on performing their own proofreading, if necessary by inserting a clause to that effect in their CONTRACTS.

The printed copy of an index is first proofread by the printer for correct spacing, alignment, wrong fonts, "outs" (words omitted), "doubles" (words set twice), wrong indentions, and, of course, misspellings and errors. Many of these mishaps will therefore already be marked on the galleys, usually in blue or green ink, and the indexer need not worry about them because these "printer's errors" will be corrected, at no extra charge, when the indexer's additional corrections are also made. The galleys or page proofs will bear some mysterious numbers and words on top of each sheet; these are reference marks for the use of the typesetters and should never be removed or crossed out. There may also be questions noted in the margin, e.g., when a typesetter is not sure whether a word in the manuscript is missing or has been deliberately misspelled, or when the spelling of a name is being queried. If the indexer thinks that the item referred to in the question does not need a correction, the question should not be crossed out, erased, or answered by just writing "OK" (which is ambiguous); the correct answer is either "OK as set" or a necessary correction.

Occasionally, the indexer may make the (mostly unpleasant) discovery that the printed index is not quite what was submitted as a manuscript because of changes made by the author or the editor or by both: subheadings displayed in indented style may have been reformatted to run-in style, or some of them may simply have been deleted; PREPOSITIONS may have been added to or deleted from subheadings or they may have been alphabetized differently; commas may have been inserted after headings; and other more or less serious tampering with the indexer's handiwork may have occurred. This happens because authors sometimes try to "improve" an index (though the result is often what a German writer facetiously called a "Verschlechtbesserung", that is "deterioimprovement"), and editors do this because they follow a publisher's house style when that clashes with the indexer's style. In most cases, the indexer will draw the shortest straw because the index is now in cold print, and any extensive changes are out of the question. Sad to say, many an index has been faulted by reviewers because of shortcomings for which not the indexer but the author or editor was to blame.

Proof Correction Marks

All corrections should be made using standardized proof correction
marks, most of which have been used by printers and typesetters
for hundreds of years. The most important of these marks are
shown in Figure 9. Complete listings of proof correction marks can
be found in the relevant national standards, namely the American
National Standard NISO Z39.22 *Proof corrections* (National Information Standards Organization 1989) and BS 5261, Part 2: *Specification
for typographic requirements, marks for copy preparation and proof correction, proofing procedure* (British Standards Institution 1976).

Mistakes in the lines of text should be indicated using only the
marks intended for that purpose, while the actual correction should
always be made in the margin, as shown in Figure 10. All corrections should be made in red ink (unless otherwise instructed by the
printer) and never in black, since a black mark on a printed line may
easily obliterate a letter or word that needs to be corrected, or may
not be noticed by the typesetter.

Additions and Changes

In principle, no changes other than necessary corrections should be
made in the text of an index at the proofreading stage, because even
the addition or deletion of a single locator is costly and, if it is not
caused by a printer's error, will be charged to the author or indexer
(depending on the provisions of the contract on this matter). Any
temptation to improve the wording of an entry must, therefore, be
firmly resisted. Nevertheless, at the galley stage it is still possible to
add or delete lines or to make other small alterations without incurring exorbitant penalties, so that, for example, the name of a person,
inadvertently omitted during indexing but afterwards discovered,
can still be inserted. At the page proof stage, however, any change
other than missed corrections made on the galleys or a new mistake
introduced in a corrected line (which happens not infrequently) is
exorbitantly costly and must be avoided. Even the addition of a
single line on a page may necessitate the resetting not only of that
page but also of one or more of the following pages. The sole
exceptions are (*continued*) lines, which can be added only when a

Mark	Meaning	Mark	Meaning
⊙	Insert period	*rom.*	Roman type
⋀	Insert comma	*caps.*	Caps—used in margin
⁚	Insert colon	≡	Caps—used in text
;	Insert semicolon	*c+sc*	Caps & small caps—used in margin
?	Insert question mark	≡	Caps & small caps—used in text
!	Insert exclamation mark	*l.c.*	Lowercase—used in margin
=/	Insert hyphen	/	Used in text to show deletion or substitution
⋁	Insert apostrophe		
⋎⋎	Insert quotation marks	ℓ	Delete
⊣N	Insert 1-en dash	ℨ	Delete and close up
⊣M	Insert 1-em dash	*w.f.*	Wrong font
#	Insert space	⌒	Close up
ld>	Insert ( ) points of space	⊐	Move right
shill	Insert shilling	⊏	Move left
⋁	Superior	⊓	Move up
⋀	Inferior	⊔	Move down
(/)	Parentheses	‖	Align vertically
[/]	Brackets	=	Align horizontally
▢	Indent 1 em	⊐⊏	Center horizontally
▢▢	Indent 2 ems	⊔⊓	Center vertically
⁋	Paragraph	*eq.#*	Equalize space—used in margin
no ⁋	No paragraph	⋁⋁⋁	Equalize space—used in text
tr	Transpose[1]—used in margin	....	Let it stand—used in text
∽	Transpose[2]—used in text	*stet*	Let it stand—used in margin
sp	Spell out	⊗	Letter(s) not clear
ital	Italic—used in margin	*run over*	Carry over to next line
___	Italic—used in text	*run back*	Carry back to preceding line
b.f.	Boldface—used in margin	*out, see copy*	Something omitted—see copy
∼∼∼	Boldface—used in text	*?/?*	Question to author to delete
s.c.	Small caps—used in margin	⋀	Caret—General indicator used to mark position of error.
≡≡≡	Small caps—used in text		

[1]In lieu of the traditional mark "tr" used to indicate letter or number transpositions, the striking out of the incorrect letters or numbers and the placement of the correct matter in the margin of the proof is the preferred method of indicating transposition corrections. (See rule 2.88.)

[2]Corrections involving more than two characters should be marked by striking out the entire word or number and placing the correct form in the margin. This mark should be reserved to show transposition of words.

Figure 9. *Proof correction marks.* Reproduced from U.S. Government Printing Office *Style manual* (1984).

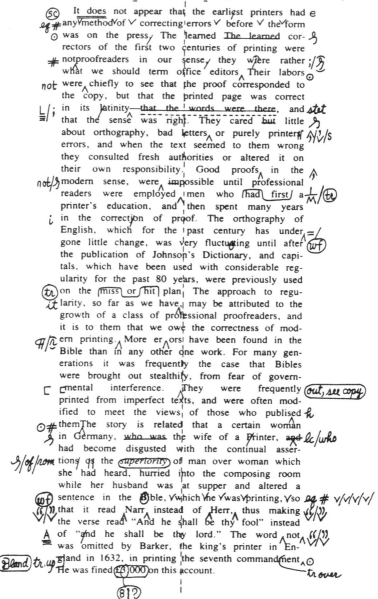

NOTE.—The system of marking proofs can be made easier by the use of an imaginary vertical line through the center of the type area. The placement of corrections in the left-hand margin for those errors found in the left-hand portion of the proof and in the right-hand margin for right-side errors prevents overcrowding of marks and facilitates corrections. (See also rule 2.87.)

Figure 10. *Specimen page showing proof corrections.* Reproduced from U.S. Government Printing Office *Style manual* (1984).

page has been set in type, so that column or page breaks (some of them inevitably BAD BREAKS) show up.

If additions or changes must be made, shorter ones can be indicated in the margin together with all other corrections (but the handwriting must be neat); additions longer than a line or two should be typed on a separate page firmly attached to the relevant galley, and a note such as "See new text" should be made in the margin so that the typesetter (who works at high speed) will not overlook the addition. No additions should be made on narrow slips taped or stapled to the galley, because they may easily be ripped off or otherwise get lost.

Procedures

It takes two to tango and to make love the old-fashioned way—and so does proofreading. An indexer who undertakes to proofread his or her own index all alone is courting disaster, because the first and most important rule of proofreading is: never proofread what you have written yourself. The best procedure is to perform proofreading with a team of two people: the indexer, who reads the printed proof, and the "copyholder" (the term used by printers), who reads aloud from the manuscript (or from the corrected galley for page proofs).

The indexer, when reading the printed proof, must above all concentrate on the graphic image of the words and their letters, not on their meaning or context, following closely what is being read aloud by the copyholder. The task is made easier by reading each line through a mask showing only one line at a time, so as not to be distracted by words on the lines above and below the one being proofread; many people prefer, however, a small ruler, covering only the lines below the one being proofread. The copyholder should read not only every word and number, but also all punctuation marks, capitalization (unless it is obvious, as in proper names), changes in typeface (words printed in italics, boldface, or small capitals), and paragraphing. In indexes, it is, of course, particularly important to read the numbers of locators clearly: 165 should be read as one-sixty-five, 408 as four-oh-eight, and the date 1354 as thirteen-fifty-four but 1,354 as one-comma-three-five-four; Roman numerals should be read as letters, e.g., LXXIV as "ell-ex-ex-i-ve" and xvi as "lowercase ex-ve-i". Mistakes are more likely to happen in numbers than in words, especially transposition of digits (69 instead of 96), so that the proofreading team must be especially careful about checking locators.

Not every indexer is, however, always in a position to have a copyholder, though husbands, wives, girlfriends, roommates, and other innocent bystanders are known to have been pressed into service. An indexer who, *faute de mieux*, must proofread his or her own work should heed the following advice and apply the tricks of the trade used by other solitary proofreaders; some of these tricks are, of course, also useful for proofreading teams.

- Do not hurry! Sure, the publisher wants the galleys or page proofs soon, but proofreading must be done carefully or not at all and will necessarily be more time-consuming than reading the same text for comprehension alone.
- Do not read words for content and meaning but for form only.
- When reading to yourself, try to pronounce each word silently.
- Do not try to read an entire line; read each word separately, including articles, conjunctions, and prepositions.
- Read the proofs several times, each time checking a different feature: spelling, especially that of names; punctuation; indentions; locators.
- Check typographical elements forming pairs: parentheses, square brackets, and quotation marks; one may be missing.
- Check typefaces: italics, boldface, small capitals.
- When spotting a mistake, look for more in the same line and in the preceding and following lines; mistakes tend to occur in clusters.
- Don't proofread for an extended period. Take frequent breaks or do other things, then return to the proofs.
- If interrupted in the middle—the phone is ringing, the baby is crying, the tea kettle is boiling, or all of the above together— mark the space or line on which you are working by a light pencil mark, a paper clip, or a colored sheet of paper between pages.
- And remember: though proofreading is sheer drudgery, and nobody will really appreciate the many dreary hours spent on it, it is the only way your index will appear in the best possible shape.

More detailed advice on proofreading will be found in the *Chicago manual of style* (1993, 3.9–39), and especially in *Mark my words* (Smith 1993), which has everything you always wanted to know on the subject in 484 pages.

BS 3700: 4.5
BS 5261, Part 2
Chicago manual of style: 3.9–39, 17.43, 17.63–64
ISO 999: 6.4.2
NISO Z39.22

PUNCTUATION

Texts are made more readable by the judicious use of punctuation marks, but in an index they should play only a minor role and should be used as sparingly as possible. On this issue, indexers, textbooks, guides, and standards are of one mind, with the sole exception of two divergent practices regarding commas versus spaces after headings.

Commas

Traditionally, commas have been put between the last word of a heading and its first locator, as prescribed by the *Chicago manual of style* (1993, 17.57) and other American style manuals. But a (mainly British) trend towards as few punctuation marks as possible is reflected in BS 3700, 7.1.4.1 which recommends to leave only a space. Both NISO Z39.4 and ISO 999 7.4.5 allow the use of a comma, other punctuation marks as needed, or two spaces. All standards recommend not to put commas after headings but to leave only a space, except when a heading ends in a numeral (which may be mistaken for a locator); in this (rather rare) case the use of either a comma or a colon is recommended. The colon is preferable, because it is quite distinct from the commas that may separate several locators, and thus avoids any possible confusion, e.g.,

vitamin B 12: 13, 15

Spacing used instead of a comma after a heading should be two typewriter spaces wide or one em space in print.

Commas after subheadings	*Spaces after subheadings*
Watson, James Dewey	Watson, James Dewey
biography, 46–47; Cold Spring	biography 46–47; Cold Spring
Harbor, 44–45, 62, 67; col-	Harbor 44–45, 62, 67; col-
laboration with Crick, 111–114,	laboration with Crick 111–114,
124–129, 136; crystallography,	124–129, 136; crystallography
137–138; discovery of DNA	137–138; discovery of DNA
structure, 181–182; disser-	structure 181–182; disser-
tation, 66, 68	tation 66, 68

Which style to follow will probably depend on a publisher's house style, and the indexer will have little choice in the matter, which, after all, is a somewhat trivial one. In run-in subheadings, a comma between the last word of a subheading and its first locator adds visual clutter to the already crowded typographical image, so that at least in this case a plea may be made to use spaces in lieu of commas. A comparison of the two styles of punctuation shows that, although there is no difference in length, the image of the paragraph without commas is clearer and therefore easier to comprehend.

Commas are used in three other instances: (a) to separate several locators; (b) between surname and inverted forename(s); and (c) after the first part of an inverted COMPOUND HEADING, a form that should only be used as a cross-reference and not as a main heading, e.g.,

indexing, automatic *see* automatic indexing

Commas should *not* be used before *see* and *see also* references, because if, as discussed under CROSS-REFERENCES, they follow immediately after the heading from which they refer, they form part of an unbroken phrase that does not need any punctuation whatsoever.

Periods (Full Stops)

Periods are normally not needed in index entries, except in a name that displays an organizational hierarchy, e.g.,

> Baltimore. Department of Transportation. Interstate
> Division. Design Section

Periods may also be used in ABBREVIATIONS, but often they are omitted, especially in acronyms, e.g., AFL-CIO, BBC or NATO.

The *Chicago manual of style* (1993, 17.15–16) prescribes a period before *see* and *see also* references following a main heading in indented style, but all other indexing standards recommend leaving only a space before cross-references or show this practice in their examples.

Colons

Because of its separating function in text passages, this punctuation mark is used where it is particularly important to distinguish clearly between elements in an index entry. The most frequent applications are:

1. To separate a main heading from its subheadings when these are displayed in run-in style, the first one being on the same line as the main heading. (When the main heading is set one line above the run-in subheadings, as in the Watson example above, no punctuation mark at all is needed after the main heading.) A comma after the main heading might be ambiguous; in the entry

> railroads: American 347, 351; bridges 235; British 321–327;
> signalling systems 132

the colon makes it unmistakably clear that the subheadings refer to railroads in general; if the entry were punctuated

> railroads, American 347, 351; bridges 235; British 321–327;
> signalling systems 132

a user would at first be led to think that the entry is on American railroads and may be baffled by the following subheading for "British".

2. To distinguish in locators for articles in periodicals between the number of a volume and that of an issue (see Table 6, p. 289).

3. To indicate relationships between terms in a COMPOUND HEADING instead of (or sometimes in addition to) PREPOSITIONS, as in the *Current technology index*, from which the following entry is taken:

POLYTHENE : Creep : effect of temperature

(which is intended to convey the phrase "Effect of temperature *on* the creep *of* polythene); note the use of en-spaces before and after the colons to enhance their visual effect.

4. As noted above, a colon should also be used to separate a heading ending in a numeral from its first locator.

Semicolons

Although almost indistinguishable from a colon in shape as well as in its use in text passages, the semicolon has important functions in index entries in cases in which the use of colons only would make an entry ambiguous. Four different purposes are served by semicolons:

1. To separate subheadings in run-in style.

2. To break up a long string of run-in subheadings into two or more paragraphs in order to group different kinds of subheadings (e.g., biographical items and titles of works in a writer's biography), each paragraph except the last one should end with a semicolon; *see also* GROUPED ORDER.

3. To distinguish between several personal names following a *see* or *see also* reference, because commas, already used to separate surnames and forenames, would be confusing:

Chichester
    bishops 3, 152, 617 *see also*
        Arundel, John; Peacock, Reginald;
        Story, Edward
    mayors 218, 347

Other items listed after a *see* or *see also* reference are also best separated by semicolons, e.g.,

buffalo *see* bison; water buffalo

4. To distinguish in locators for articles in periodicals between the number of an issue and that of a part (see Table 6, p. 289). Also, to distinguish between individual locators consisting of volume and page numbers in a string of such locators, e.g.,

tomatoes **3,** p. 188; **4,** p. 154, 216; **6,** p. 27, 334

Parentheses

These punctuation marks (known in the U.K. as "brackets" or "curves") are used in three instances:
 1. All QUALIFIERS are enclosed in parentheses.
 2. Obsolete or alternative names (including maiden names, instead of the word "née") are most economically indicated in this manner, e.g.,

Berwyck (Berwycke, Berwyk) *see* Berwick
Johnsson, Mary (Baxter) 37, 58

 3. To enclose the year of publication in a locator for an article in a periodical (see Table 6, p. 289).

Quotation Marks

"Quotes", as they are known for short, are used when direct quotations from a text are used as index entries, such as sayings of persons, titles of articles, or chapter headings from another work quoted verbatim. However, the distinction made by some style manuals as well as by Knight (1979, p. 163) between titles of long poems, which are to be italicized, and those of short ones, which are to be put in quotes, is silly and does not serve any particular purpose. None of the style manuals states at what point a short poem becomes a long one or how titles of medium-length poems (anything longer than 10 but shorter than 30 stanzas?) are to be treated. Since poems of any length are products of creative minds to the same extent as plays, novels, and works of visual arts whose titles are customarily italicized, there seems to be no good reason why poems should not be treated likewise.
 Entries for terms indexed as vocabulary items (or lexemes in

linguistic terminology) must be put between quotes to distinguish them from the same terms used semantically, e.g., "index", when referred to as a word, not as an object, is printed between quotation marks in the index to this book.

Quotes are also necessary for the indication of nicknames, e.g., Cody, William F. ("Buffalo Bill") or O'Neill, Thomas P. ("Tip") (the popular and colorful Speaker of the U.S. House of Representatives from 1977 to 1987), and for the names of fictitious characters in order to distinguish them from names of real persons, e.g., "Colonel Blimp" or "Olive Oyl", two famous cartoon characters.

But quotation marks used by an author in a text in order to highlight a word or phrase, or to give it a special meaning which it would not otherwise have, should never be transferred to the index, where the quoted word or phrase will stand alone, representing a concept just like any other heading and where the quotes do not add any further meaning. For example, in Daniel J. Boorstin's *The Americans: the national experience* (1965) the author writes on page 81 about the "Lynch Law" of the South; the index lists this as "Lynch law" . . . 81, 452. The quotes in the text were presumably put there because, as the author points out, that "law" was not a written one but just an evil tradition. On page 452 the same phrase is used without any quotes, which clearly shows that the quotation marks in the index are superfluous.

Question Marks

The sole application of this punctuation mark in an index entry is to indicate uncertainty of a date or the form of a name, e.g.,

    Bacon, Roger (1214?–1294)
    Kohn (Cohen, Cohn?), Moses 37, 42

Other Punctuation Marks

Normally, no other punctuation marks should be used in index entries, but if they are used for a special purpose, e.g., asterisks or square brackets for locators of ILLUSTRATIONS, they must be explained in an INTRODUCTORY NOTE.

Arrangement

All punctuation marks without any exception, and irrespective of whether they appear before, inside, or after a word, abbreviation, or acronym, are disregarded in alphanumerical arrangement. *See also* APOSTROPHES and HYPHENATION.

ALA: 1.2
Chicago manual of style: 17.15–16; 17.57
ISO 999: 7.4.5
BS 3700: 7.1.4
NISO Z39.4:

QUALIFIERS

Whenever the meaning of a heading is ambiguous or may become so in a particular context, it must be clarified by a word, phrase, or numerical expression, known as a qualifier. In most instances, ambiguity is caused by HOMOGRAPHS, words written identically but having different meanings.

For *topical headings,* a term indicating the field, discipline, or context should be chosen as a qualifier, e.g.,

parties (entertainment)
parties (law)
parties (politics)

Homographic PERSONAL NAMES consisting of forenames only are traditionally qualified by numbers or epithets (or both) for popes, emperors, kings, and other rulers and by place of birth, occupation, or appellation for persons who lived in antiquity or in the Middle Ages, e.g.,

Francis
Francis I, Roman Emperor
Francis III, King of France
Francis IV, Duke of Modena
Francis Joseph I, Emperor of Austria
Francis of Mayonne
Francis, Saint, of Assisi
Francis, Saint, of Sales
Hippocrates of Chios
Hippocrates of Cos
Plato (philosopher)
Plato (poet)

Modern homographic personal names are qualified by dates of birth and death, occupation, place of birth or work, or by some other identifying word or phrase. When several members of a family and more than one generation are indexed, qualifiers indicating kinship must be used even if only some of the forenames are homographs; the surname need not be repeated for every family member, and their given names may be indented under the full name of the first person listed alphabetically, e.g.,

Smith, Alexander (son of Richard) 27
    Alice (wife of John) 90
    Alice (wife of Richard) 27
    Bartholomew (nephew of John) 92
    David (grandfather of Richard) 33
    David (son of Richard) 29
    John (brother of Richard) 91
    Matthew (uncle of Richard) 37
    Richard 27, 65, 109
    Richard (son of Richard) 107
    William (son of Bartholomew) 90

Homographic CORPORATE NAMES are qualified by the name of the place in which the corporate body has its headquarters or offices; nationwide organizations, especially political parties, are qualified by the name of the country, e.g.,

Labour Party (Great Britain)
Labour Party (South Africa)
University of Alaska (Anchorage)
University of Alaska (Fairbanks)

PLACE NAMES are generally qualified by the name of a country, province, or other larger geographical area even if they are not homographs, unless the context removes any potential ambiguity, e.g., in a book on England it is unnecessary to qualify Birmingham because it will not be confused with its namesake in Alabama.

Homographic TITLES of documents are qualified by the name of the author, e.g.,

Ave Maria (Bach-Gounod)
Ave Maria (Schubert)

Identical periodical titles are qualified by place of publication, e.g.,

Natura (Amsterdam)
Natura (Milan)

The PUNCTUATION of qualifiers added by an indexer should always be a pair of parentheses, except for the personal names of saints, popes, sovereigns, and other rulers (mostly known by their forenames only) which are separated from their qualifying epithets by a comma, as shown above in the example of personal names. Qualifiers should not be italicized, as is the custom in some library catalogs.

In alphanumeric arrangement, the numerals or letters of a qualifier are all taken into consideration, continuing those of the heading; for homographic headings, they form the distinguishing elements which determine their alphabetization (the parentheses being disregarded, since they are punctuation marks), e.g.,

George
George V, King of Great Britain
George (1301–1343)
George (Anglo-Norman poet)
George (Dr.)
George (Family)

BS 3700: 5.2.1.3; 5.2.3.5; 5.3.1.4; 5.3.1.8; 5.3.3.1; 5.3.4.1
ISO 999: 7.2.1.3(c); 7.3.1.2(c); 7.3.1.3; 7.3.3.1; 7.3.4.1; 7.4.2.2; 8.5
NISO Z39.4:

REFERENCE WORKS

The following types of reference works should be at the indexer's elbow at all times for quick reference, spelling, or verification of names of persons, events, and objects, and for guidance on standard practices. The reference works listed below have proven to be particularly useful for indexing. They are reasonably priced (most of them cost less than $100 in the U.S.). A much more extensive list with evaluative annotations (now in need of updating) is in Bakewell (1987).

Dictionaries

General:

The American heritage dictionary of the English language. 3rd ed. Boston: Houghton Mifflin, 1992.

Chambers English dictionary. New York; Cambridge: Cambridge University Press, 1992.

Merriam-Webster's collegiate dictionary, 10th ed. Springfield, MA: Merriam, 1993.

The new shorter Oxford English dictionary. New York: Oxford University Press, 1993. (This two-volume work is based on the revised 1989 edition of the complete *OED,* including 500,000 definitions and 83,000 illustrative quotations in full-size type.)

The Random House dictionary of the English language. 2nd ed., unabridged. New York: Random House, 1987. (Contains also dozens of tables of facts and figures, concise French, German, Italian, and Spanish dictionaries, a basic manual of style, a table of proofreader's marks, and an atlas.)

Special:

There are literally hundreds of dictionaries in all fields and disciplines. Those currently available are listed in *Books in print,* which can be found in most public libraries and in many bookstores. The most widely used dictionaries for LEGAL TEXTS and MEDICAL TEXTS are listed at the end of the respective sections. Comprehensive one-volume dictionaries in the fields of science and technology are:

Academic Press dictionary of science and technology. San Diego, CA: Academic
   Press, 1992.
McGraw-Hill dictionary of scientific and technical terms. 5th ed. New York:
   McGraw-Hill, 1994.

Encyclopedias

The Columbia encyclopedia. 5th ed. New York: Columbia University Press,
   1993. (The most comprehensive and recent one-volume desk encyclopedia.)
The concise Columbia encyclopedia. 3rd ed. New York: Columbia University
   Press, 1994. (About half the content and a third of the price of its big
   sister.)

Almanacs and Yearbooks

The statesman's yearbook. London: Macmillan. Annual.
Whitaker's almanack. London: Whitaker. Annual.
The world almanac and book of facts. New York: Newspaper Enterprise Asso-
   ciation. Annual.

Biographical Dictionaries

The Cambridge biographical dictionary. New York: Cambridge University
   Press, 1990.
Chambers biographical dictionary. 5th ed. Cambridge: Cambridge University
   Press, 1990.
The concise dictionary of national biography. Oxford: Oxford University Press,
   1992.
Webster's new biographical dictionary. Springfield, MA: Merriam, 1983.

Gazetteers

Chambers' world gazetteer. Cambridge: Cambridge University Press, 1988.
Webster's new geographical dictionary. Revised ed. Springfield, MA: Merriam,
   1988.

Thesauri

Lists of synonyms and antonyms:

The Oxford thesaurus: an A–Z dictionary of synonyms. Laurence Urdang.
    Oxford: Clarendon Press, 1991.
The Oxford thesaurus: American edition. Laurence Urdang. New York: Oxford University Press, 1992.
Roget's thesaurus of English words and phrases. London: Longmans, 1987.
    (The original work in its latest and updated edition. Many other editions exist, some of them arranged alphabetically.)

Controlled Indexing Languages:

Thesauri and lists of subject headings in many fields and disciplines are published frequently and are often updated periodically. The *Library of Congress subject headings* (*LCSH*), issued annually since 1989, covers the entire field of knowledge but is not intended for the analytical indexing of books or periodicals; it uses inverted headings extensively, and its vocabulary is often outmoded and even offensive to certain persons and ethnic groups, despite some attempts made in recent years to revise the terminology. *Sears list of subject headings* (1991), an abridgement and modification of *LCSH* intended for small and medium-sized American public libraries, is even more limited as a source for indexing terms.

Typographical Guides and Style Manuals

Chicago guide to preparing electronic manuscripts for authors and publishers.
    Chicago: University of Chicago Press, 1987.
The Chicago manual of style. 14th ed. Chicago: University of Chicago Press, 1993. (Chapter 17, "Indexing", is available separately.)
Rules for compositors and readers at the University Press, Oxford. 39th ed. Oxford: Oxford University Press, 1983.

REVISION OF INDEXES

An index may have to be revised in three different situations: (a) for annual almanacs and similar yearbooks of facts; (b) for a book in a second (or third, etc.) revised edition; and (c) when an inexperienced indexer's work of inferior quality is rejected by an author or editor and is to be reworked by another indexer.

In yearbooks, a large amount of data remains virtually unchanged from year to year, but new names and facts are added, while obsolete or unnecessary ones are eliminated. The revision of yearbook indexes is generally performed by the publisher's own staff of indexers, who may add, delete, and revise data throughout the year while the text is being rewritten and edited, so that the new index is virtually ready when the last page of the book has been set in type. Various computer-assisted techniques for this type of ongoing revision of an index have been developed, all of them tailormade for a particular project. Rarely will the compilation and revision of a yearbook index be commissioned from a freelance indexer, and this is in any case not a job that one person working alone could successfully complete within the short time allowed for the completion and printing of the index, because yearbooks are published against very tight deadlines.

The revision of an index for a revised edition of a book must be considered from the point of view of its cost-effectiveness. Is it better to save portions of the previously compiled index to an earlier edition or to compile a new index from scratch? The answer to this question depends on several factors. If the revision of the text has been only slight and the revised parts, sections, or paragraphs can easily be identified (perhaps with the author's help), it may be worthwhile to retain the previous index and to revise it, although having to change most of the locators will be a tedious and time-consuming task. A somewhat cumbersome method for doing this (based on index galleys mounted on larger sheets of paper and marked in the margin for page numbers of indexed passages in the previous and present edition of a book) has been described by Simpkins (1985). If, however, the previous index needs extensive revision, it is more cost-effective to compile an entirely new index which may at the same time also be a better one (the indexer having learned from mistakes and omissions in the previous index). After all, nothing, least of all an index, is ever perfect, and it is well known that not only will the same text be indexed differently by different indexers, but it will also be indexed differently by the same indexer doing the same job at a later time. In most cases,

looking carefully at the previous index, noting deficiencies or mistakes, possibly considering a better layout or typographical format,
and then proceeding with the compilation of a new index while
keeping in mind the desirable or needed improvements, will take
much less time and effort than laborious attempts to save as much
as possible of the index to the earlier edition. It may, however, not
always be easy to persuade an editor of the need for a new index,
because that person may have the fallacious notion that a "slight
revision" of the previous index would be a quick and easy job, and
would therefore be cheaper.

Regarding the application of band-aids to a badly mangled job,
an indexer should not touch such an offer with a 10-foot pole. In
most instances, the job will effectively amount to the compilation
of a new index yet be a source of frustration if not despair, because the bulk of what the other indexer has produced, other than
perhaps some straightforward name entries, will have to be discarded (if it had been any good, the index would not have been
rejected).

A related but quite different situation arises when an index is left
unfinished because of illness or sudden death and another indexer
is asked to complete the job. Since every indexer has a personal
style, it may not be easy to match the previous indexer's way of
compiling the index, and already existing entries may have to be
reworked to dovetail with those of the new indexer, thus involving
more or less substantial revisions. Such a job will have to be tackled
with great care and circumspection, yet may still turn out to be not
quite satisfactory.

Finally, a word of warning to novices in indexing: no revision of
an index should be attempted as a means of getting experience or
landing possible future "real" indexing jobs, even though editors
not infrequently offer such revision or rescue jobs to beginners,
thinking this to be easier (and cheaper!) than compiling a new
index. The result is in most cases a bad index, or one that is even
worse than a rejected one, but it may nevertheless be accepted
because there is no time to commission yet another and better index. This is one of the reasons why some truly horrible and worth
less indexes find their way into print, only to exasperate users of an
otherwise useful and well-written book. Revision of an index, if
undertaken at all, is a task that demands experience and a thorough

acquaintance with the principles and rules of indexing if it is to yield a satisfactory outcome.

ROMANIZATION

Names and words written in any script other than the Roman one must be rendered in Roman letters if they are to appear as parts of a text intended for Western users, who are usually familiar with the Roman script only. This can be achieved by *transliteration* (the substitution of one or more Roman letters for each foreign letter) or by *transcription* (the rough approximation of the pronunciation). Since almost all systems for the rendering of names and words in non-Roman scripts into Roman are a mixture of both methods (with the exception of Chinese and Japanese, for which only the pronunciation can be indicated), the umbrella term *Romanization* is widely used for the conversion of foreign scripts into the Roman one*.

The conversion of one script into another has always been one of the thorniest problems in the long history of written communication among various peoples and cultures. In ancient times, Sumerian, Babylonian, Assyrian, Egyptian, Persian, and a host of other names had to be rendered into the different scripts used by those people, and into the Hebrew script of the Bible. The Romans had to Latinize names and words from Greek and a host of other languages spoken and sometimes written in their empire; the Arabs had to convert Greek names into their script when they translated the works of Greek scientists, while Arabic names and words in turn were later Latinized in the Middle Ages, not without being thoroughly mangled in the process. Chinese and Japanese names were transcribed into European languages since Marco Polo's days, while Russians had and still have to render all non-Russian names and words into their Cyrillic script. But the increasing importance

---

*The words "Roman" (when referring to the alphabet) and "Romanization" are capitalized in order to distinguish them from "roman", the name of the upright-style typeface.

of Western European languages and in particular English in global affairs has made Romanization of Russian, Arabic, Chinese, Korean, Japanese, and many other foreign names and words a necessity for not only linguists and historians but also everybody from business people to journalists, including most authors and indexers.

Since even the best Romanization is always a more or less inadequate substitute for the original form of a name or word, it would be helpful to provide indexes of names or titles in the original script for the benefit of users who *do* know that script. This is sometimes done in works on Scriptural texts, which may have indexes in Hebrew and Greek, or in international bibliographies listing the original works of, say, Russian or Japanese authors. For example, the author indexes of *Indexing and abstracting: an international bibliography* (Wellisch 1980, 1984) feature Arabic, Chinese, Hebrew, Japanese, and Russian names in their original scripts as well as in Romanization. But since in most cases the compilation of a non-Roman index will need the services of an expert on the foreign language and script involved, as well as special printing facilities (especially for Chinese script), it entails additional high costs and is, therefore, seldom undertaken.

If non-Roman entries are made, they must be displayed in a separate index and must not be interfiled with Roman-alphabet entries, as discussed under GREEK SCRIPT.

Authors who deal with persons, places, and events in countries whose languages are written in non-Roman scripts must necessarily use Romanization, but they are often entirely unaware of the existence of Romanization schemes, sometimes inventing their own or using different schemes indiscriminately*. Indexers of books are in most cases only indirectly concerned with Romanization, because they are seldom if ever called upon to Romanize names and words in a text. They must, as in other matters of form and style, follow the usage of an author as far as possible, unless the Romanization meth-

---

*T. E. Lawrence, in his *Seven pillars of wisdom* (1935, p. 25), remarked that "there are some 'scientific systems' of transliteration, helpful to people who know enough Arabic not to need helping, but a wash-out for the world. I spell my names anyhow, to show what rot the systems are." He certainly had a point there. Incidentally, he was also a most meticulous, if idiosyncratic, indexer of his work in its first limited edition of 1926.

od is highly idiosyncratic or inconsistent, in which case the indexer may wish to refer the matter to the editor.

When compiling a periodical index, however, in which different authors' Romanization of their own names as well as those of other people may vary slightly or even considerably, the indexer must necessarily play a more active role regarding Romanization. Authors' names must, of course, be rendered the way they want them, except for those who Romanize their names in various forms, a phenomenon not uncommon among Indic writers: a journal article by, say, Chaudhary may be followed by one in another or even in the same journal written by Chaudry, Choudry, Chowdhury, or a few other forms of that very common Hindi family name, all of which are the same person, but whose names may appear twice or three times in the index in an abstract journal. The habit of Indic writers to indicate their forenames by initials only does not make identification of a person any easier. If it can be ascertained that two or even three forms of names refer to the same person, cross-references ought to be made. Regarding variant Romanizations of other names and words, in the interest of consistency (and for want of anything better), the schemes used by national libraries and those found in large encyclopedias are preferable to any others because the names of persons and places appear in those sources in an authorized and therefore widely known form. Library Romanizations are, unfortunately, bedeviled by the lavish use of DIACRITICS, but it is quite possible to leave these out without impairing the resulting Romanizations, which will still in all essentials remain the same, as shown in the following examples.

LC Romanization	*Simplified Romanization*
el-'Aqqād, Abbās Maḥmūd	el-Aqqad, Abbas Mahmud
Siniakov, I͡Uriĭ	Siniakov, Iurii (or Yurii)

Romanization Schemes

If King Solomon, the purported author of Ecclesiastes, had been confronted with the bewildering multitude of Romanization schemes which have been designed, including those for his own Hebrew, he would have extended his famous saying "Of making many books there is no end" (Eccles. 12:12) to include them, too, the more so since their application often causes "a weariness of the flesh" like that of "study", as stated in the conclusion of the same verse.

National and international standardization organizations, governments, language academies, scientific societies, and international conferences, as well as philologists, anthropologists, and missionaries have produced Romanization schemes for most of the world's languages and dialects. Many of these are, however, either too simplistic or too complex, and those designed for international use or for library purposes are not very practical for everyday applications, because they are designed with two mostly incompatible goals in mind. One is the substitution of Roman letters for foreign ones in such a way that it will be possible to convert the Romanized version of a name or word into its original form, a process known as back-transliteration; this is of interest only for linguists, catalogers, and some other specialists and makes it necessary to use a large number of diacritics, some of which may have been created especially for the Romanization of a particular script but mean nothing to the layman, add visual clutter, and may be difficult to produce in print, as the examples above show. The other goal is to provide at the same time a more or less accurate clue to pronunciation, and this is for most people the more important thing. The problems of Romanization are, however, caused not only by the incompatibility of the two goals, but also by the large number of official, semi-official, "popular", and individually developed but mutually incompatible Romanization schemes which now exist for almost every major non-Roman script. Matters are made still worse by the fact that most Romanization schemes are language-specific, that is, they are tailored to the pronunciation habits and spelling conventions of speakers and readers of a particular language. A Russian name, for example, may be Romanized as *I͡Ushkevich* by the Library of Congress, as *Yushkevich* by the British Library, as *Iouchkevitch* in the French Bibliothèque Nationale (before 1960), and as *Juškevič* in German library catalogs, that is, not only in four different Romanized forms, but also in four different alphabetical positions.

The principal sources of Romanization schemes designed for English-speaking users are the following: in the U.S., the *ALA-LC Romanization tables* (1991), covering the scripts of more than 140 languages in 50 tables, and the *Romanization guide* of the U.S. Board on Geographic Names (1994); in the U.K., the schemes published by the British Standards Institution and by the Royal Society (for details of which see the Bibliography); and internationally, the transliteration schemes developed by the International Organization for Standardization (ISO), some of which are identical (or nearly so) with some U.S. and U.K. Romanization standards.

Major Non-Roman Writing Systems and Their Romanization

The following non-Roman writing systems and the schemes designed for their Romanization are briefly described in the approximate order of their book production as recorded in the *Statistical yearbook* published by Unesco, except that Chinese, Japanese, and Korean writing systems are treated together because they share a common script.

Cyrillic. The Cyrillic alphabet (which derives its name from St. Cyril, a Greek monk and missionary to the Slavs who is credited with its invention) is used to write Russian, Ukrainian, White-Russian, Serbian, Macedonian, and Bulgarian; it is also used by more than 60 non-Slavic languages in the former Soviet Union, for which special letters have been designed in addition to the letters of the Russian alphabet in order to express sounds not found in Russian. The most widely used Romanization scheme is that of the Library of Congress; in simplified form (that is, minus most of its diacritics, it is employed by the major American abstracting and indexing services and databases. Another scheme is used by the U.S. Board on Geographic Names (BGN) for the Romanization of geographic names. In the U.K., a scheme designed by the Royal Society has long been used, and the British Standard BS 2979:1958 *Transliteration of Cyrillic and Greek characters* is almost identical with it; the introduction to that standard states "when avoidance of ambiguity in back transliteration is not a paramount consideration, all accents, diacritics, etc. may be omitted in English rendering"— exactly what is recommended here. The International Standard ISO 9 *Transliteration of Slavic Cyrillic characters into Latin characters* (1986*b*) is almost never used in English-speaking countries because it is based on the system used in Yugoslavia to convert Serbian into Croatian script, which uses many diacritics and is unfamiliar to English readers.

Chinese. The Chinese developed a logographic writing system, that is, one in which each grapheme stands for a concept. The script is thus essentially independent of pronunciation (similar to our system of writing numerals, in which the grapheme 3 may be pronounced differently in English, French, German, etc. but always conveys the meaning of "three counting units"). The script can therefore be used by languages as different from Chinese as Japanese, Korean, and, formerly, also Vietnamese. Since words are written as indivisible graphemes (the "characters") and not analytically by individual letters, the script cannot be transliterated but only transcribed, indicating the *pronunciation* of characters; each character is pronounced as a syllable, of which there are about 420 in Mandarin, the most widely spoken and the official dialect. Since there are tens of thousands of characters, many of them share the same pronunciation (a situation similar to English words written differently but pronounced the same, e.g., steal/steel, yet on a vastly larger scale). In addition, each syllable may be pronounced in a variety of tones (four in Mandarin, but up to eight in other dialects); these tones are generally disregarded in Romanization, although systems for their expression have been designed.

Two major Romanization systems are currently in use. The older one is the Wade-Giles system, invented by two British diplomats and philologists. Until about 1980 it was virtually the only one used in English literature and library catalogs; it is still being used by the Library of Congress and for the Romanization of texts in the Republic of China (Taiwan). The other system, Pinyin ("Spelled sound"), was officially promulgated by the People's Republic of China in 1958 and is now widely used by the Western media and in contemporary literature on China, and has also been adopted by the British Library, the French Bibliothèque Nationale, many other European national libraries, and in the International Standard ISO 7098 *Romanization of Chinese* (1982). The *Chicago manual of style* (1993, Table 9.2: [340–341]) and BS 7014 *Guide to the Romanization of Chinese* (1989a) provide conversion tables from Wade-Giles to Pinyin and vice versa. The differences between the two schemes are substantial and in many cases affect the alphabetization of a name, e.g.,

Wade-Giles	Pinyin
Chou En-lai	Zhou Enlai
Mao Tse-tung	Mao Zedong
Tseng Yu-ho	Zeng Youhe

The Romanization system used in an index must obviously follow the one used in the text, sometimes with cross-references from one form to the other. When in doubt, the Pinyin system should be used, especially since recent Chinese names are often available only in Pinyin Romanization.

Japanese. The Japanese language is as different from Chinese as is English, but since the 6th century A.D. the language has been written in Chinese characters called *kanji,* which are pronounced in Japanese (that is, not as they are pronounced in Chinese). The *kanji* are supplemented by a syllabary of 48 signs, the *kana,* which are written in two forms, *katakana* and *hiragana.* The Romanization scheme used in English-speaking countries is known as the Hepburn system (designed by the American missionary James C. Hepburn); a somewhat different scheme, the *Kunrei-shiki* ("Official style"), is used in Japan. The British Standard BS 4812:1972 *Romanization of Japanese* provides Romanizations only for the *kana* syllabaries. English spelling of Japanese names should follow *Kenkyusha's new English-Japanese dictionary* (1980).

Korean. The Korean language is also quite different from Chinese but has been written in Chinese characters from the 3rd century A.D. until quite recently. An indigenous alphabet, designed by King Sechong in 1446, originally named *Ŏn-mun* ("Word-sentence") but now known as *Han-gul* ("Great letters"), was for a long time disdained by Korean scholars as inferior to Chinese characters and was, therefore, not widely used until the end of the 19th century, but was employed by missionaries. Since 1949, the alphabet, under yet another name, *Choson Muntcha* ("Korean script"), is used exclusively in North Korea, and it is also employed in a system mixed with Chinese characters in South Korea. The Romanization scheme for Hangul, designed by two Americans in 1939, is the McCune-Reischauer system. Substantially different systems have been used in North Korea since 1957 and in South Korea since 1959; in 1989, an effort was made by the two countries to arrive at a single Romanization system.

Arabic. The Arabic alphabet is used to write the classical Arabic language and (with some adaptations) Persian, Pushto, Urdu, Sindhi, and Malayalam; it was also the script of Turkish until 1928, when the Turks decided to adopt the Roman alphabet. It expresses essentially only consonants, while vowels are indicated by diacritics. The Romanization employed by the Library of Congress is widely used, although its rich repertory of diacritics may safely be ignored without adverse effects, as shown in the example of el-Aqqad above. The British Standard BS 4280:1968 *Transliteration of Arabic characters* and the International Standard ISO 233 *Transliteration of Arabic characters into Latin characters* (1984*a*) are virtually identical with the Library of Congress scheme, but a version that is probably better suited for most indexing purposes, *Part 2: Arabic language—simplified transliteration* has been issued in 1993 as ISO 233-2. The scheme used by the BGN for the rendering of Arabic place names differs in some details from ISO 233. The Romanization scheme employed by the *Encyclopaedia of Islam* (1954) is a mixture of several different schemes, resulting in unfamiliar forms of names; it should, therefore, not be used as a model.

Greek. The Greeks learned alphabetic writing from their Phoenician trading partners, whose writing system, as also those of all later Semitic scripts, had only consonants. (The names of most Greek letters are still Phoenician; alpha, beta, gamma, etc. mean nothing in Greek, but meant ox, house, and camel, respectively, in Phoenician.) The great achievement of the Greeks was the addition of vowel letters, some of which were Phoenician consonants for which the Greek language had no use. Classical Greek is still Romanized essentially as the ancient Romans did; modern Greek, however, in which some letters and letter combinations are pronounced differently, should have its own Romanization scheme, but only the Library of Congress and the BGN have one, whereas the British Standard BS 2979:1958 (discussed above under Cyrillic) and the International Standard ISO/R 843 *Transliteration of Greek characters into Latin characters* (1968) try (not very successfully) to combine the Romanization of classical and modern Greek.

Hebrew. The Hebrew alphabet is also a direct descendant of the Phoenician one; its 22 letters indicate consonants and semi-vowels, while vowels are written, if needed, by a system of diacritics invented in the Middle Ages. A large number of Romanization schemes have been designed for Hebrew since the Renaissance, when German Protestant scholars first began to study the Holy Tongue. The best current scheme is the one designed by the Israeli Academy of the Hebrew Language (1957), which is also the official one used by the Israeli government for the translation of laws, for the postal service, and for street signs and maps. The scheme has two versions, one of which is for general and popular purposes, while the other is designed for scholarly use; the two versions are compatible with each other. The Library of Congress uses an adaptation of a scheme designed for the *Jewish Encyclopaedia* (1901–1905) which differs considerably from the Israeli scheme, both in its transliteration of certain letters and in its application, which is far from uniform. The International Standard ISO 259 *Transliteration of Hebrew characters into Latin characters* (International Organization for Standardization 1984*b*) is virtually identical with the Israeli scheme. In the interest of easier application, *Part 2: Simplified transliteration* has been published in 1995 as ISO 259-2. The *Encyclopaedia Judaica* (1972) employs two different Romanizations; one is for Biblical names and linguistic topics, and another one is used for other names and topics, but these two schemes are not consistently applied. For this reason, the Romanizations should not be considered as authoritative models.

Detailed tables of these and other Romanization schemes, as well as a comprehensive discussion of Romanization and its problems, will be found in Wellisch (1978).

Chicago manual of style: 9.86–126; 17.114–126
ISO 999: 7.3.7
NISO Z39.4:

SINGULAR OR PLURAL?

This question arises frequently when a term that has been chosen as a heading is used in the text in the singular as well as in the plural. While this may be a matter of style in narrative text, the issue does not, in fact, depend on the wording of a text, but rather on the nature of a term. Fortunately, in the English language the decision on whether to use singular or plural is in most cases easy to make.

As a general rule, when the question as to quantity of objects expressed by a term asks "How many?", the term should be indexed in the plural; when the question asks "How much?", the term should be indexed in the singular. Put differently, terms for *countable* objects are indexed as plurals, e.g.,

> airplanes
> houses
> trees

whereas *mass* or *collective* terms (even if they have plural forms) are always indexed as singulars, e.g.,

> blood
> food
> water
> wood

Also, all *abstract* terms are always indexed as singulars, e.g.,

> freedom
> jealousy
> personality

Austin (1984, p. 106) observed that this rule is intuitively applied by all of us in everyday language; Lewis Carroll's Walrus talks to the carpenter

> . . . of many things—
> Of shoes—and ships—and sealing-wax—
> Of cabbages—and kings—
> And why the sea is boiling hot—
> And whether pigs have wings*

*Lewis Carroll. *Through the looking glass*, ch. 4.

putting all count words in the plural, and the two mass words ("sealing wax" and "sea") in the singular.

The main exception to the rule is the case when the singular and plural of a term have entirely different meanings; when both forms happen to appear in a text, both must also be indexed separately, e.g.,

>   damage / damages
>   paper / papers
>   security / securities

In some fields, such as anatomy, botany, cookery, music, or zoology, certain terms are used in the singular because the plural, though referring essentially to the same concept, has different connotations, e.g.,

>   lamb [as a cookery term, non-countable]
>   lambs [agricultural term, countable]

Indexes to books in these fields must take such conventions into consideration.

A "solution" of the singular vs. plural dilemma which should never be applied in an index (though some textbooks allow or even recommend it) is the addition of the plural ending s in parentheses, e.g.,

>   dog(s) 27, 38
>   home(s) 48, 51

or even worse, because ungrammatical:

>   antibody(ies) 247, 253

This is clumsy, unsightly, and does not really solve the problem but only evades it.

BS 3700: 5.2.2.2
ISO 999: 7.2.2.2
NISO Z39.4:

SOCIETIES OF INDEXERS

Indexing, abstracting, and the compilation of bibliographies are truly international activities, not only because indexers, abstracters, and bibliographers deal with materials in many languages and formats, but also because their work has to be done in virtually every country that has a publishing industry and a population of users of written communication in all its forms. Yet, for some reason, despite this worldwide need and interest in indexing, abstracting, and bibliography, only practitioners in the English-speaking countries have felt the need for professional associations of indexers and abstracters, and only two other such specialized societies exist so far in other parts of the world, namely in the People's Republic of China and in Japan.

The activities of the societies of indexers and the efforts of their members have been instrumental in raising the quality of indexes and increasing the proficiency of indexers. The societies also endeavor to draw the attention of publishers to the importance and value of good indexes, and they have had a decisive influence on the development or revision of national and international standards on indexing and related matters. Membership fees are moderate compared to those of many other professional associations and should make it possible for anyone active or interested in indexing and abstracting to join the international community of indexers and abstracters.

The Index Society

The first professional association of people interested in indexing and bibliographic work was founded in 1877 by Dr. Henry Benjamin Wheatley (1838–1917) and a number of his friends. Wheatley was a noted bibliographer and indexer who edited and indexed, among many other works, the diaries of Samuel Pepys in 1906; he served as the new Index Society's first secretary and was the author of the first modern textbook on indexing, *How to make an index*. The aim of the Society was to provide indexes for historical, scientific, and other important works that lacked them, and to compile bibliographies on various subjects. At the end of its first year, the Society had some 170 members who paid an annual fee of one guinea. Among them were such luminaries as the economist and logician William Stanley Jevons and Sir George Grove, the historian and lexicographer of music. The Society's first publication, written by its founder, was *What is an index?*, and it was followed by a number of indexes and bibliographies compiled by various members and published between 1879 and 1891, but lack of financial support forced the society to merge with the British Record Society, which performed similar work for original records.

The Society of Indexers (SI)

Exactly 80 years after the foundation of that first professional association of indexers, Gilfred Norman Knight (1891–1978), a lawyer and civil servant who had taken up indexing as a spare-time activity in the 1920s, conceived the idea of establishing a forum for people who, like himself, were indexing books, although, according to his own testimony, "when . . . the need for such a Society as ours first occurred to me, I was not acquainted with a single other person who worked in the same field". An advertisement, put in *The Times Literary Supplement* by Knight in 1956, resulted in replies from several dozen people, and the Society of Indexers was formally launched by 65 members in 1957. One year later, the first issue of *The Indexer,* the Society's professional journal, appeared, and it is still the only periodical in the Western world devoted specifically to all aspects of indexing; it is now shared by all four societies of indexers in English-speaking countries, whose members contribute articles, and it has subscribers in more than 40 other countries. The SI publishes also a quarterly *Newsletter* and an irregular series "Occasional papers in indexing".

Membership in SI stood at nearly 1,000 in 1994 and is "open to any individual or corporate body whose present or previous employment or activities are directly connected with the purpose and objectives of the Society." An annual general meeting is held (generally in September), at which the Society's officers are elected. A *Register of indexers* was established in 1968 and comprises those SI members whose competence in the compilation of indexes has been formally recognized by the Society's appointed assessors. An important part of SI's activities is the training of indexers by means of workshops and seminars as well as by an open-learning course administered by the SI, and providing training through manuals, tutorial support, and formal tests.

The Wheatley Medal, an annual award for the best book index published in the U.K. during the previous three years, originally established by the Library Association (LA) in 1960, has since 1968 been awarded by a joint committee of the LA and SI; it not only honors the recipient indexer but is also intended to make publishers aware of the value and importance of good indexes.

Other areas in which the SI is active include contractual relationships between indexers and publishers or authors, copyright and royalties, and participation in the work of the British Standards Institution, whose standards on indexing, alphabetization, and other related issues have been developed with the aid of SI members. It is a tribute to the high quality of these standards that several of them have been adopted as models by the International Organization for Standardization for its international standards.

Close ties are maintained with the three sister societies overseas, not only through the publication of *The Indexer*, the journal common to all of them, but also through the exchange of information and newsletters, and the participation of members from other societies in the SI biannual conferences. One of these, held in 1978 to celebrate SI's 21st birthday, was attended by more than 100 indexers from 16 countries on five continents. This event was also the last one presided over by G. N. Knight, who had then just put the finishing touches on his *Indexing, the art of* (1979), often referred to in these pages, which was published posthumously and summarized his lifetime experience in indexing over a hundred books and other publications including the 1976 edition of the British Standard on indexing (BS 3700).

The American Society of Indexers (ASI)

Shortly after the foundation of SI, indexers in several other countries, among them 45 in the United States, enrolled as members. By

1968, some library science students at Columbia University in New York thought that the time had come to form an American professional organization of indexers, and their professor of classification and indexing, Dr. Theodor C. Hines, organized a first informal meeting of interested persons. A press release announcing the intention to form a professional indexing society, published in library and book trade journals, resulted in responses from over one hundred people, and in 1969 ASI was formally established. One of the Columbia students who by then had graduated, Alan R. Greengrass, was elected president *pro tem*, and Dr. Jessica L. Harris (now Milstead) was elected secretary-treasurer *pro tem*. The first annual meeting took place in 1969, and Dr. Charles L. Bernier, a former editor of *Chemical Abstracts*, was elected president. Since then, each ASI president has served for one year. Robert J. Palmer, a freelance indexer who had been an overseas member of SI, served as ASI's corresponding member of SI and initiated talks about ASI's formal affiliation with SI; he was also instrumental in drawing up ASI's constitution.

It was no coincidence that ASI was founded in New York, where a large number of American publishers are located, and for some time most of its members came from New York and its vicinity or from other major cities on the East Coast. Gradually, membership expanded to other parts of the U.S., and ASI has now more than 1,100 members in 25 regional chapters throughout the country. Most members are freelance indexers or owners of indexing and editing businesses, and many of them specialize in certain fields, such as legal and medical indexing, or periodical indexing, while others are working as all-round back-of-the-book indexers. Indexers and abstracters working as salaried employees of database producers and other abstracting and indexing services have also joined the ranks of ASI, and a sizable number of members are teachers of abstracting and indexing at library and information science schools of several universities.

ASI publications include: the bimonthly *Key Words* (formerly the *ASI Newsletter*, 1970–1992); the *Proceedings* of its annual meetings; a number of shorter publications on various aspects of indexing, ranging from *Indexing: a basic reading list* to *Managing large indexing projects* and *An indexer's guide to the Internet*; a model contract, *Recommended indexing agreement* (1980); and a *Guide to indexing software*

(Fetters 1986–   ) which is regularly updated as new or improved software is being developed. A *Register of indexers* which lists the names and specialties of ASI members (but does not imply any endorsement by ASI) is also published annually and sent to publishers and other potential index customers. A directory of indexing courses offered by some 50 academic and commercial institutions appears from time to time.

An American counterpart to SI's Wheatley Medal, The H. W. Wilson Company Award for Excellence in Indexing, conferred on the best American book index of the previous year, was established in 1978 and awarded for the first time in 1979; it carries a prize of $1000 and certificates for the indexer and the publisher of the book. An award for the best periodical index is under consideration.

ASI maintains liaisons with a number of other professional organizations in the library and publishing fields, foremost among them the American Society for Information Science, the American Library Association, and the Association of American Publishers. Particularly important is ASI's participation in the work of the National Information Standards Organization (NISO), the successor of the Z39 Committee of the American National Standards Institute, with which NISO is affiliated. NISO's standards on indexing, abstracting, and bibliographic work have been developed with the help of ASI members, who either chaired committees or were members of them; in this way, ASI has had a major impact regarding current American standards on indexing, abstracting, thesaurus construction, electronic manuscript preparation, proof correction, Romanization, and several other topics of interest to ASI members.

ASI's annual meeting, at which officers are elected, is held in the spring and is always combined with lectures and workshops on current issues and problems in indexing and abstracting. The 1993 annual meeting celebrated the 25th anniversary of ASI with a two-day forum at which prominent indexers and information scientists presented papers, published as *Indexing, providing access to information* (1993). Workshops, seminars, and meetings are also organized at national mid-winter meetings as well as by the local chapters.

The Indexing and Abstracting Society of Canada/Société Canadienne pour l'analyse de Documents (IASC/SCAD)

A Canadian professional forum for indexers and abstracters was first established as an Index Committee of the Bibliographic Society of Canada in 1969. It published an occasional newsletter, but did not provide an adequate framework as a nationwide organization. In early 1977 the Committee on Bibliographic Services for Canada (CBSC) of the National Library Advisory Board convened a Canadian Abstracting and Indexing Services Workshop whose 18 participants, representing Canadian A&I services, recommended that an association be formed to provide an organizational framework for professional abstracters and indexers in Canada. In response to this recommendation, the CBSC sent invitations to interested persons and organizations, and at a meeting in the same year the IASC/SCAD was formally established; in 1978 it was affiliated with SI. The society has about 150 members who receive the quarterly newsletter *IASC/SCAD Bulletin*, published since 1978, which deals with both general and specifically Canadian indexing matters, and it maintains a *Register of indexers available/Répertoire des indexeurs*. Like its American counterpart, with which it maintains cordial relations, IASC/SCAD holds its annual meeting in the spring at various places in Canada, always combined with the presentation of papers and discussion of professional matters. Local workshops and meetings on current issues in A&I are also organized from time to time, and IASC/SCAD maintains contacts with Canadian organizations in the library and publishing fields.

The Australian Society of Indexers

A Society of Indexers in Australia was started by about thirty members in 1972, after H. Godfrey Green, a professional indexer and the corresponding SI member for Australia, had recruited friends and colleagues for that purpose. This society, which had about 100 members, lasted until 1976, when its annual general meeting decided to rename it the Australian Society of Indexers and affiliated itself with the SI.

The society has about 200 members in three branches, located in Melbourne, Sidney, and Canberra, where its annual meetings are held in rotation during the month of March. The branches conduct workshops and courses on various aspects of indexing. The society publishes a *Newsletter* (monthly, except in January and December) as well as a register *Indexers available* which is updated every 18 months. In 1995, the society hosted an International Conference near Melbourne which was attended by indexers from many countries.

Nihon Sakuinka Kyokai (Japan Indexers Association)

The Japan Indexers Association was founded in Tokyo in 1977 in order to promote modern methods of bibliography and indexing in Japan. At the end of its first year, the association had more than 100 members. Ten years later this number had risen to 250 of whom 143 came from university libraries or were employed by academic institutions; 29 worked for publishers and booksellers, and 26 for professional societies; 23 were librarians in national or public libraries, and 22 were special librarians; the rest came from school and private libraries.

From its beginning, the association published a very well-produced quarterly journal *Shoshi Sakuin Tembo* (Journal of the Japan indexers association), which deals with all aspects of indexes and bibliographies, including their production with the aid of microcomputers, and has occasionally carried Japanese translations of articles from *The Indexer*. The association also issued two books of more than 200 pages each, *Shoshi Sakusei Manyuaru* (Manual on the compilation of bibliographies, 1980) and *Sakuin Sakusei Manyuaru* (Manual on the compilation of indexes, 1983).

Since 1980, annual workshops on topics in indexing and bibliographic work have been organized, and an annual general meeting is held every year in July.

Zhong-guo Suo Yin Xue Hui (Chinese Society of Indexers)

The CSI was established in December 1992 in Shanghai at a conference attended by 200 representatives of libraries, information centers, and publishers. After one year, membership had grown to 450 individuals and 30 institutions. It aims at promoting theoretical research on indexing, seeks to disseminate knowledge of it, and to improve its quality. It offers training courses in indexing, plans to publish indexes to modern Chinese scholarly works, and intends to translate foreign works on indexing into Chinese. Its annual meetings take place at the end of the calendar year in one of the major cities of China.

The addresses of the societies of indexers are:

American Society of Indexers, P.O. Box 386, Port Aransas, Texas 78373.

Australian Society of Indexers, GPO Box 1251, Melbourne, Victoria 3001, Australia.

Chinese Society of Indexers, University Library, Hua-dong Normal University, Shanghai 200062, People's Republic of China.

Indexing and Abstracting Society of Canada / Société Canadienne pour l'Analyse de Documents, P.O. Box 744, Station F, Toronto, Ont. M4Y 2N6, Canada.

Japan Indexers Association, c / o Nichigai Associates, 1–23–8 Omori Kita, Ota-ku, Tokyo 143, Japan.

Society of Indexers, 16 Green Road, Birchington CT7 9JZ, United Kingdom.

SPECIFICITY

If you happened to look up EXHAUSTIVITY before you came upon this topic, you already know that it is its (her?) twin sister and that it is one of the two main criteria by which the quality of an index can be evaluated. Specificity refers to the extent to which a concept or topic in a document is identified by a precise term in the hierarchy of its genus-species relations. For example, in the hierarchy

"silk blouses" is the most specific term. Assuming now that silk blouses are mentioned in a text, should they always be indexed under that term or rather under "blouses" (because the text mentions also other fabrics), under "women's clothes" (because the text deals also with skirts, gowns, and other women's apparel), or even just under "clothes"? Although it is generally desirable that an item in a text be indexed as specifically as possible, the answers to those questions depend first of all on the text itself. If it mentions only silk blouses, then that term will generally be the best one for the index because it will provide direct access to the item, using normal English word order. (Inverted terms such as "blouses, silk" or "blouses, made of silk" should not be used; *see* COMPOUND HEADINGS.) If blouses made of other fabrics are also mentioned, it is better to use the heading "blouses", subdivided by the specific names of fabrics:

> blouses
>   cotton 34
>   nylon 29
>   rayon 31, 35
>   silk 27

Obviously, indexing silk blouses under "women's clothes" would not be specific, but if that topic is also treated in a general way in the same text, cross-references may be made from the general to the specific terms:

> women's clothes 37–39
>   *see also* blouses, gowns, hats, skirts

To the old question "How specific is specific?", which in one form or another has always been asked by indexers, there was really no good answer until research into the effectiveness of indexes showed that, while exhaustivity is essentially a matter of indexing *policy*, specificity depends, next to the terminology of the text itself, on the indexing *language* used.

In a back-of-the-book index, the terminology used by the author and the degree of specificity in the description or discussion of objects, events, or ideas will largely govern the specificity of the index. The indexing of journal articles, patents, or reports, on the other hand, will in most cases be done with the help of THESAURI or other types of controlled indexing languages, and it can only be as specific as the compilers of such tools choose them to be. That, in turn, will depend on the perceived or anticipated need for detail on the part of prospective users of documents. Thus, in a thesaurus for the field of engineering, the term "education" may be the only one for this concept, without any more specific terms, but in a thesaurus for the field of education there will be a number of more specific terms, such as elementary, high school, college, graduate, special, vocational, and other types of education, whereas the term "engineering" may not be further specified. Consequently, an article on postgraduate education for chemical engineers will be indexed under "chemical engineering" and "education" when using the engineering thesaurus, while the same article, indexed for a social science audience and using the education thesaurus, will be found under "postgraduate education" and "engineering". The answer to the question "How specific is specific?" is, therefore: you can only be as specific as your indexing language allows you to be.

Another admonition that used to be given to indexers is: "Be specific, be specific—don't be too specific!" This is not as facetious as it may look at first sight. Overly specific terms, especially when used for concepts or topics that are dealt with only casually or marginally, may hinder or even obstruct retrieval of relevant information. For example, in a history of the American Revolution, the text mentions that a British customs duty on imports to the American colonies was imposed in 1767 on glass, lead, paint, paper, and tea. The text makes it clear (and anyone who has taken American History 101 will know) that it was the duty on tea that most infuriated the colonists and led to the famous "Boston Tea Party". It would thus be not only superfluous but actually misleading to specify in the index all the commodities on which duties were levied, with the sole exception of tea, because this is one of the focal points in the book, whereas neither glass nor lead, paint nor paper are mentioned any further. Thus, an index entry for this topic might be

import duties   import duties 171
   on commodities 171   on tea 171, 183, 187–191
   on tea 171, 183, 187–191

When indexing collections of articles or their abstracts (either in a cumulative index to a run of a PERIODICAL or for a bibliographic database, high specificity tends to limit the retrieval of information to only those documents that will satisfy precisely a stated search formulation, that is, it will result in high *precision* but low *recall* (the number of relevant retrieved documents). Low specificity will, of course, have the opposite effect: it will result in high recall but low precision (Cleverdon 1972; Buckland & Gey 1994). An indexing language of low specificity (such as the traditional lists of fixed subject headings which are intended for the brief and very general indexing of books in small libraries) is unsuitable for the indexing of periodical articles and other relatively short but information-rich documents.

BS 6529: 5.4
ISO 999: 7.2.1.1
NISO Z39.4:

SPELLING

English in its written form is notorious for having the worst spelling of any major language, in the sense that the spelling of words does not in most instances give any clue to their pronunciation and must, therefore, be memorized for virtually every word, a formidable mental feat and one of the reasons "why Johnny can't read".

Dictionaries became, therefore, so indispensable for English-speaking people that for a long time every home in which people were literate (and quite a few in which they were not) had at least two books: the Bible and a dictionary. "Spelling bees" were until quite recently a popular spectator sport, and dictionaries are still the perennial best-sellers, second only to the Bible. Since the mid-1980s, electronic spelling checkers have been available, though they are not going to replace dictionaries, but only augment them. Virtually all word processors and most typewriters now have such built-in devices, relieving authors and indexers to a large extent from the time-consuming task of looking up unfamiliar or doubtful spellings in dictionaries. Still, there are many instances when either the limited capacity of spelling checkers will not extend to the verification of scientific or technical terms or the spelling problem is of a kind for which spelling checkers cannot be used: such as decisions on variant regional spellings (primarily the differences between British and American spellings); distinguishing between nearly homographic but semantically different words, such as principal/principle; the spelling of proper names; and Romanizations of names and words.

As in many other matters of form, in back-of-the-book indexes the spelling chosen by the author must generally be followed in the index, unless the author's spelling is inconsistent or highly idiosyncratic; but for collective works and periodicals, a single authoritative spelling must be adhered to. In many cases, a publisher's house style will be the decisive factor, and in case of doubt the indexer should confer with the editor.

Authorities

The dictionaries listed under REFERENCE WORKS will suffice in virtually all cases where spelling has to be verified, and seldom if ever will it be necessary to appeal to the supreme authority of the *Oxford English dictionary*, now in its vastly improved, corrected, and enlarged edition, and accessible from a multitude of angles in its electronic form. When a doubtful spelling is encountered in a highly specialized text, the author is often the best authority, especially for neologisms.

British Versus American Spelling

George Bernard Shaw's quip about the British and Americans being divided by a common language pertains, of course, also to spelling. In general, as far as indexing is concerned, this will not cause any major problems: British texts will normally be indexed by British indexers, and their indexes will follow British spelling conventions; the same is true for American texts, indexers, and spelling; but in Canadian texts, both British and American spellings (though not for the same words) may appear (Avis 1983; Rasmussen 1992).

There are instances when the matter of spelling cannot easily be decided as, for example, for collections of articles originally published on both sides of the Atlantic and perhaps also on the Western rim of the Pacific, reproduced photographically from the original publications, and then to be indexed.

Fortunately, most of the variant spellings occur in the endings -er/-re, -or/-our, -ce/-se (e.g., center/centre, color/colour, licence/license), or in the suffix -ise/-ize and its derivatives -isation/-ization, so that alphabetization and, therefore, findability is generally not affected; but gaoler/jailer or estrus/œstrus and other such variant spellings which do affect alphabetization may need cross-references. Although the suffix spellings -ize and -ization are the preferred American ones (and are, according to *The Random House dictionary of the English language* (1987), now also increasingly accepted by British publishers), it must be kept in mind that there are at least 26 words from "advertise" to "surprise" which end in -ise also in the U.S.

Regardless of the spelling chosen for an index, the original spelling of titles (especially those of poems) must always be retained.

Proper Names

The problems that may arise regarding PERSONAL NAMES and PLACE NAMES are discussed in those sections. As to the latter, similar but different names for places in foreign languages and English, such as Praha/Prague or Moskva/Moscow, are not matters of spelling (as some textbooks would have it) but rather of form, yet there may also be genuine spelling variants, especially if a place name has been rendered in ROMANIZATION, e.g.,

Addis Ababa / Addis Abeba
Khartoom / Khartoum / Khartūm

Variant Romanizations may also result in quite different spellings of
other names and words, e.g.,

baksheesh / bakshish
bas mitzvo / bath mitzvah
Koran / Qur' ān
tarboosh / tarbush

Latin Plurals

A few terms frequently employed in the information retrieval literature in general, and in that of indexing in particular, are loanwords
from Latin and are, therefore, often written in Latin plural forms,
e.g.,

focus / foci
thesaurus / thesauri

(although a few thesauruses have occasionally been sighted). Not
so, however, for *indexes* and *appendixes,* which were already spelled
in their English plural form by Shakespeare when referring to written text (*see* INDEX: THE WORD, ITS HISTORY AND MEANINGS).
Indices and appendices (the proper Latin plurals) should be left to
mathematicians and surgeons, respectively, and have no place in
indexes or appendixes and in writings about them.

Obsolete Spellings

Names of objects and corporate bodies or TITLES of works in obsolete or antiquated spelling must be indexed exactly as given, not in
modernized form, e.g.,

Mermayd (ship)
A nevv booke of destillatyon of vvaters (title)
Ye Olde Video Shoppe, Inc. (firm)

The use of *v* for *u* and *vv* for *w* (as in the example of a title above) may cause a problem in arrangement: if arranged as written, the title in obsolete spelling will not be arranged next to the same title published in a later edition in modern spelling. In this case, the *v* or *vv* should be arranged as *u* or *w*, but this can, of course, be done only manually.

STANDARDS

A standard is "something considered by an authority or by general consent as a basis of comparison; an approved model"*, and standardization—in the sense both of designing standards and of applying them—has long since become part and parcel of our daily life: one could not change a light bulb were it not for standardized threads on its base which fit standardized lamp sockets, and one could not plug in the lamp were it not for the standardized prongs on the plug that fit into a standardized wall outlet to feed standardized 110 or 220 volt electrical current to the standardized filament inside the standardized glass bulb. Such examples could be multiplied thousands of times, but it would be a mistake to believe that standards came into use only with the increasing impact of technology and science on daily life since the beginning of the Industrial Revolution. The earliest standardization of a manmade and mass-produced product occurred more than 5,000 years ago, when the people of Mesopotamia, whose only building material was clay, discovered that sun-dried or kiln-fired bricks had to have the same dimensions if one wanted to build straight walls with them. Most present standards concern physical properties—measurements, quantities, dimensions, tests of strength and durability, and many others—but standardization has also been extended to intellectual tasks and their proper execution. In this field, too, what is probably the oldest intellectual standard goes back

*The Random House dictionary of the English language, 2nd ed.

more than 3,500 years, to the Semitic tribes on the eastern rim of the Mediterranean, who either invented alphabetic writing or were the earliest known users of it. They established a fixed order of the letters, ranging from *A* to *T*; nobody knows why *A* was followed by *B* and so on, but once that order had been established, it became a standard, and one that has survived with only minor changes and a few additions to this day. It is also the one that is the most basic indexing standard, without which almost no index can be compiled.

Standardization of Indexing

Indexing is a creative activity which, though always dependent on somebody else's creativity—the text of a document—is bound to reflect the indexer's capabilities and talents (or lack of them). The indexing process itself thus defies standardization: the text of each book, periodical, or other document is unique, and each one needs a different index. Not only that, but it is well documented that the same text, indexed by several indexers, will result in as many slightly or even substantially different indexes, and even the same indexer will produce varying indexes for the same text at different times (Cooper 1969; Zunde & Dexter 1969; Tarr & Borko 1974; Leonard 1977; Rolling 1981; Markey 1984; Chan 1989; Saracevic 1991). Although the methods of these researchers are not always comparable, and only one team (Reich & Biever 1991) investigated the use of a thesaurus as an aid to consistency, they all agree that "indexing consistency, like consistency of many other human intellectual tasks, is affected by a number of factors, and no matter what, it is not very high" (Saracevic 1991, p. 83).

The technical aspects and details of indexing, however, do lend themselves to standardization. Since the 1950s, indexing standards have been developed by national and international organizations, ranging from guidelines for the analysis of documents and comprehensive standards on the construction of indexes to alphabetization, indexing terminology, the construction and use of thesauri, Romanization, and the preparation of electronic manuscripts. The most important of these standards are listed on pages 508–509 (BSI), 514–515 (ISO), and 519 (NISO), and they are referred to frequently in various sections of this book.

Standardization Organizations

Two organizations are primarily responsible for the development of national standards on indexing and related topics in the English-speaking world, namely the British Standards Institution (BSI) in the U.K. and the National Information Standards Organization (NISO) in the U.S. The BSI, an independent national body, issues standards in virtually all fields and on several thousands of subjects, technical, scientific, and intellectual. NISO is a specialized organization, devoted to developing standards concerned with information, library work, and publishing; it succeeded Committee Z39 of the American National Standards Institute (ANSI) with which NISO is now affiliated as an independent body. All standards issued by NISO are authorized as American National Standards by ANSI. Since standardization in the U.S. is a decentralized activity, rules and codes of practice published by other professional organizations have attained the status of de facto standards for indexing, e.g., the filing rules issued by the American Library Association and the Library of Congress, and the style manual of the University of Chicago Press, although the latter in particular is often at variance with national standards.

The International Organization for Standardization (ISO)*, comprising some seventy national standardizing bodies including BSI and NISO, has developed a large number of standards on information, among them several on indexing and related topics; some of these are based on or are revised versions of BSI or ANSI (now NISO) standards. Those published until 1987 have been collected in *Documentation and information* (ISO 1988).

The work of standardization for the information field in general and that of indexing in particular is carried out by committees, composed of experts on indexing and abstracting and by representatives of organizations which have an interest in the matter, including librarians, publishers, database producers, and abstracting and indexing services. Although it is well known that committees, when charged with the task of designing a horse, tend to come up with a creature that looks more like a camel, the current standards on

---

*The acronym ISO, reflecting the earlier name, International Standards Organization, was retained after the organization changed its name to the present one.

indexing are remarkably horselike, and the few camel-like features that sometimes mar their appearance are the inevitable result of compromises that have to be made in committee work. Moreover, all standards are subject to periodic reviews by the representatives of organizations participating in the work of standardization and are either reaffirmed or, more often, revised in the light of experience with the application of their provisions. The British Standard on indexing, BS 3700, for example, first issued in 1964, was revised in 1976 and again thoroughly revised in 1988, partially in order to adapt its provisions to computer-assisted indexing.

The Use and Abuse of Indexing Standards

K. G. B. Bakewell, an eminent British indexer, teacher of indexing, and prolific writer on the subject, once asked "Why are there so many bad indexes?" (1979). Most of the causes he found can be traced to ignorance or neglect of good indexing practices prescribed or recommended by indexing standards. Many self-styled but untutored "indexers" were and still are compiling horrible and monstrous "indexes" which are worse than no indexes at all because they are produced without even the most basic knowledge of the principles of indexing and are, therefore, a hindrance rather than a help for the user. Sad to say, among such clumsy and amateurish indexers are the hapless authors whose publishers force them to compile their own indexes, as well as their wives or other relatives who are often pressed into service for the same purpose on the fallacious assumption that anyone who can read, let alone write, a book can also index it.

But even more experienced indexers who manage to get steady work from publishers often compile flawed indexes, either because they insist on following outmoded and even counterproductive rules or invent their own, blithely disregarding what current standards prescribe or recommend. Some of them will even discuss in the pages of professional journals indexing "problems" which have long since found their solution in standards and codes of practice, largely because they are ignorant of them, but sometimes also in order to ride a particular hobbyhorse.

If more indexers would abide by the provisions of standards, there would be far fewer flawed and outright bad indexes, and many a debate on the merits or otherwise of a particular indexing practice, often generating more heat than light, could be laid to rest. Disregard for indexing standards is, however, not limited to some indexers. More often, it is the publishers and editors who refuse to accept indexes compiled according to the provisions of standards regarding, for example, alphabetization, capitalization, and other technical details and insist on following their own house styles, even if they have not been revised for decades or are based on outmoded practices.

Does this mean that standards and codes of practice are always models of perfection (as, by definition, they ought to be)? Of course not, and the very fact that they are revised from time to time is proof of either their incompleteness or their inherent flaws. But revisions are almost always undertaken with the aim of improving what was already a good and accepted practice or of accommodating new developments that did not yet exist when the previous version of a standard was compiled. Only rarely are revisions made in order to satisfy a transient fad, even if opponents of a particular provision sometimes claim such to be the case, as witness the controversy surrounding the treatment of names beginning with MAC in BS 3700:1988.

Standards, like any other work of fallible human beings, are never perfect, but they generally embody the best available guidance, and any indexer seeking to compile a good and useful index will always be well advised to follow current standards as closely as possible. On the other hand, if indexers feel that a provision or rule in a standard is not well thought out, or that it results in cumbersome or otherwise unsatisfactory practices, they should not hesitate to let their representatives at the standardizing organizations (normally the respective SOCIETIES OF INDEXERS) know about it, because only in this way can the work of standardization progress for the benefit of makers and users of indexes alike.

All national and international standards are available exclusively from the respective national standards organizations. This is, unfortunately, a somewhat cumbersome arrangement when a BSI or ISO standard is to be acquired in the U.S. or vice versa, but it is the result of mutual agreements among the world's standardizing organizations.

The respective addresses are:

British Standards Institution, 2 Park St., London W1A 2BS, England.

International Organization for Standardization, P.O. Box 56, CH-1211 Geneva, Switzerland.

National Information Standards Organization, 4733 Bethesda Avenue, Suite 300, Bethesda, MD 20814, USA. e-mail: nisohq@cni.org

STRING INDEXES

A string index is one "in which the description part of each index entry is a string of terms and connectives joined together by computer software according to regular and explicit rules, and in which each indexed item normally has two or more index entries with overlapping descriptions" (Craven 1986, p. 191). All string indexes (except KWIC indexes which do not need any human input other than the construction of a stop list for function words and the operation of keyboarding) share two basic characteristics: (a) a human indexer analyses a document, identifies the terms that are to form the index strings, and assigns the proper codes for their computer manipulation; (b) a computer will then generate index strings in such a way that every term coded as an access point will become the first term of a string, while the rest of the string will display the context of the access term and be in correct grammatical order (i.e., there will be no inverted phrases or other convolutions that are contrary to normal human use of language).

The earliest and most primitive string indexes were the KWIC and KWOC indexes described under KEYWORDS. The strings consist of words occurring in the titles of documents; so-called "unimportant" function words, such as articles, prepositions and conjunctions, while printed, are automatically eliminated as access terms by a stop list. No coding is needed, and each term in a string except function words automatically becomes an access term, either printed in the middle column of a KWIC index or in the margin of a

KWOC index. Grammatical order is automatically assured by the fact that a title, in order to be intelligible, must be grammatically correct. (If such is not the case, so much the worse for the title.)

The most sophisticated and complex string indexing system was PRECIS (Preserved Context Index System), developed by Derek Austin and others for the *British national bibliography (BNB)*, which used it for two decades (1971–90) to provide subject access to some 40,000 books listed annually. When the *BNB* became available in an interactive online format, the features of PRECIS designed to produce the printed version became obsolete; it was replaced by a new indexing system, named COMPASS (Computer Aided Subject System) that made use of some basic principles of PRECIS, but not of its complex coding system that produced multilevel index headings.

The abandonment of PRECIS by *BNB*, its sponsor and principal user, spelled the virtual doom of the system. It is now used in its original form only in Canada (mainly due to its versatility in a bilingual environment) by the National Film Board of Canada and for instructional purposes by the School of Library Services of Dalhousie University in Halifax, Nova Scotia. A simplified adaptation has been applied to film and video exhibits in Un Musée . . . pour rire, an international museum of humor in Montreal, Quebec (Jacobs & Arsenault 1994).

The principles of PRECIS exercised, however, a considerable influence on modern indexing theory and practice, particularly through its rules of analysis of a text and its treatment of COMPOUND HEADINGS. In addition, experiments showed that the basic principles of PRECIS could be applied to many languages, including highly inflected ones and those whose grammar differs radically from English, such as Hungarian and Chinese. For these reasons it is worthwhile to consider here briefly the basic features of PRECIS. A complete presentation of the system is *PRECIS: a manual of concept analysis and subject indexing* (Austin 1984); a shorter version is *PRECIS: a primer* (Dykstra 1985).

When indexing a document, an indexer first constructed a title-like phrase (not necessarily including terms taken from the title) that summarized the topic of the document in concise and syntactically correct form. This string was then coded according to a set of rules, using some 30 "operators" and codes. This ensured that (a) the context in which an access term appeared would always be preserved; and (b) that all strings would be in normal syntactic form (that is, no inverted phrases were permitted), connected by appropriate prepositions and conjunctions which indicated who (or what) did something to whom, when, and where. Each string consisted of three parts: the *lead* (the access term); the *qualifier* which provided the context for the lead; and the *display*, which always formed a subheading, resulting in the pattern:

Lead. Qualifier
   Display

The lead had to contain at least one term, but the qualifier and the display were not always needed in every string. All terms in a string (except for function words) were then displayed as access terms by "shunting" the three parts, performed automatically by a computer according to the operators and codes assigned to each term in a string by an indexer. The following examples demonstrate applications of the PRECIS system.

Example 1. A document on the evaluation of the professional education of nurses will be indexed by the following strings:

Nurses
   Professional education. Evaluation
Professional education. Nurses
   Evaluation
Evaluation. Professional education of nurses

Example 2. A document on costs of coal-fired power stations compared with the costs of nuclear power stations will be indexed by the following strings:

Power stations
   Coal-fired power stations. Costs compared with costs
     of nuclear power stations
Coal-fired power stations
   Costs compared with costs of nuclear power stations
Costs. Coal-fired power stations
   compared with costs of nuclear power stations

Power stations
  Nuclear power stations. Costs compared with costs
    of coal-fired power stations
Nuclear power stations
  Costs compared with costs of coal-fired power stations
Costs. Nuclear power stations
  compared with costs of coal-fired power stations

PRECIS indexing resulted in index entries that were tailormade for each document, and which were therefore of much higher quality than traditional preconceived and static subject headings. They also provided more and better access points to users of bibliographic databases, for which PRECIS had been specifically designed. The advantages of higher quality and easier access exacted, however, a high price: the number of separate index strings for any document was seldom less than three and could be as large as a dozen or more, which added considerably to the length, and therefore to the costs, of the printed version of *BNB* and other databases that used PRECIS.

Several other string indexing systems whose complexity falls somewhere between the two extremes of KWIC and PRECIS have been invented, but most of them remained experimental projects. Only one system, NEPHIS (NEsted PHrase Indexing System), designed by Timothy C. Craven, has been successfully applied to the indexing of documents on a larger scale. It is much less complex than PRECIS. It uses only four manipulating codes, namely the symbols @, ⟨, ⟩, and ?, it is easy to learn and to use, and it can be run on a microcomputer, though the necessary software is, so far, not commercially available.

Similar to PRECIS, in the NEPHIS system the indexer first formulates a statement summarizing the subject of the document, preferably using only nouns or prepositional phrases, though adjectives may occasionally be used when a noun phrase would be too awkward. The parts of the string providing the context for the lead term, which are "nested" or imbedded in the string, are coded by the appropriate symbols, and the computer program then generates the index strings, in which each term at the beginning of a nested phrase is displayed as an access term, with the rest of the phrase providing the context.

Example. A document on the use of numerical data in the humanities and in the social sciences will result in the following coded input string, in which "Numerical data", "Data", "Humanities and Social Sciences", and "Social Sciences and" are nested phrases. The symbol @ indicates that "Use" is not to be an access term.

@Use?of ⟨Numerical ⟨Data⟩⟩? in ⟨Humanities? and ⟨Social Sciences? and ⟩⟩

This string then generates the following index entries:

Data. Numerical -. Use in Humanities and Social Sciences
Humanities and Social Sciences. Use of Numerical Data
Numerical Data. Use in Humanities and Social Sciences
Social Sciences and Humanities. Use of Numerical Data

NEPHIS has been applied to the indexing of bibliographies, periodicals, and to back-of-the-book indexes; the last application has been described by Anderson & Radford (1988) who used their own software.

SYMBOLS

Symbols are tricky things: their number is unlimited, the same symbol may mean many different things, the same thing may have many different symbols, they are not easy to describe (Dyson 1992), and they are difficult if not impossible to index—yet, indexed they must be if they appear in the text of a document.

Why Must Symbols Be Indexed?

Until about the 1980s, indexers were not overly concerned with symbols. In his textbook on indexing, G. N. Knight (1979, p. 128) still thought that "It is not easy to imagine circumstances in which a symbol may have to be used as the keyword of a heading", but allowed that a symbol "might well come as the second word and so affect the order where there are several headings with the same keyword". It was, of course, well known that mathematical, astronomical, chemical, and other scientific texts contained symbols that sometimes had to be indexed (and Knight gave a few examples of these), but, even in those types of text, symbols were generally not very numerous and could more or less easily be dealt with in an index. Little did anyone in the late 1970s foresee the proliferation of symbols in texts, and especially in the technical manuals for computer software which must now be indexed to guide users to the many dozens of different symbols for commands, instructions, and applications, ranging from punctuation marks to icons.

But not only software users need index entries for symbols. People may wish to find a symbol for a particular object, activity, or idea, or they may wish to find the name or meaning of a symbol they have seen but do not know. Designers of symbols may need to verify whether a symbol similar to or even exactly like the one they have in mind already exists, and if so, whether it is protected, e.g., as a trademark. For all of these needs, symbols must be made retrievable in indexes, not only by the name of things that are symbolized (which is fairly easy to do), but also by their graphic features (which cannot be done as easily).

What Is a Symbol?

A symbol is "something representing something other than itself by association, resemblance or convention".* For the purposes of indexing, only graphic symbols, or *graphemes* in linguistic terminology, need to be considered. Thus, a short vertical stroke, in and of itself, is not a symbol; it becomes one when it is associated in somebody's mind with another thing for which it may stand as a kind of shorthand expression. The short vertical stroke may be the graphic representation of the number one or of a high frontal lax

---

*This definition, from *The American heritage dictionary of the English language,* avoids mentioning the term *sign;* the distinction made in philosophy between sign and symbol is not relevant in the context of indexing.

vowel (as in "bit"), i.e., the letter I; it may represent the chemical element iodine or indicate electrical current; or it may be a symbol for several other things—all depending on the context in which the symbol appears.

The most frequently used graphic symbols are, of course, numerals and letters, but their treatment in indexes is taken care of by long-standing rules of mathematics and alphabetizing, respectively. All other graphic symbols pose three problems, namely: in which *form*, in what *order*, and *where* to represent them in an index.

Form of Representation

All symbols have names or designations, otherwise it would be impossible to talk or write about them, or to explain what they stand for. The names are different depending on the field of application, but within one such field any symbol can, in principle, have only one name: the symbol O always means only the 15th letter of the English alphabet, and no other; it signifies only zero, and no other numeral; it means oxygen, and no other element in chemistry and physics; only one blood type, and so on. (The different names for an oblique stroke—diagonal, fraction, separatrix, shilling, slant, slash, solidus, virgule—are an exception, rarely found elsewhere in the various symbol nomenclatures.) Since users of a text in which symbols are treated as symbols may be expected to know their names in the given context, the easiest and most straightforward form of entry for any symbol is its name or designation, spelled out in full, followed by the symbol itself in parentheses and by its locators, e.g.,

infinity (∞) 37, 42

Such an entry should, of course, be made only if the *symbol* for infinity is discussed in the text, and not for the *concept* of infinity which, if also dealt with in the same text, should have a normal entry, with that for the symbol as a subheading, if needed, e.g.,

infinity 80, 84, 96
   symbol (∞) 37, 42

This method fails, however, to do two things: it does not help a user who remembers the shape of a symbol but does not know or remember its name; and it is not helpful for many software symbols, which either signify a phrase (e.g., an instruction to do something) or are icons whose function cannot always easily be expressed by a succinct heading. Consequently, there is a need to display the symbols themselves, which in turn raises the question of their arrangement.

Order of Representation

The virtually infinite variety of shapes in which symbols may appear effectively precludes any order that assures in and of itself that any uninitiated user would automatically find a particular symbol within an array of differently shaped ones, the way we all know that the letter M is somewhere in the middle of the Roman alphabet, more precisely between the letters L and N, and in no other place. The same is true of any number written in Arabic numerals in the decimal system. This is so because every literate person has to learn these ordering systems by heart as a child and retains this knowledge throughout life. No such universally known and recognized ordering system exists for symbols, yet users may want to find symbols in indexes to texts dealing with astronomy, biology, chemistry, geology, engineering, the military, linguistics, genealogy, and heraldry, to name only a few fields that employ symbols frequently, not to mention arbitrary symbols sometimes invented ad hoc by authors for certain concepts or purposes, as well as icons, the symbols used on monitors to produce pictorial effects. Icons are discussed at length in software manuals, and there are often several dozens of them; but their shapes are more often than not quite arbitrary and their meanings are not always immediately obvious, nor do they always have succinct names or descriptions. For example, in a particular software application, the image of a pencil in an icon is indeed named "pencil" and is used to draw lines, but the image of a butterfly net is called a "selection net" and is used to "select a non-rectangular drawing area for editing", something that can only be learned from the printed manual and so is not common knowledge.

It is therefore necessary to show symbols in an index in their physical shapes, and three possible methods may be used for this purpose, depending on the nature of the text and the amount of symbols to be displayed.

Alphabetical order. Each symbol is first displayed in its graphic form in a separate list, followed by its name or description in alphabetical order, e.g.,

‖   align 12
[|]   brackets 17
     close up 10
     delete 9

for an index of proof correction marks. This method, while easy to explain to users, will necessarily disperse related symbols, but so does alphabetical arrangement of entries in all indexes. It is probably best to use it when the number of symbols to be displayed is small, say, no more than a dozen or so.

Classified order. All symbols referring to a particular class are displayed together, further subarranged either alphabetically or in an order readily recognized by users familiar with the discipline or field, e.g., icons for editing, drawing, coloring, etc., each group arranged by name or instruction; another example would be symbols for the planets which, if only a few, may be subarranged alphabetically from Earth to Venus (which would be abhorrent to astronomers) or, if all nine appear, in the order of their distance from the sun, that is,

☿   Mercury
♀   Venus
⊕   Earth
♂   Mars
♃   Jupiter
♄   Saturn
♅   Uranus
♆   Neptune
♇   Pluto

Authorized list order. This is actually a variation of the classified order method. Symbols are listed in the order in which they are found in authoritative sources, such as major dictionaries or style manuals. In this case, too, the source of the listing must be clearly indicated in an introductory note.

A set of symbols that are frequently used in software texts may be arranged by two different ordering systems. The most widely accepted one is the *American National Standard Code for Information Interchange (7-bit ASCII)* (ANSI X3.4) (American National Standards Institute 1986), whose acronym ASCII is pronounced "askee". It is virtually identical with the International Standard ISO 646 *Information processing: ISO 7-bit coded character set for information interchange* (International Organization for Standardization 1973). The ASCII standard assigns a three-digit code to each numeral and letter, as well as to a few dozen symbols, e.g., the numeral 0 is 048, 9 is 057, *A* is 065 and *a* is 097, a dollar sign is 036, and a comma is 044, and so on for a total of 256 codes. ASCII codes are predominantly employed in the realm of microcomputers, and if a text deals only with symbols covered by these codes it makes sense to list symbols in ASCII order, because the prospective users of manuals and guidebooks on microcomputer software can reasonably be expected to be familiar with it. Thus, a sequence of entries for commands occurring in a software manual, where symbols are the only distinguishing elements in otherwise homographic headings, may be arranged in ASCII order, e.g.,

Heading	*ASCII code*
ESC$	036
ESC/	047
ESC@	064
ESC\	092

The other system for the ordering of symbols used in computer contexts is the Extended Binary Coded Decimal Interchange Code (EBCDIC), used by IBM for texts dealing with mainframe computer software. Symbols in indexes to such texts may therefore have to be ordered in EBCDIC sequence. Since the curse of Babel has struck also man-made computer languages and their ordering systems, there is no compatibility between ASCII and EBCDIC, nor do they list the same set of symbols.

Both systems may in the future be superseded by Unicode, a universal character encoding system, developed by the major

American computer firms. *The Unicode standard: worldwide character coding* (Unicode consortium 1991) and the identical International Standard ISO 10646, *Universal character set* (International Organization for Standardization 1993) use 16-bit encoding, cover all major modern scripts (including Chinese, Japanese, and Korean), and provide for 65,000 unique characters, including all diacritics needed for scripts using the Roman, Arabic, and Hebrew alphabet, and a large number of symbols commonly used in mathematics, physics, chemistry, and computer programming. The system is, however, not designed as a sorting device for symbols.

Whichever system is used for ordering symbols in an index, an INTRODUCTORY NOTE must make it clear which one has been chosen. A double entry in the verbal part of the index, followed by the image of the symbol, should always be made, e.g.,

♀ Venus 48, 62   *and*   Venus (♀) 48, 62

If none of the three ordering methods is applicable, symbols must be displayed in random order, e.g., in the sequence in which they appear in the text.

Alphanumeric Arrangement of Symbols

Since symbols other than numerals and letters have no intrinsic and generally accepted order, their place in an alphanumeric sequence must be determined. All current ALPHANUMERIC ARRANGEMENT rules stipulate that symbols (including PUNCTUATION marks) should be disregarded, and headings beginning with or containing symbols be arranged as if the symbols did not exist at all, that is, not as the equivalent of a space.* This "solution" of the problem accommodates the requirements of automation, since computers are programmed to recognize only numerals and letters for alphanumeric sorting. The examples in the rules make it clear that only the arrangement of name and title headings containing symbols was considered when the "disregarding" rule was conceived (probably be-

---

*The only exception is the AMPERSAND which, when not disregarded, may optionally be arranged as though spelled out in the language of the heading.

cause symbols appear only seldom at the beginning of titles, and those intended to conceal names were mainly used in late 18th- and early 19th-century books but are now rarely encountered; so it was thought that the problem could be solved by just ignoring it).

This rule is, however, actually unworkable for headings in which symbols are essential elements that must be displayed and cannot be disregarded, such as index headings for commands in software manuals or for other symbols in scientific and technical texts. The rule also confuses users searching for names or titles, because its application in indexes or library catalogs results in arbitrarily truncated (and therefore alphabetically misplaced) or ambiguous headings, as shown in the right column of Fig. 11.

Headings beginning with a symbol should therefore be arranged ahead of numerals and letters (in the order chosen for their display,

Headings in alphanumeric order	Arranged as verbalized double entries (Not in A-Z order)	Arranged by disregarding symbols (ALA rule 1.2)
& see ampersand	—	$100 a year
***, countess of	[Christ]mas star	100% American
†mas star	Countess of	The £100 wager
$100 a year	100 [dollars] a year	ampersand
$$$ and sense	[Dollars] and sense	$$$ and sense
The £100 wager	The 100 [pound] wager	B*** de B***
100% American	100 [percent] American	Bch, A.
ampersand	—	C# ballad
B...ch, A.	B[aru]ch, A.	***, countess of
B*** de B***	—	†mas star
C# ballad	C [sharp] ballad	——on, Nicolas
——on, Nicholas	—	& see ampersand
Xmas greetings	[Christ]mas greetings	Xmas greetings

Figure 11. *Arrangement of symbols.* The initial symbols of the first six headings in the left column are arranged by their verbal equivalents, i.e., ampersand, asterisk, etc.; the middle column shows the verbal double entries (where needed) for the headings in the left column; in the right column, the headings are arranged according to rule 1.2 of the *ALA filing rules.* Note that in this arrangement, the title *$$$ and sense* can only be found under "and sense", and the reference to the ampersand symbol could not be found at all because it would be alphabetized at *see* which would be absurd.

as discussed above), and their arrangement value should be equivalent to that of a space. Headings inside of which symbols appear should be arranged in their normal alphanumeric sequence. When explication of a symbol is necessary in order to understand the meaning of a title or name, a double entry should be made in which the verbal equivalent of the symbol is given in brackets, to indicate that the substituted term is not part of the actual heading, as shown in the middle column of Figure 11. When symbols have no known or intended verbal equivalent, it is left to the discretion of the indexer whether and how to explicate them.

ALA: 1.2
BS 1749: 4.3
BS 3700: 6.2.1.3(c)
ISO 999: 8.1
LC 1.3; 18
NISO Z39.4:

TABLES

Tables accompanying text present data either in list form or in a form that shows relationships among a number of factors in a way that is easy to comprehend and cannot be discussed or explained verbally with equal ease and clarity. Tabular displays of lists and numerical data are mostly found in scientific, technical, and sociological texts, whereas texts in the humanities tend to have mainly tables of lists, such as chronologies. Whether lists of items or numerical data, the information content of tables considerably augments and enhances that of the textual part of a work, and it is therefore difficult to understand why tables for the most part are only perfunctorily treated in indexes, or are even not indexed at all.

The technical parts of a table for numerical data are: the *num-*

ber and *caption*, set above the table itself; the *boxhead*, which identifies the items in the columns by *column headers* (and sometimes by *column subheaders*); the *stub* (the first column), which identifies the items in the rows under the boxhead; and the *cells* which show the numerical or verbal data; the entire matrix of cells constitutes the *field*. A table may also have *footnotes* which either elaborate on or document any part of the table. The parts of a table are shown schematically in Figure 12.

Any of these parts, excepting only the data in the field, may have to be indexed, depending on their importance relative to the text. At the very least, the caption of a table ought always to be indexed. In many instances, the items listed in the stub will also have to be indexed, particularly if they are not mentioned elsewhere in the text. For example, a table of poisonous mushrooms, their growing areas, growing seasons, colors, and antidotes may be referred to only in general terms in the text, while the names of individual species and their conditions are not further discussed because the author relies on the tabular display. Likewise, a history of the Roman Empire may include a complete list of all emperors and their reigns, but the text may not treat all of them and may contain information only on the more important ones. In both instances, every name should be indexed, as it would be if it had appeared in the text itself. Column headers may also be indexable if they convey important information not elsewhere mentioned in the text.

Numerical data in the field of a table are not indexable as such, but they themselves serve as indexes of the relationships between

Stub ↓		Table no. Caption		
Column header	Column header	Column header Column subheader	Column subheader[a]	←Box head
Item 1	Cell	Cell	Cell	
Item 2	Cell	Cell	Cell	←Field
Item 3	Cell	Cell	Cell	

[a]Footnote

Figure 12. *Parts of a table.*

items and data in the cells. Tables of numerical data in reference works are often used in this way, e.g., the data in the table below, showing the melting and boiling points of various substances, measured in degrees centigrade, will index the fact that water freezes at 0° and boils at 100°.

Substance	Melting point	Boiling point
Ethanol	−114	78.5
Mercury	−39	357
Water	0	100

If items indexed in a table also have text locators (as will often be the case), the locators for their tabular place may be marked with the letter *t* or enclosed in brackets (a kind of visual indication that the locator is for something rectangular, i.e. a table), e.g.,

fly mushrooms 134, 136, 142t   *or*   fly mushrooms 134, 136, [142]

Such indicators of locators referring to tables must always be explained in an INTRODUCTORY NOTE.

TECHNICAL MANUALS AND REPORTS

In the absence of a collective term, this heading must serve to cover a great variety of publications, most of which are in need of detailed indexes but get often only rather shoddy ones (sometimes produced by so-called "embedded indexing modules", the deficiencies of which are discussed under EQUIPMENT). Many times, they are even left without any finding aids to their often complex contents.

Some of the most common types are: owner's manuals and operating instructions from cars to pencil sharpeners; service manuals for technicians who keep equipment and machinery in working order; software and hardware manuals; standards prescribing di-

mensions, measurements, materials, testing procedures, and many
other activities, operations and objects for the proper working of
which agreement by producers and users is vitally important; rules
and regulations, ranging from collections of statutes and ordinances
to the rules of parliamentary procedures, and down to the bylaws of
the local branch of the Knights of Montezuma; a series of Progress
Reports on a new process for the manufacture of widgets, culminat-
ing in a *Final report on Widget Mark IV,* submitted to management
and consultants; and periodically issued reports of corporations,
financial institutions and societies.

Many of these and other such publications, especially technical
or financial reports, are disseminated only to a limited audience and
are not published commercially, nor are they for sale in bookstores,
and they are often not even available from the issuing firm or
organization. Others, such as owners' manuals, come with the appliances, equipment and tools the use of which they are intended to
explain, while computer software and hardware manuals, for example, are published both by manufacturers and by commercial publishers, and have an audience of hundreds of thousands.

Some technical manuals and reports comprise only a few pages
and can be read through in a few minutes; if so, they probably do
not need an index. Anything larger than 8 to 10 pages, or more
complex and time-consuming does need an index in which the
details covered by the text are listed, specified and made easily
retrievable.

The general principles and requirements of indexing apply, of
course, also to manuals and reports, but their contents and structure
are such that procedures and techniques for their indexing differ in
several respects from the indexing of books and periodicals.

Terminology. Many authors of technical manuals or reports, and
some novice indexers tend to think that indexing such documents
can be done quickly and easily, even "automatically", because there
seem to be few if any problems with "hard" terminology. After all, a
manual or report is intended to present "Just the facts, ma'am", and
lots of them. For example, in an owner's manual of a kitchen ap-
pliance the parts and their details are generally clearly labeled and
described (although this is not always the case regarding the workings, effects and possible malfunction of those parts). Thus, seldom
if ever will an indexer of technical matters encounter the problem of

having to choose terms conveying concepts that are not explicitly stated in the text but only implied, as is so often the case in historical and biographical works and in other writings in the humanities or social sciences. On the other hand, a new and complex concept involving several interrelated operations, conditions, and effects may not (or not yet) have a descriptive name, and such a phenomenon may challenge an indexer's ingenuity in finding an appropriate term. For example, the term "downloading", now so familiar to every computer user, had not yet been coined in the late 1970s, although the operation was being performed and described in the literature in various ways, and had to be indexed.

The popular idea that writers on scientific and technical matters are using "hard", that is, stable and unambiguous terminology is a misconception. Scientific and technical terminology is as much subject to synonymy, homonymy, and jargon as that of other fields, and it does change rapidly, sometimes within a decade or less, even for a relatively narrow special topic such as AIDS (Bierbaum et al. 1992). Thus, sci-tech writers are as liable to use inconsistent terms, technobabble, and neologisms known only to insiders and experts as are writers in other fields. An experienced indexer of technical manuals has stated:

> [U]ntil editors and readers are automated, even the most technical of manuals will be written and read by human beings, with all their faults and foibles and fuzzy thinking, and it will take another human being to help them find what they want in the text (Mertes 1993).

To make matters worse, some technical manuals and many reports are written by several people, each of whom is responsible for a particular aspect or feature of a product, operation, procedure or exposition of data, etc., but they may not always use the same terms for the same concept or thing. In many instances, there is no editor who would ensure that terms are employed consistently and that abstruse jargon is avoided. While engineers may write about a "hydro-magnetic combobulator", the average user of the machine to which it is attached may only know it as a "thingamajig" sitting below the motor, where it is hellishly difficult to get at when it has to be cleaned or replaced (as the manual prescribes). It is therefore important to employ headings for both technical and commonly known or "plain English" terms, linked by ample CROSS-REFERENCES, whenever there is a risk that the user will not readily understand the professional terminology of the text. This means that often collaboration between an indexer and the editor (if there is one) or with the writer of the text is required. The aim must always be to produce an index that is comprehensive as well as readily intelligible to the intended audience which may range from first-time users who are unfamiliar with even the most basic technical terms, to experienced specialists who think in jargon terms and cryptic acronyms.

It is also often necessary to display in an index of a technical manual several aspects or features of a product or object which, though stated explicitly in several different parts of the text, can be properly understood only when put in relation to each other. For example, in a software manual, every task, menu option or command may be stated explicitly, but in addition to listing them separately, the index must draw together the information under appropriate headings so as to provide the enduser with a synoptic overview of the relationships that obtain among these operations.

Finally, an indexer must understand the environment in which technical manuals are compiled, and how the sometimes severe time constraints and constantly shifting conditions under which writers must often work may affect their products. The resulting inconsistencies, redundancies, and other flaws must be reconciled and sometimes even missing information may have to be supplied by the indexer who must also be thoroughly familiar with the topic and terminology of the field for which a manual or report is being written.

Depth of indexing. Indexes to manuals and reports need a particularly high degree of EXHAUSTIVITY and SPECIFICITY so that no detail, procedure or rule, however small or seemingly insignificant, remains unindexed. The writer or editor of the text, when working with an indexer, may occasionally object to the inclusion of a minor detail in the index, claiming that "everybody will know that"; being immersed in the topic, it may be difficult for that person to imagine how anybody who has to use, apply, or perform whatever the manual or report says, could not be equally knowledgeable. The indexer may have to persuade the writer or editor of the need to include even such "self-evident" details in the index.

Form of headings. Typically, each section and sometimes even each paragraph of a manual or report has its own heading, often couched in terms of an action, such as "How to merge files" or "When to rotate tires". Writers of manuals acting as their own indexers, particularly those who use "embedded indexing modules" for that purpose, tend to employ such section or paragraph headings also as index terms, not realizing that entries beginning with "how" or "when" are unlikely to be sought in an index. The proper way of dealing with such headings is to convert them to a noun or a noun phrase and a modifying subheading, with corresponding DOUBLE ENTRIES, if needed, to facilitate retrieval both from the point of view of the action and that of the object acted upon, e.g.,

files	*and*	merging	sorting
merging		files	files
sorting		lists	letters

Such transformations of text headings to multilevel index headings cannot be accomplished "automatically" by any kind of indexing software, but only by a human indexer, fraudulent claims to the contrary by unscrupulous vendors notwithstanding.

Subheadings. Users of technical manuals often turn to the index when searching for the solution of a problem, and they want to find the relevant text passage as quickly as possible, because time is of the essence. Main headings should therefore be as clear and concise as possible, and their subheadings should be displayed in indented style which is much more easily scanned than run-in style. Indented style also allows the display of sub-subheadings which are frequently necessary in indexes of a technical nature, but are virtually impossible to display in run-in style, and it encourages serendipitous browsing among index entries—an important search technique often employed by users of technical matter. The saving of space by the display of entry arrays in run-in style is not worth the aggravation caused to busy users of technical manuals by the slow and difficult scanning of that style, especially when set in small type, as is often the case.

Acronyms of the names of organizations, objects, operations, etc., as well as other ABBREVIATIONS tend to appear in manuals and reports more often and in large quantities than in any other type of publication. Care must be taken to index all of them and their explications, either by means of DOUBLE ENTRIES or, if more than a couple of subheadings follow the full name, by a CROSS-REFERENCE to the acronym.

Illustrations. Photos, diagrams, flow charts or maps are often the only places where a particular object or operation is shown and labeled, while the text may only say "see Figure 3", without specifically mentioning the name of the object or operation. Sometimes, the text does not refer to illustrations at all, leaving it to the hapless user to make the necessary connection. It is therefore important to index illustrations not only by their captions, but also to list labeled items in them, whether or not they also appear in the text. The elusive combobulator mentioned above may become intelligible only when seen in a photo or diagram.

Locators. Manuals and reports are often not paginated continuously (as is the case in most books) but in sections marked by letters or by chapter numbers, resulting in locators such as A-17, C-25 or 3.1, 5.39; LOOSE-LEAF PUBLICATIONS are almost always paginated in this manner.

The text may also be divided into numbered paragraphs, and using these rather than page numbers as locators has the advantage of pinpointing the exact place of an item on a page; it also makes it possible to reuse unchanged entries in a revised index, whether or not page numbers have been changed.

Index format. The material covered may make it advisable or even necessary to provide MULTIPLE INDEXES for items that cannot or not easily be integrated into a single alphabetical sequence of index entries, or which can be more quickly scanned by users if listed separately. Such items may be numbers of parts for equipment or machinery, alphanumeric designations of regulations or rules, code numbers of forms, software commands, SYMBOLS other than letters or numerals, and so on.

Typography. Many manuals, such as instructions for use and maintenance of mass-produced consumer goods, are generally designed by professionals and produced by conventional printing processes, because many thousands of copies are needed. It may be assumed that an index to such a publication will also be professionally printed (though that assumption may not always turn out to be justified). But manuals and reports that are intended for a limited audience and have a short life span are almost invariably produced from typed masters or by means of desktop publishing software and multiplied on office copiers. In that case, the person responsible for the physical creation of the document (most often a typist) may have only little or no knowledge of the TYPOGRAPHY suitable for an index, and must therefore be specially instructed in these matters by the indexer, unless the index has been produced in camera-ready or machine-readable form.

Revisions. Manuals may physically resemble pamphlets or books, but the feature that most of all distinguishes them from the latter is the fact that they are frequently revised and reissued, often with only minor changes made necessary by a new or changed design feature of the equipment, machinery, software, etc. described in the text. To be sure, some books also may appear in revised editions, but the time lag between the first and any subsequent second or revised edition is normally measured in years, and the index to such an edition is almost always compiled anew for reasons discussed under REVISION OF INDEXES. Not so with manuals or rule books and the like which may be revised annually or even several times a year.

Since a large number of entries in the index to the previous edition of a manual may still be valid, it is only natural to think that the index, if produced by "embedded indexing modules", can be recycled for the current edition. The assumption is that the software will now index only new or changed text portions, while the resulting changes in locators for already existing index entries will be taken care of automatically, and deleted text will result in the deletion of index entries and locators. Experience has shown, however, that such automatic additions, deletions and revisions of existing text may cause problems, such as missing locators for items on pages from which a portion of the text has been deleted, or conversely, "ghost" entries for changed or deleted parts of text (Wittmann 1992).

If revisions of a manual are fairly extensive, it is in most cases best to compile a new index. But if changes in the text of a manual are minor and few in number, an index prepared with the aid of specialized indexing software need not be redone from scratch: the software will allow the indexer to merge new entries with existing entries or delete superfluous or redundant ones, using only a small number of keystrokes. But the new entries will still have to be

formulated and integrated with the existing ones by a human indexer, so as to ensure proper relationships among main headings
and newly added subheadings, and correct locators for all entries,
old and new.

THESAURI

The term "thesaurus" is the Latin form of a Greek word, originally
meaning "treasure store". In the 16th century it began to be used as
a synonym for "dictionary" (a treasure store of words), but later it
fell into disuse. Peter Mark Roget resurrected it in 1852 for the title
of his dictionary of synonyms. The purpose of that well-known
work is to give the user a *choice* among similar and related terms
when the one first thought of does not quite seem to fit. Almost
exactly one hundred years later, in the early 1950s, the term "thesaurus" began again to be employed as the name for a word list, but
one with the exactly opposite aim: to *prescribe* the use of only one
term, a "descriptor", for the indication of a concept that may have
synonyms. Similar to *Roget's thesaurus*, a thesaurus for indexing and
information retrieval also lists terms that are *related* to a descriptor.

What Is a Thesaurus?

The latest revision of the American Standard *Guidelines for the construction, format and management of monolingual thesauri* (NISO
Z39.19–1993) (1994) defines a thesaurus as

> A controlled vocabulary arranged in a known order in which equiva-
> lence, homographic, hierarchical, and associative relationships among
> terms are clearly displayed and identified by standardized relation-
> ship indicators, which must be employed reciprocally. Its purposes
> are to promote consistency in the indexing of documents, predomi-
> nantly for postcoordinated information storage and retrieval systems,
> and to facilitate searching by linking entry terms with descriptors.

The *descriptors* or *preferred terms* are those terms which, in the domain of the thesaurus, best describe a concept, while any synonymous terms for the same concepts will be referred to the descriptor by means of cross-references and should not be used in indexing or searching. A thesaurus thus functions first of all as a tool for *synonym control.* As an example, "automobiles" are also called autos, cars, or motorcars (and were once known as horseless carriages), but only the preferred term will be a descriptor in a particular thesaurus, all others being synonyms which are only cross-referenced to it.

A descriptor is always a member of a genus-species hierarchy: automobiles are a species of the genus motor vehicles and have themselves subspecies, such as ambulances, passenger cars, sports cars, campers, vans, etc. A thesaurus displays these *hierarchical relationships* by indicating whether a term is a *broader term* (BT), that is, a genus, or a *narrower term* (NT), a species, e.g.,

```
automobiles
   BT motor vehicles
   NT ambulances
      campers
      fire engines
      hearses
      sports cars
      vans
```

Most descriptors also have *associative relationships*, that is, when thinking of term *A* one is apt to think also of terms *B, C,* etc., which may be associated with *A* (but not hierarchically), such as accidents, drivers, garages, repairs, etc., which may come to mind when thinking about automobiles. Such *related terms* (RT) are always displayed reciprocally, e.g.,

```
automobiles       garages
   RT garages        RT automobiles
```

A special case of associative relationship is the *whole-part* relationship, which differs from a hierarchical relationship; e.g., automobiles have bodies, chassis, engines, and wheels, etc., which are not species of the genus automobiles but are parts of them. The whole-part relationship is generally regarded as an associative one and is, therefore, labeled RT, but in some thesauri the whole-part relationship is labeled BTP (broader term, partitive) or NTP (narrower term, partitive).

Uses of a Thesaurus

A thesaurus may be used in different ways, depending on whether it is employed as a tool for indexing or for searching and retrieval of information. The type of document to be indexed will determine how a thesaurus is used, as will be discussed in more detail below. (The use of a thesaurus as a tool for the retrieval of information from a database is outside the scope of this book.)

Back-of-the-Book Indexing

For an index to a book written by one author, the terminology of the text will generally determine the choice of terms for headings, and there may be relatively little need for synonym control. The indexer may, however, still need to become familiar with the scope and general terminology of the field treated in the work and may wish to consult a thesaurus devoted to that field in order to find out about the authenticity of the terms employed by the author, their correct SPELLING, HYPHENATION, the existence of synonyms for certain concepts, and terms related to descriptors in various ways. If so used, a thesaurus works exactly like Roget's: it suggests synonymous (or nearly synonymous) and related terms that may be useful either as main headings or as CROSS-REFERENCES in addition to the terms preferred by the author of a work.

Indexing of Collective Works

For the indexing of PERIODICALS and other collective works such as monographs written by several authors or conference proceedings, in which the contributors may have used variant terminology when dealing with the same concepts, the use of a thesaurus is virtually a necessity and the only effective means to achieve consistency in the choice of terms and the display of relationships in an organized and helpful manner. The application of descriptors will, however, depend on whether the index is to be displayed in printed form or online.

As stated in the definition, thesauri are primarily intended for indexing as well as for searching and retrieval from *post-coordinated* systems, in which an indexer may assign several descriptors to documents, while users may combine those descriptors to form search statements. Therefore, the descriptors in a thesaurus are deliberately formulated so that they will be helpful for searches by means of Boolean operators (AND, OR and NOT), that is, the descriptors are either single words or, if they are compound terms, they have been carefully constructed along the lines discussed under COMPOUND HEADINGS. For the most part, however, compound terms are avoided in thesauri in order to allow the combination of two or more terms by Boolean operators. This means that many compound terms which would be perfectly valid and useful in a printed index will be split into their component parts in a thesaurus.

Indexers producing printed indexes (whether for books or for collective works) in which main headings and subheadings are *precoordinated* and in which Boolean operators for post-coordinated searching cannot be used will, therefore, use thesauri primarily for synonym control and for the indication of related terms. Regarding compound terms, those listed in a thesaurus in their compound form (that is, not split into their components), e.g., "Heat treatment" or "Social class", may safely be used in a printed index, but those that are split, with an instruction to index under each part separately, e.g.,

Cotton spinning USE Cotton + Spinning

should not be used in that form in any printed index.

Adopt, Adapt, or Construct?

Thesauri have been compiled for hundreds of fields and specialties, and more are being constructed every year. A few are devoted to entire disciplines or broad areas, such as the *Thesaurus of ERIC descriptors* (1990) for the field of education, but most are for more limited domains within fields from architecture to zoology.

Many database producers (who are not necessarily also the publishers or vendors) have developed their own thesauri, which have then found wide application in the field or discipline covered by the database. Examples of these are the *Medical subject headings* (*MeSH*) (1971–   ), now included, together with several other medical thesauri, in the *Metathesaurus* (1990–   ), designed and maintained by the National Library of Medicine of the United States, and the *Inspec thesaurus* (1972–   ) of the Institution of Electrical Engineers, covering physics, electrical and electronic engineering, and information technology. These and many other thesauri compiled by and for bibliographic databases are periodically revised and updated. Information on English-language thesauri (including multilingual ones containing English-language sections) is available from the Thesaurus Clearing House, The Library, Faculty of Library Science, University of Toronto, 140 St. George St., Toronto, Ontario M5S 1A1, Canada. *Thesauri used in online databases* (Chan & Pollard 1988) lists 122 items, though a large number of these controlled vocabularies are not really thesauri at all, but just traditional subject heading lists or term lists which are not intended to serve as sources for terms usable in post-coordinated searching. Since the book provides many examples of descriptors or headings for each vocabulary, it is easy to judge their relative quality and to decide on their usefulness or otherwise for an indexing operation.

A decision to *adopt* a particular thesaurus should be based on the following major criteria.

1. *Authority.* A thesaurus should be the product of an organization known for the quality of its work and considered to be an authority by those who work in the field covered. A thesaurus compiled by one person may occasionally be acceptable if it has proved its value in practical application, but such one-person efforts are seldom revised and brought up to date at reasonable intervals, and most of them remain impressive but slowly decaying monuments to the diligence of their compilers.
2. *Practical experience.* A thesaurus should have been in use for several years, and it should be possible to check its quality and

application in either a printed version or online for its effectiveness in indexing and searching.

3. *Revision.* A thesaurus should be revised either continuously or at stated intervals. Continuous revision is achieved by publication of supplements or updatings at least once a year. A thesaurus that has not been updated for three to five years is probably not a good candidate for adoption, because terminology in virtually every field is changing more or less rapidly, and a thesaurus that is more than five years old is bound to contain outmoded or obsolete terms while missing those for recent developments and discoveries, especially in science and technology.

4. *Format.* A thesaurus should be presented in a format that makes it easy to use. Distinctive typographical layout, clear relationship indicators (and not too many different ones), and alphabetical listing of descriptors as well as their classified (hierarchical) display are among the more important characteristics of a useful format. The display of thesauri in online form, which is sorely in need of improvement and should respond to requirements that are different from those for printed thesauri, has been discussed by Weinberg (1988).

Adopting a thesaurus for an indexing operation implies strict adherence to its choice of descriptors and its synonym control, because only consistent application of a thesaurus will assure continuity and consistency in indexing as well as a high rate of success in retrieval. On the other hand, this does not and cannot mean rigid and unswerving application of descriptors, because some of them may not be suitable and, the longer a thesaurus is used, the more there will be a need for additional descriptors not yet included in the latest revision. Thus, adopting a thesaurus inevitably also means *adapting* it to the particular needs of the information retrieval system in which it is used. Any adaptation should, however, be performed very carefully, and only if there is a definite need for it, such as the appearance of newly coined terms which after a certain period show themselves to be widely used by practitioners both orally and in the professional literature. If such neologisms cannot be expressed by or subsumed under any of the existing descriptors or their combination without having to resort to cumbersome constructions resulting in terms unfamiliar to users of the system, then they should be incorporated into the thesaurus on a temporary basis until the next revision or updating*. Such a revision may either include the new term or contain it in a slightly different form, e.g., the term "Continuing education", added provisionally to an education thesaurus, may become "Lifelong education" in its next revision. Cross-references should then be made in the index, alerting users to the change and when it was made, so that retrospective searches can be made under both terms. Adaptation is not limited to the addition of new terms but must also include their possible synonyms and related terms as well as the elimination of obsolete terms, some of which may have been replaced by neologisms.

Indexers often seem to feel the urge to *construct* a new thesaurus from scratch, not having found a suitable one among the hundreds that already exist. Indexers who show signs of this affliction should be forcibly restrained until better counsels prevail and sanity is restored. Thesaurus-making is not an activity to be undertaken lightly by anyone as a hobby in his or her spare time. If a thesaurus is to cover an entire discipline or large field, it needs the combined efforts of a group of experienced people, including a professional programmer, working full time for an extended period (sometimes for years), with access to a mainframe computer, and—most important—a sponsor with very deep pockets. For those who still want to try their hands at this exciting but often frustrating game there is first of all the American Standard NISO Z39.19, cited above, the most comprehensive and lucid guide to thesaurus construction.

Other sources are "The thesaurus in indexing and searching: a review" (Feinberg, 1983), the textbook *Vocabulary control for information retrieval* (Lancaster 1986), and *Thesaurus construction* (Aitchison & Gilchrist 1987), a practical guide; these items display many examples from various thesauri. *Indexing languages and thesauri* (Soergel 1974) is still valuable for its exposition of the theoretical background. A brief introduction is in a two-part article (Batty & Eddison 1988/89) which ought to be read by anyone contemplating

---

*A famous example of an awkward (and incorrect) combination of terms, retained long after a new term had become a household word, is the heading "Electronic calculating machines" used in the *Library of Congress subject headings* for "Computers" for more than a quarter of a century.

the construction of a thesaurus. Specialized software packages supporting the mechanical stages of thesaurus construction and maintenance are available (Milstead 1993), but the compilation of the vocabulary and its relationships needs extensive intellectual effort and cannot be automated. *Caveat fabricator thesaurorum.*

Other Controlled Indexing Languages

Before the advent of thesauri constructed according to the recommendations of the relevant national and international standards, indexers relied on lists of terms variously known as subject heading lists, keyword lists, term lists, and similarly labeled aids to consistency in indexing. Most subject heading lists were and still are modeled on the most extensive and best-known one, the *Library of Congress subject headings* (*LCSH*) (Library of Congress 1989–   ), and are characterized by the fact that they are much more loosely structured than thesauri and are, therefore, less effective for indexing or searching. Their synonym control is much less consistent; they contain compound headings both in natural language order and in inverted form with no discernible criteria for the use of one or the other form, e.g., the same list may contain the headings "Public libraries" and "Libraries, college"; they use entire phrases as headings, e.g., "Children in literature and art"; they do not distinguish between genus-species and associative relationships; their cross-reference system is neither systematic nor consistent; they assign a number of separate yet widely dispersed headings to documents dealing with two or more different subjects without providing a mechanism for the linkage and joint retrieval of such multiple headings; and they permit the construction of strings consisting of several phrases and single words to form "headings", such as "Education, preschool—Computer-assisted instruction—Bibliography", providing access only under the first element while hiding all others from a searcher. The latest editions of *LCSH*, now grown to three thick volumes, use thesaurus-type relationship indicators (BT, NT, RT) instead of the traditional *see* and *see also* references, but this frivolous attempt to spruce up an antiquated system so as to make it seem to be the equivalent of a thesaurus has been rightly exposed as a fraud by Dykstra (1988). Anyone who asserts that changing a few labels for cross-references is all one has to do to convert a subject heading list into a thesaurus is either a fool or a knave.

Keyword or term lists are essentially stripped-down versions of subject heading lists with little or no synonym control and often lacking cross-references; they generally do more harm than good for indexing purposes.

BS 5723
ISO 2788
NISO Z39.19

TITLES

Written texts have been compiled for more than 5,000 years, but for only a tenth of this time—the last 500 years—have they had titles in the sense to which we have become accustomed. Thus, for most of the period during which texts were written, their authors did not bother to give them titles, nor were they known or could be referred to by their titles. At best, a book might become known by its first word or phrase, called their *incipit* (here begins . . .), and this custom prevailed until the end of the Middle Ages.

Titles, so indispensable for bibliographies and indexes, began to appear only in the late 15th century, shortly after the invention of printing. The first two title *pages*, prominently displaying the name of a work, appeared in 1463 and in 1470, but did not become a regular feature of books (and later of other texts and works of art) until the early 16th century. The first title indexes in the modern sense were compiled by the Swiss polyhistor Conrad Gessner for his bibliographic and encyclopedic works in the 1550s. The historical development of titles from the early incipits to our own time has been traced by Piternick (1991).

Today, titles of works are often better known than their authors, and many modern works, especially collective ones, are known and cited only by their titles. Even art works labeled "untitled" carry this appellation as their identification in bibliographies or biographies of artists, and such titles must then also be duly indexed. Titles of books are generally easy to index and pose few problems. Titles of single works cited in a text are entered as given (or suitably abbreviated if too long) and italicized, followed by the author's surname in roman type and enclosed in parentheses, e.g.,

Six wings (Sarton) 15

The subtitle of this work, *Men of science in the Renaissance,* may be omitted in an index because the main title is sufficient to lead the user to the page on which the book is mentioned (although in this example, as so often, the subtitle is actually the informative part of the title). The authors of cited titles should as far as possible be given, even if the text does not name them, which may necessitate some detective work on the part of the indexer.

Under no circumstances should a title be inverted to serve as a substitute for a topical heading, e.g., the title *Introduction to mechanical engineering* should not be used as a heading "Mechanical engineering, introduction to", much less "Engineering, introduction to mechanical", but both the title and the topic should get their own entries as

Introduction to mechanical engineering (Taylor) 57
mechanical engineering 53, 57, 61

Titles of PERIODICALS should not be abbreviated or reduced to acronyms, nor should any title words be abbreviated or omitted in headings. Abbreviations and omissions of title words are permissible only when the title of a periodical is part of a LOCATOR in a bibliographical reference.

The opposite of long titles are some extremely short and unusual ones, such as *A,* the very short title of a very long poem by Louis Zukofsky (1978), or *!,* the title of an article on factorials,* as well as *?*

*Listed in the INSPEC database, as reported in *Science* 242 (25 Nov. 1988), p. 1130.

and *1:30 AM delusion*, the last two also titles of poems*. In the past, titles such as these would have caused headaches when it came to alphabetization, but they can now be easily handled (*see* NUMER- ALS and SYMBOLS). For titles beginning with articles *see* INITIAL ARTICLES. For identical titles of works by different authors *see* HO- MOGRAPHS and QUALIFIERS.

All titles must be indexed in the exact SPELLING found in the text, even if they are spelled in obsolete or unusual ways, except when an obvious mistake has been made, in which case the indexer should alert the editor so that the mistake can still be corrected; if that can no longer be done, the indexer may add the traditional markings [!] or [sic] to indicate that the mistake is actually in the text and is not one made by the indexer.

Translated titles are normally indexed the same way as any other titles, but if the original title is also mentioned in the text, a CROSS- REFERENCE may be made, e.g.,

The magic flute (Mozart) see also *Die Zauberflöte* (Mozart)

Note that in this case the cross-reference is not italicized because the headings are.

Titles are, however, not always literally translated, especially not in music: Haydn's opera *List und Liebe* is also known under the Italian title *La vera costanza,* and Gounod's opera *Faust* is known in Germany as *Margarethe*. Some titles of musical works were never assigned by their composers but are popular or commercial titles, one of the most famous being Beethoven's "Moonlight" sonata op. 27 no. 2, actually named *Sonata quasi una fantasia* by the composer.† In such cases, a cross-reference from the alternative title to the one chosen as an entry should be made.

In BIOGRAPHIES or historical accounts of an author, both the person's life and works may be treated. This raises the question of where to index the (often very numerous) titles of the works: alpha- betically, among all other subheadings for the person; or in a sepa-

---

*Listed in the *Index of American periodical verse* (1986).

†The popular title was the idea of Ludwig Rellstab, a music publisher and critic, who likened the first movement to the feelings evoked by a boat gliding over Lake Lucerne in moonlight.

rate section at the end of the entry, in order to keep all references to works together. If the second arrangement is considered to be more helpful, it is relatively easy and convenient to list all titles alphabetically under the subheading "works". This subheading is, in any case, apt to be the very last one, since it is unlikely (though not impossible) that further subheadings will begin with the letters x, y, or z, e.g.,

Galilei, Galileo
   experiments 139–142, 144
   laws of motion 78, 84
   manuscripts 141
   scientific program 135–137
   works
      Dialogue concerning the two
         chief world systems 57, 493
      Sidereus nuncius 13, 80, 88
      Two new sciences 78, 589

Even if the subheading "works" is not the last one of an entry for an author, titles may still be listed under it because their italicization will make them conspicuous and they will not be mistaken for topical sub-subheadings.

A separate title index as one of MULTIPLE INDEXES may be called for if the text cites a large number of titles or if it is a biography about a prolific author, such as Daniel Defoe or Voltaire; or the moderns Edgar Wallace, Earl Stanley Gardner, and George Simenon, all of whom ran detective novel factories turning out hundreds of items; and the most prolific of them all, Isaac Asimov, with more than 400 works of science and science fiction, not counting innumerable articles, essays, reviews and speeches.

Title indexes are also necessary for anthologies of POETRY, quotations, and similar compilations of or about literary works.

BS 3700: 5.3.4
ISO 999: 7.3.4
NISO Z39.4:

TRAINING IN INDEXING

Formal education in indexing is offered in library and information science schools of universities as part of a more extensive curriculum leading to an academic degree. These courses are often long on theory and short on practice, particularly regarding back-of-the-book and database indexing. The American Society of Indexers conducts workshops and seminars at its branches, details of which are announced in ASI's newsletter *Key Words* and on electronic BBS. ASI also publishes the *Directory of indexing and abstracting courses and seminars*, last issued in 1992. Correspondence courses for both beginners and advanced students are offered by the U.S. Department of Agriculture's Correspondence Programs whose address is 14th St. & Independence Ave., Washington, D.C. 20250.

In the U.K., the Society of Indexers offers a self-taught course by means of training manuals, tutorials, and self-administered tests with answers where appropriate. The course consists of the following parts:

Arrangement and presentation of indexes by Pat F. Booth.
The business of indexing by Pat F. Booth and Elizabeth Wallis.
Choice and form of entries by Pat F. Booth and Mary Piggott.
Documents, authors, users, indexers by Pat F. Booth.
Information on sources and reference tools by K. G. B. Bakewell.

The manuals are available from the Society of Indexers, 16 Green Road, Birchington CT7 9JZ, United Kingdom.

One of the best ways to learn the process of translating, paraphrasing, and condensing the language of a text into terse indexing terms is to choose a chapter in a well-indexed book and index it. The journal *The Indexer* carries in each issue excerpts from book reviews which either praise indexes for their high quality or condemn them for various deficiencies. Books whose indexes get high marks should be chosen for training purposes. Comparing one's own handiwork with the existing index will show gaps and omissions, inconsistencies, instances of over-indexing, and other flaws that will inevitably be the result of a first attempt by a novice, and it will help him or her to become more proficient in the execution of the indexing process.

All relevant national and international standards, listed below, contain recommendations on various aspects of the indexing process, and these should be studied carefully.

BS 3700
BS 6529
ISO 999
ISO 5963
NISO Z39.4

TYPOGRAPHY

Ever since the first printed index was produced in 1467 (Wellisch 1986) and until fairly recently, indexers seldom had any influence on how their work would be handled by a printer. In fact, that very first index was printed twice by two rival printers, one of whom mutilated it by leaving out certain entries and misprinting others— sins that are still sometimes committed by editors and printers. Typographical matters such as choice of typeface, size of type, number of columns, capitalization of headings, and display of subheadings either were determined by a publisher's house style and book designer or were left to the judgment of the printer who converted the index manuscript into type, following tradition and sometimes a whim. Many printers considered the composition and printing of an index to be a nuisance or "oddment" because they were usually under intense pressure to finish the work as quickly as possible in order to meet a publisher's deadline for publication. All those concerned with the physical appearance of a book or other printed matter—publishers, designers, typographers, and printers—would in most cases have resented any meddling in their professional affairs on the part of an indexer, while on the other hand most indexers were largely ignorant of the principles of typographic design.

While all this is not yet altogether a matter of the past, a major and decisive change took place in the mid-1980s, when personal computers became helpful tools used by a large and steadily growing number of indexers. Publishers, many of whom had already been using computerized typesetting equipment for a decade or more, thereupon increasingly demanded or at least preferred the submission of electronic manuscripts coded for direct typesetting according to the stipulations of their house style.

This means that indexers should now be familiar with the basic principles of typography, because it is no longer enough to compile an index, but it will increasingly become common practice for an indexer to produce an index in a useful and pleasing format similar to the one that would have been the work of a trained typographic designer and printer.

When the raw entries have been properly edited, the index must be formatted, but even specialized indexing software will not always do that automatically all by itself (not to mention "embedded" word-processing or page-layout software which will not do that at all). The software must be carefully manipulated and used in an intelligent way by a human being if the index is to be more than just an alphabetically sorted list of KEYWORDS not on a stop list, printed in long lines across the width of a page, each keyword being followed by a large number of undifferentiated locators.

A Brief Glossary

The issues treated in the following paragraphs cannot be discussed without using the technical terms of typography. This glossary is intended to help those unfamiliar with the topic to understand some of its basic terms.

body type The typeface used to print the main body of the text, usually in any size from 6 to 14 points.
boldface A heavy and thick variant of a typeface.
em A unit of measurement equal to the width of the letter M of a given font.
en A unit of measurement equal to half the width of an em in a given font.
font (U.K.: fount) A complete set of type of one size and face.

italic A slanted type face; *see* ITALICS.

leading /led'ing/ The space between lines of type.

pica A measure of line width, about ⅙ of an inch, equal to 12 points.

point The basic unit of typographical measurement, equal to 1/72 of an inch.

roman Any ordinary typeface in which the upright strokes are vertical.

serif A short cross line at the end of the main strokes of a letter in some typefaces. Typefaces without serifs are called *sans serif.*

sinkage White space in addition to the top margin of a page, usually on chapter openings.

small capitals Capital letters of a font equal to the x-height of that font; often abbreviated to sm caps or s.c.

turnover line A line indented beneath another to accommodate words not able to be fit on the preceding line.

typeface The style or design of letters, numerals, punctuation marks, and symbols.

weight Lightness or darkness of a typeface when set in several solid lines without leading.

width The number of letters possible to set on a given line; also known as set.

x-height The height of the lowercase *x* in a font.

The Typography of Indexes

Typography is "the art of rightly disposing printing material in accordance with specific purpose; of so arranging the letters, distributing the space and controlling the type as to aid to the maximum the reader's comprehension of the text." This is the classical definition by the eminent British typographer Stanley Morison, the designer of the Times Roman typeface (1930). The typography of an index is more complex than that of the indexed text because an index is essentially a list which is intended to be scanned, not read the way a text is read. When reading a text, the eye of the reader discerns (and the brain comprehends) entire groups or "chunks" of as many as six or seven words, often skipping function words (articles, prepositions, and conjunctions) and words already familiar from reading previous lines; the meaning of such words is intuitively recognized from the context without actually being "read".

Not so in an index, where the eye must notice every single word or numeral. Function words such as conjunctions and PREPOSITIONS cannot be skipped, because it is just these words that convey the meaning of a heading or subheading, and the terms of an index are generally terse and compact; they must be read, not just vaguely assimilated from the context, as in reading text. Furthermore, text is read in one main direction only, line by line from left to right, whereas an index is read in two directions: first, vertically, downwards to find the right alphabetical place of a main heading and its subheadings, and sometimes upwards, to see to which main heading a subheading belongs (particularly when a subheading is at or near the top of a left-hand page and the main heading is near or at the bottom of the preceding right-hand page; *see* BAD BREAKS); second, horizontally, once the sought heading is found. To aid the scanning operation and to assure quick comprehension, index lines must be short; therefore, indexes are generally formatted in columns.

Typefaces

The choice of a typeface is normally not a matter for the indexer to decide, because the publisher's designer will have made that decision. The designer will also determine the size of the body type, and the index will then generally be set 2 points smaller. Typefaces are normally available in 6, 7, 8, 9, 10, 11, 12, and 14 point sizes for text and index; larger sizes are used for display, such as on title pages, for initials of chapters, and sometimes to separate alphabetical groups of index headings (the latter practice not recommended, as discussed below). Most books and periodicals are set in 10 point type; this means that the index will be set in 8 point or sometimes in 7 point type; anything smaller than that would be a strain on the readers' eyes, and the potential saving of space and paper is not worth their inconvenience.

Desktop publishing also entails first of all the choice of a typeface. A common mistake made by novices in this business is the lavish use of different typefaces, fonts, and sizes just because they can easily be produced on a computer with the aid of suitable software. Most desktop publishing manuals warn against this mistake, but Stanley Morison, writing half a century before the advent of desktop publishing, already had this to say:

> Typography is the efficient means to an essentially utilitarian and only accidentally aesthetic end, for enjoyment of patterns is rarely the reader's chief aim. Therefore, any disposition of printing material

which, whatever the intention, has the effect of coming between author and reader is wrong. It follows that in the printing of books meant to be read there is little room for "bright" typography (1930).

"Printing shall be invisible" is the title of another essay written by a bibliophile (Ward 1932), who similarly argued that print should be unobtrusive so as not to draw attention to itself but to convey the ideas expressed in the text. This applies even more so to an index, which should, above all, be easily legible. Only in exceptional cases will it be advisable to employ more than the three conventional fonts, roman, italic, and boldface. An example of such a case is shown in Figure 13, where the index conveys information not only on where the index entry may be found but also *about* it—e.g., the word "assassination" was first used by Shakespeare, and it is derived from the Arabic—all without using explanatory phrases or inverted headings.

Typefaces vary considerably regarding three basic characteristics:

1. The *x-height*, which to a certain extent affects legibility, is the vertical size of any letter that does not have an ascender or descender, like *a, o,* and *x*. Figure 14 shows two typefaces, Bembo and Times Roman, which have markedly different *x*-heights and therefore look as if they were of different sizes. Both, however, are set in 12 point, which is the distance from the top of capital letters and letters with ascenders, like *b, d, h, k,* and *l,* to the bottom of letters with descenders, like *p* and *q*.
2. The *width* or *set*. Figure 14 also shows how the two typefaces differ in this respect: the same letters and numerals, when set in Bembo, take up less than 3 lines, whereas in Times Roman they need 3¼ lines. Obviously, this may be important for an index because when more letters can be set in a short line, fewer turnover lines for long headings will be needed, which makes the index more legible.
3. The *weight*, for which no measurement is available because this is a matter of comparison and the subjective impression made on the reader. Figure 14 shows that Bembo is considerably lighter in weight than Times Roman.

All typefaces employed for regular text (that is, not any of the many dozens of fancy styles suitable for decorative purposes only)

Index

This index includes words in living languages for which the origin is given in the book (key words). An entry in **bold** is a key word from the English language and it is followed by its origin(s), the most recent being shown first. An entry in *italics* is a key word from another language; this language is indicated after the entry. Page references in *italics* refer to illustrations and/or the captions to illustrations.

A

aardvark Afrikaans/Dutch *147*
Aasen, Iva 129
Abenteuer German 135
aber Welsh 51
absurdity More/Latin 157
Académie Française 79
Accademia della Crusca 93
accent, American 165
accommodation Shakespeare 159
aceite Spanish 98
acme Greek 38
acre Greek/Indo-European 34
Adams, John 148, 161
adelfos Greek 37
admiral Arabic 98
adobe Spanish/Arabic 99
aeroplan Russian 186
Afrikaans 147
Age of Reason 159
agent provocateur French 83
agnostic Greek 38
agriculture Greek 38
agronomy Greek 38
agros Greek 34
aia Portuguese 108
aide mémoire French 82
ajedrez Spanish 99
ajras Sanskrit 34
alambique Spanish 99
alb Romanian 112
Albanian 12, *12-13*, 17, 28, 45, 202, *209*, *210* (2), *214*
Albigensian crusade 75, 81
álcali Spanish 99
alcázar Spanish 99
alcoba Spanish 99
alcohol Spanish/Arabic 99
aldea Spanish 99
Aldebaran Arabic 99
Aldrin, Buzz *149*
Alexander the Great 23, 41, 48, 60
Alexandra, Tsarina *186*
anaesthetic Greek 38
analgesic Greek 38
ananas Spanish 102
Andalusia Spanish/Arabic 96, 119
anemometer Greek 38
Angles 52, 133, 148
Anglo-Saxons 52, 54, 148, 150, *153*
anthropology Greek 39
anti-ballistic Greek 39
apa Romanian 114
Apfel German *131*, 134
apoplexy Greek 38
Appendix of Probius 67
Aquitani 48
Arab conquest of Spain 96–9
Arabic *21*, 23, 96
  script 20, 23
arancia Italian 88
architect Greek 39
aristocracy Greek 39
áriston Greek 41
Aristotle *36*
armada Spanish 101
armadillo Spanish 102
Armenian 12, *12-13*, 17, 28, 44, 202, 213
Armstrong, Neil *149*, 150–1
Aromanian *210*
arpent French 49
arroz Spanish 99
arsenale Venetian 88
arthritis Greek 34, 38
artichaud French 77
asbestos Greek 38
Ashkenazim 140
Assamese *12-13*, 18, 20, 21
assassination Shakespeare/Arabic 159
asthma Greek 38
astronaut Greek 39

Figure 13. *Variegated index typography.* An excellent example of the judicious use of various type fonts to convey in concise form information which otherwise could not have been presented in a conventionally printed index. Reproduced from *Words: the evolution of modern languages,* edited by Victor Stevenson. New York: Van Nostrand, 1983, by permission of Eddison-Sadd Editions, Ltd.

12 pt. Bembo
ABCDEFGHIJKLMNOPQRSTUVWXYZ-abcdefghijk
lmnopqrstuvwxyz-1234567890 - *ABCDEFGHIJKLMNO*
PQRSTUVWXYZ-abcdefghijklmnopqrstuvwxyz

12 pt. Times
ABCDEFGHIJKLMNOPQRSTUVWXYZ-abcd
efghijklmnopqrstuvwxyz-1234567890-*ABCDEFG*
HIJKLMNOPQRSTUVWXYZ-abcdefghijklmnop
qrstuvwxyz

Figure 14. *Comparison of two different typefaces. Bembo* has a low x-height, a narrow width, and a light weight; *Times Roman* has a large x-height, a large width, and a relatively heavy weight. Both typefaces are set in 12 point size, but *Bembo* seems to be smaller to the reader's eye when compared with *Times Roman.*

are about equally legible. Research into legibility and comprehension of printed text, conducted for letterpress printing since the 1930s (Tinker 1963) and for typefaces used in microform and computer technology (Reynolds 1979) yielded the following results: all currently used typefaces are about equally legible in sizes from 8 to 12 points; readers seem to prefer seriffed typefaces that are neither too light nor too bold but tend towards boldness; italics are read somewhat slower than roman type; and text printed in all-capitals greatly retards the speed of reading compared with lowercase.

Although these findings are based on measurements of ease and speed of reading continuous text of normal page width, they are even more applicable to the shorter lines of indexes set in two or three columns.

Typographic Features of an Index

Since the typographic features of most indexes will be determined by a publisher's house style and designer, as discussed above, the following recommendations pertain mainly to indexes produced by desktop publishing.

Title Page

The first page of an index should always be a right-hand (odd-numbered) page, featuring the word "Index" or the name of the specific index, e.g., "Subject index" if there are MULTIPLE INDEXES; the name of the indexer; and the INTRODUCTORY NOTE, if any.

Columns

Most indexes are set in two columns, which should be separated by a blank space 1 pica wide; the use of a vertical line is not recommended because it tends to distract the eye. In large-format books such as art books or "coffee-table" books the index may be set in three or even four columns, but for a normal book page of 5–6" (126–152 mm) width a three-column index is, in most instances, not advisable because of the resulting shortness of lines. Although an index set in three columns may theoretically provide space for about one third more index lines than a two-column format (as shown in Table 5, p. 271), a large part of that gain may be nullified by the length of index entries, many of which will need turnover lines, even for single locators; and subheadings, which have even shorter lines because of their indention, may often be separated from their locators on a following line, which makes the scanning of them somewhat cumbersome, as shown in Figure 15.

Lines

Index lines set in a single column across the page should be avoided as far as possible because they are wasteful of space. Exceptions to this are indexes of legal cases and those of first lines of POETRY, in which many lines will take up all or most of the width of a page and may even need a turnover line.

Index lines in a two-column format are between 10 and 12 picas wide, which will accommodate most headings consisting of one or two words and up to three or four locators without the need for turnover lines. Lines that are shorter than 10 picas should be avoided because they may generate many turnover lines, especially

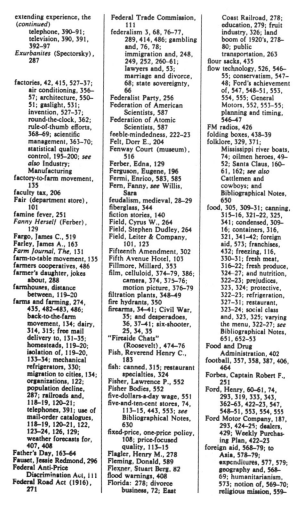

Figure 15. *Disadvantages of a triple-column index.* Three narrow columns on a page only 5″ wide generate many turnover lines which would have been unnecessary in a double-column format, e.g., in the entries for *Exurbanites*, factory-to-farm movement, Fair, *Fanny Herself*, and several others. Another awkward feature, caused by the narrow width of the lines, is the separation of many subheadings from their locators on the following line, e.g., in the entries for firearms and food.

Reproduced from Daniel J. Boorstin, *The Americans: the democratic experience* (New York: Random House, 1973), by permission.

if there are long entries for names of corporate bodies or for long titles.

Headings

Main headings should be set in the same typeface as the text, but normally 1 or 2 points smaller than the body type and with 1 or 2 point leading. Formerly, all main headings used to be capitalized, but since 1980 many indexes use capitals only for proper names, as discussed under CAPITALIZATION. This is particularly important for HOMOGRAPHS, which should also be distinguished by QUALI-FIERS, e.g.,

mercury (element)
Mercury (planet)
mercury poisoning
Mercury (Roman deity)
polish (abrasive material)
Polish (language)
Polish wheat

In complete indexes in which many headings are followed by several levels of subheadings it may be advantageous to set the main headings in capitals, small caps, or boldface, but, as emphasized above, too much variety of typeface should be avoided because it is apt to hamper legibility rather than aid it; this is particularly so for words set in capitals throughout, which are less easily legible because of the uniform height of the letters. All TITLES should be set in ITALICS. In American practice, all words in a title except articles, prepositions, and conjunctions are capitalized, whereas in British practice, only the first word and proper names in a title are capitalized. The British practice is the better one because capitalization of almost every word in a title serves no conceivable purpose but reduces legibility and obscures proper names, which are made to look the same as all other words. The American practice persists only because "we have always done it this way" and the *Chicago manual of style* (1993, 7.127) prescribes it. However, titles in American library catalogs are always displayed according to British practice, and most users are familiar with it. Therefore, it makes sense to display titles in indexes italicized but not capitalized.

Subheadings should always be set in the same point size as main headings and should be lowercased, unless beginning with a proper name. They can be displayed in indented, run-in, or hybrid style, as discussed under DISPLAY OF SUBHEADINGS. In the indented style subheadings are normally indented 1 em space under their main heading; sub-subheadings are indented 2 ems, and so on. Turnover lines are indented 1 em space deeper than the deepest indention of any heading in an entry, because they could otherwise be mistaken for subheadings; thus, in entries consisting of main headings and only one level of subheadings, all turnover lines will be indented 2 ems, but in entries with sub-subheadings turnover lines will be indented 3 ems, as shown in the correct example in Figure 16. In the incorrectly indented example, the turnover line "peace overtures" looks as if it were a subheading out of alphabetical order, and the line above seems to lack locators.

Some publishers prefer indentions of en spaces (half the width of an em space) for each level of subheadings which leaves slightly more space for each indented line, particularly for sub-subheadings and turnover lines, but results in entries that are less easily scanned.

Whichever measure of indention is used (and there are yet other variations), it is important to indent turnover lines in such a manner that they cannot be mistaken for a subheading at any level.

In a typed index manuscript each indention is indicated by moving the line 2 spaces to the right, as shown in Figure 17. In a computerscript the indentions are set by the relevant software code.

Correct	*Incorrect*
Nixon, Richard M.	Nixon, Richard M.
as President 358–373, 387	as President 358–373, 387
Cambodia policy 363–365, 367	Cambodia policy 363–365, 367
détente with Russia 369	détente with Russia 369
Vietnam negotiations and	Vietnam negotiations and
peace overtures 359, 370	peace overtures 359, 370
Watergate 367, 370, 373	Watergate 367, 370, 373
as Vice-president 261–262	as Vice-president 262–262

Figure 16. *Indention of a turnover line.*

CD–ROM   491, 492, 599, 749

 compared with online   750

 indexing for 696

CENDATA (database)   567

census data   544, 567

Chemical Abstracts

 abstractors   558

 Chemical Registry System   668

 compared with Beilstein   484

 compared with Khimiya   485

 coverage   675

 indexing

  metallurgy   618

  patents   568

  pharmacology   566

 pricing   654

 use of   463, 651

chemistry

 abstractors for   558

 databases   463, 484, 485, 526

  568, 572, 618, 722

 organic compound descriptors   633

Chicago manual of style   548

CD-ROM   491, 492, 599, 749
  compared with online   750
  indexing for   696
CENDATA (database)   567
census data   544, 567
Chemical Abstracts
  abstractors   558
  Chemical Registry System   668
  compared with Beilstein   484
  compared with Khimiya   485
  coverage   675
  indexing
    metallurgy   618
    patents   568
    pharmacology   566
  pricing   654
  use of   463, 651
chemistry
  abstractors for   558
  databases   463, 484, 485, 526, 568,
    572, 618, 722
  organic compounds descriptors   633
Chicago manual of style   548

Figure 17. *From typescript to printed index.* Left, the typescript on which indentions are marked by two character spaces for each level of indention; right, its printed form, set in 7-point Times Roman and indented 1 em at each level.

Long dashes should not be used to indicate indentions because they, too, create visual clutter. The white space left by consistent indentions is quite sufficient to guide the eye from a heading to a subheading, sub-subheading, and so on, whereas dashes, whether instead of or in addition to indentions, are always ambiguous: does one dash stand for the main heading, two dashes for a subheading, etc., or does the second dash stand for the second element of an inverted heading? The practice of printing dashes at indentions is, however, sometimes still found in indexes to legal matters and in governmental documents.

In the run-in style, the entire paragraph created by the subheadings is indented 1 em under the main heading. Sub-subheadings can, however, not be accommodated in the run-in style without resorting to further indentions within a paragraph, which results in a hybrid style (*see* example on p. 147).

Locators

All locators should be printed immediately after a heading, separated from it by a 1 em space, which is sufficient without the use of a comma after a heading. This practice is recommended by BS 3700, 7.1.4.1, while ISO 999, 7.4.5 and NISO Z39.4 allow the use of a comma, another suitable punctuation mark such as a colon, or two (typed) spaces (that is, a printed em space). The house style of most American publishers still prescribes a comma between a heading and the first locator, following the *Chicago manual of style* (1993, 17.57).

If the heading is followed by several locators, they must be separated by commas. Printing all locators immediately after a heading will result in "ragged right" lines, a design now often employed also for text in books and periodicals as being more natural and legible than right-justified lines. Under no circumstances should all locators be printed flush at the right margin of a column, the headings being connected with their locators by a line of dots, known as leaders, e.g.,

    books 53, 68
    typography 47

There is neither a utilitarian nor an esthetic reason for this obsolete style; rather, the lines of dots needed to guide the eye across a column or page create visual clutter, especially when such lines are long and the index is set in a small type size.

Running Heads

The top line of every index page except the first one must be marked with the word INDEX as running head. If a work has MULTIPLE INDEXES, each index must have its own running head, which will aid users in finding the desired part of an index quickly and easily. Because running heads for indexes are short—one or a few words only—they are best set centered on the line or at the outer margin of the page, where they will be most conspicuous. The first line of the index itself is usually set 1 or $1\frac{1}{2}$ lines below the running head.

Guidewords

In large indexes, especially those of reference works, guidewords (also known as catchwords) indicate the first and last lead terms (or their initial letters) on a page spread. They are also set up on the top line of an index page, flush left or right with the outer margins. If guidewords are used, the running head is set on the same line, either flush with the inner margins or centered on the pages.

Alphabetic Groups

The groups of entries beginning with the same letter must be separated from each other to facilitate the scanning of the index. This is best achieved by leaving one or at most two lines of blank space between each alphabetic group. The house style of many publishers prescribes setting a letter in boldface or display type between groups or as the first letter of the first heading in a group. While this may be a little bit easier on the reader's eyes and esthetically more pleasing if a suitable display letter is used, it is a waste of space. Since the display letter and the lines above and below it occupy at least 4 lines, this means that $26 \times 4 = 104$ lines (or 92 lines if there are no entries under X, Y, and Z) are needed for the fancy separation of alphabetic groups, whereas only 25 (or 22) blank lines are needed to achieve the same purpose (no line is needed before A). The 79 or 70 wasted lines are the equivalent of about $1\frac{1}{2}$ columns in an average book index, which may just make the difference between an adequate and a skimpy index if

ABERDEEN STREET: BROOKLYN
Bushwick Avenue
1923	North side	0118-A1
1941	South	0118-A2

ACADEMY AVENUE: RICHMOND
Yetman Avenue - Brighton Avenue
1935	South side - Southeast	1194-C3
1935	South side - Northwest	1194-C4
1936	South side - West	1194-C1
1936	South side	1194-C2

ACADEMY STREET: MANHATTAN
Amsterdam Avenue - Nagle Avenue
1933	North side	0672-B6
1933	North side	0672-B7

Broadway - Vermilyea Avenue
1930	South side	0672-C1
1930		0672-C2
1930	South side	0672-C3
1930	South side	0672-C4
1930	South side	0672-C5

Cooper Street - Seaman Avenue
1932		0672-E2
1932		0672-E3

Harlem River Drive
1929		0672-E1

Seaman Avenue
1932	South side	0672-D3

Vermilyea Avenue
1926		0672-D1
1927		0672-D2

201st Street (East)
1927		0672-D4

201st Street (West)
1932		0672-D6
1937		0672-D5
1937		0672-D7

ADAMS STREET: BRONX
Van Nest Avenue - Morris Park Avenue
1928		0016-A1
1928		0016-A2
1938	West	0016-A3
1938	North side	0016-A4

JEWISH NEIGHBORHOODS
n.d.	1416-E3
1901?	0869-A1
1905?	0869-C2
1905?	0869-C3
1930	0869-A6
1931	0869-B5
1931	0869-C4
1931	0869-C5
1932	0869-D1
1932	0869-D2
1932	0869-D4
1933	0869-A2
1933	0869-A3
1933	0869-A4
1933	0869-A5
1933	0869-B1
1933	0869-B2
1933	0869-B3
1933	0869-B4
1934	0869-B6
1936?	0869-C1
1936	0869-D3

JEWS
see Jewish neighborhoods

JEWS, BLACK
see Royal Order of Ethiopian Hebrews

JOAN OF ARC: STATUE
1918	0965-C5

JOHN BARRETT ESTATE
1932	1199-F1

JOHN E. BRYAN PARK
1937	0036-B3

JOHN F. KENNEDY INTERNATIONAL AIRPORT
n.d.	1292-D5
n.d.	1292-D6
n.d.	1292-D7
n.d.	1292-E1
n.d.	1292-E2
n.d.	1292-E3
n.d.	1292-E4

Figure 18. *Indexes to a collection of photos on microfiche.* In the "Street index" (left) each photo is indexed first by street name or number, then by cross streets, date, and direction of view; the locators in the right margin refer to microfiche frames. In the "Subject index" (right), only the dates and the microfiche frames are needed under each subject. Although the columnar arrangement of the entries may at first sight seem to be somewhat wasteful of space, it provides good legibility despite the use of 6-point type for the subheadings. Reproduced from *The microfiche edition of Photographic views of New York City, 1870s to 1970s* (Microfiche 1981), by permission of the publisher, University Microfilm International.

space is at a premium. Letters between alphabetic groups should, therefore, be set only if this can be done without thereby reducing the number of index entries.

Unorthodox Typography

An index must, first of all, be so designed that it achieves its purpose in the best possible way. The nature of the indexed material sometimes demands innovative and unorthodox displays of entries. Figure 18 shows solutions to an unusual problem posed by a NONPRINT MATERIALS collection.

For other topics related to the typography of indexes *see also* (CONTINUED) LINES, CROSS-REFERENCES, ILLUSTRATIONS, LATIN TERMS, LOCATORS, PROOFREADING, and PUNCTUATION. Two useful articles with many examples of good and bad index design and typography are by Kinross (1977) and Ridehalgh (1985).

BS 3700: 5.2.3.2; 7
ISO 999: 6.4.1; 7.3.4.1; 9.3.4; 9.4.1.3
NISO Z39.4:

USERS OF INDEXES

Indexers are always admonished—and rightly so—to keep in mind the prospective users of their work. Will users look for the terms that have been chosen? Does the index provide for possible synonyms? Are headings specific enough? Do they need to be modified by subheadings? Is the arrangement of subheadings easy to follow? Is it strictly alphabetical? If not, have users been made aware of the chosen principle of arrangement (chronological, numerical, etc.)? These are only a few of the considerations the indexer should constantly keep in mind while compiling the index, so it will truly be an aid and a guide for the users.

But there are two major problems concerning "users". One is that indexers normally do not know for whom they are working, nor what people will do with their indexes. Only very little is known about the use (or misuse) of book indexes, nor is there much if any feedback from readers, except for occasional critical remarks by book reviewers who may point out the shortcomings of an index or the regrettable lack of one. On the other hand, well-constructed indexes are easy to use, so that readers tend to think that it is also easy to compile them (and this fallacy is one of the reasons for the meager fees offered to indexers by some clients). Regarding printed periodical and electronic database indexes, several researchers have documented that users are often frustrated by the inadequacy of index terms, fail to use them correctly, or are confused by them (Bates et al. 1993; Siegfried et al. 1993; Larsen 1988). It seems, however, that failure to retrieve desired information is more often caused by users' faulty search strategies rather than by unsuitable indexing (Borgman 1986; Chen & Dhar 1990; Kingsland et al. 1993).

The other problem is the fact that there is no such thing as "*the* user". Users of books, periodicals and other information sources come in all shapes, sizes, and colors, and they have widely varying information needs. Even the same user, searching the index to the same book or periodical, may do so quite differently at different times and for different purposes. Still, it is possible to divide prospective index users into two broad categories.

First, there is the user who has read a book from cover to cover and afterwards wishes to find in the index the places in which a particular subject has been dealt with. Having read the book, that user knows or remembers (though not always correctly) the terminology of the author and so expects the remembered terms to be found in their proper alphabetical place.

Second, there is the user who has *not* read a book but expects its index to reveal whether or not that book contains information on a desired topic. Most often, this will be the index to a reference work, such as a general or specialized encyclopedia, a collection of laws and statutes, a standard or specification, etc., or the index to a textbook or general treatise on a broad subject. The index to a literary work intended to be read from cover to cover should also try to serve the user who has not read the book but is attracted to it by its title or subject when in search of information. Still more is this the case for scientific and technical works, which are rarely read through rather than dipped into by scientists, engineers, physicians, as well as laymen looking for information on facts, descriptions, procedures, and operations, as well as theories and ideas.

For that second category of users it is often more important to know with certainty that a book does *not* contain anything on the sought topic, since if it does not deal at all with what is being looked for, it can be quickly put aside so that the index of another book that seems more likely to be of help can be searched. The high value of a negative answer—knowing for certain that something is not as was thought or does not exist—was first recognized by Francis Bacon, who said that "major est vis instantiae negativae" (the negative instance is the more powerful one). (*Novum organum,* bk. 1, aph. 46) Also in this second category is the user who scans the index to a periodical covering a certain subject field. That user may not have read any of the articles in it, but may nevertheless expect it to contain information on a sought topic; or the user may simply look for an article in any journal covered by a general indexing database, such as *Reader's Guide to Periodical Literature,* or by a discipline-wide one, such as *Index Medicus.*

Both of these categories may be further subdivided into what has been termed "casual" index users—those who have ample time to search or browse through an index, patiently following up cross-references to synonyms or related topics—as opposed to "desperate" index users who are in a hurry because of an approaching deadline or a dire and perhaps life-threatening emergency, as vividly described by Mulvany (1994*b*, 10–11).

Finally, it has been suggested (as reported in Knight 1979, 88n) that there is a third category of users, namely, those who are browsing through indexes to find odd or unexpected aspects of a subject, and that this is mainly done by students in search of a theme for a term paper. Even though there may be a kernel of truth in this assertion, the indexer need not be concerned about it. An index entry is made because the indexer decided that an item in a document is indexable and may be helpful to a potential user—even if that user is an inexperienced student, hunting up "odd" facts.

ZEN AND THE ART OF INDEXING

There is no affinity between Zen and the art of indexing. To the contrary, the teachings of the Buddhist sect and the requirements of indexing are diametrically opposed: the former disdains reality as it is conveyed through the senses as vain and empty and shuns reliance on sacred scriptures; the latter pays close attention to the world as it is perceived and reflected in the written word. No *koan* on indexing, such as "What is the locator of an item on an unnumbered page?", is known to have been composed by an ancient Zen master. But for this book a topic beginning with the letter Z had to be found, and in the absence of one pertaining to indexing, the heading chosen for this section (with apologies to Robert Pirsig) seemed to serve as well as any other.

Now that I have your attention, this may also be an opportunity to tell you the story of the letter Z. It was originally the seventh letter of the Phoenician alphabet and was written almost exactly the way it is now; its name, *zayin,* meant weapon (a twisted dagger). When the Greeks adapted the Phoenician alphabet to their language, it became the sixth letter (since the one preceding it in the Phoenician alphabet, pronounced like *w,* was of no use to the Greeks), and it was renamed *zeta.* The Latin language, in turn, had no need for the voiced sibilant sound it represented (the same for which z is most often used in English, as in *zone*). But when the Romans embraced Greek culture and Greek loanwords entered the Latin language, the letter Z was needed to transliterate such words as ZΩNH ("girdle"), which became the Latin word *zona.* Still, the Romans relegated the "foreign" letter to the end of the alphabet, where it has remained ever since.

BIBLIOGRAPHY

The bibliography lists all works referred to in the text, except those listed in the section REFERENCE WORKS and at the end of the sections LEGAL TEXTS and MEDICAL TEXTS. Dates of ISO and NISO standards marked 199X indicate that the standard is in preparation.

ABHB: the annual bibliography of the history of the printed book and libraries. 1973– . Dordrecht; London: Kluwer.

Academy of the Hebrew Language. 1957. [Rules for the transliteration of Hebrew script into Roman script.] Jerusalem: Academy of the Hebrew Language. (In Hebrew.)

Aitchison, Jean; Gilchrist, Alan. 1987. *Thesaurus construction: a practical manual.* 2nd ed. London: Aslib.

ALA-LC Romanization tables: transliteration schemes for non-Roman scripts . . . (1991). Edited by Randall K. Barry. Washington, DC: Library of Congress.

American Library Association. 1968. *ALA rules for filing catalog cards.* 2nd ed. Chicago: American Library Association.

American Library Association. 1980. *ALA filing rules.* Chicago: American Library Association.

American National Standards Institute. 1977. *Bibliographic references.* New York: American National Standards Institute. (ANSI/NISO Z39.29)

American National Standards Institute. 1985. *Abbreviation of titles of publications.* New York: American National Standards Institute. (ANSI Z39.29)

American National Standards Institute. 1986. *Information systems—coded character set—7-bit American National Standard Code for Information Interchange (7-bit ASCII).* New York: American National Standards Institute. (ANSI X3.4)

American Psychological Association. 1994. *Thesaurus of psychological index terms.* Washington, DC: American Psychological Association.

Anderson, James D.; Radford, Gay. 1988. "Back-of-the-book indexing with the Nested Phrase Indexing System (NEPHIS)". *The Indexer* 16:79–84.

Anderson, M. D. 1966. "The length of book indexes". *The Indexer* 5:3–4.

Anderson, M. D. 1969. "Chapter headings". *The Indexer* 6:116–118.

Anderson, M. D. 1971. *Book indexing.* Cambridge: Cambridge University Press. Revised edition 1985.

Angel, Dennis; Tannenbaum, Samuel W. 1977. "Work made for hire under S.22". (In: *The complete guide to the new copyright law* . . . Dayton, OH: Lorenz Press.)

Anglo-American cataloguing rules. 1988. 2nd ed., 1988 revision. Ottawa; Canadian Library Association; Chicago: American Library Association; London: Library Association.

Apicius. 1936. *Cookery and dining in imperial Rome* . . . rendered into English by Joseph Dammers Vehling. Chicago: W. M. Hill. Reprinted New York: Dover, 1977.

Art & architecture thesaurus. 1994. 2nd ed. New York and Oxford: Oxford University Press.

Austin, Derek; Dykstra, Mary. 1984. *PRECIS: a manual of concept analysis and subject indexing.* London: British Library.

Avis, Walter S. 1983. "Canadian English in its North American context". *Canadian Journal of Linguistics* 28:3–15.

Bakewell, K. G. B. 1979. "Why are there so many bad indexes?" *Library Association Record* 81:330–331. Addendum: 449. Comment: 451.

Bakewell, K. G. B. 1987. "Reference books for indexers". *The Indexer* 15:131–140, 195–196.

The Barnhart dictionary of etymology. 1987. New York: H. W. Wilson.

Bartlett, John. 1992. *Bartlett's familiar quotations.* 16th ed. Boston: Little, Brown.

Barzun, Jacques; Graff, Henry F. 1970. *The modern researcher.* Rev. ed. New York: Harcourt, Brace & World.

Bates, Marcia J.; Wilde, D. N.; Siegfried, S. 1993. "An analysis of search terminology used by humanities scholars: the Getty Online Searching Project report no. 1". *Library Quarterly* 63:1–39.

Batty, David; Eddison, Betty. 1988. "Introduction to the world of thesaurus building". *Database* 11 (6):109–113.

Batty, David. 1989. "Thesaurus construction and maintenance: a survival kit". *Database* 12 (1):13–20.

Beare, Geraldine. 1989. "Local newspaper indexing projects and products". *The Indexer* 16:227–233.

Beghtol, Claire. 1986. "Bibliographic text theory and text linguistics: aboutness analysis, intertextuality and the cognitive act of classifying documents". *Journal of Documentation* 42:84–113.

Bell, Hazel K. 1989. "Indexing biographies: lives do bring their problems." *The Indexer* 16:168–172.

Bell, Hazel K. 1990. "Indexing biographies: the main character". *The Indexer* 17:43–44.

Bell, Hazel K. 1991*a*. "Bias in indexing and loaded language". *The Indexer* 17:173–177.

Bell, Hazel K. 1991*b*. "Indexing fiction: a story of complexity". *The Indexer* 17:251–256.

Bell, Hazel K. 1992*a*. "Distortion and mutilation: it can happen to us". *The Indexer* 18:40–41.

Bell, Hazel K. 1992*b*. *Indexing biographies and other stories of human lives.* London: Society of Indexers. (Society of Indexers occasional papers on indexing, no. 1)

Bell, Hazel K. 1992*c*. "Should fiction be indexed? The indexability of text". *The Indexer* 18:83–86.

Bellardo, Trudi. 1991. *Subject indexing: an introductory guide.* Washington, D.C.: Special Libraries Association.

Bellardo, Trudi. 1993. "Indexing from A to Z". [Book review.] *Information Processing & Management* 29:678–679.

Bentley, Nicholas; Slater, Michael; Bugis, Nina. 1988. *The Dickens index.* Oxford: Oxford University Press.

Bierbaum, E. G., et al. 1992. "Subject control of the literature of Acquired Immunodeficiency Syndrome (AIDS)". *Information Processing & Management* 28:89–98.

Bishop, A. P.; Liddy, E. D.; Settel, B. 1991. "Index quality study, part 1: Quantitative description of back-of-the-book indexes". (In: *Indexing tradition and innovation: Proceedings of the 22nd annual conference of the American Society of Indexers.* Port Aransas, TX: American Society of Indexers, pp. 15–51.)

Blair, David C.; Maron, M. E. 1985. "An evaluation of retrieval effectiveness for a full-text document-retrieval system". *Communications of the ACM* 28:289–299.

Blair, David C. 1986. "Full text retrieval: evaluation and implications". *International Classification* 13:18–23.

Blair, David C. 1990. *Language and representation in information retrieval.* New York: Elsevier.

Blanken, Robert R. 1971. "The preparation of international author indexes, with particular reference to the problems of transliteration, prefixes, and compound family names." *Journal of the American Society for Information Sciences* 22:51–63.

Bliss, M. 1990. "From neo-classicism to Nepal: the making of RILM's third cumulative index". *Fontes Artis Musicae* 37:149–164.

Bonzi, Susan. 1990. "Syntactic patterns in scientific sublanguages: a study of four disciplines". *Journal of the American Society for Information Science* 41:121–131.

Boodson, K. 1975. "Indexing a bibliographical guide". *The Indexer* 9:93– 100.

Boolootian, Richard A. 1976. *Elements of human anatomy and physiology.* St. Paul: West Publishing Co.

Boorstin, Daniel J. 1965. *The Americans: the national experience.* New York: Random House.

Booth, Pat E. 1987. "Thesauri: their uses for indexers". *The Indexer* 15:141– 144.

Borgman, Christine. 1986. "Why are online catalogs hard to use? Lessons learned from information-retrieval studies". *Journal of the American Society for Information Science* 37:387–400.

Borko, Harold; Bernier, Charles L. 1978. *Indexing concepts and methods.* New York: Academic Press.

Boulding, Kenneth E. 1956. *The image: knowledge in life and society.* Ann Arbor: University of Michigan Press.

Bradley, Philip. 1989. "Indexes to works of fiction: the views of producers and users on the need for them". *The Indexer* 16:239–248.

British Library. 1980. *BLAISE filing rules.* London: British Library.

British national bibliography. 1950– . London: British Library.

British Standards Institution. 1958. *British standard for transliteration of Cyrillic and Greek characters.* London: British Standards Institution. (BS 2979:1958)

British Standards Institution. 1968. *British standard for the transliteration of Arabic characters.* London: British Standards Institution. (BS 4280:1968)

British Standards Institution. 1972. *Romanization of Japanese.* London: British Standards Institution. (BS 4812:1972)

British Standards Institution. 1976. *Specifications for typographic requirements, marks for copy preparation and proof correction, proofing procedure.* London: British Standards Institution. (BS 5261, Part 2:1976).

British Standards Institution. 1984. *British standard recommendations for examining documents, determining their subjects, and selecting indexing terms.* London: British Standards Institution. (BS 6529:1984)

British Standards Institution. 1985a. *British standard recommendations for alphabetical arrangement and the filing order of numerals and symbols.* London: British Standards Institution. (BS 1749:1985)

British Standards Institution. 1985b. *Specification for the abbreviation of title words and titles of periodicals.* London: British Standards Institution. (BS 4148:1985)

British Standards Institution. 1988. *British standard recommendations for preparing indexes to books, periodicals and other documents.* London: British Standards Institution. (BS 3700:1988)

British Standards Institution. 1989a. *Guide to the Romanization of Chinese.* London: British Standards Institution. (BS 7014:1989)

British Standards Institution. 1989*b*. *Page sizes of books*. London: British Standards Institution. (BS 1413:1989)

British Standards Institution. 1989*c*. *Recommendations for references to published materials*. London: British Standards Institution. (BS 1629:1989)

British Standards Institution. 1989*d*. *Specification for code for bibliographic identification (biblid) of contributions in serials and books*. London: British Standards Institution. (BS 7187:1989 ≡ ISO 9115:1987)

British union catalog of periodicals. 1955–1958. London: Butterworth.

Bruner, Katherine Frost. 1984. "On editing and indexing a series of letters". *The Indexer* 14:42–46.

Buckland, Michael; Gey, Fredric. 1994. "The relationship between recall and precision". *Journal of the American Society for Information Science* 45:12–19.

Burneston, George I. 1994. "Atlas indexing at the National Geographic Society". (In: *The changing landscapes of indexing: the proceedings of the 26th annual meeting of the American Society of Indexers, San Diego, California, May 13–14, 1994*. Port Aransas, TX: American Society of Indexers, pp. 1–7.)

Calkins, M. L. 1980. "Free text or controlled vocabulary: a case history step-by-step analysis . . . plus other aspects of search strategy". *Database* 3:53–67.

Carey, G. V. 1963. *Making an index*. 3rd ed. Cambridge: Cambridge University Press.

Carrow, D.; Nugent, J. 1981. Comparison of free text and index search abilities in an operating information system. (In: *Information management in the 1980s: Proceedings of the American Society for Information Science 40th annual meeting, Sept. 26–Oct. 1, 1977*.) White Plains, NY: Knowledge Industry Publications.

Cerf, Christopher; Navasky, Victor. 1984. *The experts speak: the definitive compendium of authoritative misinformation*. New York: Pantheon Books.

Challenges in indexing electronic text and images. 1994. Edited by Raya Fidel [et al.] Medford, NJ: Learned Information.

Chan, Lois M.; Pollard, Richard. 1988. *Thesauri used in online databases: an analytical guide*. Westport, CT: Greenwood Press.

Chan, Lois M. 1989. "Inter-indexer consistency in subject cataloging". *Information Technology & Libraries* 8:349–357.

Chen, H.; Dhar, V. 1990. "User misconceptions of information retrieval systems". *International Journal of Man-Machine Systems* 32:673–692.

Chicago guide to preparing electronic manuscripts for authors and publishers. 1987. Chicago: University of Chicago Press.

Chicago manual of style. 1994. 14th ed. Chicago: University of Chicago Press.

Churchill, Winston S. 1950. *The hinge of fate*. Boston: Houghton Mifflin. (The Second World War. Vol. 4)

Churchill, Winston S. 1983. *Churchill's history of the English-speaking peoples*. Arranged for one volume by Henry Steele Commager. New York: Greenwich House.

Cleveland, Donald B.; Cleveland, Ana B. 1990. *Introduction to indexing and abstracting*. 2nd ed. Littleton, CO: Libraries Unlimited.

Cleverdon, Cyril W. 1972. "On the inverse relationship of recall and precision". *Journal of Documentation* 28:195–201.

Coates, Eric J. 1960. *Subject catalogues: headings and structure*. London: Library Association.

Cohen, Barbara E.; Nickerson, Alexandra. 1995. An office out of the home. *Key Words* 3 (1), Jan.–Feb.:11–15.

Collison, Robert. 1962. *Indexing books: a manual of basic principles*. London: Benn.

Collison, Robert. 1972. *Indexes and indexing*. 4th rev. ed. London: Benn.

Columbia-Granger's index to poetry. 1990. 9th ed. New York: Columbia University Press.

Cooper, William S. 1969. "Is interindexer consistency a hobgoblin?" *American Documentation* 20:268–278.

Corbett, Maryann. 1992. "Indexing and searching in statutory text". *Law Library Journal* 84:759–767. Reprinted in *Key Words* 3(1), Jan.–Feb. 1995:7–10.

Cragg, F. 1902. "Book indexes". *Library Journal* 27:819–821.

Craven, Timothy. 1986. *String indexing*. Orlando, FL: Academic Press.

Crystal, David. 1971. *Linguistics*. Harmondsworth: Penguin Books.

Crystal, David. 1984. "Linguistics and indexing". *The Indexer* 14:3–7.

Cunningham, Ann Marie; Wicks, Wendy. 1992. *Guide to careers in abstracting and indexing*. Philadelphia: National Federation of Abstracting and Information Services.

Cutler, Anne G. 1970. *Indexing methods and theory*. Baltimore: Williams & Wilkins.

Dabney, Daniel P. 1986a. "The curse of Thamus: an analysis of full-text legal document retrieval". *Law Library Journal* 78:5–10.

Dabney, Daniel P. 1986b. "A reply to West Publishing Company and Mead Data Central on 'The curse of Thamus'." *Law Library Journal* 78:349–350.

Debrett's peerage and baronetage. 1803– . London: Debrett's Peerage.

A dictionary of American English on historical principles. 1936–1944. Chicago: Chicago University Press.

Diodato, Virgil; Gandt, Gretchen. 1991. "Back of book indexes and the characteristics of author and nonauthor indexing: report of an exploratory study". *Journal of the American Society for Information Science* 42:341–350.

Diodato, Virgil. 1991. "Cross-references in back-of-book indexes". *The Indexer* 17:178–184.

Diodato, Virgil. 1994*a*. "Duplicate entries versus *see* cross-references in back-of-the-book indexes". *The Indexer* 19:83–87.

Diodato, Virgil. 1994*b*. "User preferences for features in back of book indexes". *Journal of the American Society for Information Science* 45:529–536.

Directory of indexing and abstracting courses and seminars. 1992. Port Aransas, TX: American Society of Indexers.

Documentation and information. 1988. 3rd ed. Geneva: International Organization for Standardization. (ISO standards handbook 1)

Dorner, Jane. 1992. "Submitting works on disks: authors' stipulations". *The Indexer* 18 (1):35–36.

Durant, Will; Durant, Ariel. 1965. *The age of Voltaire.* New York: Simon & Schuster. (The story of civilization. Part 9)

Dykstra, Mary. 1985. *PRECIS: a primer.* London: British Library. Revised reprint: Metuchen, NJ: Scarecrow Press, 1987.

Dykstra, Mary. 1988. "LC subject headings disguised as a thesaurus". *Library Journal* 113 (March 1):42–46.

Dyson, Mary C. 1992. "How do you describe a symbol? The problem involved in retrieving symbols from a database". *Information Services and Use* 12:65–76.

Editors on editing: what writers need to know about what editors do. 1993. 3rd ed., edited by Gerald Gross. New York: Grove / Atlantic Monthly.

Edwards, Shirley. 1993. Investigation of a computer-assisted indexing system for its practical application in a production environment. (Unpublished report, presented orally at the 56th annual meeting of the American Society for Information Science, Oct. 23–28, Columbus, OH, and summarized in *Key Words* 1 (9):15.)

Encyclopaedia Judaica. 1972. Jerusalem: Keter.

Encyclopaedia of Islam. 1954– . 2nd ed. Leiden: Brill.

Encyclopedia of science and technology. 1992. New York: McGraw-Hill.

Encyclopedia of world art. 1959. New York: McGraw-Hill.

Facts on file yearbook. 1941– . New York: Facts on File.

Fairthorne, Robert A. 1974. "Temporal structure in bibliographical classification". (In: *Ottawa conference on the conceptual basis of the classification of knowledge, Ottawa, 1971.* Pullach / München: Verlag Dokumentation, pp. 404–412. Reprinted in *Theory of subject analysis: a sourcebook.* Littleton, CO: Libraries Unlimited, 1985, pp. 359–366.)

Farrow, John F. 1991. "A cognitive process model of document indexing". *Journal of Documentation* 47:149–166.

Feinberg, Hilda. 1983. "The thesaurus in indexing and searching: a review". (In: *Indexing specialized formats and subjects.* Metuchen, NJ: Scarecrow Press, pp. 260–281.)

Fetters, Linda. 1986– . *A guide to indexing software.* Port Aransas, TX: American Society of Indexers.

Fetters, Linda K. 1994. *Handbook of indexing techniques: a guide for beginning indexers.* [Port Aransas, TX]: Fetters InfoManagement.

Fidel, Raya. 1987. *Database design for information retrieval.* New York: Wiley.

Fidel, Raya. 1991. "Searchers' selection of search keys: II. Controlled vocabulary or free-text searching". *Journal of the American Society for Information Science* 42:501–514.

Fidel, Raya. 1992. "Who needs controlled vocabulary?" *Special Libraries* 83:1–9.

Fidel, Raya. 1994. "User-centered indexing". *Journal of the American Society for Information Science* 45:572–576.

Frohmann, Bernd. 1990. "Rules of indexing: a critique of mentalism in information retrieval theory". *Journal of Documentation* 46:81–101.

Fugmann, Robert. 1982. "The complementarity of natural and indexing languages". *International Classification* 9:140–144.

Fugmann, Robert. 1992. "Illusory goals in information science research". (In: *Classification research for knowledge representation and organization. Proceedings of the 5th International study conference on classification research, Toronto, Canada, June 24–28, 1991.* Amsterdam: Elsevier, pp. 61–68.) (FID 698)

Furnas, G. W. et al. 1987. "The vocabulary problem in human-system communication". *Communications of the ACM* 30:964–971.

Gateway software and natural language interfaces: options for online searching. 1988. Edited by James A. Benson and Bella H. Weinberg. Ann Arbor, MI: Pierian Press.

Gesnerus, Conradus. 1548. *Pandectarum sive partitionum universalium . . . libri XXI.* Tiguri: Excudebat Christophorus Froschoverus.

Gibson, John. 1989. "The highlighting / underlining syndrome". *The Indexer* 16:253.

Gomez, L. M.; Lochbaum, C. C.; Landauer, T. K. 1990. "All the right words: finding what you want as a function of the richness of indexing vocabulary". *Journal of the American Society for Information Science* 41:547–559.

Graham, Gordon. 1992. *What publishers do: from authors to readers.* Chatham: Butterworth.

Grant, Rose. 1990. "Cookbook indexing: not as easy as ABC". *American Society of Indexers Newsletter* no. 98 (May–June):1–4.

Guide to indexing and cataloging with the Art & architecture thesaurus. 1994. Edited by Toni Petersen and Patricia J. Barnett. New York and Oxford: Oxford University Press.

Hagler, Ronald. 1991. *The bibliographic record and information technology.* 2nd ed. Chicago: American Library Association.

Haig-Brown, Richard. 1979. "On citing Acts of Parliaments and related law". *The Indexer* 11:205–208.

Harman, Donna. 1994. "Automatic indexing". (In: *Challenges in indexing electronic text and images.* Medford, NJ: Learned Information, pp. 247–264.)

Havlice, Patricia P. 1987. *And so to bed: a bibliography of diaries published in English.* Metuchen, NJ: Scarecrow Press.

Hewitt, A. R. 1969. "Legal indexing". (In: *Training in indexing.* Cambridge, MA: MIT Press, pp. 152–166.)

A history of the Jewish people. 1976. Edited by H. H. Ben-Sasson. Cambridge, MA: Harvard University Press.

Hjørland, Birger. 1992. "The concept of 'subject' in information science". *Journal of Documentation* 48:172–200.

Hlava, Marjorie M. K. 1984. "How to build a database". (In: *Private file creation/Database construction.* New York: Special Libraries Association, pp. 1–22.)

Hodge, Gail M. 1992. *Automated support to indexing.* Philadelphia: National Federation of Abstracting and Information Services. (NFAIS report series #3)

Hodge, Gail M. 1993. "Computer-assisted database indexing: the state-of-the-art". (In: *Indexing, providing access to information: looking back, looking ahead. The proceedings of the 25th annual meeting of the American Society of Indexers.* Port Aransas, TX: American Society of Indexers, pp. 33–44.) Reprinted in *The Indexer* 19 (April 1994):23–27.

Hoffman, Herbert H. 1976. "How the indefatigable H*Y*M*A*N* K*A*P*L*A*N* got filed by the foiling rules". *U*N*A*B*A*S*H*E*D Librarian* (21):11–12.

Houissa, Ali. 1991. "Arabic personal names: their components and rendering in catalog entries". *Cataloging & Classification Quarterly* 13:3–22.

Humphrey, Susan M. 1994. "Knowledge-based systems for indexing". (In: *Challenges in indexing electronic text and images.* Medford, NJ: Learned Information, pp. 161–175.)

Hunnisett, R. F. 1972. *Indexing for editors.* Cambridge: British Records Association.

Iivonen, Mirja. 1990. "Interindexer consistency and the indexing environment". *International Forum on Information and Documentation* 15 (2):16–21.

Index of American periodical verse. 1971– . Metuchen, NJ: Scarecrow Press.

Indexers on indexing: a selection of articles published in The Indexer. 1978. Edited by L. M. Harrod. New York: Bowker.

Indexing, providing access to information: looking back, looking ahead. The proceedings of the 25th annual meeting of the American Society of Indexers. 1993. Port Aransas, TX: American Society of Indexers.

Indexing specialized formats and subjects. 1983. Edited by Hilda Feinberg. Metuchen, NJ: Scarecrow Press.

Indexing: the state of our knowledge and the state of our ignorance. 1989. *Proceedings of the 20th annual meeting of the American Society of Indexers, New York City, May 13, 1988.* Edited by Bella H. Weinberg. Medford, NJ: Learned Information.

INSPEC thesaurus. 1973– . London: Institution of Electrical Engineers.

International Organization for Standardization. 1968. *International system for the transliteration of Greek characters into Latin characters.* Geneva: ISO. (ISO/R 83).

International Organization for Standardization. 1973. *Information processing: ISO 7-bit coded character set for information interchange.* Geneva: ISO. (ISO 646)

International Organization for Standardization. 1981. *Documentation and information—Vocabulary—Section 3a: Acquisition, identification, and analysis of documents and data.* Geneva: ISO. (ISO 5127–3a)

International Organization for Standardization. 1982. *Romanization of Chinese.* Geneva: ISO. (ISO 7098)

International Organization for Standardization. 1983*a. Documentation and information—Vocabulary—Part 1: Basic concepts.* Geneva: ISO. (ISO 5127–1)

International Organization for Standardization. 1983*b. Information and documentation—Vocabulary—Part 2. Traditional documents.* Geneva: ISO. (ISO 5127–2)

International Organization for Standardization. 1984*a. Transliteration of Arabic characters into Latin characters.* Geneva: ISO. (ISO 233)

International Organization for Standardization. 1984*b. Transliteration of Hebrew characters into Latin characters.* Geneva: ISO. (ISO 259)

International Organization for Standardization. 1985*a. Documentation: Methods for examining documents, determining their subjects, and selecting index terms.* Geneva: ISO. (ISO 5963)

International Organization for Standardization. 1985*b. ISO bibliographic filing rules . . .* Geneva: ISO. (ISO/TR 8393)

International Organization for Standardization. 1986*a*. *Information processing —Text and office systems. Standard Generalized Markup Language (SGML).* Geneva: ISO. (ISO 8879)

International Organization for Standardization. 1986*b*. *Transliteration of Slavic Cyrillic characters into Latin characters.* Geneva: ISO. (ISO 9)

International Organization for Standardization. 1987*a*. *Documentation— Bibliographic identification (biblid) of contributions in serials and books.* Geneva: ISO. (ISO 9115)

International Organization for Standardization. 1987*b*. *Documentation— Bibliographic references—content, form and structure.* Geneva: ISO. (ISO 690)

International Organization for Standardization. 1993. *Transliteration of Arabic characters into Latin characters—Part 2: Arabic language—simplified transliteration.* Geneva: ISO. (ISO 233–2)

International Organization for Standardization. 1993. *Universal character set.* Geneva: ISO. (ISO 10646)

International Organization for Standardization. 199X. *Documentation— Rules for the abbreviation of title words and titles of publications.* Geneva: ISO. (ISO 4)

International Organization for Standardization. 199X. *Information and documentation—Guidelines for the content, organization, and presentation of indexes.* Geneva: ISO. (ISO 999)

Intner, Sheila S. 1984. "Censorship in indexing". *The Indexer* 14:105– 108.

Jacobs, Christine; Arsenault, Clément. 1994. "Words can't describe it: streamlining PRECIS just for laughs!" *The Indexer* 19:88–92.

Japan Indexers Association. 1980. *Shoshi sakusei manyuaru.* [Manual on the compilation of bibliographies.] Tokyo: Nichigai.

Japan Indexers Association. 1983. *Sakuin sakusei manyuaru.* [Manual on the compilation of indexes.] Tokyo: Nichigai.

Jennett, Sean. *The making of books.* 1967. 4th ed. New York: Praeger.

The Jewish encyclopaedia. 1901–05. New York: Funk & Wagnall.

Johnson, Samuel. 1952. *The letters of Samuel Johnson* . . . Collected and edited by R. W. Chapman. Oxford: Clarendon Press.

Kaback, Stuart M. 1992. "Online patent information: who needs indexing? We do, naturally". *World Patent Information* 14:198–199.

Keen, E. Michael. 1977. "On the generation and searching of entries in printed subject indexes". *Journal of Documentation* 33:15–45.

Keen, E. Michael. 1978. *On the performance of nine printed subject index types* . . . Aberystwyth: College of Librarianship Wales. (British Library R&D report 5475)

Kenkyusha's new English-Japanese dictionary. 1980. Tokyo: Kenkyusha.

Kilgour, Frederick, G. 1993. "Locating information in an Egyptian text of the 17th century B.C." *Journal of the American Society for Information Science* 44:292–297.

Kilmartin, Terence. 1983. *Guide to Proust: remembrance of things past.* London: Chatto & Windus.

Kingsland III, Lawrence C. et al. 1993. "Coach: applying UMLS knowledge source in an expert searcher environment". *Bulletin of the Medical Library Association* 81:178–183.

Kinross, Robin. 1977. "The typography of indexes". *The Indexer* 10:179–185.

Klein, Ernest. 1966–67. *A comprehensive etymological dictionary of the English language.* New York: Elsevier.

Knight, G. Norman. 1968. "Book indexing in Great Britain: a brief history". *Journal of Library History* 3:166–172. Reprinted in *The Indexer* 6:14–18.

Knight, G. Norman. 1970. "The problem of copyright: an indexer's triumph". *The Indexer* 7:17–18.

Knight, G. Norman. 1979. *Indexing: the art of.* London: Allen & Unwin.

Korycinski, C.; Newell, Alan F. 1990. "Natural language processing and automatic indexing". *The Indexer* 17:21–29.

Krause, Michael G. 1988. "Intellectual problems of indexing picture collections". *Audiovisual Librarian.* 14:73–81.

Lancaster, F. W. 1986. *Vocabulary control for information retrieval.* 2nd ed. Arlington, VA: Information Resources Press, 1986.

Lancaster, F. W. 1991. *Indexing and abstracting in theory and practice.* Champaign, IL: University of Illinois. Graduate School of Library and Information Science.

Langridge, D. W. 1989. *Subject analysis: principles and procedures.* London: New York: Bowker-Saur.

Larsen, G. 1988. "End-user searching and the human aspect". *Online information 88: Twelfth international online information meeting.* Medford, NJ: Learned Information.

Lawrence, T. E. 1935. *Seven pillars of wisdom.* London: Cape.

Leacock, Stephen. 1942. *My remarkable uncle, and other sketches.* London: John Lane, The Bodley Head.

Lee, David. 1991. "Coping with a title: the indexer and the British aristocracy". *The Indexer* 17:155–160.

Leonard, I. E. 1977. *Inter-indexer consistency studies, 1954–1975: a review of the literature and summary of study results.* Champaign, IL: University of Illinois. Graduate School of Library Science.

Levin, Bernard. 1989. Don't come to me for reference. *The Times* (10 Nov.).

Lewis, D. B. W.; Lee, Charles. 1948. *The stuffed owl: an anthology of bad verse.* London: Dent.

Library of Congress. 1980. *Library of Congress filing rules.* Washington, D.C.: Library of Congress.

Library of Congress subject headings. 1989– . Washington, D.C.: Library of Congress.

Liddy, Elizabeth D.; Bishop, Ann P.; Settel, Barbara. 1991. "Index quality study, Part II: publishers' survey and qualitative-assessment". (In: *Indexing tradition and innovation: Proceedings of the 22nd annual conference of the American Society of Indexers.* Port Aransas, TX: American Society of Indexers, pp. 53–79.)

Liddy, E.D.; Jorgensen, Corinne L. 1993. "Reality check! Book index characteristics that facilitate information access". (In: *Indexing, providing access to information: looking back, looking ahead. The Proceedings of the 25th annual meeting of the American Society of Indexers.* Port Aransas, TX: American Society of Indexers, pp. 125–138.

Liebscher, Peter. 1994. "Hypertext and indexing". (In: *Challenges in indexing electronic text and images.* Medford, NJ: Learned Information, pp. 103–109.)

List of initial articles. 1991. *Cataloging Service Bulletin* (52):26–29.

Maddocks, Hugh C. 1988. *Generic markup of electronic index manuscripts.* Port Aransas, TX: American Society of Indexers.

Malone, Dumas 1948–1981 *Jefferson and his time.* Boston: Little, Brown.

Managing large indexing projects: Papers from the 24th annual meeting of the American Society of Indexers, San Antonio, Texas, May 23, 1992. 1994. Port Aransas, TX: American Society of Indexers.

Marchionini, Gary. 1994. "Designing hypertexts: start with an index". (In: *Challenges in indexing electronic text and images.* Medford, NJ: Learned Information, pp. 77–89.)

Markey, Karen. 1984. "Interindexer consistency tests: a literature review . . ." *Library & Information Science Research* 6:155–177.

Matthews, Joseph R.; Williams, Joan F. 1984. "The user-friendly index: a new tool". *Online* 8 (3):31–35.

McCarthy, Sherri. 1988. *Personal filing systems: creating information retrieval systems on microcomputers.* Chicago: Medical Library Association.

McGraw-Hill encyclopedia of science and technology. 1992. 7th ed. New York: McGraw-Hill.

McGraw-Hill encyclopedia of world art. 1968. New York: McGraw-Hill.

McIntosh, Ronald. 1990. *Hyphenation.* Bradford (U.K.): Computer Hyphenation.

Meads, Jon A. 1985. "Friendly or frivolous?" *Datamation* 31 (1 April):96–100.

Medical subject headings. 1971– . Bethesda, MD: National Library of Medicine.

Meltzer, M. 1981. "Indexing the correspondence of Lydia Maria Child". *Microform Review* 10 (Winter):16–17.

Mertes, Kate. 1993. "Anything but cut and dried". *Key Words* 1 (8):1, 20–21.

Metathesaurus. 1990– . Bethesda, MD: National Library of Medicine.

Miller, George A. 1956. "The magical number seven, plus or minus two: some limits on our capacity for processing information". *Psychological Review* 63:81–97.

Miller, Samuel. 1803. *A brief retrospect of the eighteenth century.* New York.

Milstead, Jessica L. 1983. "Newspaper indexing: the *Official Washington Post Index*". (In: *Indexing specialized formats and subjects.* Metuchen, NJ: Scarecrow Press, pp. 189–204.)

Milstead, Jessica L. 1984. *Subject access systems: alternatives in design.* Orlando: Academic Press.

Milstead, Jessica L. 1992a. "No, you cannot be replaced by a computer". *Key Words* 1 (2):1–2.

Milstead, Jessica L. 1992b. Methodologies for subject analysis in bibliographic databases. *Information Processing & Management* 28:407–431.

Milstead, Jessica L. 1993. "Thesaurus management software". (In: *Encyclopedia of library and information science* 51, *Supplement* 14. New York: Dekker, pp. 389–407.)

Moore, Donald. 1990. "The indexing of Welsh personal names". *The Indexer* 17:12–20.

Morison, Stanley. 1930. "First principles of typography". *The Fleuron* 7. Reprinted in *Books and printing.* Rev. ed. Cleveland: World Publishing Company, 1963, pp. 239–251.

Moys, Elizabeth M. 1992. "Legal vocabulary and the indexer". *The Indexer* 18:75–82.

Moys, Elizabeth M., et al. 1993. *Indexing legal materials.* London: Society of Indexers. (Society of Indexers occasional papers on indexing, no. 2)

Mulvany, Nancy C. 1990. "Software tools for indexing: what we need". *The Indexer* 17:108–113.

Mulvany, Nancy C. 1994a. "Embedded indexing software: users speak out". (In: *The changing landscapes of indexing. The proceedings of the 26th annual meeting of the American Society of Indexers, San Diego, California, May 13–14, 1994.* Port Aransas, TX: American Society of Indexers, pp. 41–47.)

Mulvany, Nancy C. 1994b. *Indexing books.* Chicago: Chicago University Press.

Mulvany, Nancy; Milstead, Jessica. 1994. "Indexicon, the only fully automatic indexer: a review". *Key Words* 2 (6):1, 17–23.

Names of persons: national usages for entry in catalogues. 1977. 3rd ed. London: International Federation of Library Associations and Institutions. *Supplement.* 1980.

Names of states: an authority list of language forms for catalogue entries. 1981. London: International Federation of Library Associations and Institutions.

National Information Standards Organization. 1988. *Electronic manuscripts: preparation and markup.* Bethesda, MD: NISO. (NISO Z39.59)

National Information Standards Organization. 1989. *Proof correction.* Bethesda, MD: NISO. (NISO Z39.22)

National Information Standards Organization. 1994. *Guidelines for the construction, format and management of monolingual thesauri.* Bethesda, MD: NISO. (NISO Z39.19–1993)

National Information Standards Organization. 199X. *Abbreviations of titles of publications.* Bethesda, MD: National Information Standards Organization. (NISO Z39.5)

National Information Standards Organization. 199X. *Indexes and related information retrieval devices.* Bethesda, MD: NISO. (NISO Z39.4–199X)

National Newspaper Index. 1979– . Belmont, CA: Information Access Corporation.

NewsBank. 1970– . New Canaan, CT: NewsBank.

Noel-Todd, Alex. 1989. "What's in a name? The Statute book and popular titles". *Law Librarian* 20:29–34.

Oliver, Sunday. 1993. "Keeping books". *Key Words* 1 (5):15–17, 22.

Orbach, Barbara. 1990. "So that others may see: tools for cataloging still images". *Cataloging & Classification Quarterly* 11 (3/4):163–191.

Orwell, George. 1984. *Nineteen eighty-four.* Oxford: Clarendon Press.

The Oxford companion to the English language. 1992. Oxford; New York: Oxford University Press.

The Oxford dictionary of English etymology. 1966. Oxford: Clarendon Press.

The Oxford English dictionary. 1888–1933. Oxford: Clarendon Press. *Supplement.* 1972–1987.

The Oxford English dictionary. 1989. 2nd ed. Oxford: Clarendon Press.

Penrose, Roger. 1989. *The emperor's new mind: concerning computers, minds, and the laws of physics.* New York; Oxford: Oxford University Press.

Penrose, Roger. 1994. *Shadows of the mind: a search for the missing science of consciousness.* Oxford, New York: Oxford University Press.

Pepys, Samuel. 1970–83. *The diary of Samuel Pepys: a new and complete transcription.* Edited by Robert Latham and William Matthews. London: Bell & Hyman.

Peterson, Candace. 1994. "Newspaper indexing". (In: *Managing large indexing projects.* Port Aransas, TX: American Society of Indexers, pp. 11–14.)

Piggott, Mary. 1991. "Authors as their own indexers". *The Indexer* 17:161–166.

Piternick, Anne B. 1991. "From incipits to colon counts: a natural history of titles". *Scholarly Publishing* 22:170–183.

Piternick, Anne B. 1992. "Name of an author!" *The Indexer* 18:95–100.

Pountain, Dick. 1987. "Sorting out the sorts". *Byte* 12:275, 276, 278, 280.

Prynne, William. 1633. *Histriomastix . . .* London.

Rasheed, Muhammad Abdur. 1989. "Comparative index terms". *International Library Review* 21:289–300.

Rasmussen, Lisa. 1992. "Selected linguistic problems in indexing within the Canadian context". *The Indexer* 18:87–91.

Readers' guide to periodical literature. 1900–   . New York: H. W. Wilson.

Recommended indexing agreement. 1990. Port Aransas, TX: American Society of Indexers.

Reich, Phyllis; Biever, Erik J. 1991. "Indexing consistency: the input/output function of thesauri". *College and Research Libraries* 52:336–342.

Reynolds, Linda. 1979. "Legibility studies: their relevance to present-day documentation methods". *Journal of Documentation* 35:307–340.

Richardson, Samuel. 1755. *A collection of the moral and instructive sentiments, maxims, cautions, and reflections, contained in the histories of Pamela, Clarissa and Sir Charles Grandison . . .* London.

Ridehalgh, Nan. 1985. "The design of indexes". *The Indexer* 14:165–174.

Rolling, Loll N. 1981. "Indexing consistency, quality and efficiency". *Information Processing & Management* 17:69–76.

Rombauer, Irma S.; Becker, Marion Rombauer. 1975. *The joy of cooking.* Indianapolis: Bobbs-Merrill.

Rothman, John. 1983. "Is indexing obsolete? Keyword indexing and free-text searching". (In: *Indexing specialized formats and subjects.* Metuchen, NJ: Scarecrow Press, pp. 22–33.)

Rowley, Jennifer. 1994. "The controlled versus natural indexing languages debate revisited: a perspective on information retrieval practice and research". *Journal of Information Science* 20:108–119.

Salton, Gerard; McGill, Michael J. 1983. *Introduction to modern information retrieval.* New York: McGraw-Hill.

Sandlin, Leslie M. et al. 1985. "Indexing of smaller circulation daily newspapers". *The Indexer* 14:184–189.

Saracevic, Tefko. 1991. "Individual differences in organizing, searching, and retrieving information". (In: *Proceedings of the 54th ASIS annual meeting 1991, vol. 28. Washington, D.C., October 27–31, 1991.* Medford, NJ: Learned Information, pp. 82–86.)

Schickele, Peter. 1976. *The definitive biography of P.D.Q. Bach.* New York: Random House.

Schuegraf, E. J.; Van Bommel, M. F. 1993. "An automatic document indexing system based on cooperating expert system design and development". *Canadian Journal of Information and Library Science* 18 (2):32–50.

Schuyler, Peri L. et al. 1993. "The UMLS Metathesaurus: representing different views of biomedical concepts". *Bulletin of the Medical Library Association* 81:217–222.

Scientific style and format: the CBE manual for authors, editors, and publishers. 1994. 6th ed. New York: Cambridge University Press.

Sears list of subject headings. 1991. 14th ed. New York: H. W. Wilson.

Shatford, Sara. 1986. "Analyzing the subject of a picture: a theoretical approach". *Cataloging & Classification Quarterly* 6 (3):39–62.

Shatford Layne, Sara. 1994. Some issues in the indexing of images. *Journal of the American Society for Information Science* 45:583–588.

Sher, Dena N. 1994. "Poetry in indexes". *The Indexer* 19:102–104.

Shoshi Sakuin Tembo. [Journal of the Japan Indexers Association.] 1977– . Tokyo: Nichigai Associates.

Siegfried, S.; Bates, Marcia J.; Wilde, D. N. 1993. "A profile of end-user searching behavior by humanities scholars: the Getty online searching project report no. 2". *Journal of the American Society for Information Science* 44:273–291.

Silvester, June P. et al. 1994. "Machine-aided indexing at NASA". *Information Processing & Management* 30:631–645.

Simpkins, Jean. 1985. "Producing a revised index". *The Indexer* 14:209.

Simpkins, Jean. 1990. "How the publishers want it to look". *The Indexer* 17:41–42.

Smith, Peggy. 1993. *Mark my words: instruction and practice in proofreading.* 2nd ed. Alexandria, VA: Editorial Experts.

Snow, Bonnie. 1992. "Trade names in medicine: searching for brand name comparisons and new product news". *Database* 15 (3):99–105.

Soergel, Dagobert. 1974. *Indexing languages and thesauri: construction and maintenance.* Los Angeles: Melville.

Spence, Matthew. 1993. "How to get clients". *Key Words* 1 (4):4–7, 21.

Spiker, Sina. 1953. *Indexing your book: a practical guide for authors.* Madison, WI: University of Wisconsin Press.

Starting an indexing business. 1994. Port Aransas, TX: American Society of Indexers.

Svenonius, Elaine. 1976. "Natural language vs. controlled vocabulary". (In: *Proceedings of the 4th Canadian conference on information science, London, Ontario, May 11–14, 1976.* Ottawa: Canadian Association of Information Science, pp. 141–150.)

Svenonius, Elaine. 1986. "Unanswered questions in the design of controlled vocabularies". *Journal of the American Society for Information Science* 37:331–340.

Svenonius, Elaine. 1994. "Access to nonbook materials: the limits of subject indexing for visual and aural languages". *Journal of the American Society for Information Science* 45:600–606.

Tarr, Daniel; Borko, Harold. 1974. "Factors influencing inter-indexer consistency". (In: *Proceedings of the 37th ASIS annual meeting, Atlanta, Georgia, October 13–17, 1974.* Washington, D.C.: American Society for Information Science, pp. 50–55.)

Tenopir, Carol; Lundeen, Gerald. 1988. *Managing your information: how to design and create a textual database on your microcomputer.* New York: Schuman.

Thaxton, L.; Redus, M. E. 1975. "Of migraines and Maddox: the making of the *Atlanta Constitution index". RQ* 14:225–227.

Theory of subject analysis: a sourcebook. 1985. Edited by Lois May Chan, Phyllis A. Richmond, Elaine Svenonius. Littleton, CO: Libraries Unlimited.

Thesaurus of ERIC descriptors. 1994. 13th ed. Phoenix, AZ: Oryx Press.

Thomas, Dorothy. 1983. "Law book indexing". (In: *Indexing specialized formats and subjects.* Metuchen, NJ: Scarecrow Press, pp. 153–179.)

Thomas, Dorothy; Mulvany, Nancy. 1994. "Periodical indexing: design, management, and pricing". (In: *Managing large indexing projects.* Port Aransas, TX: American Society of Indexers, pp. 15–22.)

Thornton, J. L. 1965. "How I indexed Dickens's letters". *The Indexer* 4:119–122.

Thring, Sir Henry. 1877. "A new index to the statute law". *Law Magazine* 4th series, 8:491–512.

Thurber, James. 1981. *Selected letters of James Thurber.* Boston: Little, Brown.

Tibbo, Helen R. 1992. "Abstracting across the disciplines: a content analysis of abstracts from the natural sciences, the social sciences, and the humanities . . ." *Library and Information Science Research* 14:31–56.

Tibbo, Helen. 1994. "Indexing for the humanities". *Journal of the American Society for Information Science* 45:607–619.

Tinker, Miles A. 1963. *Legibility of print.* Ames, IA: Iowa State University Press.

Training in indexing: a course of the society of Indexers. 1969. Edited by G. Norman Knight. Cambridge, MA: MIT Press.

Unicode Consortium. 1991. *The Unicode standard: worldwide character encoding. Version 1.0.* Reading, MA: Addison-Wesley.

United States. Board on Geographic Names. 1994. *Romanization systems and Roman-script spelling conventions.* Fairfax, VA: Defense Mapping Agency.

Updike, Daniel. 1962. *Printing types: their history, forms and use.* 3rd ed. Cambridge, MA: Harvard University Press.

Van Herwijnen, Eric. 1994. *Practical SGML.* 2nd ed. Norwell, MA: Kluwer.

Vergil, Polydore. 1534. *Anglicae historiae libri XXVI . . .* Basileae: Apud Io. Bebelium.

Vickery, Brian; Vickery, Alina. 1992. "An application of language processing for a search interface". *Journal of Documentation* 48:255–275.

Wall, R. A. 1980. "Intelligent indexing and retrieval: a man-machine partnership". *Information Processing & Management* 16:73–90.

Wall, R. A. 1993. *Copyright made easier.* London: Aslib.

Ward, Beatrice. 1932. "Printing should be invisible". London: Privately printed. Reprinted in: *Books and printing*. Rev. ed. Cleveland, OH: World Publishing Co., 1963, pp. 109–114.

Webster's third new international dictionary of the English language. 1961. Springfield, MA: Merriam.

Weinberg, Bella H. 1981. *Word frequency and automatic indexing*. New York: Columbia University. Unpublished DLS dissertation. University Microfilm International # 83–27316.

Wellisch, Hans H. 1972. "A flowchart for indexing with a thesaurus". *Journal of the American Society for Information Science* 23:185–194.

Wellisch, Hans H. 1978a. *The conversion of scripts: its nature, history, and utilization*. New York: Wiley.

Wellisch, Hans H. 1978b. "Early multilingual and multiscript indexes in herbals". *The Indexer* 11:81–102.

Wellisch, Hans H. 1980. *Indexing and abstracting: an international bibliography*. Santa Barbara, CA: ABC-Clio. [19th century-1976.]

Wellisch, Hans. H. 1981. "How to make an index, 16th century style: Conrad Gessner on indexes and catalogs". *International Classification* 8:10–15.

Wellisch, Hans H. 1984. *Indexing and abstracting 1977–1981: an international bibliography*. Santa Barbara, CA: ABC-Clio.

Wellisch, Hans H. 1986. "The oldest printed indexes". *The Indexer* 15:73–82.

Wheatley, Henry B. 1878. *What is an index? A few notes on indexes and indexers*. London: Longmans, Green.

Wheatley, Henry B. 1902. *How to make an index*. London: E. Stock.

Wheeler, Martha Th. 1957. *Indexing: principles, rules and examples*. 5th ed. Albany, NY: New York State Library.

White, Howard D. 1992. "External memory". (In: White, Howard D.; Bates, Marcia J.; Wilson, Patrick. *For information specialists: interpretations of reference and bibliographic work*. Norwood, NJ: Ablex Publishing Corp., pp. 249–294.)

Wilson, Patrick. 1973. "Situational relevance". *Information Storage & Retrieval* 9:457–471.

Wilson, Patrick. 1977. *Public knowledge, private ignorance: toward a library and information policy*. Westport, CT: Greenwood Press.

Wittmann, Cecelia. 1990. "Subheadings in award-winning book indexes: a quantitative evaluation". *The Indexer* 17:3–6.

Wittmann, Cecelia. 1991. "Limitations of indexing modules in word-processing software". *The Indexer* 17:235–238.

Zukofsky, Louis. 1978. *A*. Berkeley, CA: University of California Press.

Zunde, Pranas; Dexter, Margaret E. 1969. "Indexing consistency and quality". *American Documentation* 20:259–267.

INDEX

Entries are filed word-by-word. **Boldface** locators indicate extensive treatment of a topic. Locators following a modified main heading indicate references to minor topics. Locators followed by an asterisk (*) indicate illustrations; locators followed by *n* indicate footnotes; locators followed by *t* indicate tables.